INSIDE
ROOM 40

The Codebreakers of World War 1

INSIDE
ROOM 40

The Codebreakers of World War 1

PAUL GANNON

Ian Allan
PUBLISHING

Inside Room 40
Paul Gannon

First published 2010

ISBN 978 0 7110 3408 2

Published by Ian Allan Publishing

an imprint of Ian Allan Publishing Ltd, Hersham, Surrey KT12 4RG.
Printed in England by CPI Mackays, Chatham, Kent ME5 8TD.

Visit the Ian Allan Publishing website at www.ianallanpublishing.com
Distributed in the United States of America and Canada by BookMasters Distribution Services.

Contents

Acknowledgements 6

List of Tables 6

Introduction 7

Chapter 1 Germany's War Signals 10

Chapter 2 Room 40: Birth of a Legend 21

Chapter 3 Code Capture 37

Chapter 4 Codes and Ciphers 44

Chapter 5 Message Makers 66

Chapter 6 Message Takers 72

Chapter 7 Message Breakers 81

Chapter 8 Counter-blockade 96

Chapter 9 'For You the War Is Over' 110

Chapter 10 'The Pillars of Hercules Have Fallen' 119

Chapter 11 Inside Room 40 139

Chapter 12 Codebreakers 154

Chapter 13 The Spanish Interception 171

Chapter 14 'Most Secret, Decipher Yourself' 186

Chapter 15 '97756 = Zimmermann' 198

Chapter 16 On Timing and Treacheryv 208

Chapter 17 Applied Intelligence 218

Chapter 18 War, Revolution and Peace 238

Chapter 19 After the War 244

Epilogue 251

Notes 257

Bibliography 274

Index 280

Acknowledgements

My thanks for assistance with research, reading some of the draft chapters, providing photographs or other essential contributions go to David Williams, Antony Hoogman, Tim Matschak, Alan Cargill, Lynne Walsh, Reg Atherton, Robert Dudley and Ronan Scaife. The staff of the Churchill Archives Centre, Churchill College Cambridge and the National Archives, Kew. Also to Mark Beynon who commissioned this book.

Tables

Table 4.1   Sample entries from the SKM codebook system
Table 4.2   Two-part code example
Table 4.3   The *Handelsschiffsverkehrsbuch* (HVB) codebook system
Table 4.4   *Verkehrsbuch* (VB) codebook system
Table 4.5   A simple cipher
Table 4.6   Enciphering a coded message
Table 4.7   SKM cipher method
Table 4.8   Breaking a transposition cipher
Table 6.1   Wireless sets in use from Marconi and Telefunken, 1909–1914
Table 12.1   Sample army field message
Table 12.2   Codewords for spelling-groups
Table 12.3   Common spelling-groups
Table 15.1   Partially reconstructed 13040 codebook
Table 16.1   Zimmermann telegram timetable
Table 16.2   Changes to the Zimmermann telegram between
             sending and publication in the USA
Table 17.1   Gross tonnage of merchant shipping losses,
             January–December 1917

Introduction

On 17 January 1917, Nigel de Grey, a young naval intelligence officer, hurried to the office of his wartime superior, Captain William Hall, Director of Naval Intelligence. Once inside, de Grey impatiently spluttered out his question. 'Do you want to bring America into the war, sir?'

The short, dapper captain, known to his subordinates and colleagues as 'Blinker' Hall because of his rapidly blinking eyes, was immediately alert. 'Yes, why?' he exclaimed.

De Grey brandished a piece of paper, exclaiming 'I've got a telegram here that will bring them in if you give it to them'.

The war was at a critical stage. A dreadful, bloody stalemate on land and sea was consuming lives at an awful rate. The military offered no obvious way of breaking the deadlock. America's entry to the war, however, could sway the balance and bring the slaughter to an end. But neither America's government nor its people wanted to join the Europeans' imperial war. If de Grey was not exaggerating the import of his intelligence, then whatever it was he had discovered could be decisive in determining the outcome of the war.

De Grey was one of the handful of people who worked in Room 40 of the Admiralty in central London. Their task was to break German naval and diplomatic codes. This particular telegram had been sent from Berlin, via Washington, to the German representative in Mexico. De Grey, and a colleague Dilly Knox, had managed to make out only some passages of the message. But what they had revealed was enough to send de Grey dashing off to Hall's office. In the telegram the German Foreign Secretary, Arthur Zimmermann, proposed that Germany and Mexico join forces in waging war – 'conduct war jointly; make peace jointly' – against the United States. When the telegram's contents were fully decoded and revealed to the American public, America was propelled into joining the war, ensuring Germany's defeat.

This intercepted message is Room 40's most renowned achievement. Yet, the 'Zimmermann telegram' was just one of many tens of thousands of wireless and telegraph cable messages systematically intercepted throughout the war and decoded by Room 40, and also by its little known War Office equivalent, MI1(b). While the existence of these codebreaking activities was kept quiet during the war, various details were exposed soon after the fighting had ended. But it was only in the early 1980s, that a semi-official account of Room 40 was written by Patrick Beesly (a naval intelligence officer at Bletchley Park, the Second World War equivalent of Room 40).

Beesly had access to at least some of the Room 40 archives and his book became the standard work on the subject. In the quarter of a century since then, little new material has been published on Room 40. But many previously secret documents have been opened at the National Archives in Kew, West London, including several on the Zimmermann telegram and on the secretive MI1(b). As the centenary of the outbreak of the cataclysmic Great War approaches, it is time to review the story of Room 40, to see what the archives can tell us now.

History, it is frequently asserted, is written by the victors. And this case certainly seems to fit that aphorism. Assuming that we do not dwell too long on what might actually be meant by 'victory', Britain was clearly among the states that determined the shape of the peace settlement imposed at Versailles. British codebreakers in the First World War peeped into the secret military, naval and diplomatic messages of Germany and its allies, and also into the diplomatic messages of neutrals, including the USA, Spain, the Netherlands, Greece and Switzerland. British codebreaking was part of the overall effort that achieved victory. And, by bringing America into the war, codebreaking was critical in determining who would be the winners and the losers. So the codebreaking story would seem at first glance to be a classic case of history written by the victors through the documents that they have selected to leave us in the archives. But it is not such a simple matter.

A few years ago I wrote a book about the Second World War and British codebreaking at Bletchley Park, including the creation of the world's first electronic computer, Colossus.[2] That book was based on documents, now in the National Archives at Kew, which were preserved at the end of the war. Much of the documentation associated with that project had been destroyed. The surviving documents did include quite a few intelligence 'appreciations' and interpretations drawn from intercepted messages, but very, very few of the original intercepts still existed (though recently a million such documents have been 'discovered'). For the purposes of recovering the overall story, there were many administrative documents as well as some substantial technical works.

However, while researching for this new book about British codebreaking activities in the First World War, I found the situation to be near enough the reverse. There is a dearth of administrative files, technical documents and of intelligence appreciations and the like. Much of what happened inside Room 40 and MI1(b) remains hidden, lost probably for ever as it is unlikely that many, if any, more documents will turn up (though some were 'found' by GCHQ in 2005). On the other hand, available at Kew for anyone to view are many thousands of the original unalloyed intercepted messages (mainly translated into English but with quite a few in original encoded/encrypted form and some partially or wholly decoded).

This book tells the story of the First World War and the story of Room 40 and of MI1(b) partly through these German intercepts. In that sense it is history intercepted, decoded and translated by the victorious side – but as written by the vanquished. The intercepts allow us to hear the voice of German military and naval commanders and officers (seldom, though, of the lower ranks), and also of diplomats, politicians and spies. There are orders couched in military jargon, often about apparent trivia such as switching on harbour lights, but also informing us of debates between diplomats, civil servants and politicians about strategy. Combined, the intercepts reveal how the German military and government understood and tried to organise the war they were fighting. The geographical spread and range of topics covered in those messages is astounding. They reveal how Room 40 and MI1(b) gave British military and government leaders an extraordinary oversight of their enemies' activities on every continent and on every ocean of the land war, the sea and air war, the espionage and sabotage war, and the propaganda and diplomatic war. The First World War was truly global, with fighting in many regions, not just the Western Front and the North Sea. Other nations had large-scale codebreaking operations, but what distinguished the British effort was its systematic nature. With Room 40 and MI1(b) we see the origins of the shadowy bodies that have industrialised codebreaking.

Yet this is also a story about people. The cast of characters that peopled Room 40, and its military equivalent, is as replete with brilliant academics and potty eccentrics as the more renowned codebreakers of Bletchley Park in the Second World War. A few accounts from the individuals, who toiled night and day between 1914 and 1918, have survived and allow us to get a feel for what it would have been like inside Room 40 or MI1(b) and to glimpse behind the mask of command and the veil of secrecy.

Chapter 1

Germany's War Signals

No one really expected war in 1914. Even after the Archduke Franz Ferdinand, crown prince of the Austrian Hapsburg Empire, was assassinated in Sarajevo on 28 June, few imagined that war was on its way – let alone a war that would be without previous parallel in death, injury, agony, starvation, disease and economic and social dislocation. David Lloyd George, the British Chancellor of the Exchequer, was an enthusiastic reformer and moderniser. Before the war he had been occupied with laying the foundations of the welfare state in Britain, introducing pensions, unemployment benefits and health insurance. He had other great projects for mid-1914 – reform of the House of Lords, Ireland, votes for women. 'I cannot recall any discussion on the subject [of an imminent war] in the Cabinet until the evening before the final declaration of war by Germany,' Lloyd George later wrote in his *War Memoirs*. 'We were much more concerned with the threat of imminent civil war in the North of Ireland.' On the day before Germany declared war the Foreign Secretary, Lord Grey, briefed ministers on the 'situation' in Europe. It was very grave, he told them, but still hopeful. Yet, even if war still seemed avoidable, the British government took some important measures to prepare for its outbreak, banning, on 2 August, all unauthorised wireless use, and on 3 August ordering the impounding of all amateur wireless sets.

The diplomatic holiday season was just getting underway. Many diplomats and politicians were away from the national capital cities as the crisis exploded onto the scene. The diplomats of the European 'Great Powers', mainly aristocrats, were unable or unwilling to break with the socially essential tradition of attending their country estates during high summer. Opportunities in the early days to limit the war to a minor conflict in the Balkans were lost because diplomats were not in their offices. Any lingering prospects of defusing the situation evaporated in the summer heat. Instead, the Great Powers were drawn into widening the conflict, constrained by commitments to their alliances, and propelled into war by their own precipitate demands from one state to another, transmitted around Europe by telegraph to empty Foreign Offices. When a satisfactory reply to an ultimatum was not received in the short time allowed, war was declared.

Austria sent its declaration of war to Serbia on the 28 July by telegraph – the first time war had been declared by telegram. Russia and Germany, supporting respectively Serbia and Austria, declared war on each other within five days.

Russia's involvement threatened to drag in its Entente allies, France and Britain. But 'even then,' said Lloyd George, 'I met no responsible Minister who was not convinced that, in one way or another, the calamity of a great European war would somehow be averted.' However, Germany's plans for war with Russia involved knocking out France to its west, before the more sluggish Russian army had time to mobilise to its east. Once France had been defeated, Germany could turn to deal with Russia having thus avoided a 'two-front war'. So, once Russia and Germany declared war on each other, Germany was committed to launching an attack on France. This made it almost inevitable that Britain would join in. Britain – and its Empire – would be vulnerable if the European continent were dominated by a vigorously expansive Germany, especially if it took control of Channel ports. When it became clear that Germany's military attack on France would begin with an attack on neutral Belgium, Britain had its *casus belli* – or at least one that made a suitable justification for war for the population that would have to fight it.

Britain sent an ultimatum to Germany demanding a declaration, by midnight European time (11pm British time) on 4 August, of respect for Belgium's neutrality. Lloyd George described it as a 'day full of rumours and reports, throbbing with anxiety. Hour after hour passed, and no sign came from Germany. There were only disturbing rumours of further German movements towards the Belgian line. Then evening came. Still no answer.' The Prime Minister, Foreign Secretary and Home Secretary were 'all looking very grave'. Shortly after 9pm a telegraph message, sent from the German Foreign Office to the German ambassador in London, was intercepted by the British Censorship office, installed at the main international telegraph cable exchange in London. The message was translated and immediately sent to the anxious huddle of senior ministers. It read, the 'English Ambassador has just demanded his passport shortly after seven o'clock declaring war'.

This confusing message was the first news they received from Germany in response to the ultimatum. No word reached London from the British ambassador in Berlin (the German authorities having held up his telegram reporting on his meeting with the German Foreign Secretary). 'We were at a loss to know what it meant,' said Lloyd George. It might indicate an attempt by the German navy to take pre-emptive action against British ships or harbours. Ministers debated whether they should use the intelligence gained from the intercepted message to begin mobilisation without waiting for the deadline to be reached. They also pondered whether to order the start of naval operations previously scheduled to happen only on the commencement of hostilities – such as cutting German international submarine telegraph-cables to isolate it as much as possible from the outside world. 'Should this intercept,' the ministers debated, 'be treated as the commencement of hostilities … should we unleash the savage dogs of war at once or wait … and give peace the benefit of even such a doubt as existed for at least another two hours?' They waited, but that did not avert war.

***

Ten years earlier, in 1904, British warships were ordered to begin intercepting any foreign wireless transmissions they picked up, sending copies on to London. Records of some of these pre-war intercepts still exist, though the earliest surviving copies of such messages date only from March 1914 onwards. These surviving messages were taken by wireless operators on Royal Navy ships – such as *Glasgow* on patrol in the South Atlantic. Other surviving intercepts were telegraph messages sent by Germany over British international telegraph cables operated by the Eastern Telegraph Company, ETC. The volume of intercepts increased as war drew closer. The Naval Intelligence Division employed an officer, Fleet Paymaster C. J. E. Rotter, to study the intercepts before the war. During the war, Rotter became a vital member of the navy's codebreaking team, rapidly becoming one of the best codebreakers. It is possible that he may have deciphered messages before the war, but there is no direct evidence to support this suggestion. As far as is known, none of the messages were decoded before November 1914, when German codebooks were captured and methods of breaking the ciphers had been developed.

However, we can now look at some of these intercepted messages and observe how Germany prepared for war and then signalled its start to distant German naval and merchant ships and to its far-flung colonies. Some of the decoded messages reveal that Germany took early preparations for distributing cipher keys and codebooks, making them ready for use in the event of war. For example, on 20 March 1914, a message sent in the name of the Kaiser to the German Legation in Montevideo contained instructions about which ciphers were to be issued to which secret agents in Buenos Aires and Rio de Janeiro. On 5 May, the *Admiralstab* (Admiralty staff) in Berlin sent details of the distribution of new ciphers to the German cruiser *Königsberg* at Dar es Salaam, in the colony of German East Africa. Other messages, for example one on 18 March, contained instructions to seek potential supplies of coal and places where discreet re-coaling of German warships could take place if, or when, war did break out. Yet others, such as a message sent by cable on 9 April from Berlin to a German gunboat in Manila, record the details of ships surveying the waters near both German and British territories in the Far East.

After the assassination of Franz Ferdinand on 28 June, the tone of the messages changes. The abrupt telegrams now convey a tension and apprehension which was absent from the earlier signals. As the political crisis deepened, both the German and the British navies were put 'on alert' in July 1914. This was something that could be done without provoking war in the way that 'mobilisation' of armies inevitably meant war would take place. On 7 July, the *Admiralstab* sent a telegram to a gunboat, *Eber*, which was undergoing boiler repairs at Cape Town – in the British territory of South Africa. The *Eber* was warned that the 'political situation at home [is] not free from difficulty. Development is to be expected in eight to ten days. When is your boiler cleaning finished?' Later the same day the captain was told to 'conclude no written agreements of any description with [the] Consul General. Destroy any that exist.' In mid-July the German cruiser *Scharnhorst* at Yap, in the German-controlled Marshall Islands, was informed that an 'Austro-Hungarian note has been presented to Serbia July 23. Political development cannot be foreseen. Await further developments at Penope Island.' On 26 July, the warship *Königsberg,* still stationed off the East African coast, was advised that 'diplomatic relations have been broken off between Austria and Serbia. Tension between Dual Alliance [Germany and Austria] and Triple Alliance [Russia, France and Britain] possible. It is presumed that England will maintain an expectant attitude.' Other messages forwarded to the *Königsberg's* captain provided intelligence about the movement of what Berlin thought to be French warships also off East Africa (though, as was noted when the message was eventually decoded by the British codebreakers, they were actually British warships).

Most of the above messages were intercepted by the Eastern Telegraph Company. But on 26 July a message is entered in the log book kept by the British codebreakers as having been intercepted by an Admiralty wireless station at Dover. This is the first of several messages intercepted by Admiralty land-based wireless stations, as opposed to warships or commercial telegraph cable stations. The message informed the commander of the German High Sea Fleet that 'we have received news that Russia has broken off [peace time] manoeuvres and sent the troops back to their depots [indicating intended mobilisation]'. The message also urged the naval commander to 'hasten the return of Wilhelm'.

Even though the political situation in Europe had been getting steadily worse in July, Kaiser Wilhelm II had gone off on his usual summer cruise in his imperial yacht, *Hohenzollern*, to the Norwegian fjords (where his captive guests were subjected to his excruciatingly adolescent practical jokes). Cancelling his trip might have given the impression that Germany was eager to exploit the crisis following the assassination of Franz Ferdinand. Going through with it was intended to signal that everything was normal. But once war seemed inevitable it was vital to ensure the Kaiser's safe and speedy return. Wilhelm's absence from Germany also meant that his frantic belated attempts to cool things down and to avoid war were futile. Russia had mobilised: war was now certain.

On the 29th the *Eber* in Cape Town was told to 'leave on some plausible pretext and go to Luederitz Bay [in German South-West Africa]'. The captain dragged his vessel out of the harbour 'in a hurry, half [her] boiler tubes not working and in a heavy sea'. The next day the German navy's main wireless station, at Norddeich in northern Germany, told the cruiser *Strasburg* that 'war has broken out between Austria and Serbia … in the present state of affairs the English Channel is still passable'. The same day coded wireless messages were broadcast by the German high-power wireless station at Nauen, near Berlin, the world's most powerful wireless transmitter, capable in the right atmospheric conditions of sending messages as far as southern Africa and Asia. These messages, sent to unnamed recipients, ordered the bringing into play of preparations for coal supplies and secret re-coaling places. And a plain language message was sent to all German merchant ships: 'Threatened with danger of war. Enter no English, French or Russian harbours.' The merchant captains were also told to keep an eye on movement of foreign warships and to report them to the *Admiralstab*.

The next day, all German merchant ships were ordered to sail immediately for the nearest neutral port to avoid being captured by British or French warships. Cruisers stationed at German colonies in Africa and Asia were told to start attacking Allied shipping. Berlin instructed the cruiser *Dresden*, 'Do not come home but carry on cruiser warfare [ie, attacking enemy warships and merchant ships flying enemy flags]. We will send coal.' German agents in South America, Spain, Portugal and other places were told to start clandestine operations. Details of payments for agents were transmitted to distant posts. In return Berlin received intelligence reports – some of them no doubt of value, but many made up of wild rumours, such as the one relaying the tip that 'a secret confidential agent reports that on Thursday 15,000 Englishmen [will] arrive in Alexandria [in Egypt] from Malta' on 2 August. German colonies, vulnerable to Allied attacks, were told to keep Berlin well informed about what happened far from the homeland. 'Send regularly by wireless short messages on the political situation. The big wireless station here [at Nauen] is open for reception continuously by night and day … all telegrams to be enciphered.'

***

The World War had begun. Some of the first warlike actions were taken on a global scale as Germany and Britain each attacked the other's cable and wireless communications networks. While the armies poured into mobilisations centres preparatory to murderous battle in northwest and central Europe, British and German navies and secret services engaged in a minor war at sea. The *Königsberg* left Dar es Salaam, while Graf von Spee's cruiser squadron sailed from Germany's Chinese colony, and its only major naval base outside the homeland, Tsingtao. A few other German cruisers also set sail with the intent of attacking British warships, merchant ships and also British wireless and cable stations at remote locations such as Fanning Island and the Cocos Islands. These were tiny specks of land thousands of miles from any continental mass. All the same they were vital hubs in Britain's global network of submarine telegraph cables. The web of cables enabled Britain to administer its colonies (most importantly India), co-ordinate with its Dominions (Canada, Australia and New Zealand), conduct its trade and finance, and direct the Royal Navy's policing of the seas. In fact very little damage was done to British communications systems and the British ability to communicate to or from virtually anywhere in the world was unimpaired.

Meanwhile, British and Australasian ships left their ports to hunt down German cruisers, leading first to a defeat for the Royal Navy at Coronel, and then to a victory at the Falklands (see below), so that with only a little difficulty the oceans were cleared of German ships by the end of 1914. At the same time naval expeditions carried forces to invade German colonies and islands, in large part to destroy or to take over and incorporate the German wireless stations. One after another, Germany's global chain of wireless stations was closed down. The wireless station at Dar es Salaam was put out of action on 9 August. That at Yap, in the Pacific Caroline Islands, was closed on 12 August (this prevented direct wireless communication from Graf von Spee's squadron to Berlin and from then on any messages had to be passed on to cable stations, thus coming within the grasp of British-owned cable companies, although it appears that such messages were not intercepted). On 24 August the station in Togoland was destroyed by the Germans themselves to prevent it falling into British hands. Germany's wireless station at Samoa fell to a New Zealand force on 29 August.

Such operations turned seamlessly into the acquisition of Germany's colonies and expansion of the British Empire.[3] Samoa serves as a good example of the process. The operation was being put together even before the war had started. On 2 August an Admiralty memo raised the idea. 'An expedition from New Zealand would serve a useful purpose if sent to capture Samoa, where Germany has a harbour and a wireless station: the island should be occupied and held. … This is quite a feasible operation. If hostilities break out, it would be well to accept all offers from the Dominions to attack German Colonies. Besides being a powerful threat, it will stimulate the imperial idea.' Although New Zealand's help was sought for the Samoan operation, it was made clear that any territory that was acquired would not belong to New Zealand and, at the end of the war, it would be placed 'at the disposal of the Imperial Government' in London.

The Naval Intelligence Division was able to provide some information about the wireless station on Samoa. It was a fairly powerful Telefunken set with a maximum transmission range of 2,000 nautical miles, was located 8 miles inland and was served by a 400-foot high mast. The intelligence report added that the island was home to 544 'whites' (of whom 329 were German and 132 British), 1,000 'colonial', 1,300 Chinese and up to 20,000 natives. 'Practically no military resistance is expected.' The expedition was told to capture the wireless station undamaged so it could then be used to contact other British wireless stations – and also to 'intercept and report signals from unknown sources'. According to one ex-naval officer, the first actual use by the Royal Navy of intercepted German messages took place when the captured Samoan wireless station picked up a message from von Spee's *Scharnhorst* on 4 October 1914. The signal was encoded in the 'secret German mercantile code [ie, HVB, see Chapter 3], which had already been captured'. So, when decoded, the message revealed that von Spee's squadron was sailing from the Marquesas to Easter Island. This message is not recorded in the log book of messages cited elsewhere in this chapter. Though the codebook had been captured it had not by then reached London. Also the cipher system, if one was used, had not been broken at the Admiralty in London. It is possible that the Australians who first captured the codebook were using it themselves and may have broken the cipher key before the Admiralty's cryptographers did so in London, and it is also possible that no cipher was employed on this message.

The New Zealanders also took two other German wireless stations: Nauru in the Marshall Islands and Herberthihe in the New Pommern Islands. Towards the end of September, Duala in the Cameroons fell to a British and French force. In mid-November, Japan took control of Tsingtao, with token British military assistance. However, the South African force sent into German South-West Africa took a little longer to finish the job and the capital, Windhoek, with its wireless station, held out until May 1915.

Plans existed too for cutting German submarine telegraph cables. The British telegraph cable maintenance ship *Telconia* left port early on 5 August 1914, as soon as the war started, and headed out into the North Sea, steaming towards Emden near where the Dutch-German border meets the coast. A few miles off the shore the ship swung its grappling gear – intended for lifting up damaged cable for repairs – out over the side of the ship and dropped it down into the grey waters. According to the historian Barbara Tuchman, the 'heavy grappling irons were plunged into the water, dragged along the bottom, and hauled up, bringing with them an eel-shaped catch, dripping mud and slime, that clanged against the ship's side with a metallic sound. Several times the manoeuvre was repeated, and each time the eel-like shapes were cut and cast back into the sea.' The severed cable ends were later recovered, reconnected and integrated into the Allied cable network. Altogether five cables were cut: two linking Germany with America, one to Brest in France, one to Vigo in Spain and one to Tenerife in North Africa. All of Germany's independent cable links to the outside world were put beyond use, except for some German-owned cables linking West Africa and South America which could not be cut as both ends of the cables landed on neutral territory.

Within a few weeks of the war's outbreak Germany's international communications had been severely constricted. Cable communications were limited to a few nearby neutral countries (in particular Sweden and Denmark). Wireless gave it a few more outlets. Germany could continue to send messages from its wireless stations at home – the high-powered station at Nauen near Berlin, and a fairly high-powered naval station at Norddeich. Germany also owned two wireless stations on the soil of a neutral country that lay beyond the reach of the British. These were based in the USA and remained in use. However, the American government imposed strict controls. The Germans could only use a codebook or cipher if the USA was given a copy so that US censors could monitor what was being transmitted. This severely limited their usefulness. This brief summary of the closing down of German communications has taken us slightly ahead of our story. We can step back briefly to the start of the war, and see how it was expressed in intercepted German wireless signals.

***

Back in early August, the outbreak of war was marked by a bombardment of wireless and cable messages from Berlin and Norddeich. To help boost morale at the start of the struggle a message on 5 August to all warships from the *Admiralstab* cancelled all outstanding punishments for breaches of discipline. More importantly, arrangements were made for cruisers to meet up with supply ships, carrying essential fuel and food supplies, at quiet points on the coasts of South America, Africa and chains of volcanic islands in the Asian seas. When Germany and Austria sought to strike an alliance with Turkey two German warships, the *Göben* and *Breslau*, were instructed by a wireless message on 4 August to head as quickly as possible to Constantinople (present-day Istanbul). They were chased by a small British patrol. But lacking the gun power to take on the German ships, the British commander turned back – to face ignominy for not upholding the suicidally aggressive honour of the Royal Navy. The German ships made it into the Dardanelles and the Black Sea, encouraging Turkey to enter the war and then wreaking havoc for the next few years. The 'escape' of the two ships from the clutches of the feared Royal Navy was an important propaganda victory for the German navy, damaging the Navy's zealously maintained reputation. Berlin was delighted to hear of even such a minor success and wanted more details. On 11 August Berlin sent a message to the captain of the *Göben*, 'His Majesty the Kaiser directs the captain to send in a report of your escape.' Propaganda was to become a key part of the First World War both on the home fronts and in neutral countries. On 12 August the powerful German wireless stations at Nauen near Berlin sent out a joyous message: 'Our army has won a decisive victory at Mülhausen, Alsace, against the French Army Corps. Spread the word.' Details of other victorious clashes of arms were similarly reported, for example on the 20 August, celebrating 'incomparable bravery' by German forces storming and conquering a strongpoint on the Western Front.

The log of intercepts is silent between 23 August and 9 September – except for a single message intercepted in Shanghai on 6 September. This reported that the Japanese were expected to arrive off the coast of Tsingtao, Germany's concessionary territory on the coast of mainland China, acquired in 1898 to great national pride. In early November Japan, symbolically aided by a few British troops, fully conquered the territory that had given the Kaiser so much cause for satisfaction. The apparent German wireless silence – or perhaps it was difficulties at the British listening stations in successfully intercepting signals – ended on 9 September, with a message from Nauen to Windhoek, in German South-West Africa, giving details of British blockading lines off the African coast. A few days later, on 22 September, another message from Nauen to Windhoek reported that 'all lines of communication have been compromised except perhaps no. 163'. This meant the disruption by the Royal Navy of the coal and supplies bases set up around African sea routes to provide for German cruisers.

From then on such messages become quite common. Around this time the British, through much immensely good luck, came into possession of the three main German naval codebooks (see Chapter 3). And, following French success in late September in breaking German army cipher 'keys' in northwestern France, the British also worked out how to break the German navy cipher keys (codes, ciphers and keys are discussed in Chapter 4). A message dated 21 October (intercepted by the Naval Board in Melbourne, Australia) was sent from Nauen to the German ship SS *Roon*. It had been sent in a non-secret, commonly used public code, but with a secret cipher. It reported that 'my activity has been rendered difficult because the collier has been detained by the government. Nevertheless 1500 tons of coal are stored for use in case of necessity at Fjilatjap [Java] on board steamer Sydney.' This could stand as an example of many such messages reporting on the German struggle to sustain, and the British to crush, German cruiser warfare on the high seas. But what makes it interesting for our story is the combination of the use of the public codebook and the secret cipher. All the other messages we have cited were secured with secret codebooks and secret ciphers. But for this message, the code used was the common *ABC Code*, a publicly available commercial codebook (see Chapter 4). A codebreaker could guess that a certain word would be contained in the message, but in enciphered form. A handwritten note in the log of the messages records: 'It was from this message that 'Key B' was discovered, by guessing the [codeword] for "*Roon*". ' We will look more closely at the methods used for breaking codes and ciphers in later chapters.

Among the last few messages recorded in the log book are several relating to the small squadron of German cruisers, led by Admiral von Spee, which left Tsingtao at the outbreak of war (to escape being caught in harbour by the Japanese). They steamed erratically from one remote Pacific island to another, looking for opportunities to sink a few British merchant ships, damage some telegraph cable and wireless stations, and, most important of all, seek out coal so that they could keep on the move (and all the while whittling away their irreplaceable supply of shells). On 1 November Spee's ships were attacked, suicidally, by a smaller British squadron at Coronel in the southern Pacific, off Chile. The commanding officer, despite facing overwhelmingly negative odds, feared that his reputation would be damaged if he did not attack, as happened to the captain (mentioned above) who let the *Göben* and *Breslau* off the hook as they rushed for the safety of the Black Sea.

The encounter with Spee's cruisers, at Coronel was a shock to the Royal Navy – its first major defeat at sea for many decades. But Spee, aware that he would sooner or later be trapped, lost belief in his squadron's ability to survive and he considered making a dash through the British blockade back to Germany. Eventually Spee's ships were enticed (quite possibly by false leads planted by British naval intelligence) to attack the Falkland Islands in the southern Atlantic. Spee received a report from a German agent in Punta Arenas that there were no British warships at the Falklands, but this was incorrect. Spee took the bait and, on 8 December, his ships were destroyed by a more powerful British squadron.

Interception of wireless signals played a role in the battles of Coronel and the Falklands, and in the hunting down of a lone German cruiser, *Emden*, which was causing havoc in the Indian Ocean. The Royal Navy ship, *Glasgow*, was present at both battles and used 'direction-finding' techniques to locate the enemy. According to one historian, 'In the last resort … [German] cruiser warfare failed because the Germans could not conceal the movements of their ships. A steady stream of clues as to their whereabouts were picked up, often with great rapidity, sometimes in real time, and circulated with efficiency by the British between the Admiralty, local commands and pursuing naval units on the worldwide wireless and cable network.'

The Royal Australian Navy had its own codebreaking unit, set up in August 1914, consisting of one senior naval officer, Frederick Wheatley. He received intercepted wireless messages sent to and from German ships and cable messages sent via Montevideo. Wheatley cracked a new cipher used with the German merchant shipping codebook (the HVB, see Chapter 3). The messages sent in the new cipher key were mainly connected with arrangements for coaling and supply ships to meet Spee's ships off the west coast of South America. It is possible that Wheatley's success in breaking the new HVB cipher key in early November contributed to the eventual destruction of Spee's squadron at the Falkland Islands. It is also possible that Wheatley's achievement helped British codebreakers to break German ciphers.

A footnote to the story is found in a file in the National Archives which records that a copy of the German SKM codebook (see Chapters 3 and 4) was sent out to the South Atlantic for the *Glasgow* because its wireless telegraphy officer, Lieutenant Stuart, had intercepted and logged many signals (some of which we have seen earlier in this chapter). The file records, 'It is greatly to his credit that so careful a watch was kept though he cannot have guessed the remarkable results to be obtained ... after the success of [Room 40] in the late months of 1914, a copy of a captured German signal book was sent to the South America Station and Stuart made such excellent use of it and the material he had so carefully collected that he was able ultimately to decipher a signal made by *Dresden* on [8 March 1915] giving the destination as Juan Fernandez where she was found and destroyed by *Glasgow* and other ships. This is one of the very few instances of the deciphering of an enemy signal which led to immediate and definite results'.[4] Unfortunately, the full extent of codebreaking activities in the southern hemisphere in the first year of the war remains unknown and the scene of our story shifts from southern waters to northern ones.

Chapter 2

Room 40: Birth of a Legend

Once the war started, German wireless messages passing through the ether were plucked from the airwaves by amateur wireless enthusiasts in Britain, entirely on their own initiative, and by the privately owned Marconi Company. Copies of the intercepted messages were sent to the Admiralty in London. Because no one at that arthritic institution had given any thought to intercepting enemy communications, there was no plan to deal with the messages sent in by the amateur sleuths. So the messages piled up on the desk of the director of the Admiralty's naval intelligence department, Captain Henry Oliver. The semi-official history of Room 40, written by a Second World War naval intelligence officer, Patrick Beesly, says that, 'Oliver realised their potential value but had no staff who were not already fully occupied and certainly none with the slightest idea of how to set about the problem of codebreaking. One day in the first half of August, Oliver was walking across to the United Services Club in Pall Mall for lunch in the company of his friend the Director of Naval Education, Sir Alfred Ewing. "It struck me," Oliver recounts, "that he was the very man I wanted." He knew that Ewing had some interest in ciphers, because they had recently talked of "a rather futile ciphering mechanism" which Ewing had devised. They had also discussed "novel methods" of constructing ciphers. Oliver said that the development of Naval education would receive little priority during the war and offered Ewing the task of devising means of codebreaking and setting up of a small codebreaking team organisation. Ewing promptly accepted.' This is the official story of the birth of British codebreaking in the First World War – a truly British tale of bumbling amateurishness that just about helps the country pull through in its hour of crisis.

The story has grown in the re-telling. One retired British Admiral has it that Oliver 'had these messages on his desk and was trying to make up his mind what to do with them when he chanced to meet Sir Alfred Ewing … [who] had made a lifelong study of cryptology as a hobby and [who] asked to be allowed to study the messages'. The point that gets exaggerated is the chance nature of the whole affair. There was no insight into the potential usefulness of the enemy intercepts. Ewing's meeting with Oliver was just good luck befalling slothful civil servants taking long leisurely lunches and strolls in the sunny summer heat through a verdant St James's Park. Even as the country went to war, decisions on whom to appoint to vital posts depended upon who one happened to be lunching with. As one historian puts it: 'In the inimitable manner of which the British are so proud, it was amateurs who came to the rescue of a torpid officialdom.'

It is now clear, however, that this standard account is in good part a cover story, created to provide a plausible narrative to accompany details of codebreaking activities that leaked into the public realm after the war. The cover story emerged in piecemeal fashion. For each leak, there had to be an official story to explain it away. The various little cover stories then get repeated and added to, evolving into legend. Writers add or alter details to show a little originality in their new account and to avoid copying existing accounts too obviously and too closely. So the legend accumulates dubious details. 'Revisionist' historians have questioned the legend, pointing to documentary evidence that contradicts it in some way or other. One Italian historian, Alberto Santoni, has suggested that the British cover story was invented so as to give the impression that the British success at codebreaking during the First World War was pure good luck and was unlikely to be repeated in a later conflict. His view, and that of others, is that British interception and codebreaking operations were systematic. They were undertaken from as early as March 1914 if not much earlier, probably as early as 1904. After the war, British security services cleverly hid the truth. They downplayed British skill and experience with codebreaking. The cover story was thus a key part of this cunningly effective British deception plan – with the result that Germany and others underestimated the skill of British wireless interception engineers and cryptographers with stunning results in the Second World War. But this takes matters too far. It is too dependent on our subsequent knowledge of the British success at codebreaking in the Second World War. And, anyway, the documentary evidence shows that post-war spy chiefs and politicians repeatedly publicised their ability to intercept and decipher the communications of the new enemy, Soviet Russia.

What actually happened is certainly not quite as amateurish and dependent on luck as the British cover story implies. Yet neither was it anywhere near as coolly planned and implemented as some historians would have it. It is possible now to reconstruct a more nuanced account of the founding of Room 40 and its almost forgotten military counterpart, MI1(b), by bringing together a variety of documentary sources now available at the National Archives at Kew, West London, and the Churchill Archives Centre at Cambridge. The official story was not created purely for public consumption, but was also passed on internally to those who worked for the British codebreaking organisation itself, providing a handy internal account of the origins of their own organisation. The more that historians peek behind the curtain of secrecy, the more they discover about the extent of British intelligence activities in the decades before the First World War. Their work has uncovered a long but slender history to British interception and codebreaking, going deeper than previously acknowledged, establishing that Room 40 and MI1(b) developed from marginally more foresight than the inherited accounts would suggest.

***

By the end of the 19th century Britain controlled the world's main submarine telegraph cables. Virtually all other governments had to rely on British cables]to communicate with their overseas ambassadors, military attachés and overseas forces. In some instances – such as when British and French troops came close to armed conflict on the Upper Nile at Fashoda in 1889 – the British made use of their control of the cables to expedite British messages and delay French ones. In the case of the Fashoda Incident, as it became known, the British monopoly on rapid telegraphic reports from the region meant that the French government, lacking full knowledge of the situation, backed down and military conflict was avoided (to Britain's advantage).

Within Britain the interception of telegrams was illegal under the Post Office Act of 1837. But this Act of Parliament was not applicable abroad. The 'Indian' government was not prevented from intercepting Russian telegrams passing through India and Persia. The great concern of the British civil servants governing India was Russia's designs on the 'jewel in the imperial crown'. The Great Game – the name given to the struggle between Britain and Russia during the latter half of the 19th century for influence on the borders of India – was one of the key dynamics of European Great Power politics. British fears often focused on local rulers within India who might conspire with Russia. In 1879 letters between the late Amir of Afghanistan, Shere Ali, and the Maharajah of Kashmir fell into British hands. The then Viceroy, Lord Lytton, wrote that 'part of it is in a cipher of which the key is yet to find', implying that someone, somewhere was active in looking for the key.

In 1904 Major G. R. M. Church and Captain G. S. Palmer were sent to Simla to start systematic efforts to intercept Russian messages and break their codes and ciphers. They were searching for evidence of links between Russia and political opponents to British rule, and also intelligence about the emerging conflict between Russia and Japan. Church had been a telegraph censor in Aden in 1900, so had some experience of eavesdropping and maybe of codebreaking too. There was some token resistance to the idea of intercepting the Russian telegrams. The acting Viceroy, Lord Ampthill, was worried that 'the regular interception of correspondence telegraphic and otherwise is contrary to all English practice'. All the same, he acceded to it.

There was a hiccup in 1909 when the newly arrived British minister in Persia, George Barclay, stopped supplying intercepts to Simla. He wrote,

'There was a very great danger of being found out in this spy work, [so] it seemed to me so all-important to avoid even a remote risk of incurring further mistrust on the part of the Russians that I put a stop to the practice.' His concern was that Britain and Russia were mending their traditionally poor relations and becoming allies, so nothing should be done to disturb the new friendship. Persia was a potential flashpoint and events there could wreck the growing entente. His argument seems to be a utilitarian one, rather than abhorrence at the ungentlemanly prospect of reading someone else's mail. But, at another level, his concern is based on the assumption that the Russians would have been angry – and surprised – if they found out what was going on. The Russians and the Japanese both used wireless interception widely in their war of 1905 (at which the Russians suffered a serious defeat) and were more likely to be surprised if Britain did not intercept messages than annoyed if they did.

Snooping, however, had become so useful – or so addictive – that the Indian government simply found other, more willing, places to intercept Russian messages. In 1912, the Viceroy of India informed the India Secretary, back in London, that 'in the Army Department [in Simla] they have succeeded in discovering the Russian, Persian and Chinese ciphers, and they are now able to decipher any telegram despatched from, or arriving in, India, or passing along Indian telegraph lines. Thus I was able to give you the other day the contents of a telegram from the Russian Consul at Bushire to the Russian Minister in Tehran, and we are able to control all the telegrams sent by the Persian Consul General to his own Government. We have quite a large file of Chinese telegrams that have been deciphered and that are quite interesting.'

***

Turning from diplomatic interception to army intelligence, there are documentary records of the British army gaining access to Russian and Turkish codes and ciphers in the 1870s and 1880s. For example, in 1875 the British military attaché in St Petersburg came into possession of some Russian enciphered messages and the appropriate cipher key. During the Egyptian 'campaign' of 1882, tapping of cables revealed that the opposing Egyptian army was intercepting British traffic. British army intelligence made use of their intelligence in an offensive way and sent a few false orders over the telegraph cables hoping to mislead their opponents.

Further opportunities for interception and decryption came at the turn of the century with the Boer War. Both sides tapped telegraph cables to listen in on the other in southern Africa. Britain could listen in elsewhere too. In 1901 during secret negotiations, the British allowed Louis Botha, the Boer commander, to communicate in code with the Boer's president, Paul Kruger, in exile in Europe – via British-controlled cables. The British army then took copies of the messages and decoded them. The British claimed that the messages revealed nothing which they did not already know. Coincidentally or not, from about this time the British Committee for Imperial Defence started to think systematically about the role of submarine telegraph cable networks in time of war. 1904 seems to be the key date – it was that year that the interception unit was set up at Simla and that British warships were first ordered to intercept and send on naval wireless messages from all around the world's oceans.

The Admiralty did not get around to setting up a proper intelligence department until the late 1880s. It got off to a pretty ropy start. In 1888 there was something of a panic at the Admiralty over rumours that the French navy was being mobilised at the port of Toulon, and possibly also Cherbourg, for an attack on the Royal Navy. British attempts to find out whether these rumours were true or not came to nought. So, it was embarrassingly necessary to ask the well-informed Italian and German ambassadors in Paris for their views (which scotched the rumours). Soon after, reports of new harbour works and railway line at Dunkirk became attached to an impression that they were to be used for launching an invasion of Britain. The naval officer sent to check out these stories had limited command of French and found that when he asked for direction to the sea (*mer*) it was thought that he was asking to be pointed towards his mother (*mère*). Despite these difficulties he was able to smooth concerns, reporting that the rumours were got up by scaremongers. In 1889, following a visit to the Paris Exhibition, the same hapless intelligence officer was responsible for mongering a scare on his own account. He was particularly impressed by a huge artillery gun on display, reporting back to the Admiralty about the fearful threat it seemed to pose. Only later was it learned that the gun was made of papier mâché.

Both the Army and the Navy Intelligence Departments grew, becoming more effective (and more professional) in the last decade of the 19th century and the first years of the new century. Military and naval attachés at overseas embassies contributed lots of intelligence in the run-up to the war. Intelligence officers were installed in distant naval commands. They provided immediate tactical intelligence to their local commander. They also telegraphed back to London more strategic information for collation and assessment. All the same, even as late as 1914, there was no intelligence officer in the flagship of the Australian squadron. And when war broke out in the middle of that year, a Royal Navy squadron ordered to destroy a German wireless station on a remote spot in the Pacific Ocean, Rabaul on New Guinea, returned without carrying out the mission because it lacked intelligence on the location of wireless station on Rabaul and had failed to find it. A second, better informed, naval force had to be sent back to finish off the job. Also, not every senior naval officer was fully convinced that intelligence was necessary, and least of all intelligence gathered from intercepted messages.

***

All the same, by 1914 many officials and commanders had some experience with interception and codebreaking. According to one historian, 'By July 1914 many Indian and diplomatic authorities, including [Sir Edward] Grey [the Foreign Secretary] and two successive permanent under-secretaries, Charles Hardinge and Arthur Nicolson, and at least three officers in the Boer War who achieved high command during the Great War, Henderson, Kitchener and Milne, had some practical experience with the use of signals intelligence. The same may be true of the two British commanders-in-chief on the Western Front, for both John French and Douglas Haig commanded columns in 1902 which had received copies of the captured Boer codebook. Moreover, Haig was the head of the Indian general staff and his intelligence chief during 1914-17, John Chateris, was a member of the Indian intelligence branch when the Indian codebreaking bureau was at work. ... Before August 1914 the British Authorities had already decided to form cryptanalytical organisations during any war. ... The army and probably the navy had incorporated limited preparations for signals intelligence into their planning for major wars. The intelligence authorities of Britain's fighting services planned to establish cryptanalytic bureaus in time of war and had at least an elementary idea of what this would entail.' There were attempts by both the army and the navy to acquire German and Turkish codebooks before the war started. They were not always very successful. The Admiralty's intelligence division paid out for a copy of a German naval codebook, but it proved to be a worthless forgery (this incident obviously rankled and later in the war British agents sold a fake copy of a British Emergency War Code to the Germans and used it to feed false information at a suitable time).[5]

As we saw in Chapter 1, German wireless messages were intercepted, copied and kept by wireless operators at the Admiralty in London at the beginning of May 1914 and by wireless operators on at least one Royal Navy warship at least as early as March 1914. The bulk of the messages intercepted between March and July are recorded as being sourced not from wireless but from the cables of the Eastern Telegraph Company (as Germany communicated with its consuls and military attachés in places such as South America out of reach of wireless transmitters based in Germany). Telegraph companies copied and filed the text of messages passing through their offices for operational reasons (messages often had to be repeated when garbled and thus repeated or clients might complain at a later date about alleged shortcomings of a transmitted message). Such copies could easily find their way to the Admiralty if the telegraph company was willing to co-operate. During late July, as the international situation grew more fraught, the number of intercepted wireless messages increased. They are recorded as having been intercepted by the Admiralty at London or Dover, Portpatrick,

Scotland, as well as Royal Navy ships and wireless stations in places such as Cape Town and Kingston (in Ontario). Intercepts from the Marconi Company start to be recorded from the end of July. A message was intercepted at a new Admiralty 'policing' station, Stockton, on 1 August. By 3 August the number of Admiralty stations taking messages increases and one entry reads, 'Taken at Admiralty, Chelmsford, Towyn, Stockton, etc.' A single officer in the Naval Intelligence Division, Fleet Paymaster Charles Rotter, received the messages and attempted to make some sense of them – but at the time he lacked access to the codebooks, so it would have been very difficult to break the cipher, except in cases where public codes were used.

The standard account, as we have seen, is that on the day war was declared or sometime in early August (the accounts vary), Oliver is supposed to have had that lunch appointment with the Director of Naval Education, Alfred Ewing. They were old pals and by coincidence Oliver had, on a previous occasion, chatted with Ewing about his amateur interest in the art of cryptography – the breaking of secret codes and ciphers. So, Oliver, according to one account, scooped up the messages piling up on his desk, stuffed them in his pocket and then set out for lunch to walk to that lunch at the United Services Club. The idea of two very senior naval officers, in the first days of the war, ambling amiably through the park, is not quite in the same league as the story of an insistently insouciant Francis Drake finishing off a leisurely game of bowls before slipping away to meet the Spanish Armada. But it is surely just as much of a legend. The start of the war would have meant an immense amount of work for Oliver. As head of Naval Intelligence he had to ensure a flow of reliable information needed for a wide variety of naval operations. Several such operations had been planned for the first days of war, such as cutting German undersea telegraph cables, invading German colonies in Africa and Asia to destroy their wireless stations, clearing the oceans of German warships, and arranging the convoy of troop ships across the Channel (and from the distant dominions of Canada, Australia and New Zealand). All these missions needed good intelligence on the whereabouts of German warships and forces. Oliver also needed to supply intelligence to those whose job it was to protect the home fleets in Scotland and around the Channel. And Oliver was no slouch. Indeed, he had a reputation as an extremely hard worker. Later in the war, after his promotion in November 1914 to Chief of Naval Staff, he hardly ever left his office, having a camp bed where he napped for short periods. He added to his own workload by refusing to delegate, and drafted naval orders personally.

One military historian has described the scene in the 'war room' at the Admiralty in London, shared by the navy's Operations and Intelligence divisions at the start of the war: it was, he says, 'wild, thousands of telegrams littered about and no-one keeping a proper record of them'. There is, thus, no reason to assume that the workaholic Oliver, on the extremely busy first day of the war (or thereabouts) would have found time for a relaxing lunch with an old chum. He may well have arranged a lunch appointment with Ewing. But it would surely have been a working lunch, not an opportunity to catch up with a pal. Obviously Oliver wanted to see Ewing for some important reason to do with the war. The reason was that one of Oliver's tasks was to sort out the pressing challenge of setting up the pre-planned codebreaking unit within the Admiralty. He had already identified Ewing as the man for the job. Oliver later recalled, 'Before 1914 the [naval] intelligence department had been trying without success to decode wireless ciphers. I wanted to put a big man on it.'

Ewing was a big man figuratively speaking only. His son later wrote, 'In private Ewing often expressed the regret that he was not taller, and remarked that a tall man can be impressive even when whispering brainless balderdash, whereas a short man like himself, in order to get the same result, must stand on tiptoe and shout solid sense.' If this is true, then Ewing must have learned very early in life how to raise himself up on his toes and bawl loudly, for he was marked out as a special student by his lecturers from his first days studying engineering at Edinburgh University. He was a 'very serious student' and his professor recommended that he be employed, initially unpaid, during his vacations at a telegraph cable manufacturing plant in East London (the centre of the world's cable manufacturing industry). He assisted engineers performing electrical testing of cables. His diligence brought payment and, despite his tender years, he was sent to South America to help with cable repairs. Ewing first came into contact with codes at this time. He suggested to a colleague that they should encode their telegrams to each other when working in foreign countries to ensure commercial secrecy. He also learned to appreciate the importance of changing the code frequently to maintain confidentiality.

In 1878, aged only 23, he was appointed a professor of mechanical engineering at Tokyo University and given the task of setting up an engineering studies department. While there, fascinated by earthquakes that frequently shook the country, he invented the basic design for the 'seismograph' which measures earthquake intensity. Measuring the moving earth is not an easy task, as the measuring device needs to be able to stay stable while the earth itself judders and jumps. He also worked on magnetism, coining the term 'hysteresis'. He was then offered a newly established chair of engineering at Dundee University. It was a step up, but not enough to occupy his burning ambition. His son said, 'putting it bluntly, it is perhaps not unfair to say that all the time he was in Dundee he was working hard to get out of it'. His shameless self-promotion bore fruit in 1890 when he was appointed professor of mechanical engineering at Trinity College, Cambridge. Here he worked as hard as ever, successfully establishing engineering as a subject fit to be studied in the refined world of Cambridge.

But even this was not enough for him. As his son wrote, 'his energy, his capacity and appetite for work became almost insatiable; no grist was too small for his mill. Nor was he afraid to let other men see that he meant to succeed, and meant to get all the work he could, and the reward of that work.' As well as his academic duties, he took on a role as an engineering consultant for big industrial projects, as author of encyclopaedia articles and as an expert witness in court cases (which he found 'pleasantly remunerative as well as excellent sport'). He was not short on expounding his opinions and views about the future, although not necessarily with any great foresight, such as 'foretelling the time when the car would lead to the solution of one of the great social problems – that of relieving the congestion of the towns by bringing folk out into the country'.

In 1902 Ewing was invited to become Director of Naval Education. The navy's leadership, in part at least, had begun to realise that the technical challenges of modern warships demanded a complete overhaul of the education and training of both officers and ratings. New methods of selection were needed. New schools and training establishments were to be set up. And a new curriculum had to be devised. But 'some of the old school did not relish the idea of an engineer rising to be an Admiral. Others considered that the [existing system of] competitive examinations should not be abolished … other diehards thought that the change was an indictment against all previous Boards of Admiralty and hinted that the character of the scheme was too exclusive. One leading traditionalist, Admiral Lord Charles Beresford, protested that 'under the new scheme of Naval Education a civilian settles the curriculum and issues reports upon the results, without showing how the results are obtained. … What is required at this critical moment is the abolition of the office of the Director of Education and the reconstitution of the Committee of Education of the Admiralty, composed of naval officers.' Nevertheless Ewing's tough character ensured that 'the initial plan was adhered to'. One of his favourite arguments was that while it took only two years to build a battleship, it took nine to mould a naval officer.

Ewing rose to the top with the aid of his considerable self-confidence and some extremely sharp elbows. His achievements at Tokyo, Dundee, Cambridge and at the Admiralty show that he was entirely capable of beating many a taller chap when it came to doing a good job. His ability to build an organisation from new, to pick the right people and to get the job done, meant that, however squat his physical shape, he was a big man, eminently suitable for a big job. Ewing's interest in ciphers was also somewhat more professional than suggested by the references to his personal hobbyist's attraction to the arcane subject of cryptography. His early work with telegraph cables first brought the use of codes to his attention. Later, while at the Admiralty, Ewing sat on a pre-war Admiralty committee on codes and ciphers, including studying the potential use of machines to encipher and decipher messages (though one of Ewing's detractors within Room 40, William F. Clarke, later wrote that his experience on the committee 'taught him little or nothing'). Probably the 'futile' cipher machine was connected with this work. Ewing started work on his new task immediately after his meeting with Oliver.

Within a day or two, a handful of the navy's modern languages teachers found themselves being contacted and asked to volunteer, for a short while, for special duties. They were told to report to the office of the Director of Naval Education at the Admiralty in London. The first of these volunteers were Alastair Denniston, W. H. 'Bill' Anstie, and two naval instructors about whom only their surnames are known: Curtis and Parish.[6] Alastair Denniston was a key member of Ewing's staff, becoming his deputy. In 1914, he was a 33-year-old German language teacher at Osborne, with absolutely no knowledge of codes or ciphers. He was an excellent linguist, having studied at the Sorbonne and Bonn Universities, rather than a British university. He had also written a German grammar book, which was widely used in British schools. He was the son of a medical doctor and proved to be a sportive child and young adult. In 1908 he won a bronze medal at the London Olympics as a member of the Scottish hockey team, but his real talent lay in his love of languages and he was marked out as a fine linguist. After the war he became head of Room 40's successor, the Government Code and Cipher School, GC&CS. Despite some concern in the 1930s about his appointing friends and relatives to important secret posts, he retained that position until 1941. Denniston was also a short man, and it is claimed that he was known to colleagues as the 'Little Man'.[7] Bill Anstie was another languages teacher, from the Royal Naval College at Dartmouth. During the war he played a key role in breaking many different German cipher keys and working out the contents of codebooks. A fellow cryptographer, William F. Clarke, later described Anstie as 'a charming fellow who once shocked Sir Alfred Ewing by pinning up the notice of a sweep in Room 40 with the first prize a copy of the German codebook'. For both Denniston and Anstie, Ewing's call for volunteers led to new, unexpectedly absorbing careers. Yet for the first week or so they were floundering, overwhelmed by the seemingly insoluble task they had taken on of making sense out of long lists of meaningless letters or numbers. Their first job was to spend time learning some of the basics of the codes and ciphers.

Within a week of getting started Ewing received a visit from Colonel MacDonogh from the War Office where a similar organisation had been set up under an officer with 'experience of deciphering in the Boer War'. In the run-up to war the War Office had a single officer in its intelligence division looking at intercepted messages, the Librarian of the General Staff. (In December 1914, when the German military ciphers had been cracked, the cryptographers decided to look back at old intercepted messages which were stored by the

Librarian; they discovered 'some perfect specimens ... intercepted on 13 and 14 November 1913'.) The urgent military need in late August 1914 was to halt the headlong German assault, via Belgium, into northern France. A British Expeditionary Force was quickly put together and transported to France by the third week of August, though the French were unsure if they could rely on the British force to turn up. The future commander-in-chief of the army, Douglas Haig, for example, wanted to keep the army back in Britain until later in the year when a bigger army could be assembled, despite the risk that the French army would collapse if not helped soon. Right up to the last minute the army high command argued about where the British forces should assemble – towards northeast France or closer to the Channel (and the escape route home if things went terribly wrong). The speed of the German advance and the attempts of the French and British to organise a defence meant that the airwaves were thick with Allied and German wireless traffic. There were plenty of messages to be plucked out of the ether if anyone could be found to look at them. At first the messages were intercepted by army wireless units, there being no dedicated interception station, and the messages were passed to the BEF's intelligence unit in northern France.

The War Office in London also had a central intelligence section with its own codebreaking department before the war. But the BEF's intelligence operations were not controlled from London (as was the case with the Admiralty). The War Office's 'contribution was at the strategic level, providing training, a central repository of information and longer-term back up to field units'. Its name went through various changes, but I will stick throughout with its best-known name MI1(b), standing for Military Intelligence department 1, section B. It was headed by Brigadier-General Anderson, the officer brought out of retirement. During the Boer War, he had been involved in tapping telegrams sent between Boers in southern Africa and their supporters in Europe. In 1912, he established 'very close relations' with the French cryptographic bureau, one of the most advanced in Europe. Although he retired in 1914, he was either brought back or he volunteered his services. He was assisted by Major Church from the codebreaking unit at Simla. Several others also joined the team. Four of them – Lieutenant G. Burnett, Captain Shirley Goodwin, Mr H. C. Steel and H. E. C. Tyndale – joined in at the beginning of August, but left in mid-September and nothing is known about why they joined or about why they left. J. St. Vincent Pletts, an employee of the Marconi Company, who joined the small cryptographic team on 11 August, was one of the first of a handful of civilian recruits to the section. He was followed by Oliver Strachey (brother of the controversial author Lytton Strachey) who joined on 26 September 1914. He came from the Indian civil service. His background may have been reliably high class, but he and his spouse were not too careful about keeping his appointment secret. His wife wrote to her mother that Strachey had been assigned 'to decipher codes and piece together scraps of wireless messages picked up from the enemy'. Despite boasting to relatives, Strachey was to prove to be an extremely good cryptographer and stayed in the post-war codebreaking unit set up under Denniston in 1918/19. He was joined in MI1(b) by another civilian, C. Bryans, on 4 October, and two army officers, 2nd Lieutenant G. C. Crocker on the 5th and Lieutenant A. J. Quarry on the 8th.

Ewing's and Anderson's organisations were told to merge, or at least to work as one unit. Given the military situation, they were to concentrate on military messages from the Western Front. Naval work was given second place. As Denniston later put it: 'The prenatal life of the cryptographic section began.' Denniston and Anstie were dispatched to the War Office, across the other side of Whitehall, while Parish, Curtis and a new recruit, Lord Herschell, manned the watch from Ewing's tiny office in the Admiralty. There is no record of how Herschell became involved. He was way above even Ewing's fairly elevated social status. His father had been a Lord Chancellor under Gladstone. The young aristocrat himself was a Lord-in-Waiting to Edward VII and then to George V. Herschell was also a personal friend of the Spanish king. He was a very good linguist. However, Herschell was not a natural cryptographer. Within a couple of months he was taken off cryptographic work and given the job of translating captured German documents. When he finished that, the new head of the Naval Intelligence Division, Captain William 'Blinker' Hall (who replaced Oliver in November 1914) kept him as one of his personal assistants or 'fixers'. Another codebreaker, William F. Clarke who joined Room 40 in 1916, described Herschell as 'only a sort of honorary member'.

***

Wireless technology was fairly new and rather clumsy to use in 1914. Wireless sets were large, heavy and unwieldy. They also needed their own generators to provide power and a mast to hold up an aerial. Several horses and wagons were needed to transport the equipment for a single wireless station. While size and power did not matter on ships, on land they were serious drawbacks. Wireless was transportable, not portable. So, early in the war, wireless sets were issued only to the headquarters of the commanders of the individual 'corps' and 'armies' (each army being a grouping of several 'divisions' and each army being a grouping of two or three corps) and also to cavalry formations (which had horses and wagons for transport and also had the task of undertaking reconnaissance for intelligence). The first German army wireless messages were heard during the French and British retreat after the battle of Mons in the last week of August. The retreat threatened to turn into a rout and it was even feared that Paris might be reached by the German troops. As the German front advanced and moved deeper into French territory, the retreating French armies destroyed the telegraph network, making it useless to the advancing German troops. This pushed the Germans to rely even more on wireless.

MI1(b)'s first intercepted message was picked up quite early, possibly on 9 August. A log book records that the message 'seems' to bear this date, but this is not certain. Unfortunately there appears to be no record of the intercept or what happened to it. The first challenge was to get good-quality intercepts. As one cryptographer noted, 'At this time and for weeks following, the reception of the intercepted messages seemed to present great difficulty to the operators of our stations – accuracy was very rare and in some cases the errors were very gross.' Things improved in early September so that the cipher officer at the British Expeditionary Force's GHQ, Captain Henderson, reported that the operators were now able to distinguish between French and German wireless signals. A few days later, Henderson suggested that many more messages could be picked up if a dedicated wireless interception station was set up.

According to Denniston, 'It was the time of the German advance into France and their movements could be dimly observed from the study of the *en clair*.' The speed of movement, the need for immediate communication, the volume of wireless traffic, and the difficulties of handling codes and ciphers under fire, all combined to overwhelm the wireless operators in General Georg von der Marwitz's cavalry corps. The operators stopped wasting time with ciphers and started sending their messages in plain language. Soon the practice spread to other army units and within a short time the German army had effectively abandoned use of ciphers. These plain language messages, as commanders tried to rally and regroup their armies, gave their British and French counterparts useful forewarning of German movements in the run-up to the stemming of the German advance at the 'First Battle of the Marne' at the beginning of September. This is considered by military historians to be a decisive clash, marking the failure of the German attempt to knock out France in a single powerful blow. The German army had reached the limits of its logistical capability and it was beginning to lose coherence of purpose as its forward momentum stalled. A gap opened up between two German armies which the French and British were quick to exploit, aided by the intercepts giving away German positions, plans and conditions. The French commander-in-chief, Joseph Joffre, said that 'German wireless stations were one of our most precious sources of information'. According to one historian, the 'French and British forces intercepted at least some fifty [wireless] messages in plain language from German divisions, corps, armies and army groups … [gaining] otherwise unavailable insights into the collapse of enemy command and the yawning gap in its line during mid-September 1914. Victory on the Marne was no miracle. Over the next two months similar *en clair* transmissions (combined with the solutions of encoded German traffic) warned the British Expeditionary Force of the precise time, location and strength of six full scale attacks on its front … Without this material, the British Expeditionary Force might well have lost the race to the sea, or even have been destroyed.' Ironically, this happened only a few weeks after the Russians had committed the same error, leading to a spectacular German victory at the Battle of Tannenberg.[8]

The French cryptographers were more advanced than the British. A French army cryptographic bureau already existed at the start of the war and was fairly well practised in intercepting German wireless traffic – little surprise given the enmity that existed between France and Germany ever since the Franco-Prussian War of 1870–71 in which France was invaded and Paris came under siege. The French bureau initially concentrated on careful logging and analysis of German messages – where were they sent from and to whom, at what time, how often, and what could be inferred from these facts when they were collected for hundreds of messages. This, now known as 'traffic analysis', allowed the French to begin to draw up a picture of the structure of the German army. Although only a few German senior command units were equipped with wireless, they generated a significant amount of traffic, reaching a crescendo during October. Following the check on the German advance at the Battle of the Marne, the fighting turned into a series of flanking movements which came to a stop only when the Swiss border was reached in the south and the Channel in the north. The head of the French cryptographic bureau, Colonel Cartier, looking back on these hectic first days at the end of the year, wrote, 'I need not tell you of the overwork I have had to sustain since the end of July. I have managed to cope with it, though I was often afraid I should succumb.'

The first major cryptanalytic breakthrough came from the careful logging of all the intercepted German messages in early September. A plain language message was intercepted asking, '*War ist Circourt?*' ('Where is Circourt?'). A reference number pointed to a previous enciphered message. The French cryptographers guessed that message probably contained the word '*Circourt*' and started to play around with the message. They checked what happened if they assumed that a set of characters in the cipher text represented *Circourt* in cipher. No doubt it took many fruitless attempts to locate the right solution. But once they eventually found *Circourt* in the cipher text, they were well on the way to solving the cipher (see Chapter 4). Before the beginning of October they worked out the full key. The news spread quickly through the French army and even outside the military. A senior officer hurriedly issued orders to keep quiet about it. However, the Germans appear not to have heard the news and made no attempt to change the key they were using until 17 October. It took the French just four days to break the new key. When the key was changed again at the start of November it took three days, and the next change after that was cracked in just one day. It seems likely that this breakthrough was made thanks to the capture of some German documents and in particular a copy of the German army's instructions for using ciphers. The French got hold of this document at the end of August or very early in September because their translation of it from German into French is dated 2 September. This would have told the French cryptographers that the cipher methods were based on a simple transposition system (see Chapter 4). This meant that the actual letters of the plain language message would exist somewhere in the intercepted message, making the guessing of 'cribs' (words very likely to be in the message, such as '*Circourt*') a suitable way of cracking the cipher. The haul of captured documents also included a list of 'call-signs', used by German military wireless operators to call up different stations, and the identity of the military unit for each call-sign.

One decrypt revealed to the French that the Kaiser was planning a visit to near the front in Belgium. The French decided to use the information and to welcome him with a bombing raid. But again the story spread like wildfire – a report even appearing in the columns of the newspaper *Le Matin* citing intercepted messages as the source of the information for the planned raid. This did come to the notice of German intelligence and an apparently more complex cipher system was introduced. In fact the new system was not significantly more secure. And anyway the French had built up a good enough knowledge of the German military messages that they had enough information to work out the new system using cribs. They soon cracked the new cipher.

It was on 2 October that the French delivered the captured cipher instruction documents to the British army codebreakers and informed them that they had broken the key used for the German military messages. The translated German cipher instruction document made its way to MI1(b) in London and was referred in reports as 'Exhibit II'. Two days later further intelligence reached London 'from Captain Henderson and his analysis of the system [based] on the surmise that Exhibit II is correct'. On 3 October MI1(b) received some momentous news from GHQ in northern France. A cipher key of some 20 characters had been worked out by the British cryptographers at GHQ. The cipher used a 'double transposition' technique (see Chapters 4 and 9) following the system described in 'Exhibit II'. The British military cryptographers used the key – *zumsturmwehrrechts* – to crack German messages dating back to 22 September. The details of this achievement are very sketchy; it seems that a specific set of circumstances was needed. Messages enciphered using a slightly more complex system than the most basic cipher could at that stage only be deciphered if two or more intercepted messages, of the same length, with very few errors and enciphered with the same key, were available (this technique is described in outline in Chapter 9). 'These circumstances have but rarely been met with,' noted one cryptographer.

'No time was lost in getting down to decipher,' said Denniston. Watchkeeping in the War Office was reorganised and more people were needed. Herschell and another newcomer to Ewing's team, R. D. Norton, were set to working on military messages during the day, but based at the Admiralty building in Ewing's office, while Denniston and Anstie remained working at the offices of the War Office codebreaking team. MI1(b) was established in Room 219 of the War Office buildings on Whitehall. The room was easily big enough for the staff and all the papers and books they rapidly gathered. A powerful wireless receiving station was erected at South Lawn, near Oxford, and a direct telegraph line was set up between the station and the Admiralty so that intercepted messages could be sent on as soon as they had been taken down by the intercept operators (previously telegrams had to be sent via Oxford and passed through several hands, introducing delays and errors).

The two British cryptographic teams now began to organise their work in a systematic fashion. The Admiralty and the War Office worked together, forming four pairs of staff, each pair having a cryptographic expert and a German language expert. Three pairs maintained 24-hour watch, working 8 hours each, with the fourth pair covering time off. One of the civilians in MI1(b), C. Bryans, started another important job and set about compiling a dictionary of German words found in deciphered messages. As will be seen in later chapters, such dictionaries were to play a vital role when it came to working out the content of new German codebooks. Another civilian, J. St. Vincent Pletts, contributed some ground-breaking technical expertise by inventing a machine 'to lessen the labour in finding a key'. Unfortunately we have no more information on this key-finding machine.

This was all to pay dividends in the future. In the autumn of 1914, from the surviving fragments of information about the early days of British cryptography in the First World War, we can see that the combined unit had acquired important German documents and learned how to break German army cipher methods. Within the first three months of the war a solid foundation had been put together for the next four years. However, while some success was being found on the battlefields, back at the Admiralty, Ewing and his helpers were making no progress on the naval intercepts. Given the nature of the events in the battlefields of northern Europe, this was not seen as immediately crucial. As many hands as possible had to be made available for the army's codebreaking needs and work on the naval messages was confined to the night watch. However, some events had already taken place that would change all that.

Chapter 3

Code Capture

Following the great naval Battle of Trafalgar in 1805, the Royal Navy established dominance of the seas around Britain and northwestern France. But the French navy could still inflict damage on isolated naval and merchant ships in remote seas. The French islands of Île de France and Bourbon Island (now Réunion), located east of Madagscar in the southwesttern reaches of the India Ocean, provided bases for marauding French warships. In 1810 the Royal Navy was intent on revenge for ships recently lost to raiders from the island. The aim was to take Grand Port, 'one of the loveliest spots on the island – the ruins of the old Dutch town set against a backdrop of mossy mountains, hunched along the skyline like crouching green lions, the waters lapping placidly around the bay of sparkling turquoise'. The idyllic-seeming bay was not very welcoming to seafarers, thanks to corals lurking a few feet below the surface. It was also protected by well-placed guns. And, about four miles offshore, there was a small islet, Île de Passe, with its own fort and battery of guns covering the approaches. An attack from the sea looked very unlikely to succeed as it would first be necessary to get past Île de Passe – unless some deception was employed.

In August 1810 a single British ship, *Sirius*, approached the Île de Passe one evening shortly after dark. Some 70 armed men landed and quietly took control. No one on the main island knew of the islet's capture. The French codebook used for communications between ships, the Île de Passe and Grand Port was seized before it could be destroyed. A few days later some French warships approached Île de France, bringing along with them some captured British merchant ships and British civilians. The sight of a strange warship close to Île de Passe raised concerns among the approaching French ships. But the British sent signals in the proper code, giving the approaching ships false information about the British supposedly being elsewhere. Satisfied, the French ships started their approach, only to find themselves being fired on. However, bad luck and incompetence wasted the advantage gained by use of the captured codebook and it took some time before Île de France was finally captured and the seas secured for the unhindered growth of Britain's Empire and trade. In this chapter we will see how the British managed to capture some German codebooks early in the First World War.

In later chapters we will see how well, and also how badly, the intelligence revealed by the captured codebooks was used.

Even in August 1914 the war was a global one. The capture of some German documents, including important codebooks, took place during August in two quite coincidental events in opposite parts of the world – in the chilly waters of the eastern Baltic and on the balmy seas off the coast of Australia. In October or November a third event took place, this time somewhat closer to home, in the North Sea. The most immediately important of these events was that which took place in the Baltic. Here the Russians captured two or three of the copies of the main German naval 'signal' book and other papers about secret communications (we will look at codes and ciphers in Chapter 4). Known as the *Signalbuch der Kaiserlichen Marine*, SKM, (Signal Book of the Imperial Navy) it was a major trophy for the Russians as all the copies of it should have been destroyed by the German ship's captain and crew. The ship was the cruiser *Magdeburg*, 446 feet (136m) long, weighing over 4,500 tons, which had been built in 1911. It was a very modern and well-equipped vessel with 373 crew members. On 2 August, the *Magdeburg* and another cruiser, *Augsburg*, set out to bombard the Russian naval port of Libau. The sortie achieved little. The German ships 'fired some twenty rounds into the deserted harbour, which [like other ports] had been blocked by the Russians by the sinking of detained German merchantmen in the entrance'.[9] The operation was embarrassingly ineffective for the German navy. As the great Battle of Tannenberg got underway between the German and Russian armies, the *Admiralstab* (German Admiralty staff) came under pressure to do something to relieve the pressure on the German troops. So on the night of 25/26 August, the two cruisers and other ships were sent off to reconnoitre in the Gulf of Finland. On their way home the ships became separated in thick fog. At 12.14am on 26 August the *Magdeburg* ran aground either on some rocks or on a sandbank (sources vary) near Odenshol lighthouse, off the coast of Estonia. She could not free herself. Nor did an attempt by one of the other German warships to tow her off have any success.[10] The captain, fearing that Russian ships could not be far off, ordered preparations for the destruction of secret documents, including the copies of the SKM codebook and other secret documents such as charts of German minefields. Some documents were burnt, but the three copies of the SKM were spared so that it would still be possible to communicate with the other ships. One copy was held on the bridge, one in the wireless room (where the cipher instructions and other secret documents were also kept) and one in the captain's cabin. Explosive charges were placed so that the ship could be blown up before the Russians arrived. But some of the charges went off prematurely and the crew started to abandon ship without first destroying any more secret papers.

Just at that moment several Russian ships appeared and at 4.10am started firing. The *Magdeburg's* captain tried to organise a fightback but, 'by 7am resistance had been given up'.[11] The Russians boarded the partially damaged German ship and found the captain's copy of the SKM codebook. Two further copies were recovered from the sea. The Russians decided that they would keep the waterlogged copies and that they could spare the dry copy. Count Constantine Benckendorff, son of the Russian ambassador to London and a former cipher officer, was given the task of accompanying the codebook on its sea voyage to the north of Scotland.[12] There he disembarked and took the train to London. On 13 October he handed the codebook to Winston Churchill, the Navy minister, known by the traditional title of First Lord of the Admiralty.

Churchill described the incident in his account of the war, published under the title of *The World Crisis:* 'At the beginning of September, 1914, the German light cruiser *Magdeburg* was wrecked in the Baltic. The body of a drowned German under-officer was picked up by the Russians a few hours later, and clasped in his bosom by arms rigid in death, were the cipher and signal books of the German Navy and the minutely squared maps of the North Sea and Heligoland Bight. … The Russians felt that as the leading naval Power, the British Admiralty ought to have these books and charts … [later in October] I received from the hands of our loyal allies these sea-stained priceless documents. We set on foot at once an organization for the study of German wireless and for the translating of the messages when taken in. At the head of the organization was placed Sir Alfred Ewing'.

Over the years this seemingly fanciful story has been repeated many times – despite the fact that, as has also been widely reported, the copy of the codebook at the National Archives at Kew has clearly never been in contact with any sort of water, let alone immersed in a briny sea. The improbability of the idea of the codebook-clasping corpse has even been cited by conspiracy theorists as 'evidence' that the entire story of the capture of the codebook is a fake. But Russian sources suggest that one copy was indeed found grasped in the arms of a drowned German sailor. No doubt Churchill was told of this and could not resist adding the extra sparkle to his story, so applied it to the British copy. There are other 'errors' in Churchill's account – such as the misleading placing of the appointment of Ewing and the setting up of his organisation as happening *after* receipt of the codebook in late October. But the most conspicuous feature of Churchill's account is the colour – the dead sailor gallantly clasping to his bosom the secret codebook, perhaps either heroically intending that it would sink with his drowning body or, in understandable desperation, hoping that it might act as a tiny life raft.

Around the other side of the world another German codebook had already been captured. This time it was a merchant codebook, the

Handelsschiffsverkehrsbuch, HVB, (Merchant Ships' Transport Book). It was captured on a German-Australian merchant ship, the *Hobart*, moored off Melbourne on 11 August, by a boarding party from the Royal Australian Navy. The boarding party wore civilian clothes and claimed that they were customs officials in an attempt to trick the captain – who did not know that war had broken out – into granting them easy access to the ship. When their ruse was uncovered, the captain attempted to remove secret papers from a hidden space behind a panel in his cabin. He was arrested and the papers seized. It appears that the Royal Australian Navy did not appreciate that they should pass on details of their find to London and sat on them for the next four weeks – or perhaps the Australian cryptographic unit set up at the beginning of the war wanted exclusive use of the codebook. They eventually realised that they should supply a copy to the Admiralty. On 9 September it was finally sent by boat to Britain, arriving at the Admiralty at the end of October, a couple of weeks after the SKM had made its way there too.

A third codebook, the *Verkehrsbuch*, VB, (Transport Book) was also recovered, allegedly, from the North Sea during November. A small skirmish took place in shallow waters off the coast of the Dutch island of Texel between five British ships and a much inferior German squadron of four smaller vessels, all of which were quickly sunk. One of the masters of the stricken German vessels put all his ship's confidential documents into a lead-lined chest and ditched it over the side. The chest was then miraculously trawled up from its resting place on 30 November by a British trawler. Among the prizes was a copy of the VB. By early December this book too had found its way to Ewing's team. The term used to describe this find – miraculous – is not my choice, but that of the codebreakers themselves. According to a post-war internal history, 'A trawler by an almost incredible coincidence caught up in her net a series of secret documents – an incident that became known as "the Miraculous Draft of the Fishes".'[13] This may be another cover story. The Director of Naval Intelligence, Blinker Hall, later claimed that the VB was recovered from the North Sea 'by trawlers sent out for that purpose'. However, Hall's claims are to be treated with caution.[14] The VB codebook was used by military attachés stationed at German embassies as well as by various units within the navy such as submarines. Version III of the VB was used for *Auswaertigen Amts* (German Foreign Office), *Reichskolonialamts* (Reich Colonial Office) and *Kriegsnachrichtenwesens* (the War Communications Authority), so in the longer run it turned out to be of critical importance.[15]

By the end of autumn 1914 Ewing's team had in their hands three very important documents. The bulk of the daily messages sent out by the German Imperial navy were coded with the SKM, so it had the potential to reveal much about German naval operations. Before the three codebooks had been captured, most of Ewing's staff were working on army messages for the War Office. So in November, after the codebooks had been received, Assistant Paymaster Charles Rotter was transferred to Ewing's team from the Naval Intelligence department where he was the main German language expert. Rotter was the officer who had looked at intercepted messages before the war earlier at the Admiralty (see previous chapter). Some writers have suggested that Rotter had been active in cryptography for some years. No doubt he had spent some time trying to break the German messages that had been collecting in the run-up to the war, but there is no evidence to suggest that he had any success, although this cannot be ruled out. Denniston recalled how the atmosphere at the Admiralty changed towards the end of October following some visits by a Russian military man. An unknown person – Rotter – was then noticed working in a small room that became out of bounds. 'Then one fine day [Ewing] remarked that it was blowing hard in the German Bight and in reply to direct questions explained what was afoot.' The details of the windspeed in the Bight came from an intercepted weather report that Rotter had deciphered and decoded. Once Rotter found out how to break the cipher keys, the naval codebreakers were able to start deciphering and decoding the German naval messages sent in the SKM and other codes. William F. Clarke later wrote that Rotter was 'the founder of Room 40's success by his work on early captured documents'.[16] Rotter noticed that the German wireless operators had made a serious error by 're-ciphering' the message numbers. Whether this means that they put the telegram number in clear in the message text and also enciphered within the cipher text, or whether they re-used the numbers within the cipher text of different messages is not clear. But some sort of mistake of this type gave Rotter an entry into the German cipher system used with the SKM. No doubt he was helped by the discoveries of the French military codebreakers on the Western Front and by Australian codebreakers who, at the end of October, had broken a German cipher key used with the public ABC Commercial Codebook (see Chapter 1). Rotter was Room 40's first cryptographic expert. He stayed with Room 40 for the duration of the war and later went on to become Director of Statistics at the Admiralty. When the Second World War started, recalled Clarke, 'in 1939 [Rotter] sent some money to give his old colleagues a drink at Bletchley Park'. He died in 1948.[17]

Although the naval codebreakers had been told about the French and British armies' success with German ciphers, the navy did not return the favour. Ewing kept the breakthrough secret from the army codebreakers in MI1(b). The acquisition of the SKM was to be kept fully under wraps. Its value was so great that no word could be allowed to slip out about its capture. So it followed that the breaking of the cipher had be kept quiet too. What's more Ewing now wanted his staff back from the War Office. There was now plenty of naval work for them to be getting on with. So when relations between the War Office and the Admiralty began to fray, Room 40 and MI1(b) went their own ways.As one of the naval cryptographers on loan to the War Office later commented: 'One is bound to admit that signs of jealousy were not absent even in this small section of men drawn from many branches of civil life.' Success, it seems, could not be shared.

The first major break in relations between the two units was the result of a most serious military incident – the damaging of a senior military man's honour. Denniston later recalled, 'It must be remembered that all this time civilians deciphered and translated the messages, which all concerned the Western Front and were of immediate value to the Intelligence Section of GHQ [General Headquarters of the British Expeditionary Force in France] whither they were transmitted by wire and daily bag. But it must also be remembered that they were also deciphered and translated in the Admiralty and if [generally] of no immediate value, they were occasionally of extreme interest and could hardly be concealed from those in supreme control.' MI1(b) passed its information up through the army command to the Minister of War, who happened to be a soldier, Lord Kitchener. Ewing's people forwarded their information up to the First Sea Lord, Jacky Fisher, and the First Lord of the Admiralty, Winston Churchill. This worked well most of the time. But one day some information from an intercepted message, concerning the treatment by the Germans of Indian prisoners, was delayed on its way to Kitchener. Churchill, however, was informed promptly and it seems that, in a meeting with Kitchener, he talked about the latest intelligence. Kitchener was outraged at what he perceived to be the deep injury done to his dignity incurred by being informed by the First Lord of the Admiralty about something to do with the War Office. Relations at the working level soured as each team then tried harder to please its own superiors.

It is possible that MI1(b) had some hint of what had happened at the Admiralty and wanted part of the action. Certainly, the Admiralty did pass on to MI1(b) some intelligence derived from its naval intercepts. For example, in late 1914 when it intercepted a message revealing the current keyword in use with German military cipher system on the Eastern front, details of the keyword ('*ConstantinopleWienBerlin*') were forwarded to MI1(b). However, they did not pass on any hint about the source of the intelligence. General Anderson, in charge of MI1(b), asked Room 40 how it had discovered the keyword, but got no response. At that time wireless traffic on the Western Front had dropped away, with mobile battles turning into static trench war where more secure wire telegraphy and telephony could be used. So, MI1(b) was looking for things to do. It asked Room 40 for closer co-operation several times, aware perhaps that something was going on. It was, said Denniston, 'now clear that the Admiralty cryptographic section had found a task which concerned the navy alone and that there might be an enormous outlet for their energy … relations between the two offices were already somewhat strained and the new activities in the Admiralty were a closely guarded secret and a definite breach occurred'. There was also pressure from the naval colleges to return their teachers who were needed for the new term in September. With two exceptions – Denniston and Anstie – the instructors duly gave up their secret work and went back to teaching naval recruits. Ewing had to look elsewhere for staff. His first resort was to withdraw from joint work with MI1(b). Unfortunately the separation was messy and left a legacy of bitterness and non-co-operation which persisted until Ewing was edged out in mid-1916. Denniston, later head of the joint army, navy and Foreign Office cryptographic unit between 1919 and 1941, commented, 'Looking back over those years, the loss of efficiency to both departments caused originally by mere official jealousy is the most regrettable fact in the development of intelligence based on cryptography.'

With the return of those who had been working at the War Office, Sir Alfred Ewing's room at the Admiralty was now becoming rather crowded. In the early days Ewing had continued to receive visitors connected with his work as Director of Naval Education. The codebreakers had to put all their papers away in a cupboard so that none of the outsiders might pick up any hint of the true work of Ewing's office. However, now even this was too risky and all visitors were banned. The sensitivity of senior naval officers brought this period to an end when a young civilian codebreaker, unaware of the deference normally expected by the higher beings at the Admiralty, refused entry to Ewing's office to the very important personage of the Assistant Secretary to the Admiralty. What with the overcrowding and the need for quiet and for security, it was decided that the codebreakers should have their own accommodation. A room in a distant corner of the old Admiralty buildings, where no unexpected visitors would ever find their way, was found and the section moved into Room 40 OB (for 'old buildings'). This gave Ewing's team its home and its name. With access to the codebooks, and methods in hand to break the cipher keys, 'Room 40' was ready to become one more cog in the great war machine.

Chapter 4

Codes and Ciphers

In 1898 a pioneer of the electric telegraph, Charles Bright, claimed that the telegraph meant that 'peoples have been brought more in touch with each other, so also have their rulers and statesmen. An entirely new and much-improved method of conducting diplomatic relations between one country and another has come into use with the telegraph wire and [submarine] cable. The facility and rapidity with which one government is now enabled to know the "mind" – or, at any rate, the professed mind – of another, has often been the means of averting diplomatic ruptures and consequent wars during the last few decades. At first sight, the contrary result might have been anticipated; but, on the whole, experience distinctly pronounces in favour of the pacific effect of telegraphy.'

It is true that the telegraph lay behind much of the extraordinary growth of peaceful national and international cultural and commercial activities of the second half of the 19th century. But Bright was over-optimistic. The telegraph also supported the military power of colonial governments and enabled their 'minor' wars, fought by and large not on European soil and not against European foes, but in Africa and Asia and against local forces (and for whom they were major conflicts). Europe's large-scale wars were few – the Crimean War (where the telegraph played a role in the later stages) and the 'wars of German unification' culminating in the Franco-Prussian War of 1870–71 (where the railway and the telegraph took on a central role, especially in underpinning the German 'knock-out' style of attack). With the invention of the wireless, telegraphy was able to spread its tentacles further, beyond the reach of metal cable. In the early 20th century, as Europe drifted into total war, the availability of effectively instant communication between governments did little to retard its approach. And, the telegraph and the railway meant that war, once declared, would come more quickly and in greater intensity than anyone imagined. Once the war started, cable and wireless technologies, primarily developed as tools of trade, were applied, often seamlessly, to military ends. One important aspect of commercial telegraphy was the use of codes.

Initially such codes were developed because the senders of telegrams wanted to reduce the length of messages and thus the cost of sending them. The rapidly growing network of telegraph links, both within individual countries and between them (across land borders and as submarine cables across even the widest oceans), carried a vast amount of telegraphic traffic for governments and the military, for commerce and for the private individual. The telegraph was an essential tool for many types of business. But it could be costly to use. Senders of telegrams – even prolix military and government administrators – soon learned to use short sentences, developing what became known as 'telegraphese'. Telegrams were charged by the word, so keeping messages to as few words as possible made sound sense. The long leisurely style of the handwritten letter – 'May I trouble you to send at your earliest convenience the sum of one hundred pounds sterling' – was replaced by short sharp messages – 'Send 100 pounds soonest'.

But even this was insufficiently economic for companies that had to send hundreds or thousands of telegrams. So special codes were devised to wring out every last drop of excess 'wordage'. Codes were effectively dictionaries with lists of plain language words and phrases in alphabetical order – thus the term 'codebook'. But instead of having a definition alongside each entry, there would be a 'codeword'. So the codeword for 'send' might be DJTB, for 'sent' DJTC, for 'sentiment' DJTD, and so on. Some codes gave a group of numbers as the codeword, rather than a group of letters (so 'sent' might be 8350, 'send' 8351, 'sentiment' 8352, etc). These are called 'code-groups' rather than codewords, though they are effectively the same thing. Codes could make messages shorter by allocating a single codeword (or code-group) to represent a phrase and not just a single word. So there was a codeword for 'pay'. But other codewords would also be offered for related entries such as 'pay by cash', 'pay by cheque', 'pay by telegram', 'pay today', 'pay in 30 days', 'pay in full', 'pay on satisfactory completion of the contract', 'pay with 10% discount', 'pay with 25% discount', and so on. At the receiving end, decoding involved looking up in the codebook each codeword in a message and checking its original meaning.

There are two ways of squeezing even more savings out of a codebook. First, it can be made larger. So codebooks with as many as 50,000 or more entries were quite common in industry and commerce. The more entries, the greater the potential for contraction of the length of messages. However, this came at the cost of being more cumbersome to use. This not just a matter of manual handling of a very big codebook, but more importantly of gaining the skill of knowing what codewords were available. Second, a codebook can be tailored more closely to the needs of its users. Customised codebooks were produced in their hundreds and thousands for every type of industry or commercial activity from shipping merchants and railway companies to shoe-makers and agricultural suppliers. As one writer has put it, 'There were codes for bankers, brokers, canned goods, clothing, coal, coffee, … seeds, ship brokers, shipping, sugar, tailors, textiles, theatres, ticket brokers, tobacco. … To open these books is to feel the life pulse of the business. The Waste Merchant's Standard Code offers a consignment of *cast iron scrap, excessively rusty* with [the codeword] IQUA.' The devising of codes for specific industries and types of business became a significant economic activity in its own. While a general codebook might offer 10:1 contraction, a well-designed, purpose-built codebook might reach 20:1 or 30:1. These codebooks were expensive to compile and thus expensive to buy, though for a busy company soon repaid their initial cost. All the same, changing circumstances meant that they soon had to be updated or replaced. The historian of codebreaking, David Kahn, observes: 'A code once compiled does not retain its value forever. A code reflects the world at a particular instant, and as the world moves on it outmodes the code. … Ironically, the better a code is at its moment of its compilation, the more closely its vocabulary fits the business requirements of its time, the more rapidly will it become obsolescent.' That observation applies to military codebooks too.

Codebooks became a common part of everyday life. Even tourists could buy codebooks so that they could keep in touch with family and friends at relatively cheap telegraph rates. Such codebooks were 'public' in that anyone could buy a copy and use it. Some were marketed specifically because they had a very wide range of users. The most commonly used public codebook was the *ABC Code*, devised by a shipping manager. It went through dozens of editions between 1874 when it was first published and the outbreak of the First World War when its use was global. Indeed, we saw in Chapter 1 how some of the German wireless and cable messages intercepted in the run-up to and around the outbreak of the war, were sent in the *ABC Code* (though then made secure by enciphering it). Other codebooks, such as those for very obscure industrial sectors, sold fewer copies and so were more expensive, but were still public, and two competing companies might use the same code. Those companies, organisations and individuals who wanted more secrecy would devise their own codebook (or pay someone to devise one for them). Many a company dreamed up its own codebook for communications that had to be entrusted to the public telegraph networks (as did Sir Alfred Ewing in his days as a young engineer working for a cable company). The basic principle was exactly the same. An alphabetical dictionary with entries for words and phrases would be accompanied by a corresponding list of codewords or code-groups. If a user wanted extra security, the coded message could be 'enciphered' using some system or other (see below).

The three main German codebooks captured early in the war, the *Handelsschiffsverkehrsbuch*, HVB, the *Verkehrsbuch*, VB, and the *Signalbuch der Kaiserlichen Marine,* SKM (and other German military and diplomatic codebooks that we will meet in later chapters), were all derived from the basic telegraphic codebooks of the time. They were not designed with secrecy in mind. These three codebooks had much in common, but were also quite specific in their own way. Each needs a short description. But before looking at the individual codebooks, a comment is necessary about the sources for the remainder of this chapter. There is a section on codes and ciphers in a multi-volume 'secret history' of the naval war written in the early 1920s by Frank Birch, with help from William F. Clarke. Both joined Room 40 in 1916 and stayed on after the war to write the historical documents now lodged in the National Archives in Kew. Both men, their writings show us, were extremely arrogant and brimming with sarcasm. The codes and ciphers section is generally attributed to Birch, who was a historian (a 'rather dull' one according to one writer). Despite his profession, Birch has left us with a distinctly obscure historical source. Unfortunately, in the chapter on codes and ciphers, one of the most important in the document, Birch is at his most obscure, allowing allusion and ladlings of opinion to dominate; it is someone writing to show how clever he is. Someone in the Admiralty commenting on this chapter in 1921 wrote: 'I have read this chapter very carefully. It seems a pity that more has not been written on this subject, which would be of all absorbing interest to an N. O. [Naval Officer] engaged on ciphering duties. This particular work fails chiefly in that throughout … it is written in a style which I feel sure no one except a super civilian will understand. … As it stands this work is a danger if it can be understood at all. A detailed criticism would fill many pages.'

However, in the National Archives there are also several captured German documents, including copies of the three main codebooks and several other papers, among them the original German instruction books for the some of the cipher systems used with the codebooks. By comparing Birch's obscurantist text with these German documents it has been possible to put together a more comprehensible account of the German naval codes and ciphers. Unfortunately there remain plenty of apparent contradictions. For example, Birch insists that one particular type of cipher (that used with the VB codebook as described later in this chapter) was not used until much later in the war. However, the German booklet of instructions for the cipher technique is dated 1908. From the archival material I have described three types of cipher known to have been used with a particular codebook at some time or other in the war. However, there were many more types of cipher than I have recounted here and there were often several different types of cipher in use with any one codebook at any one time. Thus, it is not possible to be absolutely precise about which cipher was used with which codebook and at which period of the war.

***

The SKM is an impressive tome. It looks, if anything, like one of the oversized Bibles only ever seen propped up on a lectern in a cathedral. The copy of the SKM held in the archives at Kew is far too heavy to hold up like an ordinary book and, like a large Bible, would have had to rest on a table or stand of some sort when it was used. It weighs much more even than a book of its size should, as its covers are lined with lead to aid its sinking if thrown overboard.

To the British observer the likeness to a Bible is heightened by the large Gothic lettering of the early pages of the codebook and especially the large print spelling out its full name: *Signalbuch der Kaiserlichen Marine*. At the top left-hand corner of the title page in small Gothic type, but underlined, is the word *Geheim!* (Secret). Lower down on the same page is the Kaiser's coat of arms and next to it an official stamp of the *Kaiserlichen Marine*, the Imperial navy. On the next page, among a series of general instructions and observations, one line is printed in heavy type: 'If the danger arises that the *Signalbuch* could fall into enemy hands, it must be thrown overboard or destroyed (by burning).' The comparison of the SKM codebook with the Bible is not entirely based on its great size and impressively archaic-looking typeface. Figuratively speaking the SKM was the German naval signaller's bible. It was not just a codebook. Indeed, it was not even primarily a codebook. It was, as its title suggests, a book about all types of naval signalling. Having grown out of traditional signalling techniques from the pre-wireless days, using flags and semaphore, it was designed for ease of use for signallers working in emergencies and under fire, not for the needs of people who needed to send secret telegraph messages without undue complication or difficulty.

The SKM was not used at all for cable telegraphy and it preceded the invention of the wireless. The SKM's wireless telegraphy code section was thus added as an afterthought. In modern jargon it was a 'bolt-on'. The '*FT*' (*Funktelegraphie* – W/T or wireless telegraphy) section, though the biggest part of the codebook, is thus only one of several sections in the SKM. The book starts off with several pages of pretty, colourful images of idealised signalling by flags, semaphore and lamps (for which there was a special version of the Morse code), a section on '*Evolutions signal*' (ie, ships' tactical movements around one another in both normal sailing and in naval battles), before moving on to '*FT Namen*' (wireless telegraphy 'call-signs') and then to the various codes which are our main interest. Even within the wireless telegraphy section there was not one codebook, but several. There was a dictionary of words, a list of ship names and a geographical place-names list, plus several smaller sections for compass bearings, map grid-references and so on. This may have eased the task of designing the wireless telegraphy section of the codebook and integrating it with the existing signals book, but it introduced serious weaknesses. These failings were exploited by Room 40 later in the war when new versions of the codebook were published and were not hand-delivered by drowned German sailors but had to be 'reconstructed' by skilful cryptography (see Chapter 12).

The basic system was extremely simple and gave a three-letter codeword – such as AAB or EVT or NLT – to represent a plain language letter, word, name or phrase. So, for example 'security' (*Sicherheit*) was represented by RTL; 'land (*Land*) by LZA, 'on land' by LZB, 'distance oneself from land' by LZG, 'land out of sight' by LZI and 'land in sight' by LZJ, and so on. The dictionary was in alphabetical order so the user would look up the word or phrase to be encoded and use the codeword. The three-letter codewords were also in alphabetical order (indeed in the codebook itself they form the left-hand column, with the plain entry in a right-hand column). Some examples are given in Table 4.1 of SKM entries (with translation of the meanings as an additional third column).

Table 4.1

Sample entries from the SKM codebook system

AÄB = a

AÄC = ä

AÄD = ab   [a common German prefix]

AÄE = abändern-ung   [alter/amend – alteration/amendment]

AÄF = abgeändert   [altered/amended]

AÄG = in Abänderung   [in amendment/in alteration]

...

DOI = Burg   [castle]

DOJ = Burge, Burgen   [guarantee]

DOK = Burgerlich   [civilian (authorities) also middle class/bourgeois]

DOL = Burgermeister   [mayor]

DOM = Burgerschaft   [citizenry]

DON = Burgschaft   [company]

DOÖ = Büro   [office]

DOP = Bursche   [boy, fellow]

...

DOX = Canadier   [Canadian]

DOY = Cardiffkohle   [Cardiff coal]

DOZ = Celsius-Grade   [Celsius/Centigrade degree]

DOa = Cent   [cent (money)]

DOg = Chance   [chance, prospect]

...

LYA = Lage   [situation]

LYÄ = augenblickliche Lage   [momentary situation]

LYB = in der Lage   [in the situation]

LYC = kritische Lage   [critical situation]

LYD	=	politische Lage	[political situation]
LYE	=	politische Lage hat sich gebessert	[political situation has improved]
LYF	=	politiche Lage	[strategic situation]
LYM	=	tactische Lage	[tactical situation]
LYP	=	Lagern -ung	[store, storage]
LYQ	=	Lagerschale	
LYR	=	Lagune	[lagoon]
LYS	=	lahm, -heit	[lame/tired, lameness/tiredness]
LYT	=	Lage is gefäerlich	[situation is dangerous]

Example: original message: 'political situation [of] mayor changed; prospect [for acquiring] Cardiff coal changed; situation difficult', would be coded as 'LYD DOLAÄF DOG DOYAÄF LYJ'.The person receiving the message looks up each codeword to uncover the original meanings.

(source:ADM137/4156)

It will immediately be obvious that there are some special letters, such 'Ä', 'α' and 'γ', in the three-letter codewords. This extends considerably the number of codewords available for use beyond what would be possible with just the basic 26 letters of the alphabet (though the need for extra combinations was due to the wasteful structure of the codebook). It is worth pointing out that for some time the Room 40 cryptographers were unaware of the full number of these extra characters; in particular they missed the distinction between 'A' and 'Ā'.This had the effect on one occasion of Room 40 passing on wrong map references to the Admiralty, which in turn lessened the trust of senior Admiralty officers in Room 40's intelligence because they knew that the map references were mistaken, for example, because a German ship was known to be in one place (in map reference area 'Ā' only to be told by Room 40 that it was elsewhere (in map reference area A).This minor technical difficulty was soon overcome, but the distrust lingered.

Both the plain language entries and the codewords were arranged in alphabetic order. This meant that a single list only was needed for both encoding and decoding.A plain language word or phrase beginning with 'a' is likely to have a codeword beginning with 'A' (or a closely placed letter in the alphabet). Similarly a coded message with a codeword beginning with 'A' is likely to represent a plain language entry beginning with 'a' (or perhaps 'b') in the original meaning.A very basic technique for improving codebook security would be to allocate the codewords in random rather than alphabetical order (see Table 4.2). However, this requires two lists, whereas the simpler structure adopted for the SKM (and also the VB and HVB) requires only one list. With a 'one-part' code, if a codebreaker knows that 'ATW' means 'army' and 'ATY' means 'army group', then it is certain that ATX is also a variant of 'army', such as 'army camp' or 'army corps'. With a 'two-part' code, knowing the plain meaning of one codeword (ATW) does not offer any clue to the plain meaning of another similar codeword (ATX). More complex means of breaking such codebooks are necessary. Later in the book (see Chapter 12) we will see how the codebreakers had to devise machinery to break two-part (or 'hatted') codes in a practical timescale.

Table 4.2 Two-part code example

Part 1 for encoding

Arrange	= GHR
Arrange immediately	= AAC
Arrange on arrival	= RTL
Arranged	= WEF
...	
Motive	= WBV
Move	= AAD
Move as soon as feasible	= NAE
...	
Trade	= WWN
Trade embargo	= AAB
Trade note	= LRF

Part 2 for decoding

AAB	= Trade embargo
AAC	= Arrange immediately
AAD	= Move
AAE	= Despatch
...	
LRF	= Trade note
...	
NAE	= Move as soon as feasible

The basic outline of the SKM is thus quite simple – a 'one-part' codebook with alphabetic entries. However, as pointed out above, the SKM was in effect grafted onto an existing manual and system of naval 'signalling'. This meant that the simple structure was complicated by the extra sections that were simply borrowed, unmodified, from the signals book. Codewords for compass bearings began with an X so, for example, 299 degrees was XOI. Codewords for times always began with a Y. The grid boxes used to determine location at sea on German maps were given codewords beginning with Z. Thus a very high number of codewords within actual messages began with an X, a Y or a Z. Another feature was the list of ship names. This assigned a two-letter code to each ship in the German navy (including merchant ships). This two-letter code was preceded by a standard extra character, the Greek letter ß ('beta'). But the unadorned two-letter code was also used as a 'call-sign' when one wireless operator wanted to call another ship or a ship wanted to identify itself to others. Analysis of call-signs, effectively the names of user organisations, is the first task of eavesdroppers. But more important, these features added a structure to the coded messages that could be detected in the enciphered messages, helping the process of breaking the cipher key. As Birch noted, 'These complications were all of a nature to puzzle the German coder and assist the English decipherer.'

The SKM's origins in naval signalling affected the codebook in other ways. It meant that it contained masses of signals for 'elaborate forms of tactical manoeuvring [at sea], many of them now out of date ... and this was not unnatural: for it was based on [code]books designed solely for visual signals, which only friends might see, and not with [cable] telegraphy or wireless which was certain to fell into malevolent hands'. As Birch pointed out, the SKM even had a codeword, GÜK, for *fiendlich Flaggschiff rammen* – ram the enemy flagship – a tactic left over from the age of sail, if not that of the galleys, and most unlikely ever to be used. Another great weakness was that the codebook simply was not changed often enough – indeed the copy captured in August 1914 stayed in use by the German navy, despite their having some idea of its loss, until 1917. All in all, the SKM was a mess. This meant it was a gift to the British codebreakers. When it was updated the new codebook inherited the structural weaknesses, so the British cryptographers were able to start working out the new code from knowledge gained with the old one. (The skill of 'reconstructing' a codebook from scratch is covered in Chapter 12.)

The *Handelsschiffsverkehrsbuch* (in full, '*Handelsschiffsverkehrsbuch für den chiffrierten verkehr mit Deutschen Handelsschiffen*' (HVB – 'Merchant ships' transport book for enciphered traffic with German merchant ships') was primarily for use by merchant ships, but was used by warships as well, especially if they needed to communicate with merchant ships. It was also used by Zeppelin airships on both naval reconnaissance and bombing flights. Each entry is represented by a four-letter codeword: *König* (king) is represented by SCZR; '*wie viel lokomotiven sind erfordelich*' (how many locomotives are required') by SPGC. As with the SKM, the HVB codebook was a 'one part' system with plain and codewords in alphabetical order.

It also had its own regularities. Though the book was alphabetical, it started its codewords with DABC (not AAAA or anything in between). The DA—codewords all represented ship and squadron names of German and foreign navies (see examples in Table 4.3). Code entries with K—, L— and M—were devoted to proper names and letters or combinations of letters for spelling out words not in the word list (see examples in Table 4.4). Code entries OABC to OAKN were assigned to grammar and grammatical descriptions, such as *punkt* (full stop) or 'the next group is in plural'. The words and phrases in the *wörterbuch* (dictionary) were given codes between OALB to PZWV or between RABC to VPKC. In theory, the use of four-letter codewords meant that many more possible codeword combinations were available for use. However, this advantage was thrown away. The only letters of the alphabet that were used in any codewords were A, B, C, D, F, G, K, L, M, N, O, P, R, S, T, U and V. This is only 17 of the possible 26 letters of the basic alphabet. More noticeably still, only 12 of them – D, G, K, L, M, O, P, R, S, T, U and V – would ever appear as the first letter in a codeword. These restrictions aided the breaking of the ciphers used with the codebook.

The HVB in fact had two sets of codewords. The second, consisting of 'pronounceable nonsense words', was designed for sending messages by telegraph cable. So, *König* could be coded as SCZR, or as 'mukop emari'. This type of nonsense word was commonly used for telegrams. They were carefully designed not to be similar sounding and to exclude situations where a small error in tapping out the Morse code would send a quite similar set of letters but with a totally different meaning.

Table 4.3 The *Handelsschiffsverkehrbuch* (HVB) codebook system

cable codeword	W/T codeword	plain word (meaning)	
babac igapo	DAKC	Gazelle	(ship name)
babac agefu	DAKF	Gefion	ditto
babac ihave	DAKG	Geier	ditto
babac ihebo	DAKL	Gneisenau	ditto
babac ihuli	DAKM	Göben	ditto
…			
gosid ehige	MSZK	Vigholm	(place-name)
gosid ehyra	MSZL	Vigo	ditto
gosid ekica	MSZN	Vigsö Bucht Dänemark	ditto
gosid elavo	MSZO	vih	(syllable for spelling out words)

gosid emari	MSZP	vik	ditto
gosid emego	MSZR	Vikerö Fjord	(place-name)
gosid enafy	MSZT	vil	(syllable for spelling out words)
gosid eneci	MSZU	Vila, Port	(place-name)

The third main German naval code, the *Verkehrsbuch* (VB) translates as the 'transport book', but this does not give an adequate impression of its users. Submarines and small patrol boats used it instead of the SKM for communications at sea. Also it was used by the German naval and military attachés located at foreign diplomatic posts or posted alongside foreign military forces. Some diplomatic traffic also used the VB, and also communications between the German navy and the army. The VB differed from the other two main naval codebooks in that the codewords were 'code-groups' of five numbers rather than letters. Thus 'embargo' was represented by 38256. The code-group 63389 meant: *'Telegram [nr] [vom] [betr] ist eingetroffen [im]'* (Telegram [number] [from] [concerning] has arrived [at])' – the bits in square brackets are optional meanings that will be obvious to the user from the context. The numbers used to make up the code-groups consisted of two parts: a three-number *stammzahl* or 'root number', derived from the codebook page number, and a two-number *eindzahl* or 'end number' derived from the number on the page of the plain language entry (each numbered 00 to 99). The codebook starts on page 100 with grammatical entries; pages 101–250 contain code-groups for proper names and for combinations of letters for spelling out words not in the word list; 251–280 contain a list of ships, banks and their branches, telegraphic routes, cable offices and so on. Pages 281 to 712 (the end of the book) form the main word list or dictionary. One section in the dictionary gives a series of code-groups for encoding single and pairs of plain language letters. These code-groups can be used to spell out words which do not exist in the dictionary or any other list of plain entries.

Table 4.4 *Verkehrsbuch* (VB) codebook system

Note: the page number gives the first three numbers of the code-group and the individual entry gives the last two numbers (so that Alkmaar = 105 55 and Fray Bentos = 148 17).

Page 105

50 Alistro

51 alj

52 alk

53 Al-Kalah

54 Al-Khelb

55 Alkmaar
56 all
57 äll
58 alla
59 alle
60 allem
61 allen
62 aller
63 Allerheiligen B.   [All Saints' Day]
64 alles
…

Page 148
11 Franz
12 französisch   [French]
13 fras
14 Fraserburgh (Scottl.)   [Scotland]
15 Fraternité, Fort de la
16 fray
17 Fray Bentos
18 fre
19 fred
20 Frederica
…

Page 257
60 Torpedoboat D3
61 Torpedoboat D4
…
67 Torpedoboat D10
68 Torpedoboat S11
69 Torpedoboat S12
…

Page 270
00 A
01 AÄ
02 AB
03 AC
…
57 ÄZ

58 B
59 BA
60 BÄ
61 BC
...
Page 302

08 Artillerie	[artillery}
09 Schwere Artillerie	[heavy artillery]
10 Uberlegene Artillerie	[superior artillery]
...	
12 Artillerieabteilung	[artillery detachment]
13 Artilleriefeuer	[artillery fire]
...	
28 Artilleristenmaat	[artillery trooper]

Frank Birch, writing after the war, commented that all three of the codebooks possessed many common features, 'and, great as were the single and especial disadvantages of each, the defects which they had in common were glaring'. The books were too large (both physically and in the number of entries) to be used without difficulty. The SKM offered some 300,000 three-letter codewords for word and positional entries alone, but, reckoned Birch, probably not more than 5,000 were ever used. On the other hand, despite the mass of entries, a simple meaning such as *Helgoland* (Heligoland) required two codewords. On the excessive number of useless entries Birch fully exercised his loquacious extravagance: 'The chief significance of this defect, of these albequestrian propensities, is one which may, perhaps, occur less readily to the layman than to the cipher expert. The expert knows that in such a book only a very few of the groups can be used and in guessing a [cipher] key on it, he knows that when he has [worked out] two letters he can guess with fair accuracy the remaining one' (or in the case of a four-letter code, the remaining two letters). And this was still possible, 'even if he has no knowledge whatever of the sense of a message or even the meaning of a single group in the book. It was indeed on this principle alone that the keys on the successor to the SKM, the FFB, were originally solved.' Ideally, all the codewords in a codebook should be used in a roughly equal number of times each (to foil codebreakers for whom frequency analysis is the key tool). Commonly occurring entries such as 'full stop', place-names, ship names, naval unit names and so on all present severe challenges for the designer of effective codebooks. None of the main three codebooks made use of basic techniques aimed at defeating frequency analysis, such as employing 'dummy' groups (meaningless entries used to pad out the message and upset cryptographers using frequency analysis) or 'substitute' codewords (offering several alternative code combinations for common plain meanings such as 'full stop').These, said Birch, 'afford the key-guesser a considerable amount of difficulty'.

Birch poured scorn on the one-part nature of the codebooks. 'Yet of all the defects common to German codebooks the most striking and the least excusable consisted in the order in which the [codewords] occurred. Early codebooks had never been formed with any great regard for cryptography. They never set out to defeat organised research. As long as one message could not readily be deciphered that was enough. German codebooks consisted each merely of one book in which [plain language entries] were arranged alphabetically down the page and codes (letters or numbers) were arranged against them on the left hand side in alphabetical or numerical order. The realisation of this defect came very late to the German [naval] authorities.They were slow to remedy it. It can easily be remedied by having two books, one for coding and one for decoding … [otherwise] once the key is obtained and the sense of a few [codewords] fixed, [the cryptographer] is able, with great ease, to fill in the remainder.To the key-getter it is almost of equal assistance. Certain parts of the alphabet occur more commonly than others; and in certain classes of messages the [codewords] most commonly used will all occur on the same page [of the codebook] … It was on this principle that many German naval codebooks were read in the [Admiralty in London] before any of them fell into British hands.' Birch concluded that the devising of German naval codebooks 'was bad, unimaginative and lacking in the first essentials of secrecy, brevity and speed of replacement'.

***

Frank Birch also excoriated the German ciphers. 'To cipher plain language so that it may be hard to [decrypt for] the enemy and easy for a friend is difficult; it needs patience and mutual confidence and understanding: for wide and general use it is dangerous … so [the German navy] decided to supplement [by] ciphering such defects of existing [codebooks] as were realised … [But] the system of [ciphering] adopted was radically bad … by its simplicity it helped the German as little as it hindered the British [cryptographer] …They caused little trouble to the expert English decipherer, sitting at ease with a number of copies of signals intercepted and forwarded by the most expert English wireless operators, [but] were a constant source of nuisance and confusion to a barely trained German depending upon the "intake" of one wireless operator and lacking in time, ingenuity and skill to rectify small errors. … The actual method[s of ciphering] remained in use, though not in general use, to the end of the war'.[18] Birch records that at least eight different naval codebooks were used at one time or another and the cipher systems that were used with each codebook were often changed. 'During the currency of any codebook there were always two and often three or four different methods of ciphering it in force at the same time.'[19] Thus it is only possible in the remainder of this chapter to introduce some of the cipher systems known to have been used at one time or other with a particular codebook. We will come across some more cipher systems in later chapters.

A cipher in modern meaning usually implies the use of a 'key', which can change and is used to encipher particular messages, and a process or set or rules for using individual keys. Breaking a cipher thus involves two stages: firstly identifying the process, and secondly working out the key for any particular message.

Most often we now think of the key as a word (often called a 'keyword') or a set of numbers. But two of the three ciphers which we will look at in the remainder of this chapter did not use a keyword. The 'key' in these cases was a small printed booklet. Each booklet contained a pair of tables – one for enciphering and one for deciphering – with a set cipher-letter as a substitute for each code-letter in a codeword. The key and the process are effectively the same thing in such a simple cipher. In the third cipher to be dealt with below, there was indeed a keyword system used in a formalised way.

We will start with the *Chiffreschlüssel zum HVB* (Cipher key to the HVB). At the top of the page of the German instruction booklet is the injunction, 'to be kept apart from the HVB' – so that the two items could not be captured at the same time. There are some simple instructions and a table, with the code-letter on the left and the cipher-letter on the right (see Table 4.5). The second table lists the cipher-letter on the left in alphabetical order and its code-letter equivalent on the right to allow for easy deciphering. This is just about as simple a cipher as can be conceived (indeed it is effectively the same as a simple two-part codebook). The same substitution was the same every time the same code-letter occurred (until a new table of substitutions was introduced). As the cryptographer's most important technique for breaking ciphers is a 'frequency analysis' of the number of times each letter of the alphabet (or number) is used in the enciphered message, this steady, unchanging system of substitution will not hide any pronounced frequency 'bulges' in the coded message(s). Now, this might not matter if the codebook has been well designed to filter out any statistical distortions in the frequency of use of letters. But, as we have seen, only 12 letters of the alphabet were ever used as the first letter in the HVB codewords. This fact alone gave the codebreakers a head start when it came to tackling new ciphers or codebooks.

Table 4.5

A simple cipher

To cipher:	To decipher:
A – I	A – E
B – L	B – K

C – D	C – M
D – S	D – C
E – A	E – Y
F – M	F – T
G – X	G – P
H – Z	H – Z
I – O	I – A
K – B	K – W
L – N	L – B
M – C	M – F
N – V	N – L
O – U	O – I
P – G	P – V
R – T	R – X
S – W	S – D
T – F	T – R
U – Y	U – O
V – P	V – N
W – K	W – S
X – R	X – G
Y – E	Y – U
Z – H	Z – H

Note: J and Q are not used.

We can look at an example from the original German instruction book, using the 'nonsense' codewords used by the HVB codebook. An enciphered message was always preceded by a call-sign and its location plus a special codeword, 'kisah aciba', which meant that 'the contents of this message have been enciphered with the HVB key'. Table 4.6 shows the coded message from the steamship *Neckar* to an address in Bremen informing it of the ship's expected arrival at Shanghai.

Table 4.6

Enciphering a coded message

Full coded message:

Elond Bremen kisah aciba hanib ynixe kukib uroli mifob alyri fysuc ixonu bugik arecu

Full enciphered message (note 'Elond Bremen kisah zivol' not enciphered, as described in text):
Elond Bremen kisah aciba zivol evora bybol ytuzo comul ineto mewyd oruvy lyxob itady

Note: kisah aciba = codeword for 'the contents of this message have been enciphered with the HVB key'. It is not enciphered.

German original	English translation	codeword	enciphered word
Fuer Admiralstab der Marine	to the Admiralty Staff	hanib ynixe	zivol evora
Bei eingetroffen	arriving	kukib uroli	bybol ytuzo
15, Juni	15 June	mifob alyri	comul ineto
Shanghai		fysuc ixonu	mewyd oruvy
Neckar		bugik arecu	lyxob itady

Such a simple cipher is not very secure, especially if it is not changed very frequently. For skilled cryptographers, which is what many members of the Room 40 team rapidly became, a cipher like this was hardly any extra effort. It was quite easy, using frequency analysis, to work out a new key or table of substitutions when one was introduced. We saw in Chapter 1 that several German messages were sent out at the beginning of the war warning ships that the HVB key had been compromised and telling them to use the 'reserve' key with the HVB, to use the SKM instead. At the outbreak of war there was one key for everyday use and another in reserve. In the case of the HVB, then, Room 40 was faced with a badly designed and insecure codebook, a ridiculously simple cipher system and an infrequently changed key.

The situation was only slightly more complex in the case of the VB. The VB, as we saw earlier, used 'code-groups' with numbers instead of codewords with letters. Numbers can more easily be subjected to complex cipher techniques than letters. Addition and subtraction operations, for example, are easy to perform. But the German naval cipher designers failed to take any real advantage of this potential extra security (though German army and diplomatic ciphers did use 'subtractor' ciphers). Instead, the numerical code-groups were turned back into groups of letters by one cipher technique used with the VB. And, just as with the HVB, a substitution table was provided, though a somewhat more complicated one. The complication came about because, as we saw, the VB code-groups were made up of three numbers derived from the page number (*stammzahl* – root number) and two numbers derived from plain meaning entry number on the page (*eindzahl* – end number) giving a five-number code-group as a substitute for the plain language meaning of the codebook entry. The simplest cipher used with the VB converted the code-group of five numbers into a ten-letter codeword. The *stammzahl* and the *eindzahl* were separated and each was given a five-letter nonsense codeword. For example, a code-group 36782 (page 367, entry 82 of the VB codebook) would be represented as 367 = 'evuet' and 82 = either 'iacus' or 'voval'. The decision which nonsense word to use for the *eindzahl* was left to the cipher clerk, '*nach wahl*' – according to choice. So 36782 would be either 'evuet iacus' or 'evuet voval'. The substitution table was in effect a ten-page codebook where the *stammzahlen* were listed first, then the *eindzahlen*. No advantage was taken of the numerical codewords, and reliance was again placed in a cipher system that needed to have new keys (ie, effectively a new set of printed substitution books) published and distributed frequently.

The absence of concern for security stands in sharp contrast to the considerable effort put into the core design principle of this cipher system. The apparently nonsensical words – 'iacus', 'voval' and the like – were in fact very carefully chosen so that any errors in transmission could be corrected. The navy's instruction book for using the cipher pointed out that a fault can be generated either by the 'medium' – ie, the cable or the ether – or by the operators. The design of the 'cipher-words' prevented potentially confusing letter combinations from occurring. The annexe to the substitution book contains half a dozen pages of instructions on how to correct transmission errors and several pages of useful tables of permissible combinations, doubling the size of the whole cipher book. This cipher system was designed with the problems of inaccurate transmission in mind, not security. It no doubt reflected the needs of the time when it was designed – in the case of the copy of the cipher book in the National Archives in Kew, that was in 1908.

It is necessary to emphasise that this simple cipher applied to the navy's use of the VB codebook. When it was used for diplomatic messages a numerical 'subtractor' cipher system was used. There were many different types of 'subtractor' cipher. Each consisted of a 'key' of between three and thirteen numbers, sometimes used in groups or simply recycled. The key could be 'slid' so that the numbers were in different positions each time they were used in a message. Sometimes two keys would be used, of different lengths, one after the other, again with a system to 'shift' positions on each reiteration. Devices known as 'sliders' were employed to assist in using the keys. The key would be subtracted (without any 'borrowing') from the code-groups. At the receiving end the operator would apply the same key, adding it to the enciphered code-group numbers (ignoring any 'carry') and restoring them to their original values. Obviously this is a somewhat more difficult system to break, but it had one great problem in addition to that of devising keys. It was necessary to organise a system of sending out new keys to diplomatic representatives in foreign countries. Because of the British stranglehold on cable communications the distribution of new keys was often done by wireless message – thus giving away details of the key.[20]

When we come to the cipher system used with the SKM at the start of the war we take a seemingly big step up in extra complexity. However, even this system remains surprisingly simplistic. This type of cipher was used by the navy in conjunction with the SKM and was also used by the German army in the field (without first encoding the message, so the plain language message was enciphered directly). The cipher system depended on a keyword known to both sender and receiver. New keywords were usually distributed by some secret method – though we saw in the previous chapter how one new key (*ConstantinopleWienBerlin*) was sent out in a compromised code and under the old cipher key. I have used 'Wilhelmshaven' as the key for the example. This type of cipher is known as a 'transposition cipher' as the original letters are shuffled around, not changed as with the ciphers discussed above. The example message reads: 'The message would be coded into three letter groups using the SKM but is shown in plain for the example.'

The keyword is written out on a piece of paper. The number '1' is written underneath the earliest letter in the alphabet to occur in the message. In our example keyword the letter 'a' appears in *haven*, towards the end of the keyword, so '1' is written underneath it. There is no 'b', 'c' or 'd' in the keyword, but there is an 'e', so '2' is written underneath it; then '3' is written underneath the next earliest letter to occur, which is another 'e'. The number '4' is written underneath 'h' and '5' underneath the second occurrence of 'h', '6' underneath 'i' and '7' is under the 'l' and so on until the end of the keyword is reached (see step 1, Table 4.7). The plain language (or encoded) message is then written out in horizontal lines underneath the key, starting in the top left-hand corner (step 2). Then the columns, starting with the column numbered 1, then column number 2 and so on, are written out in a single continual horizontal line, creating a stream of letters which forms the message to be sent (step 3). At the receiving end the operator would effectively reverse the process, by writing out the keyword and numbering the columns in exactly the same way as the enciphering operator. He would then write out the message, one column at a time, starting with the first set of letters under column numbered 1, the next set under the column numbered 2 and so on. The plain (coded) message could then be read horizontally, line by line.

Two points need to be mentioned. First, it would be possible to put the final stream of letters through the whole process once again, creating a double transposition. Second, there is a further slight complexity involving the fact that the columns are usually of two different lengths (in the example some are six letters and others seven letters) and some other steps were actually involved to take account of this. But this facet need not worry us here as the basic technique is what matters in understanding the challenge facing the cryptographers (though these extra steps did increase the complexity of their task).

Table 4.7

SKM cipher method

The key is 'Wilhelmshaven' and the message is 'The message would be coded into three letter groups using the SKM but is shown in plain for the example.'

Step 1: Write out the key and then number the letters starting with the earliest letter in the alphabet (where two or more of the same letters occur give them consecutive numbers starting from the left).

W	I	L	H	E	L	M	S	H	A	V	E	N
13	6	7	4	2	8	9	11	5	1	12	3	10

Step 2: Write out the message in horizontal lines from left to right below the two lines already written out.

W	I	L	H	E	L	M	S	H	A	V	E	N
13	6	7	4	2	8	9	11	5	1	12	3	10
T	H	E	M	E	S	S	A	G	E	W	O	U
L	D	B	E	C	O	D	E	D	I	N	T	O
T	H	R	E	E	L	E	T	T	E	R	G	R
O	U	P	S	U	S	I	N	G	T	H	E	S
K	M	B	U	T	I	S	S	H	O	W	N	I
N	P	L	A	I	N	F	O	R	T	H	E	E
X	A	M	P	L	E							

Step 3: The vertical columns are then written out in number order into a single continuous horizontal stream. For the example, I have written out the continuous line twice, once with the column number to indicate its source, and once without the column number.

(1) E I ET OT (2) E C E UT I L (3) O T G E N E (4) M E E S U A P (5) G D T G H R (6) H D H U M P A (7) E B R P B L M (8) S O L S I N E (9) S D E I S F (10) U O R S I E (11) A E T N S O (12) W N R H W H (13) T L T O K N X

E I ET OT E C E UT I L OT G E N E M E E S U A P G D T G H R H D H U M P A E B R P B L M S O L S I N E S D E I S F U O R S I E A E T N S O W N R H W HT LT O K N X

Step 4: The message could be put through the same process again to give a 'double transposition'.

Step 5: The message is received at the distant end and the operator uses the same keyword to create another table and, knowing where column 1 should go, is able to write out the message column by column.

The navy distributed printed booklets containing details of the current keyword to ships and land-stations. Such booklets were supposed to be kept in a different place from the codebook so that if a vessel was captured it should be easier to prevent both codebook and key booklet falling into enemy hands. Such rules were hard to follow as it was often the same person who had to encode and encipher, or decipher and decode, messages in the same wireless room. It was also difficult to get lists of new keywords to diplomatic and military sites outside the territory of Germany, its allies and their captured lands. There were few and only intermittent means of distributing booklets physically, such as when German submarines visited foreign ports, and wireless transmission often had be resorted to.

One solution to this problem of distributing keys was to use an agreed system for *generating* keys at each end of the link. For example, on one system used between Berlin and Madrid, the day's key was derived from a word taken from a publicly available book, such as the commercial *ABC Code*, along with the date. The word was taken from a given position on a new page of the book each time a message was sent (for example, it could be the first word of the fifth line on a page, using consecutive pages for consecutive messages). An example left us by one of Room 40's codebreakers, Professor Bruford, shows a key compiled from the appropriate word from the *ABC Code* page – in this case it is the place-name *Maipol*, plus the day and the month – making *Maipol-vierzehn-mai* (Maipol-fourteen-May).

One of the easiest methods of breaking messages enciphered with this type of cipher is known as the 'anagram' method. It required certain conditions to be met: two or more messages, of the same length and enciphered with the same key (this is known as a 'depth'). Having two messages enables the codebreaker to make progress when one message does not offer any obvious word on which to move forward. The example in Table 4.8 is drawn from two real messages sent at the time. Each message has been truncated to 32 letters to keep the example to a manageable size.

Table 4.8

Breaking a transposition cipher

The two intercepted enciphered messages were:

Message 1: I S O S K I N M E D N A O T N I X T M R A A F N N T E X L T H A

Message 2: N A R S D K E K E I H R Z K R I E N K B D H K V W E K D I I B E

The two messages are written out on pieces of card, with each card containing a pair of letters (one from message 1 and one from message 2) on top of each other. A number indicating the position of the pair of letters in the messages is written at the top of each card.

1	2	3	4	...	31	32
I	S	O	S	...	H	A

N	A	R	S	...	B	E

The cards are then shuffled about and tried in different places until the two messages can both be read.

```
2 18 22 14  6 13 25 17 10 23 28  4 30  9 31 26  1 11 19 27 24 16  7 12  8  5 21 15 32 29 20  3
S  T  A  T  I  O  N  X  D  F  X  S  T  E  H  T  I  N  M  E  N  I  N  A  M  K  A  N  A  L  R  O
A  N  H  K  K  Z  W  E  I  K  D  S  I  E  B  E  N  H  K  K  V  I  E  R  K  D  D  R  E  I  B  R
```

Message 1: Station XDF is in Menin on channel RO
Message 2: To HKK two KD seven HKK four KD three BR

With a lot of mental effort it is also possible to guess the actual keyword. Actually, to be more precise, it is the keyword order (ie, the numbers at the top of each column) that is the object of desire. It is not necessary to know the actual letters of the keyword, as what matters is the *order* of the letters in the keyword in the alphabet, the keyword being just a simple and (hopefully) secret means of specifying that order (for example, keyword '*bad*' produces the same numbering as keyword '*pot*', ie, 213).

Many cryptographic experts insist that all codes and ciphers can be broken given enough messages and enough time. If this is true, then encoded and enciphered messages can be seen as secure for only a short time. The codebooks and cipher keys need to be changed frequently if security is to be retained. On this the German naval effort was completely hopeless. In the acid pen of Frank Birch: 'Even after four years' experience the German Admiralty got no further than devising a key which could be solved in three or four days but was kept in force for ten days or a fortnight, and allowed [codebooks] to remain in force for a year which could effectually be compromised in two months [and often less]'. The British cryptographers in Room 40 were blessed not only by the miraculous delivery of German codebooks into their immensely grateful hands, but also by a grossly incompetent approach to security by the *Admiralstab*. Badly designed codebooks, ridiculously simple ciphers and absurdly infrequent changes of codebooks and cipher keys were all precious gifts to the British cryptographers, as were the voluminous and powerfully transmitted wireless messages and the excessive number of actual copies of the codebooks on circulation within the navy (and thus liable to capture).

The HVB was the first codebook to be changed. A new edition was released in early 1916 (known as the AFB). The SKM was not replaced until May 1917 (by the FFB) and the VB was partly replaced in 1917 (by 'Nordo' codebook). These shortcomings gave the British codebreakers just enough of a challenge to allow them to learn their new trade before the Germans introduced tighter security measures - rather like the way not taking the full course of a prescription of antibiotics gives undesirable bacteria a chance to develop resistance.

Chapter 5

Message Makers

The Imperial navy (*Kaiserlichen Marine*) was born as a small, coastal protection force during the Franco-Prussian War of 1870–71. The war was a great victory for Germany. The Prusso-German army occupied much of northern France, laying siege to Paris. On land Germany was king. But the German navy consisted of little more than five 'ironclads' and a few auxiliary craft. The French, who had ten times as many ships, planned to exploit this naval dominance by landing an invading army in the north of Germany and by bombarding German ports. But it all came to nothing. The German coast was too far away and the ports too well defended by guns, sandbanks and sunken obstacles. The French had the 'wrong sort of navy', one designed to fight a 'blue sea' battle against the British fleet, not to transport troops or maintain a distant blockade in the grey waters of the North Sea. The French navy did bring some small comfort to the battered French nation. In the early days of the war they blockaded ports in the German Bight. Prussian naval ships remained helpless in harbour while the French captured some 40 in-bound merchant ships. Also, 'Prussia could do nothing to stop the shiploads of war-materials, which poured into Brest and Bordeaux and Marseille throughout the second half of the year,' thus prolonging Paris's resistance. 'It was a lesson not wasted on a later generation of German sailors.' That new generation oversaw the rapid expansion of the Imperial navy, fostered by the unbalanced and impetuous Kaiser, Wilhelm II, who came to the throne in 1888. His enthusiasm was widely shared. Germany had become Europe's leading industrial power. Its population expanded from 49 million in 1891 to 65 million in 1911. All the same, without its own warships Germany often had to stand by and allow others to decide the outcome of events. Wilhelm was determined to join those who could enforce their views, and an arms race was launched between Britain and Germany, each seeking dominance of the high seas.

For Britain the navy had traditionally been its main military service – such that 25 per cent of all tax revenues were devoted to it. But for Germany it was the army that was the source of power and pride. The navy, for all the Kaiser's and the public's support, was an afterthought. It was not integrated into overall military strategy. It remained subordinate to the army. Public political justification for the navy was expressed in terms that were global and imperial, but naval strategy was 'continental' (ie, directed at the politics of the European landmass), where it would serve mainly to assist the army. There was no real concept of using sea power independently. The result was a confused and unclear strategy at the outbreak of hostilities.

When the war started, senior naval officers on both sides adopted a cautious stance. In the words of a post-war British intelligence assessment: 'The theory of [modern] naval warfare was well known and firmly established; [but] its practice was an entirely unknown field. The recent Spanish-American [1898] and Russo-Japanese [1905] wars had added very little to the sum of knowledge, and, since that date, modern inventions [including long-range guns, torpedoes, submarines and aircraft] had appeared to revolutionise the whole art … the opponents in the sea war were like fencers, who, carefully trained in the theory and brought up in the traditions of the *salle d'armes,* are suddenly opposed in a duel to the death, armed with weapons of new possibilities and unknown peculiarities.' On both sides, naval officers and ratings, as well as most politicians and civilians, expected a cataclysmic naval battle to take place within a few days of the war's outbreak. The public on all sides also anticipated rapid victory on land.

Most British naval officers and ratings were keen to 'have a go' and get into action as soon as possible. But the admiral acting as commander–in–chief of the Grand Fleet, John Jellicoe, kept his big battleships out of harm's way. The Grand Fleet was moved a few days before war began to Scapa Flow on Orkney. Winston Churchill later wrote, 'The strategic concentration of the fleet had been accomplished with its transfer to Scottish waters. We were now in a position to control events and it was not easy to see how this advantage could be taken from us … If war should come, no one would know where to look for the British fleet. Somewhere in that enormous waste of waters to the north of our islands, cruising now this way, now that, shrouded in storms and mist, dwelt this mighty organisation. Yet from the Admiralty building we could speak to them at any moment if need arose.'

During the autumn smaller detachments were stationed further south at Rosyth, Harwich and Dover. One of their first tasks was to support a blockade of Germany's sea traffic, intended initially to provoke the *Hochseeflotte* (High Seas Fleet) to venture away from its home ports where, short of coal and with a prolonged run home, it would be vulnerable. The blockade would eventually be enforced by converted merchant ships strung out between the Shetlands and Norway. The Channel would be fairly easy to cut off to German surface ships. In the meantime, the Royal Navy had a lot of other responsibilities: transporting and protecting British troops crossing the Channel; bringing troops from the colonies and dominions; chasing a few German cruisers at large in the Atlantic and the Pacific; and maintaining

Britain's lines of communication with the world at large, and with the USA and the British Empire in particular. With the Royal Navy so stretched, in fact the first weeks of the war offered Germany its best chance for a surprise naval attack on Britain or the Royal Navy.

But the German Imperial navy went on the defensive too, waiting for the Royal Navy to come to it, to venture a long way from home, short of coal and with a prolonged voyage back to safety. The main German naval bases at the outbreak of war were in the German Bight – 'bight' is an old English word meaning a wide bay or a bend. The German Bight is the section of German coast between Denmark and the Netherlands where the coast turns from trending roughly northeast to north. The coastline is like a reverse L-shape, with the main ports nestling in the corner where the horizontal and the vertical sections meet. This was an excellent set-up for defence – there were few prominent landmarks, plenty of shifting sandbanks, only a few shallow, narrow channels for ships, and myriad opportunities for defensive booms and gun positions. But the very factors which made the Bight a good place for defence also made it a rather poor site for launching offensive operations. At low tide the *Hochseeflotte* could not cross the shoals and sandbanks that gave access from the German ports to the North Sea. Indeed it took two tides for the full fleet to put to sea. And there were long runs back from enemy territory. Sorties along the coast to the west were at risk of being spotted from the Dutch coast, and sailings to the north, from Denmark. The German fleet commanders convinced themselves that Dutch trawlers (and British trawlers disguised as Dutch) were watching them and passing on intelligence about German fleet movements to the Royal Navy.

The German expectation was that the Royal Navy would conduct a 'close' blockade, aiming to prevent any ships – military or commercial – from entering or leaving German ports. They sat and waited for the Royal Navy to appear off the coast, but this did not happen. Early in the war a flotilla of ten submarines was sent out first to the northwest searching for the British blockading ships. They found nothing until they turned south and saw some light cruisers and destroyers. These were in fact the outer screen of the ships defending the cross-Channel troop convoys. But the German navy thought that they were the blockading force. Another submarine reconnaissance voyage also failed to find a close blockade.[21]

The Germans had hoped their navy could sally forth and attack small squadrons of British blockading ships, whittling away the Royal Navy's superiority until its diminished Grand Fleet could be destroyed in a final conflagration. Instead the Royal Navy imposed its 'distant' blockade and German strategy was pretty useless. German naval commanders slowly came to realise that they were in fact cooped up in their secure bases with nothing for the bigger ships to do except accompany minelayers and minesweepers on their duties – hardly an honourable task in the mind of the average naval officer, especially when the German army was, at first, gathering more glory for itself in Belgium and northern France, and then held under siege in the trenches.

The cautious strategy adopted on both sides meant that the big fleets, which had dominated thinking about naval warfare in the years before 1914, became secondary. The naval war would, by and large, be fought by smaller vessels – submarines, torpedo boats, minelayers, minesweepers, monitors, armed trawlers and so on. The potential dangers these smaller vessels posed to big warships had only been vaguely appreciated before the war – everyone's attention was focused on the 'Dreadnoughts'. However, the Kaiser's refusal to allow the *Hochseeflotte* to undertake offensive operations meant that Germany was left with little alternative to attacking enemy warships, auxiliary naval craft and even merchants with small vessels, mines and submarines. This became known as *Kleinkrieg* – 'small war'. By mid-September the British commanders had come to realise that the main enemy of their warships was not the *Hochseeflotte*. A warship that could take two or more years – and vast sums of money – to build could be sent without warning to the bottom of the sea in a few minutes by mines or torpedoes. The sinking by submarines of the Royal Navy warship *Hawke* on 5 September and three more cruisers on 22 September, led Jellicoe to withdraw the Grand Fleet even further out of danger, to waters in Northern Ireland, beyond the reach of enemy submarines.

Kleinkrieg generated lots of wireless traffic. A Room 40 cryptographer noted after the war: 'The strategic position of the German fleet, assembled as it was in the different anchorages of its North Sea [German Bight] and Baltic ports, all of which must have been in telegraphic communication with each other, would, it might be imagined, have enabled the use of W/T [wireless telegraphy] to be reduced to a minimum … [however] staff work was bad … [and] the volume of W/T traffic was enormous. Important details of intended operations, dispositions of battle squadrons, cruisers and flotillas, the ordering of lights [of harbour entrances and channel-marking buoys], etc. were conveyed by this means, with the result that very definite news of contemplated movements was given to the enemy … it seems doubtful whether the Germans were aware of wide range of their wireless [signals].' The very formal organisation of German naval wireless communications was also a great help to the British. German communications were regular and stylised. The same reports were sent at the same time every day and the same routines were employed whenever ship movements were planned. After a short time Room 40 could predict the departure or arrival of ships by intercepting wireless instructions sent to the harbour lighting authorities to switch on warning lights. Similarly, returning U-boats would wireless in details of their expected time of arrival at a specified meeting point; this would be followed by more wireless traffic instructing escort vessels to meet them.

German wireless engineers underestimated the distance over which their wireless signals could be picked up, assuming that they would not reach as far as the British Isles. Wireless traffic between ships in the North Sea and Wilhelmshaven was relayed via a wireless station on Heligoland, 'owing to the belief of the sender that his W/T installation was not powerful enough to communicate directly, whereas as a matter of fact, these messages were easily picked up by British stations, much more remote'. The British interception engineers gained a significant advantage from the emphasis placed by wireless pioneers, starting with Guglielmo Marconi, on developing sensitive wireless receivers, able to detect every last lingering trace of wireless waves.

The German navy published a booklet in 1913 entitled *FT-Bestimmungen der kaiserlichen Marine* (Wireless Telegraphy Instructions for the Imperial Navy), which saw several revisions during the war but remained essentially the same throughout. The instructions applied to communications between navy wireless telegraphy stations (other rule books were published for communications with the long-distance stations at Nauen and occupied Bruges, and also for navy communications with non-navy and foreign-owned stations). The booklet informed readers: 'This book is a secret object, in times of peace or of war, in the sense of section 1 of the law against betrayal of military secrets of 3 June 1914.' The rules made it clear that use of wireless transmission was to be kept to a minimum. 'Wireless telegraphy may only be used in vital circumstances and [when] no other means of communication is available … All service units of the navy are allowed to send wireless messages, but can only use that right in emergency circumstances and those circumstances are to be assessed each time a telegram is to be sent.' Replies to telegrams too were to be made only if absolutely essential. There were equally strict rules about the use of codes and ciphers. Plain language could be used only for private telegrams (which were in any case to be severely restricted in number) or service telegrams if they had no tactical, strategic consequences for any military action and whose wording was harmless and had no connection to other wireless traffic. The instruction booklet pointed out that 'a trained wireless telegraphy discipline is the fundamental requirement for secure and fast signalling. All commanders are required to use all means to ensure compliance.'[22] As we will see in later chapters, despite these clear injunctions, wireless telegrams were often sent with abandon.

Early in the war, the global demands on the Royal Navy meant that several of the Grand Fleet's warships had to be sent away from the North Sea. In October and November, following the first sinkings of warships by U-boats, German submarines were in effective control of the North Sea – but German commanders did not realise it. This opportunity did not last long. Once von

Spee's and other cruisers were removed from other seas the Grand Fleet would be back to strength. Also new ships were due in the spring of 1915, boosting the dominance of the Grand Fleet.

The last few months of 1914 witnessed plenty of small clashes between British and German vessels, but no big battles. The first North Sea meeting between German and British warships started badly for the Royal Navy. British submarines directed British light cruisers to chase themselves. Then a British submarine launched a torpedo against a British light cruiser, which responded by trying to ram the submarine. Both the torpedo shot and the ramming attempt were failures. Later that day things went better for the Royal Navy, with three German light cruisers being sunk. One historian commented how the clash 'established a moral superiority at sea that remained to the British advantage for the rest of the war ... But the euphoria of victory helped to render less urgent the rectification of the Royal Navy's faults. Most palpable, and perhaps predictable, were the failures of command and staff work.' This was one of the few clashes that occurred before Room 40 started to decode and decipher German naval messages. Would the better intelligence now available from Room 40 outweigh the obstacles set by failures of command and staff work – or would the advantages offered by the better intelligence be thrown away?

Chapter 6

Message Takers

One day in 1903 two men, both called William, happened to visit Rome at the same time. One of them was Kaiser Wilhelm II of the German Empire. The other was Guglielmo Marconi. He was the returning hero, the Italian boy who had gone to London to turn his invention of the wireless into a commercial success. Now he was visiting the eternal city to be made a citizen of Rome. The 'other Guglielmo', as the Italian press humiliatingly dubbed the Kaiser, was there to visit the Pope. Wilhelm did not like Guglielmo. Marconi drew public attention away from the vain Kaiser, though there were deeper reasons too. Later that day the two men met as dinner guests of King Victor Emmanuel. Marconi reported: 'The Kaiser's conversation with me and his general attitude were strangely characteristic of the role of omniscience which he had already assumed at the time. After having congratulated me on my work and my wireless he proceeded to tell me that he considered that I was wrong in "attempting to obstruct wireless communications from German ships". I told William of Hohenzollern that although I thanked him for his advice I felt confident both on technical and other grounds that the course of development for wireless telegraphy which I was following was the right one ... At dinner whenever the King of Italy tried to direct the conversation towards wireless telegraphy and its achievements the Kaiser just as resolutely headed it off towards other subjects.'

The Kaiser's tetchy mood derived in part from an incident in 1902 involving his brother Crown Prince Heinrich who travelled to America on the German liner *Kronprinz Wilhelm*. Throughout the trip Heinrich (who was to become commander of the German navy's Baltic fleet during the First World War) was impressed at being able to send and receive messages via the Marconi wireless set installed on the ship. However, the return journey was on different German ship, *Deutschland*. It was kitted out with a German wireless set. The messages transmitted from this ship were not received – or were ignored – by Marconi Company wireless stations. The German ship was thus unable to send or receive any messages until it neared the German coast and came into range of German land wireless stations. Marconi claimed that the problem was a technical one, even blaming the German ship's wireless set for being out of order, but this was a lie. It is true that the German system was, at that stage, inferior, transmitting only up to about 125 miles (200km). But the reality is that there were commercial and political reasons for the Marconi Company's policy of communicating only with its own wireless sets – in modern times we could liken this to the way some retailers of 'e-book readers' limit their use to e-books also purchased through them. Wilhelm was livid. Germans and Americans shared his anger. 'What the American magazine *Electrical Weekly* described as 'malignant Marconiphobia' spread across Germany, and soon [German wireless scientist Professor] Slaby and others were writing indignant letters to the *New York Herald* complaining that they were the victims of deliberate wireless sabotage.' In response, the various German wireless developments were concentrated in a single national champion, Telefunken, to take on the Marconi Company.

The international struggle for a share of the worldwide market for wireless sets was often bitter. Between 1909 and 1914, Marconi's share of international sales inevitably fell from 67 per cent to 39 per cent as more and more manufacturers joined the market. Telefunken's share grew from 10 per cent to 33 per cent (see Table 6.1). Marconi and Telefunken equipment often appeared on the opposite sides of military conflicts. In 1911 Turkey and Italy went to war over Libya. Marconi may have been an adopted Englishman, but he was born an Italian and personally helped the Italian navy deploy his wireless sets. He later reported his satisfaction watching, from the Italian warships, the destruction by shelling of Turkey's North African shore-based Telefunken wireless stations.

Table 6.1

Wireless sets in use from Marconi and Telefunken, 1909–1914

Year	Marconi		Telefunken		Other		Total
	No.	%	No.	%	No.	%	
08 1909	161	67	24	10	55	23	240
10 1910	203	63	53	16	66	20	320
07 1912	900	37	798	33	752	32	2450
01 1913	1047	37	871	31	879	31	2797
01 1914	1521	39	1281	33	1100	28	3902

Source: Michael Friedewald, *Telefunken und der deutsche Schiffsfunk 1903-1914*.

Against this background the competition between Marconi and Telefunken was as much political as commercial, as much nationalistic as technological. 'Beyond question, the creation of [the German electrical] industry was the greatest single achievement of modern Germany,' wrote a leading economic historian. That achievement had been due to 'extensive diplomatic influence and unstinted support from government'. Britain's economic and imperial leadership seemed under increasing threat from Germany. In 1903 Germany and the USA combined to force an international agreement on Britain which finally made Marconi agree to interconnection of international wireless operations. An American admiral argued that Marconi and Britain must not be allowed to become dominant in wireless communications. 'Such a monopoly will be worse than the English submarine cable monopolies which all of Europe is groaning under.'

***

Marconi's invention of the wireless at the turn of the century was welcomed at sea, especially in the Royal Navy. It was still reeling from the shock of a major disaster at sea in 1895. Admiral Sir George Tryon ordered two columns of steamships to perform a turn in a way that meant that the leading ships were bound to collide head-on. The admiral, one of the hundreds who died in the tragedy, was a leading proponent of modernising the navy's battle tactics. Senior naval commanders were divided over whether captains at sea should have more room for initiative – as the unlucky Admiral Tryon advocated – or whether they simply needed to be able to follow precise orders without showing any initiative, as the more traditional mindset favoured. Although the disastrous collision was not the consequence of Tryon's ideas, the fact that it happened under his command weakened his case. In fact it was blind obedience that prevented any inferior officer daring to tell an admiral that he had given an incorrect order. An unchallenged order turned an error into a disaster. But it was the hand of the traditionalists that was strengthened. Control from the centre could become even stronger thanks to the wireless. The Admiralty not only allowed Marconi to test his sets at sea in its warships, it also worked with his company to transform wireless sets, with their faults and limited range, into a reliable working system that could transmit over many miles under all sea conditions. Wireless was taken up much more eagerly in the Royal Navy than in Wilhelm's Imperial navy. Admiral Tirpitz, the German navy minister, appreciated the value of wireless but thought that new equipment should be adopted only when it had been fully proven. He stuck with this rule, delaying German naval implementation of wireless. He did succumb to pressure to deploy German wireless sets, but they performed badly, so Tirpitz's opinion against early adoption of wireless was reinforced. Thus, in 1914, the German navy was faced with the urgent challenge of implementing wireless technology on its ships.

We say, rightly, that Marconi 'invented' wireless. Yet he did not invent any of the major components or sub-systems he brought together to create a simple wireless system – a transmitter, an antenna and a receiver. These he borrowed from others, saw how they could be used together, and set about integrating them into a working system. He then tinkered, tested and developed his technologies, further improving their performance step by step. On the surface it might seem as if the wireless transmitter was the key invention, being able to sending out a signal over an appreciable distance. But really it was the receiver that was at the core of Marconi's success. His first receiver was not very practical, but it worked enough to prove the idea and was soon replaced by new technologies, often developed by others. Between 1900 and 1914 there were dramatic improvements in the transmitters and antennae, but most important was the improved sensitivity of receivers. Marconi, unlike other wireless developers, was driven by the urge to transmit over longer and longer distances, and this demanded very sensitive receivers. Marconi's emphasis on receivers gave Room 40 a very significant advantage in interception of German wireless traffic when the war started.

***

The Room 40 legend has it that, at the outbreak of war, the Admiralty had only one station working at intercepting wireless traffic – Stockton – and even it was really supposed to be doing something else. Then, shortly after war broke out, two amateur wireless enthusiasts, Russell Clarke and Bayntun Hippisley, contacted the Admiralty to report that they had been picking up German messages on their private wireless sets at home and they volunteered their services. Further help came from wireless stations belonging to the Marconi Company, again under their own initiative. The Admiralty was wholly unaware that the Germans might use wireless so had taken absolutely no steps to intercept messages. From these modest beginnings an effective wireless interception service was developed. As with the overall cover story about Room 40 (see Chapter 2), this one is also close to the truth, yet not overly close. It telescopes events and it puts, once again, far too much emphasis on amateurish good luck.

Stockton is described in documents from the time as the navy's 'policing' station, listening into Royal Navy wireless traffic and checking that rules about its use were being followed. But, as we saw in Chapter 1, as war approached, several wireless stations started intercepting material, at both naval and Marconi Company sites. For example, a message on 3 August was intercepted at 'the Admiralty, Chelmsford, Stockton, etc'. Also a wireless station at the Admiralty in London and another at Dover, as well as several British warships, picked up German messages that same day. At the time, only a very few people could afford to buy their own wireless set, so amateur wireless operators were of a fairly high social standing. One such enthusiast was E. Russell Clarke, a barrister. When the war broke out, he used his personal wireless set to listen in to the airwaves to see what he could pick up. Soon he realised that he was intercepting German wireless signals. If this was true, then what he was doing was illegal. At the outbreak of the war the Defence of the Realm Act made it a crime to operate a wireless set to transmit or receive signals. All operating licences were suspended and sets were ordered to be dismantled. Denniston commented, 'It is not clear why the Police or Post Office had not sealed up their apparatus, but it can well be imagined that some rash official had tried his best on Russell Clarke and had been forced to retire the worse for wear.' Whereas the ordinary person would have been hauled off to the magistrates' court, Russell Clarke was able instead to offer his services to the Admiralty and soon had a meeting with Sir Alfred Ewing, an old friend. Or perhaps the well-connected Clarke had already had discussions with friends in high places such as the GPO and was directed to Ewing. Denniston also recalled that Clarke had done some work on improving wireless reception for the War Office previously, discovering that Hunstanton on the East Anglian coast was a good site for wireless reception. So, it seems more likely that Russel Clarke was acting on official authority and was not the intrepid amateur portrayed in the legend.

Another amateur wireless owner, Bayntun Hippisley, had dismantled his set at his home in Ston Easton, Somerset, following the instructions from the General Post Office. But he then received an invitation from an acquaintance, Sir Henry Norman, the Assistant Postmaster General, asking him to visit Norman's home in Hazelmere 'in order to write down anything sent in by W/T [wireless telegraphy] in Morse Signals, Norman having I presume by reason of his position of Assistant Postmaster General managed to keep his station in commission'. A few days later, 'Russell Clarke turned up with a request that I should return home and put my own station in commission again. This was done at the request of … Sir Alfred Ewing'. Hippisley set up a directional aerial pointing eastwards 'and some stuff obviously of Hun origin was taken and sent to [the Admiralty] from our local village post office. After a short time Sir Alfred came down to see how we got the stuff telling us that what we were sending up was of the greatest importance. He asked if we could suggest any improvement.' Hippisley and Russell Clarke gained permission to look at two new sites: on the Huntingdon road in Cambridge and a coastguard station at Hunstanton. They soon moved their wireless sets and antennae to Hunstanton and set them up there, intercepting their first messages in November. Hippisley recalled that Clarke was 'too short-sighted to be any good aloft' so he and another recruit, C. P. O. Marshal, had to raise the antenna. They then settled down to keep a watch for twenty-four hours, seven days a week. Each of the three covered an eight-hour period every day. 'It was a killing job but we kept it up till the folk at the Admiralty took pity on us and sent a relief crew.' A party of GPO telegraphists was dispatched to help maintain the watch and 'things became a bit easier after that'. But it was only the start of a long journey. Hippisley recalled that by the end of the war there were sixteen fully staffed stations in operation, 'most of them of my own construction in what was then the United Kingdom [ie, including southern Ireland] and two in Italy and one in Malta'.

Russell Clarke and Hippisley decided that a useful addition to their team would be Leslie Lambert. 'R. C. and I used to work wireless telegraphy with [Lambert] long before the War from our home stations. It struck us that he would be most useful to us when we started up at Hunstanton. ... Lambert was of course socially a cut above some folk I have to deal with. ... He was a clever conjuror and used to give shows to the Royal children. [One day at Hunstanton] I received information that some people had broken through the sentries and on arrival I found a party from Sandringham with Her Majesty Queen Alexandra who looked through the window and was surprised to find Lambert sitting writing at a desk. She called out, "Why Lambert what on earth are you doing here?" The dear lady being stone deaf did not get his answer. This episode was not entered in the log nor was it reported to the Admiralty. I had a few words with the Corps of Sentries about the break-in. He smiled at me and said they all knew her and the party were Home Guards raised from Sandringham Staff.'

Lambert became a key figure in the interception of German naval and diplomatic wireless transmissions. After the war he carried on working for GC&CS, which replaced both Room 40 and MI1(b). But Lambert had another life under a different name. As A. J. Alan he became a famous wireless broadcaster on the BBC. He wrote crime and ghost stories which he himself then read, with the aid of his monocle, and dressed always in a dinner suit, to a large and devoted audience. His was the classic 'BBC accent' of the inter-war period. A. J. Alan's true identity was kept secret until after his death. This second occupation allowed Lambert to bring together his two passions – entertaining and wireless technology. As mentioned above, the wireless enthusiast of the day was of a higher social class than nowadays and it was not a sign of geekishness to be keenly interested in wireless technology. Few if any of today's stars and celebrities have any interest in the technology of their medium – and would probably be treated as odd if they did. Lambert was a pioneer of both the content and the technology of wireless broadcasting.

A not untypical story of his, called 'My Adventure in Chiselhurst', is about how the narrator, attending an exhibition of the latest wireless equipment, meets an old friend – a wealthy stockbroker – who is suffering from a head cold. The friend invites the narrator home for dinner, to see his new wireless set imported from the USA and also to meet his new, young wife. When they get to the house, however, there is a phone call from his wife saying that she could not get home as her car has broken down many miles away. The stockbroker is told by his wife to make sure he takes some aspirin for his cold before retiring. All this the narrator infers from listening surreptitiously to one side of the telephone conversation. The pair of pals have a lavish dinner and listen to the American 'super-het' wireless. The patriotic narrator is scornful: 'Needless to say, the tall-boy [screening the radio from view] was far and away the best thing about it. When he switched it on the volume of distorted noise was so appalling that I can't think why the ceiling didn't come down.' After brandy the narrator makes his way home. Later that night the stockbroker is found dead – the result of poisoning. It is clear that the culprit is the wife but there is no evidence to prove it. The narrator gives evidence to the coroner's inquest, though he does not tell us whether he reported having listened in to his friend's telephone conversation or not. At first it looks as if the wife will get away with murder, but a final twist to the story ensures that justice will be done. The story's style and content is now rather dated (it is assumed, for example, that you will realise that the stockbroker has a team of servants on hand at home) but the narrative structure follows a classic crime story formula. What is of interest for our story is the social setting. First, the fashionable subject of wireless technology among the moneyed classes. Second, the natural acceptance by an upper-class gentleman that it was not shameful to listen in on one's friends – as long as one did not admit it.

Lambert's wireless expertise was technological and intuitive, and not scientifically based. Trial and error combined with long hours made his work a great success. One of his many technical achievements was discovering a method used by the German wireless engineers to evade interception by rapid switching of wavelengths. For a further insight into his character it is worth taking a glance at a report written at the end of the war recommending that he be kept on the staff. Among his many creditable points it is also noted, 'Lieutenant Lambert has a wireless telegraphy station at his private house in London at which he keeps watch for some hours every day and is in constant touch with International wireless telegraphy arrangements.' From 1914 through to 1918 he was to make a considerable contribution, along with Clarke and Hippisley, to improving the technical performance of the British naval wireless interception service. Their hard work was to pay dividends in both world wars. Excellence in cryptography is not a lot of use if messages cannot be intercepted. The Room 40 cryptographers benefited from Marconi's determination to develop very sensitive receivers and from the technical enthusiasm of people such as Lambert, Hippisley and Clarke.

The interception station at Hunstanton was mainly concerned with picking up the signals transmitted by the high-power German naval wireless station at Norddeich and also German military messages from the Western Front. The naval messages, broadcast 'to all ships', were of two types: weather forecasts and intelligence reports on the movement of Allied shipping. As we saw in Chapter 2, Rotter's first cipher key break was on the weather reports. But the weather data and information on British shipping was of limited value. Sometime that autumn, Russell Clarke visited Ewing at the Admiralty to discuss their work. When Clarke was shown some of the naval messages that Room 40 was dealing with he realised that there were many other messages in similar form being sent by the Germans on less powerful transmitters in and around the area of the German Bight. He told Ewing that he could get hundreds of such messages 'which if read would give the daily doings of the German fleet'. There was 'only one aerial at Hunstanton,' said Denniston, 'which was doing good work on military interception and [Ewing] was a little loath to lose good stuff for a pig in a poke. However, he agreed to a weekend trial, which was of course conclusive. From what we could read of the stuff intercepted at Hunstanton alone it was clear that we should from now onwards be able to follow every movement of the enemy provided always that they used the same key, call-signs and [code] book.' The number of sets and operators at Hunstanton was increased and the promised hundreds of daily messages were intercepted and dispatched to 'Ewing, Admiralty'.

Another aspect of wireless technology rapidly became a critical adjunct to interception. 'Direction-finding' deployed sensitive receivers and aerials which could be used to indicate the direction from which a wireless signal was being transmitted. Two or more direction-finding stations would allow the drawing of compass bearing lines on a map and the point where the lines crossed would indicate a transmitter's location (within a reasonable degree of accuracy). The impetus came from a Captain H. J. Round from the Marconi Company who set up two direction-finding stations for use in northern France in late 1914. 'This was speedily done and following their success a large network, covering the entire western front was developed.'[23] The direction-finding network revealed the location of German wireless stations, helping build up a picture of the German army's 'order of battle'. The direction-finding stations were mobile, using two lorries and one car to transport the gear and aerial from site to site. However, no sooner was the network complete than there was a decline in the use of wireless by the German army. Later, when German wireless traffic increased again it was found that direction-finding stations in France were sited too close to one another to get precise directions, so some military stations were set up in Britain, such as those at Peterborough, Westgate and Seaham.[24]

Captain Round then went to the Admiralty to set up another network of stations. The first, based at Chelmsford, experienced poor receiving conditions, so a move was soon made to Lowestoft. This first station was followed by others at Lerwick, Aberdeen, York, Flamborough Head, Birchington and five stations in Ireland, until a ring of stations sat ever watchful all along the coasts of the British Isles. Other stations followed abroad and on board naval ships.[25] The physical geography of northwestern Europe gave Room 40 a considerable advantage over the German navy when it came to direction-finding. Germany of course had its own network of direction-finding stations, but they were spread over a significantly narrower north–south range. British stations could take readings from stations located between 49 and 57 degrees of latitude, whereas German stations were limited to a spread between 51 and 55 degrees. This made their triangulation calculations less accurate. By 1917, at the height of the submarine war, the British direction-finding system offered positional information of an accuracy of about 20 miles in home waters and up to 50 miles in distant Atlantic ones.

The prolific Captain Round also developed a technique for replacing crystal sets with electronic valve receivers. These valves were ideal for amplifying very weak signals without introducing much 'noise', which meant in turn that very weak signals picked up by the aerial could be amplified sufficiently for a person or a machine to detect. The Marconi Company started to supply sets equipped with the 'Round valve' from February 1915.[26] In 1917, Russell Clarke also made important contributions to interception technology when he developed sensitive 'short wave' receivers, allowing considerably more German wireless signals to be intercepted. 'In 1917, the sending of [short wave] signals was inaugurated and so sure were the [German naval] authorities that its range was limited and that it could not possibly be intercepted by English [wireless] stations that *en clair* messages were often sent by this method. Thanks, however, to the remarkable success of the late Mr E. Russell Clarke in perfecting intercepting gear, the British intercepting stations were able to pick up most messages' thus transmitted.[27] This steady flow of technical advances led to a significant increase in the number of messages intercepted and passed to Room 40. The number rose to its maximum towards the end of 1917, then declined during 1918 when 'the enemy became rather more chary of imparting vital information by wireless telegraphy'.[28]

In the pages that follow much emphasis is laid on the success of codebreaking and on how several brilliant cryptographers uncovered the secrets of German army, navy and diplomatic communications. But we should not forget that they needed material to work on and it was scientist-technologists such as Round, practical wireless engineers such as Clarke, Hippisley and Lambert, and technocratic entrepreneurs such as Marconi, who developed the sensitive wireless receivers that provided for the supply of such material. The 'other William' had no idea how his navy was giving the game away, thanks to that pesky little Anglo-Italian and his earth-shattering invention

Chapter 7

Message Breakers

In the move to Room 40, Ewing had to give up one of the perks of his post as Director of Naval Education – his office with its fine view over Horse Guards Parade where, in more peaceful times, he would take his children, or associates he wanted to impress, to witness such flamboyant demonstrations of imperial martial pride as Trooping the Colour. With the move Ewing lost more than just his view of the parade ground. As the organisation grew it needed people with skills in such arcane fields as cryptography, objective intelligence assessment, the intricacies of the German language and the even more complex subject of naval matters. The demands of the work began to leave Ewing lagging behind his own increasingly specialised staff. Forceful, ever more self-confident codebreakers, secretive intelligence experts and canny naval officers stepped in to fill the vacuum. Ewing's role seems to have diminished in inverse proportion to the organisation's expansion.

Ewing was 59 years old in 1914. His first wife had died in 1908 and he married a younger woman in 1911, but he had far less energy than during his prime. His favourite holiday pastime was mountaineering and he regularly visited the Alps, becoming an experienced alpinist. But his age was catching up on him. On a trip in 1908 he wrote home, 'I am in pretty good walking form now. It is when I try to climb boulders that, like the sailor in the story, I feel all of a tremble. We found some boulders on the way home yesterday and I played on them enough to show me my incompetence. I am now more than ever certain that a Swiss holiday is just the thing to set one up. I already feel seven years younger, and next week hope to pull in my waist band as far as they can go.' A few days later, while Ewing and his party crossed the Theodule Pass to Breuil, they encountered a violent hail storm and were repeatedly blown off course and 'covered with ice like armour'. Once safely off the mountains Ewing observed 'that the experience was more enjoyable after the event than at the time'. A short while later some of those same climbing companions died in an accident. Ewing was seriously shaken by the news. Though he continued to climb in later years, he was much less adventurous than he had been in his early days, when he had to continually prove that he was better than other men. Climbing at the extremes is a young man's game. Older climbers have to watch others coming along behind them, stronger and perhaps more skilled, climb rock faces far smoother and ice falls far more intimidating than ever they did.

Cryptographers, like climbers, often do their most outstanding work when fairly young. The now rather well-seasoned Ewing had to face the same sense of loss – the realisation that he was no longer on top of the whole game – in his work in Room 40 as with his climbing. Subordinates and rivals began to be seen by other members of staff as the real managers of Room 40. Ewing is portrayed in the accounts that survive as more and more marginal. His organisational and self-promotional skills brought Room 40 into existence as a *cryptographic bureau* which intercepted and decrypted the core working communications of the German fleet. His contact with the universities, and especially Cambridge, brought him academics who turned into brilliant cryptographers. But his temperament proved inadequate for the task of setting up an *intelligence centre* that could exploit the information gained from the intercepts.

***

The budding organisation won vital support from the government's navy minister, First Lord of the Admiralty, Winston Churchill. On 11 November 1914, Churchill addressed a memo to Ewing and the navy's newly appointed Chief of Staff, Henry Oliver (previously met in Chapter 2 as Director of Naval Intelligence and the man who appointed Ewing). The memo read, 'An officer of the War Staff, preferably from the ID [Intelligence Division] should be selected to study all the decoded intercepts, not only current but past, and to compare them continually with what actually took place in order to penetrate the German mind and movements and make reports. All these intercepts are to be written in a locked book with their decodes, and all other copies are to be collected and burnt. All new messages are to be entered in the book, and the book is only to be handled under direction from COS [Chief of Staff]. The officer selected is for the present to do no other work. I shall be obliged if Sir Alfred Ewing will associate himself continuously with this work.' Churchill's initials on the document are accompanied by those of the First Sea Lord, Jack Fisher. Churchill had a long and intimate connection with intelligence, and 'signals intelligence' in particular, throughout his long career. No doubt the log book of decoded messages cited in Chapter 1 was the one to which Churchill referred.

Churchill's memo is often called Room 40's 'Charter', but this is a misreading. On one level it is simply a note instructing Ewing to appoint someone to handle and assess the intelligence being revealed by the decrypts (see below). On another level the memo may well have been a way for Churchill, ever conscious of his image in the eye of history, to lay an unmissable documentary mark in the records, showing his intimate involvement with Room 40 from its earliest days. But the memo's important message – the tight control of the intercepts – ensured that, far from being a charter of rights setting Room 40 free to acquire and assess intelligence, it was more of a constraining order. It created a constrictive framework around Room 40, limiting how its intelligence could be used – even to the extent of specifying exactly how decodes should be written out and secured for storage. Churchill's real concern was to ensure that no one gave away the big secret.

The tussle between making effective use of intelligence and protecting its source for future use is an age-old one and there is no easy resolution. Churchill erred far too much in the early days on the side of caution. He was insistent that only a very few people knew about the big secret – just nine people at the top of the navy were initiated into the inner circle. As well as imposing excessively tight security, Churchill's memo created another organisational problem. It appeared to place the cryptographic team under the Chief of Staff, Oliver. On his promotion to that position, Oliver was succeeded by a ruthless new director of the Intelligence Division, Captain William 'Blinker' Hall. Hall was one of the nine 'in the know'. But none of his Intelligence Division staff could be told. Nor was he allowed to be in charge of Ewing's team, who were supplying such important intelligence. Instead, Ewing reported directly to Oliver, the newly appointed chief of naval staff. He was too busy to add any more tasks to the crowded agenda of his twenty-one-hour working day. Hall, who had the energy and ideas necessary to make effective use of the intelligence bonanza, was effectively sidelined by Oliver. It was he who controlled which intelligence was used and how. Ewing, who did not like Hall, willingly played along in minimising Hall's involvement in his little empire.

Room 40 became, in the words of one Second World War naval intelligence officer, 'Oliver's private cryptographic bureau'. He would receive the intelligence, assess it and then draw up orders for the navy to react, involving Fisher and Churchill in major events, but not seeking advice from the admirals in charge of the Grand Fleet at Scapa Flow and other squadrons at Rosyth, Harwich and Dover. And he certainly did not seek any advice from the cryptographers or those who worked with them translating and analysing the intercepted German messages. Oliver might misinterpret the intelligence – assuming for example that only a small part of the German fleet was leaving port, so not sending out the Grand Fleet (see below). He would decide what snippets of intercept intelligence to pass to the commanders at sea, such as Admiral Sir John Jellicoe in charge of the Grand Fleet. When the commanders saw things with their own eyes that clashed with the intelligence they had received – such as being told that only a minor German force was at sea when they found they were facing the main

German fleet – they began to doubt the value of Room 40's intelligence generally. Churchill, obsessed with security, failed to see that this superb new intelligence source was being badly handled.

Yet, for all his failings, Churchill was a doting stepfather to his infant cryptographic organisation, giving it support and encouragement as well as providing the sustenance needed to ensure rapid early growth. Growth meant more staff. The core of the cryptographic team in Room 40 was formed by Denniston (who had obtained leave of absence from Osborne), Norton and Herschell, backed up by Parish, Curtis and Professor Henderson, but only 'where their other duties allowed'. According to Denniston, all six were singularly ignorant of cryptography but they were becoming expert analysers, filers and translators of German military telegraphs. Denniston, Herschell and Norton formed the watch, kept around the clock to receive intercepted messages. Using the techniques developed by Rotter to break the cipher, they would then attempt to decipher and then decode them. Denniston revealed, 'In the earlier stages of development new men were sought who had but two qualifications, a good knowledge of German and a reputation for discretion. Cryptographers did not exist, so far as we knew. A mathematical mind was alleged to be the best foundation but it must be noted that except for Russell Clarke and Henderson, no one had such a reputation and in fact the majority of those chosen had actually had a classical training.' Ewing's insight, and probably his most important contribution to Room 40 in the long run, was that the people needed to break the German codes and ciphers were those with a good knowledge of German and languages in general.

Late in 1914 and early in 1915 more potential cryptographers were recruited. One of the recruits, joining in December 1914, was Herbert Morrah, a well-known writer and literary critic of the day. His novels included such forgotten titles as *A Serious Comedy* and *The Faithful City*. He was also author of a book, published in 1911, called *Highways and Hedges,* where his words were appended to a set of paintings of charming rural scenes. He was editor between 1899 and 1901 of the literary magazine *The Argosy*. Frank Birch, who for a time headed the Baltic section of Room 40, wrote a short account of Room 40 in the form of a parody of Alice in Wonderland, entitled *'Alice in ID25'* and had the small pamphlet printed (with a run of around 100 copies). The story begins with Alice falling into Room 40's in-tray for incoming messages. This leads to a journey around Room 40 and other rooms, meeting the strange inhabitants. We will return to some of Birch's other caricatures later (see Chapter 11), but the Morrah that Alice meets is a 'dark, dreary creature with soft eyes … he had a box of matches in one hand and a lyre in the other. His pockets were stuffed with papers and one which stuck out a long way was marked "Weather Chart". "Have a match," he said, suddenly holding one out to her. "Thanks very much," she replied, taking it.

"That'll be a shilling," and he smiled benignantly as he held out his hand. Now Alice knew that matches were scarce, but she couldn't help protesting all the same. "Isn't it rather expensive?" she inquired. "Not at all." He shook his head. "That's the rule. Everybody gives me a shilling and I find as many matches as I can". "I think it's a very *silly* rule," said Alice, feeling rather annoyed. "But, I have to do it. I *have* to!" he exclaimed, rolling his eyes and waving his arms. "It's my War Work".' No doubt there are some in-jokes here to which we are not privy, but this is clearly telling us something about Morrah as a person and about his work – looking for 'matches' probably between different messages or with suspected cribs in the messages.

Morrah was an Irishman and, according to one colleague of his, 'a rabid Home Ruler'.This brought him into frequent conflict with a clergyman from Northern Ireland who joined Room 40 somewhat later than Morrah, the Reverend W. H. Montgomery. He was 'an Ulsterman who had to be kept on peaceful terms with H. Morrah,' said the fellow cryptographer. Alice's madcap trip through Room 40 shines some light on the spats between Morrah and Montgomery. While Alice is being shown around, Morrah happens to mention ' "Home Rule", stirring the creature [Montgomery] into action. "Did I hear you say *Home* Rule?" shouted the creature violently, while an extraordinary change came over him. "Yes, you did say Home Rule. That's it! *I* heard you! Home Rule!" And his voice grew louder and his eyes rolled and he beat his hands together and waved his arms and looked so fierce and dangerous that Alice began to feel quite frightened.'[29] Before the war Montgomery was a 'lecturer and writer on Historical subjects at Cambridge, being an MA and resident member of St John's College'. More relevant to his new task, he had also spent time in Germany and had considerable experience in translation, including the chapter on the Teutons in the *Cambridge Medieval History*. He was very good with languages, recalling at the end of the war: 'I have a considerable facility in acquiring a working knowledge of a language, [for example] I can read Dutch without having studied it and lately got up enough Polish for certain practical purposes' – by which, of course, he means cryptographic purposes. According to William F. Clarke, Montgomery 'died learning to drive a motor in 1926'. As a cryptographer he earned Denniston's highest acclamation: 'very sound'.

Two other early recruits from December 1914 were Lord Monkbretton and H. W. 'Harry' Lawrence, both of whom seem to have been recruited for their social background as much as anything. Monkbretton was a former private secretary to Joseph Chamberlain. Later, with two other socially well-connected members of Room 40, R. D. Norton (one of the original team members) and Edward Bullough (who joined in September 1915), they formed what became known as the "Gentleman's watch". Lawrence's occupation sounds an odd one as a training ground for cryptography – he was an expert on furniture and art. William F. Clarke felt he needed to record only two other items of information about Lawrence: first that he was the brother of the actor Gerald Lawrence and secondly that he was 'One of the most popular of our staff … one of our most loveable members.' Neither snippet adds anything to our knowledge of his cryptographic or linguistic contribution, but at least leaves us with some indication of his ability to fit in with his colleagues.

Among those who joined Room 40 during 1916 were 'Dilly' (Dillwyn) Knox, George Young, Nigel de Grey – all of whom were to make major contributions to Room 40's work – and several others (see Chapter 11). They were generally drawn from certain professions: naval schoolmasters, academics, the diplomatic service, wounded officers, businessmen with good connections in the city and some of the king's social circle. A few were from less obviously relevant backgrounds, such as the expert on furniture and a fashion designer. In such cases we can suspect that personal connections were what led them to be selected for Room 40. The wounded officers in the main did not get taken on to perform cryptanalytic work, but handled the routine tasks – logging incoming messages, sorting them into message types, getting them to the right people and so on. The messages arrived in a pneumatic tube from the Admiralty's communications centre, so these clerical workers became known as 'tubists'.

***

If it needed German language experts to decode and decipher, it needed a naval eye to assess what the intercepts might actually mean. The messages transmitted by the German naval command seldom spelled everything out in the form 'leave harbour at 05.00hrs to reconnoitre in the area of Dogger Bank, returning the following morning' (though on one fairly major occasion such an explicit message was sent, as we will see towards the end of this chapter). Rather there were orders to switch on harbour lights, or to make wireless contact at a certain time, or to go to a map reference or to implement secret orders. It took naval experience and intuition to work out what a set of messages might imply. To make matters worse, some of the senior British naval commanders who were sent the Room 40 decodes, became rather upset when they received translations, for example, from the German *laufen*, reporting that so and so ship would 'run' at such and such a time. Similarly it was once reported that a ship would return to port that evening 'athwartwise'. These naive translations and ugly transliterations wound their Lordships up into fits of contempt for the impertinent civilians purporting to provide them with intelligence. A naval eye was needed.

The first man appointed to fill this post was Assistant Paymaster Rotter, but his considerable cryptographic skill was wasted spending time dealing with the translated intelligence and he was needed breaking new cipher keys. Blinker Hall, rather than Ewing, was responsible for finding someone else for the job. The man he chose was Captain Herbert Hope. He was working in the intelligence division, all the while dreaming of getting sent to join the crew of a warship, but assigned in fact to compiling charts and records of German ship movements. 'Our duties,' he recalled, 'were not arduous, nor did they call for the exercise of any great intelligence, in fact they might just as well have been carried out by three intelligence clerks ... I continued at this dull occupation, cursing my luck at not being at sea, all through August, September and November.' Then he was let into the big secret. 'When I first went to Sir Reginald Hall, he first impressed on me the need for absolute secrecy and then informed me that German naval wireless telegraphy messages were being decoded in the Admiralty; the First Lord (Mr. Winston Churchill) had decreed that an executive naval officer was to be appointed to sift messages and I was detailed for the purpose.'

The new job was initially just as disappointingly tedious as the work tracking German ships. Hope sat on his own in an empty office waiting until someone brought him a few decoded messages. At first these numbered just half-a-dozen a day at most. 'These messages were not, in themselves, of great importance and in some cases were not very intelligible,' wrote Hope. 'However, I did my best by writing remarks on them which I sent to [Captain] Hall. I found out afterwards that he sent my remarks to the First Lord who sent them on to the COS [chief of staff]. I quite realise now that at that early stage my remarks were very amateurish and beside the point, and must have added to the worries of the COS [chief of staff], who by that means got prejudiced, in addition to other reasons, against my work and myself; it took a long time to break down this prejudice.' Hope told Hall that he needed to see the original decodes and to be allowed to speak directly to the interception staff, the cryptographers and translators, if he was to draw real intelligence from the messages. Hall, however, explained that, as the production of the decodes was not under his control, he was unable to authorise closer contact for Hope. This impasse was broken thanks to the irascible First Sea Lord, Jacky Fisher. One day in November, Fisher came across Herschell wandering round the Admiralty looking for Hope to deliver some decodes to him. Fisher took Herschell to Hope's office, came in and questioned Hope about his work. This at least is the accepted story, but it is quite possible that Herschell, now one of Hall's 'fixers', was told by Hall to apply his grace and charm in leading Fisher to hear Hope's story. In any event, Hope grabbed the chance and explained his difficulties to Fisher. The First Sea Lord wasted no time in instructing Ewing to initiate Hope into the 'Holy of Holies'. 'I was introduced into the Mystery on 16 November 1914,' recalled Hope. 'This was the beginning of a sphere of work which was probably unique, was absorbingly interesting and which threw me into a close relationship with probably as fine a set of fellows as it would be possible to meet.' Hope rapidly won the respect of the cryptographers and became, in their eyes, 'Our beloved chief' according to William Clarke. He saw Hope as 'the hub of Room 40 ... mainly responsible for its success'.

Hope immediately set himself up as 'censor'. Until then the full set of raw daily decodes had been sent to the privileged inner circle allowed to receive them. Hope realised that this was becoming impractical as too many messages were now being decoded. Someone had to 'decide what type of message should be sent in, as with the increasing number of them it was clear that a selection on these lines must be made'. He also kept a copy of all messages, compiling an immensely informative database of intelligence about the 'organisation and economy of the German fleet ... We were very much helped by a thorough and extensive wireless telegraphy exercise which the Germans used to carry out every night,' where every squadron and unit called up in turn and individual ships replied with their call-signs. This allowed Hope to draw a chart of the organisation of the German fleet (its 'order of battle' in the military jargon) and pass it on to Hall's intelligence division and senior commanders.

Another useful German habit was for vessels at sea in and around the Bight to transmit their position by reference to a secret grid system quite frequently. The documents captured from the *Magdeburg* included maps of the grid system used by the German navy, and the SKM included the codewords used for transmitting these grid references. So once the cipher key in use at any time had been broken, these messages could be decoded and the vessels' rough positions identified. This intelligence was not of much immediate tactical use – it was not generally possible to rush off and attack ships or submarines based on such decrypts unless there happened to be a suitable warship in the vicinity. But these messages provided good medium-term intelligence about German naval operations, especially the many minor ones by submarines and minelayers. There were other more direct advantages too. According to Hope, 'Whenever any of their vessels was at sea, she was continually signalling her position by saying what [grid] square she was in. By plotting all these positions on a chart we were soon able to establish clearly defined channels, and furthermore, it was soon seen that there were a large number of squares in which no ship ever reported herself and which remained conspicuously blank on [the plotting] chart: it was only reasonable to suppose that these blank spaces were mined areas. As soon as sufficient information was obtained, a chart was made out and circulated.'

Hope learned how to use both the routine and the unusual. 'Experience showed that the Germans were exceedingly methodical in their methods and a large number of signals were made day by day which were of great assistance in solving the new 'key' to the code when it was shifted ... [but it was also found that] any messages which were not according to routine were to be looked upon with great suspicion' as possibly indicating the start of a German naval operation. It was Hope's job to detect such signals and to guess what sort of operation was afoot so that the navy could react. But the cramped system of not passing on intelligence to those who needed it (such as commanders of the Fleet) prevented its best use. 'In a very few months we obtained a very good working knowledge of the organisation, operations and internal economy of the German Fleet. Had we been called upon by the staff to do so, we could have furnished valuable information as to movements of submarines, minefields, minesweeping, etc. But the [Admiralty] Staff was obsessed by the idea of secrecy; they realised that they held the trump card and they worked on the principle that every effort must be made to keep our knowledge to ourselves so as to be able to keep it up our sleeves for a really great occasion such as the German Fleet coming out in all their strength to throw down the gauntlet in battle ... In other words the Staff was determined to make use of our information *defensively* not *offensively*' (emphasis in original). Here Hope points to a major flaw in the Admiralty's use of the intercepts. Room 40's intelligence was seen as primarily giving advance warning of the 'really great occasion' – the cataclysmic clash of fleets of titans that everyone still expected would take place soon. The real nature of the naval war had not sunk into the mindset of the Admiralty's political leadership (Churchill) and naval commanders (Fisher, Oliver). They clung to the familiar, expecting a decisive sea battle, a Trafalgar for their generation, with them at the helm.

***

To try and break the stalemate in the North Sea, the German navy's commanders sought the Kaiser's sanction for limited assaults on the British, trying to lure isolated parts of the Royal Navy out of port. The first attack was on the British coast, on 4 November, at Yarmouth. A German squadron succeeded in crossing the North Sea, shelling a British minesweeper and two British destroyers (without causing much damage), bombarding Yarmouth, laying some mines and then escaping before the British battle cruisers under Admiral Beatty could get to the scene. Churchill later claimed that when the Admiralty first received reports of the bombardment, it was assumed that the attack must be a precursor of a more major operation elsewhere. According to Churchill, 'The last thing it seemed possible to believe was that first-class units of the German fleet would have been sent across the North Sea simply in order to disturb the fisher-folk of Yarmouth. ... Several hours of tension passed; and then gradually it became clear that the German battle cruisers were returning home at full speed and that nothing else was apparently happening.' Room 40 did not gain advance notice of this raid as it was only just beginning to learn how to break cipher keys at this time.

Embarrassed by the venture's lack of real success, Admiral Ingenohl (commander of the *Hochseeflotte)* wanted to have another go, with a bigger attack. Public anger in Britain at unpunished raids on the coast might lead to political pressure being put on the Royal Navy to split the Grand Fleet into smaller squadrons stationed along the coast to provide defence. This was exactly what Jellicoe did not want to do. The loss of von Spee's ships at the battle of the Falklands made another attack all the more important for German propaganda purposes. It also meant that British battle cruisers would be coming home from the South Atlantic, so any strike should take place before they reached British waters. Also, morale in the German navy was suffering from inactivity. The German plan was for Rear Admiral Franz Ritter von Hipper, commander of the German fleet's battle cruiser squadron (which served as the scouting forces of the *Hochseeflotte*) to take four battle cruisers, one armoured cruiser, four light cruisers and several destroyers to bombard Scarborough and Hartlepool and to lay mines in shipping lanes. Ingenohl had been forbidden to take his main dreadnought battle fleet to sea, but, without telling the Kaiser, he did send his big ships out. They were to wait just east of Dogger Bank, to attack any British forces that were at sea and draw them onto newly laid German mines. All told, 112 German vessels put to sea.

But here the events we have been discussing in this book intervened. The capture of the naval codebooks and the breaking of the cipher techniques began to produce results for the Royal Navy. Room 40's output of decoded intelligence about German naval movements meant that Britain regained control of the North Sea. Rotter's key-breaking skills were needed at the beginning of November. An error was made by a German wireless operator. A message dispatched from Norddeich to all ships was broadcast in two different forms. In one the message was coded using the standard SKM codebook, but in the second message it was partly in the VB code and partly in the SKM. 'This enabled the VB key 'A' to be quickly determined on Dec[ember] 3, the day the VB came into our hands.' Quickly, in this context, means about two weeks, for it was on 15 December that it was broken. This break was timely as the German navy was about to stir from its lair.

Room 40 was able to give forewarning as orders were sent out in the SKM code and cipher which was already compromised. At 03.27 on 14 December, an order was intercepted asking for 'extreme reconnaissance' by airships and aeroplanes to the northwest and west 'as German forces will be at sea'. A little later another message gave away the timing of the departure of Hipper's battle cruiser fleet – it would leave the River Jade at 03.30hrs and pass Heligoland at 05.30hrs. After that, apart from a couple of messages ordering transfer of control of torpedo boats, no further signals were intercepted until 03.23hrs on 15 December (when a message transferring wireless control was picked up) and then there was another gap until the following morning. Meanwhile the Royal Navy was getting itself ready to respond to this intelligence windfall.

There was insufficient warning for the raid to be prevented, but time was ample for British warships to sail into the middle of the North Sea, get to the east of the German ships and cut off Hipper's way home. While the intercepts revealed that Hipper and his battle cruisers would be putting to sea, they did not mention that Ingenohl and the *Hochseeflotte* would also sail. When the top commanders and Churchill met at the Admiralty, they concluded that the *Hochseeflotte* was not sailing. So only Beatty's battle cruisers with light cruisers and destroyers and a single squadron from the Grand Fleet were ordered to sail. Jellicoe with the main part of the Grand Fleet was ordered to stay in port. The order, drafted by Chief of Staff, Henry Oliver, told Jellicoe: 'Good information just received shows that the German First [Battle] Cruiser Squadron with destroyers leave the River Jade on Tuesday morning early and return on Wednesday night. It is apparent from information that [Ingenohl's] battleships are very unlikely to come out.' Jellicoe would have preferred to put all his ships to sea, believing that the power of the fleet should be used in a concentrated form, and not in a way that risked defeat of isolated portions of it. His appeal to the Admiralty to revise its decision was rejected. Beatty set to sea to rendezvous with the other forces east of Dogger Bank – just 30 miles from where Ingenohl, with his much bigger and more powerful force, would be sitting and waiting.

Hipper's raiding force hit bad weather as it sailed west and some ships had to return. Hipper, believing that Ingenohl's big battleships would remain on station, decided to continue with the raid. He successfully bombarded the two towns and Whitby too. Then he turned east to head home. The British fleet had put to sea shortly after the German fleet and had steamed well to the east of the German ships then turned west. For several hours the two fleets steamed towards one another, unaware of each other's exact location. The heavy seas made for moderate progress. The first sighting of each other was made about 04.20hrs when a German submarine reported sighting British ships. The first clash occurred at about 05.15hrs between advance ships 'screening' the main fleets. For two hours a scrappy battle took place in the dark between a few British destroyers and a superior German force of cruisers and destroyers, with the British ships suffering badly. During the fighting one British ship fired a torpedo towards a German cruiser. Although the cruiser managed to avoid the torpedo, its firing was reported to Ingenohl, waiting with his big ships way to the east, near Dogger Bank. Further west, as the first smatterings of light began to appear in the eastern sky, Hipper's and Beatty's ships both realised that they were facing much bigger forces than they had so far realised.

Ingenohl, worried about the threat from submarines and mines, decided to turn back to avoid risking damage to his ships and the wrath of the Kaiser. He did so shortly before Beatty's smaller force sailed to nearly the same spot. Here was the chance German strategists had dreamed of – an out-gunned, isolated part of the British fleet that could be destroyed, reducing the overall balance of naval forces between Britain and Germany to parity. But as the author of the official British naval history put it, the German admiral 'knowing nothing of the presence of our squadrons, fairly turned tail and made for home, leaving his raiding force in the air'. Fortunately for the Germans, the British made just as big a mess of the opportunity Ingenohl and Room 40 had provided them with by leaving so hastily.

By 11.00hrs extra British forces had been ordered to sea (including, far too late, Jellicoe's Grand Fleet). The two fleets were about 100 miles apart and closing on each other. At this point the morning's clear weather disappeared and cloud and rain moved in, making sighting of the enemy difficult. One British admiral said that 'they came out of one rainstorm and disappeared in another'. When screening forces met, the British commander overlooked the need to inform Beatty of the encounter. Beatty, seeing some firing in the distance, thought that it involved only one German ship and did not give chase. Then Beatty's signals officer sent, not for the last time, an ambiguous message to the light cruisers engaged with the German ships. This led to several cruisers calling off the chase. After that the British lost sight of the Germans. Hipper and his scouting fleet escaped. By this time Room 40 was intercepting more messages. One message sent by Hipper at 12.45hrs gave his position, but by the time it had been deciphered, decoded and sent out to Beatty, at 14.50hrs, it was already too late. Another intercepted message caused some alarm at the Admiralty as it was their very first indication that the *Hochseeflotte* was at sea. In fact the message recorded the position of the *Hochseeflotte* on its retreat, but this was not understood at the Admiralty. They belatedly feared that the *Hochseeflotte* was setting out to catch Beatty's battle cruisers unawares.

The first set piece action to take place with the help of Room 40's decodes had been a flop. The great naval commanders from Churchill down had, without exception, acted with arrogance and incompetence. Room 40's intelligence was misused from start to finish and communications between commanders at sea had been atrocious. Perhaps it is understandable. The generals on land had repeated rehearsals of battle-fighting between late 1914 and 1918 and, arguably, even with all this practice never quite understood what worked and what did not, or did so only late in the war. So it is perhaps too much to expect that the navy could have got everything in order for its first encounter. The question would be whether it could learn from its mistakes.

There was public anger at the outcome in both Germany and Britain. The unchallenged raids on the British coast generated hysteria. After the raid 'the mayors [of Scarborough, Whitby and Hartlepool] demanded coastal artillery and dreadnoughts anchored off the beaches. The Indian Government telegraphed that Madras must be protected'. Churchill later wrote, 'Dissatisfaction was widespread. However, we could not say a word in explanation. We had to bear in silence the censures of our countrymen. We could never admit, for fear of compromising our secret information ... [the] one comfort we had. The indications upon which we had acted had been confirmed by events. The sources of information on which we had acted had been confirmed by events. The sources of information on which we relied were evidently trustworthy. Next time we might at least have average visibility. But would there be a next time?'

In fact Churchill and the navy got their next opportunity to make something of Room 40's remarkable output a month later, in January 1915. The German navy suspected that the Royal Navy must have had some advance warning of the German fleet's movements during the attack on Scarborough. But, despite knowing of the loss of codebooks, they focused their suspicions on Dutch trawlers around the area of Dogger Bank in the centre of the North Sea. They reckoned that the trawlers must be sending details by wireless to the British, so a plan was conceived to set a trap by sailing to near Dogger Bank, hoping that the British would be drawn forth. On this occasion, Ingenohl actually sent orders for the operation to Hipper by wireless. At 22.04hrs on 22 January he told Hipper to take ships out to reconnoitre the Dogger Bank area. 'They are to leave this evening during darkness and return during darkness tomorrow.' At 23.54hrs on the same date, instructions were sent by wireless for Buoy 8 and the Alte Jade to be lit before dusk, and for the outer lights of the Jade to be switched on between 17.45hrs and 19.00hrs, for ships to leave the port.

The Admiralty first learned about the new German operation from Room 40 about midday on 23 January. It took Churchill, Fisher and Oliver until 14.00hrs to work out their response and it was not until 14.10hrs that Jellicoe and Beatty and other commanders were sent their orders. Beatty's battle cruisers, sailing from Rosyth, were first to encounter the German ships. Jellicoe's Grand Fleet was still 140 miles away from the fighting and never took part. But at least this time Room 40's intelligence had been successfully used to engineer a meeting of big warships with the British fleet out-gunning the German ships. Room 40 later decoded a message from Hipper reporting his position, speed and course. He added, 'eight large ships, one light cruiser [and] 12 destroyers in sight'. At 21.37hrs he reported, 'seven light cruisers [and] 26 destroyers following me. Behind them further clouds of smoke. Propose to attack ships, keeping in touch when in inner German Bight.' In the mêlée that followed, Beatty's flagship took a battering and had to retire from the fight, but two German ships were badly damaged; one of them, *Blücher*, eventually turned sideways and sank. The images of German sailors sliding down the great hull of the ship as it finally went under are some of the most famous photos of the war at sea and made for a great propaganda coup for the Royal Navy.

A short time later, Beatty thought he saw a submarine periscope in the waters some distance off and ordered his ships to turn away, allowing some space to build up between the British and German ships so contact was lost. In fact, Room 40 knew the rough position of German submarines and there was none in that area. But Admiralty Chief of Staff, Henry Oliver, had chosen not to inform Beatty of submarine location intelligence. Then there was another ambiguous ship-to-ship signal sent from Beatty's flagship. This led to the other German ships escaping destruction and they limped back to base. At 23.41hrs a wireless message was sent from the German naval high command to the *Hochseeflotte* 'to get up steam in all boilers'. But this was a gesture. It would be impossible for the fleet to get up steam, await the right tide, file through the shallows and sandbanks, and get to Dogger Bank in any useful timescale. More useful, perhaps, was an order to the *Hochseeflotte*, sent at 04.40hrs, telling the sailors to line up on deck and give the returning ships three cheers.

Room 40's intelligence had been better handled on this occasion than during the Scarborough raid. The encounter had been engineered, based on intercepts, and it was incompetence at sea that led to the German escape. However, it may well be the case, as Jellicoe argued, that if he had been given intercept intelligence about the German operation immediately it was available, then the Grand Fleet could have sailed almost two hours earlier. That would have allowed Jellicoe to get to Dogger Bank in time to take part in the first major naval clash of the First World War. If Beatty had known that there were no German submarines in the area he would probably have pushed his pursuit (though he may have distrusted wireless intelligence if he had received it). Oliver's personal cryptographic bureau was still incapable of becoming a real naval intelligence centre, able to assess as well as gather intelligence and ensure that commanders got all the intelligence they needed when they needed it.

One writer, Filson Young, who spent six months as an 'intelligence officer' (basically deciphering incoming wireless messages) on one of Beatty's warships was a witness to the Battle of Dogger Bank. He contrasted the laxity of talk in London with the cramped conversations permissible in the officer's wardroom on board a warship. In London, 'To know anything one had to go out to lunch, and I am bound to say that at such houses as the late Lady Paget's and Mrs. J. J. Astor's the information was generally up to date and accurate. The well-fed oracle from the War Office, carefully waiting until the servants had left the room, with a peach and a glass of port before him and his, "Well, I can soon tell the little *I* know," remains a type of those days. He would be so deep in the imparting of his information that the return of the domestics with the coffee and cigarettes was never allowed to interrupt it.' On first arriving in the battleship wardroom Young found a wholly different atmosphere. 'To my astonishment I found that it was I who was being asked for news, and, above all, for naval news. It was the first astounding revelation of the way in which the men on whom everything depended were being kept in the dark, not only as to the war in general, but as to the way in which it intimately concerned the naval arm and their own part of it. The absence of *Princess Royal* [in the South Atlantic chasing von Spee's cruiser squadron] being referred to by someone with puzzled indignation, I naturally made some reference to the mission in the Atlantic. It was my first lesson. A dead silence followed my remark. Someone said: "We are not supposed to know that," and the conversation was as soon as possible changed … What had been talked quite freely about in London was not known here, and when accidentally made known was not further discussed.'[30] Blinker Hall later claimed that he deployed agents whose job was to spread misinformation, in elevated social circles, that would be picked up by the neutral diplomats in London and passed on to German diplomats in other countries. Perhaps Young had met one of his agents. But his description of the contrast with the atmosphere on board is instructive.

In retrospect the main issue was not what the British thought about the Battle of Dogger Bank. Rather it was the effect it had on the German war leaders. After Dogger Bank the German fleet did not venture very far into the North Sea until the middle of 1916. In the first half of 1915 it made the occasional foray, but sailed no further than about 120 nautical miles from home, where it was certain not to meet a sizeable British fleet. This period provided no let-up, however, for Room 40 or the Grand Fleet. The German fleet's forays – to protect minesweeping operations in the approaches to the Bight for example – generated similar messages as those signalling an attack on the British coast. The Admiralty had no choice but to alert Jellicoe's Grand Fleet and Beatty's battle cruiser squadron and send them out to sea to meet any potential threat. Time and again the British fleet put to sea for no purpose. All the same, the German surface fleet was on the defensive. German interest in the North Sea was now diving below sea level.

Chapter 8

Counter-blockade

In November 1914 a German submarine, U-18, sailed into Scapa Flow. A British intelligence account tells the story: 'Scapa Flow was at this time the Mecca of ambitious submarine officers; all their hopes had turned in that direction, no place was so much discussed and so far no submarine had succeeded in penetrating its defences. [When U-18 sailed on 11 November its officers were] much worried by the presence of the Fishing Fleet off the Dogger Bank and the watchkeeping officer of U-18, Lt Neuerburg ... advocated their being all sent to the bottom by mines, as it was obvious they were on look-out duty.' Cooler minds sought bigger prizes. The trawlers were left to trawl and/or spy, while U-18 headed for the biggest prize of all, Scapa Flow. The 'crew strung up to the highest pitch of excitement, with the firm intention of attacking the Fleet and if possible [Jellicoe's flagship] *Iron Duke* or of perishing in the attempt. The boat rounded the point, proceeded close up to the boom, till a view could be obtained of the whole harbour.'[31] A diary kept by a crew member records what happened next: 'Then came disillusionment. All had gone! The nest was empty! There was not a single large vessel in the harbour.' Withdrawing, U-18 then made its way to the Moray Firth to shadow the Grand Fleet awaiting a chance to attack. But just south of Hoxa Sound it was rammed by a destroyer, *Garry*, and the periscope ripped off. 'The boat rose and sunk at steep angles up to thirty degrees. The men were ordered to run forward, then to run aft.' The submarine then hit the bottom and started to rise. On surfacing it was rammed again and started sinking again. 'Thank heaven no water came through. The same terrifying business we had just been through re-commenced. The boat shot upward and downward. The men rushed fore and aft ... we stumbled over loaves of bread, kettles and cooking pots from the galley.' The submarine then fell to the bottom again and with no engine or steering, the crew used compressed gas to raise it to the surface, where they surrendered to the *Garry*.

At the start of the war German U-boats were limited to patrolling the German Bight and nearby areas. When it was realised that submarines could stay at sea for longer than had been expected, they sailed further, pushing northwards to the Norwegian coast and venturing westwards too, crossing the North Sea to Harwich, the Firth of Forth, the Cromarty Firth and Scapa Flow, in search of British blockading ships and warships. For the next couple of months the U-boats were used for reconnaissance, though individual commanders also looked out for any chances to attack enemy warships – hence U-18's daring but fruitless escapade. Room 40 decoded position reports sent home by U-18 as it left harbour and headed towards the North Sea, but lost track when it stopped transmitting wireless messages. Potentially devastating though it could have been, this raid was just one small incident in the naval *Kleinkrieg* ('small war').

By the end of 1914, Room 40 was providing a sustained output of decoded messages which revealed the day-to-day operations, successes and tribulations of *Kleinkrieg*. A sample of intercepted messages from 1 and 2 January 1915 illustrates the type of information to which the British codebreakers gained access. The messages were all intercepted, deciphered, decoded and translated by Room 40 on the day they were transmitted by the German navy. At 00.03hrs the 1st Torpedo boat flotilla was sent instructions about its duties and details of its night position. At 04.47hrs a warship was ordered to sail the next day for Cuxhaven. At 06.12hrs a message was transmitted to the commander of a submarine flotilla asking for details of his plans. At 06.42hrs he reported that two U-boats were on duty in distant waters, one was ready for service, three were in Wilhelmshaven ready to sail on 4 January and one at Kiel ready for 7 January. At 08.00hrs a German warship reported its position as '4 delta, area 9'. At 15.20hrs a submarine, U-24, reported that another submarine, U-12, had found a new British minefield east of the Thornton Bank buoy. Twenty mines had been seen, but the full extent of the field was unknown. At 18.25hrs a flotilla of torpedo boats was ordered to advance west at 06.45hrs the next morning from Weser Buoy. At 06.11hrs several groups of *sperrbrecher* (minesweeping) boats were given details of where they should sail to the next day. At 03.50hrs naval command was informed that there would be no air reconnaissance that day (presumably because of poor weather). At 04.35hrs a U-boat was told that its night position was one mile downstream of the warship *Braunschweig*. At 05.20hrs a group of minesweepers was told where they should sail to. At 06.00hrs the harbour authorities were ordered to switch on some lights near the mouth of the River Jade at 21.00hrs for the warship *Albatross*. At 09.10hrs submarine U-29 was instructed to sail at 19.00hrs the next day from Wilhelmshaven to Emden.

Moving on to the beginning of February, a few more messages are of interest for revealing the sort of naval operations that took place day in, day out for much of the war. A lot of messages involved training exercises, aimed at keeping morale up during the enforced stay of the big warships in home waters. The 5th Torpedo boat half-flotilla was sent for firing practice at the Alte Jade on the evening of 2 February. The same day the *Chef der Hochseestreitkrafte,* Commander of the High Seas Forces, ordered the battery at Schillig Horn to practise firing between 11.00hrs and 16.40hrs on the 4th, 5th and 6th, 'Schillig Road to be evacuated for this purpose'. Another message from the same commander 'sent the usual signal ordering [certain vessels] to take part in W/T [wireless telegraphy] practice and observation of enemy W/T till 06.00'. A reconnaissance squadron asked for the Kiel barrier to be raised on Thursday at 13.30hrs and 21.00hrs.

A month later some decodes reveal some of the minor clashes that marked *Kleinkrieg*. On 1 May torpedo boat T162 reported that it had been in action with two armed trawlers near North Hinder, 'the leading trawler was sunk and the others scattered'. Having sunk the trawler, T162 had attracted attention and was on the run, heading for safety at Zeebrugge with a British destroyer chasing it. A series of messages allowed Room 40 to track the lamentable attempt to sail of a warship, *Pommern*. The first message at 15.30hrs on 6 February reported that *Pommern* had entered the Brunsbuttel lock and broadcast details of its wireless system. At 22.10hrs it was reported to a waiting commander that the warship 'commences passage at dusk today'. Whether the fading light was to blame is not reported, but at 22.50hrs the *Pommern* ran aground 'at Place F buoy of Alter Jade. No damage. Hope to get off at high water'. Whilst waiting for the chance to float off, the *Pommern* was told by the commander of the 1st Torpedo boat flotilla that it was detailed for submarine protection. Another ship, *Arcona,* ran aground two days later, at 21.30hrs and had to wait until 00.20hrs for the tide to rise.

The intercepts also revealed German intelligence successes. German intelligence had heard that a British air raid was planned some time between 8 and 11 February. Ten enemy aircraft were expected to attack Emden, Brunsbuttel and Kiel. Extensive air reconnaissance was requested, 'early enough for observations to be made at dawn'. On 8 February a report from Antwerp recorded that 'another trustworthy agent reports that transport of troops for Folkestone and Calais begins on 9 February'. Some intercepts even revealed details of German counter-intelligence activity. A message on 14 March addressed to the Marine Korps at Bruges in Belgium reported, 'From a reliable source ... there is an Englishman at Vlissingen [Flushing], apparently an officer, tall, slight, clean-shaven who is trying to bribe Dutch fishermen to take him with them. Off Zeebrugge they are to break down so that they have to go to Zeebrugge for assistance. This will be used for espionage.' Intelligence reports sending out details of the sailing of British merchant ships became commonplace. Another common category was reconnaissance reports from airships. An example from 4 May 1915 is typical. Zeppelin L-7 took off at 11.00hrs intending to follow a northwest by westerly course. It found nothing up as far as map square '8 epsilon' where it saw four trawlers of uncertain nationality. A short while later it had to turn from its course because the easterly wind was too strong. Its report was brief: 'Nothing seen of the enemy.' The files at the National Archives contain thousands of these kinds of messages recording the daily activities and minor operations of the Germany navy, the humdrum of

Kleinkrieg and illustrating the extraordinary detail revealed to Room 40.

However, there are few easy ways to tie up the intercepted intelligence with its exploitation by the Royal Navy. One exception concerns a German minelayer in June 1915. After a couple of successful sorties laying mines and sinking merchant ships the minelayer gave itself away by excessive use of the wireless. As recounted in a British intelligence file, 'Her success proved her undoing. She could not let the news of them wait until her return and commenced to use her wireless which led to the discovery of her position and course.' The vessel was intercepted by English light cruisers, and, on their approach, the captain sank the boat, escaping with his crew on board a Swedish sailing vessel. British ships rescued British prisoners but, because of a Zeppelin sent out to cover the vessel's return, made no attempt to capture it.[32]

But this did not add up to much and from the German point of view *Kleinkrieg* was not achieving the required shift in the balance of power in the North Sea. The Royal Navy's dominance of the seas between Britain and Germany was demonstrated by the slowly tightening British blockade of trade with Germany by neutrals. U-18's voyage into Scapa Flow came at a time when the German navy was becoming rather disillusioned with the performance of submarines. They had sunk a few British warships. But the 'strike rate' was never going to make a serious contribution to reducing the Royal Navy's predominance. On the other hand there was intense pressure on the navy to do something to help the army. The submarine offered a way forward, not by strategic choice, but by want of alternative.

***

The use of naval blockades was such a common operation and so integrated into the cultural mindset of Europeans in the centuries leading up to the First World War that there was a well-developed set of international maritime law about blockades and the capture of 'prizes'. The law was quite specific about how vessels could be stopped, boarded, searched and seized, about the types of goods that could be carried to belligerent nations, and about the monetary compensation that could be claimed in 'prize courts' (one of which was based in London and was independent from the English courts and British government, and would award damages against the government if the letter or practice of prize law demanded it).[33] The British blockade in 1914 was illegal, as only close blockades were recognised by law. Also the British imposed their own extensive list of contraband goods, most controversially treating food as contraband on the grounds that the German government had taken control of food supplies. By early 1915 the blockade was enforced by converted liners, armed only with guns powerful enough to sink U-boats. They had to spend day after day at sea, whatever the weather, patrolling the rough rolling waves between Scotland and Norway. Boarding parties would be cast to sea in small rowing boats, even in the worst gales – when a mistake in approaching the suspect vessel could mean destruction of their fragile boat and certain drowning. Once on board they would search the ship's papers for details of any potential 'contraband' goods bound for Germany, via the Netherlands or Denmark. Britain and Germany, the world's most industrialised and most urbanised countries, promised to be the most vulnerable to economic blockade. They were both heavily dependent on imports of food and materials. In Germany the blockade was seen as an act of deep aggression, aimed not at the Germany military, but at 'starving' the civilian population.

Submarines offered Germany a way to strike back, to go on the offensive. In February 1915 the German government announced that it would launch unrestricted submarine warfare on British merchant ships and those suspected of trading with the British. A message intercepted by Room 40, transmitted on 7 February from Norddeich, 'to all ships', informed them of a 'proclamation of military area around England, Scotland and Ireland. All merchant ships within the area will be destroyed.' It was left to young U-boat commanders, culturally attuned to aggression, to interpret the rules and make the final decisions on which ships to sink. But the submarine was not an ideal blockading vessel. The accepted practice of 'cruiser' warfare was for the blockading warship to stop and search a suspect vessel, then, if it was trading with the enemy, to put a crew on board to pilot the seized vessel home as a prize. But this was difficult for submarines. They did not have room to carry spare crews that could take several ships back to Germany on one sailing. That meant they had to sink any intercepted vessel, but also had to give ships' crews time to lower lifeboats. This in turn meant that they had to surface to give the necessary warning. Submarines were extremely vulnerable to being shot at or rammed when they were on the surface (whereas, under water, they were largely invulnerable). So, if they followed the rules demanded by prize law, they were forced to remain on the surface for some time, allowing the crew and any passengers to abandon ship. The Royal Navy exploited this. It employed decoy vessels, converting merchant ships to carry guns that were hidden from view until the submarine made itself vulnerable. Sometimes the decoy ship's crew would even pretend to be in panic, botching the lowering of their lifeboats in order to encourage the submarine to surface. Soon, of course, the German submarine commanders became wise to these tricks and were inevitably driven towards sinking ships without warning. This made conflict with neutrals more likely as mistakes were easily made when peering through a misted periscope lens and trying to determine whether the object in sight was an enemy or a neutral vessel, while keeping an eye out for any enemy warships.

At the start of the submarine campaign Room 40 was already getting quite a bit of information on submarine movements and the overall state of readiness of the submarine fleet. For example, an intercept of 9 March 1915 from a U-boat 'half-flotilla' reported its situation: U-24 ready for service at Emden, while U-28, also at Emden was only ready for limited service in the Bight; at Wilhelmshaven U-21, U-22, and U-30 would be ready by 27 March, the situation with U-33 was 'uncertain'; at Kiel U-32 would be ready on 11 March and U-19 on 1 April; and U-20, U23, U27 and U29 were already on 'distant mission'. Room 40 put a question mark in their transcript of the decode after U-23, presumably because it was garbled in transmission and that this was a guess. From March to May 1915 the German navy kept, on average, six submarines at sea, sinking 29 merchant vessels in March, 33 in April and 53 in May (though, to put that in context, there was an average of over 1,000 sailings of merchants to or from British ports every month).

Germany was not alone in using submarines. Britain used them for attacking enemy warships and reconnaissance, but not for blockade duties. Some intercepted German wireless messages from this period illustrate the German war against British submarines. On 3 May, German aircraft number 78 from Borkum reported that at 06.30hrs it had seen a British submarine on the surface, in 117 epsilon, which dived when the aircraft swooped to attack it. The aircraft continued to patrol the area for half an hour, hoping to catch the submarine resurfacing. At 07.15hrs between 92 and 93 epsilon it saw a half-submerged submarine, which again dived as the aircraft approached it. The submarine did not respond to any recognition signals from the aircraft, so the pilot dropped three bombs, one of which fell just in front of the bow. Then the next day the pilot of another aircraft, number 112, reported that at 14.30hrs he had sighted a British submarine in 75 epsilon and at the same time he also saw a German submarine in 84 epsilon going north. The plane warned the German vessel and then dropped three bombs on the enemy submarine which exploded near it, but apparently did no damage as the British submarine did not dive, but fired shrapnel at the aircraft, 'which burst close' to it. The shrapnel persuaded the pilot to retreat out of bombing range and so the incident ended. But it shows that, even under attack from the air, submarines were fairly safe if they could dive quickly enough or their captain had the courage to stand and shoot back. The aircraft's method of attack – dropping bombs out of the side of the plane – was not accurate enough.

***

Not all the ships sunk by German U-boats were British ships. Vessels from the Netherlands, Norway, Spain and Greece all became victims. Their governments' diplomatic protests led the Kaiser to declare, on 2 April, that no neutral vessels would be attacked. But this did not preclude problems with neutral citizens on Allied merchant ships. The intercepts reaching Room 40 included German intelligence reports sent out to submarines giving details of British grain ships expected to leave South Atlantic ports for

London, Hull, Liverpool and Leith in mid-March. The German intelligence system also watched Belgian and Dutch ships closely, feeding back information which was then broadcast by the German navy and picked up by Room 40. The Marine Corps at Bruges was informed on 10 March that Rotterdam harbour was expecting the [Belgian] steamers, *Elisabeth van België, Baron Baeyens, Hainault* and *Prasident Bunge,* all flying Dutch flags and with Dutch masts. Two days later further intelligence, from the German consul in Rotterdam, claimed that the steamers *Hainault, Prasident Bunge* and *Leopold II* had convoyed, while flying a Dutch flag, over 1,000 Belgians on board for the British army and were due to leave the Dutch port on Thursday to go to Hull. On 10 March, Room 40 intercepted a typical intelligence report sent from Norddeich 'to all ships' informing them of some prime potential targets. These were a 'large' British merchant ship, *Khim*, and another merchant, *Omrah*, which were to leave London on 12 March. The second report in the message mentioned that a 'fast steamer *Lusitania* leaves Liverpool March 13th'. Further intelligence reports followed mentioning the liner as well as other ships.

Nearly two months later, on 7 May, the *Lusitania* was torpedoed as it approached Ireland from the west having crossed the Atlantic.[34] It sank with the loss of 1,201 lives – including 128 US citizens. The *Lusitania*, one of the fastest ships on the Atlantic, was an icon of the age of the ocean-going liner. It displaced over 30,000 tons, while its four turbine engines consumed 1,000 tons of coal a day and powered it at an average speed of 20-25 knots. Its first-class accommodation was truly luxurious, with 'gold and white, glass-domed, Louis XVI dining salons and mahogany-panelled lounges and smoking rooms with huge marble mantelpieces'. Its horrific sinking was bound to attract enormous publicity in the USA, even without the American deaths. In response the Kaiser decreed that large passenger liners, even if flying an enemy flag, would not be attacked, rolling back a bit further the effectiveness of the submarine counter-blockade. Germany also suggested marking US ships in specified bright paint patterns. The USA rejected this particular offer, but seemed otherwise to accept the situation.

A short comment is called for here on the many conspiracy theories that have been developed about the *Lusitania* affair. Some authors have concluded that Churchill and other British naval leaders allowed the *Lusitania* to sail into waters where a U-boat was known to be lurking (from intercepted wireless messages decoded by Room 40) so that it would be sunk, seriously damaging German-American relations. The problem with these theories is that they rely on assumptions derived from the absence of evidence. I cannot add anything to the discussion from my research in the archives to validate these theories except to note (as in the message cited above) that the *Lusitania* was only one of several ships known to have been on the German target list. Like many conspiracy theories, this one at heart depends on an efficient and seamless synchronisation of the actions of two conflicting parties. The German submarine captain, for example, was intending to return home but belatedly changed his mind because the mist cleared shortly before the liner sailed into his sights. Also, efficiency in the assessment and handling of signals intelligence was not the British naval command's strong point at the time. It is a mistake to focus on the handling of intelligence related to this one incident without putting it in the context of the general tendency to impart less information than was necessary, even to the commander-in-chief of the Grand Fleet, let alone to broadcast it to commercial vessels.

Germany put more submarines to sea from the summer of 1915 onwards and sinkings increased sharply: 114 in June, 86 in July, 107 in August and 58 in September. And the 'strike rate' improved too, rising from 10 ships sunk for every one submarine lost between March and May, to 35 to one from June to August. Room 40 picked up the signals sent when the U-boats left port, when they were out on duty, and when they returned home. For example, on 19 May 1916 a typical message from the command to the Heligoland outposts read, 'Tomorrow morning proceeding out from Heligoland to the north, U-27 eastward of Arum Bank. U-21, U28 to the Ems River.'[35] Such intercepts gave the British regular and comprehensive accounts of U-boat departures, positions during operations every two hours, operational reports and their plans to return to port. As the network of direction-finding stations came into operation a new source of information became available. In March 1915, for example, a direction-finding station picked up 'suspicious' wireless signals, thought to be German submarines, located at 56 degrees 16 minutes North and 4 degrees and 45 minutes East at 11.00hrs. By 06.00hrs the next day the source of the signal had moved to another location. Several other reports the same day, from the direction-finding stations, provided evidence of other submarines in and around the waters surrounding the British Isles.

All this intelligence pouring into Room 40 was hardly used at all. Just as naval and military historians, ever since the war, have concentrated their writings on the big battles, most particularly the Battle of Jutland in 1916, so at the time the navy's senior commanders overlooked the chance of using Room 40's intelligence offensively against the submarine war. The log book of telegrams sent out by the section of the Naval Intelligence Division responsible for tracking U-boats, E1, giving naval units warnings of sightings, confirmed and unconfirmed, of German submarines shows that the intelligence was derived from a pretty wide variety of sources. Most come from naval or merchant ships, coastguards and the like. But the general public too kept the Admiralty informed. To quote one example, Mr Thomas Glen of Prestatyn, North Wales, reported in early February 1915 having seen several times lately submarines off the coast near the holiday resort of Rhyl. He also reported having seen 'powerful searchlights'. The Senior Naval Officer at Liverpool was asked to investigate. However, the log book contains no messages of the sort that we have seen Room 40 was decoding nor even the intelligence derived from direction-finding stations. The naval chief of staff, Henry Oliver, did use Room 40's decodes to protect especially valuable cargoes, holding a special ship back in port until the coast was clear, so to speak, or re-routeing them away from dangerous waters, but in general merchant ships, their crews and passengers, not to mention their valuable cargoes, were on their own. In fact, the officer responsible for plotting U-boat positions in the navy intelligence division, in section E1, was not allowed to see the product of Room 40's work until 1917 when Blinker Hall took full control of Room 40. In turn, Room 40 was not allowed to know the locations of British warships and merchants.

After the sinking of the *Lusitania* the submarine offensive continued, but under much stricter rules forbidding the sinking of passenger ships and neutral merchant vessels. On 19 August, a German submarine sank a British steamer, *Arabic*, causing the death of 44 passengers and crew, four of them US citizens. This led to more anger in America and strong protests from President Woodrow Wilson. The Kaiser hoped to find a solution by forbidding his submarines from sinking passenger liners unless the passengers and crew could be saved. But this was an almost impossible condition and on 18 September the German *Admiralstab* instructed naval commanders to withdraw all submarines from the Channel and the Western Approaches, temporarily ending the submarine blockade of Britain (though submarine warfare continued in the Mediterranean, to where several now-redundant U-boats were moved and where, also, there were few US ships to kick up a fuss). A Room 40 history, written at the end of the war, observed, 'It must have been particularly galling to the [German] naval authorities to be obliged from political considerations to curb the activities of the submarine commanders who had been exhibiting the greatest prowess during August … Apart from all other considerations, the sinking of the *Lusitania* came to be generally regarded by the German navy as a capital political error … [although, initially] it was received with extraordinary rejoicing by the German public at large and was an endless source of encouragement to those who suffered most from the Allied blockade.'

A British intelligence account says, 'From numerous articles appearing in the German press at the beginning of 1916 it is evident that disappointment with the results of submarine warfare was widespread in Germany.'[36] A newly appointed aggressive naval commander, Vice Admiral Reinhard Von Scheer argued for a more generally aggressive policy by the navy. Again, the objective was to entice the Royal Navy out to sea. He recognised the numerical superiority of the British fleet, so did not want a mass battle, but all the same hoped that he could goad the British into sending out smaller squadrons upon which he could pounce. There was a brief resumption of submarine warfare in March and April 1916, but this was called off due to US diplomatic pressure. The early months of 1916 also saw attack and counter-attack by both navies, hoping to pick off a few enemy warships or lesser vessels. A German raid on the English coast – with attacks on Lowestoft and Yarmouth – was fairly successful. Poor command and bad weather delayed the arrival of the Grand Fleet, so it did not get to sea in time to cut off the raiders on their return journey. This was despite advance warning given by Room 40. British attempts to entice the German fleet to sea were equally unsuccessful. 'It is against this background of raid and counter-raid with both sides baiting traps – Jellicoe to catch the *Hochseeflotte* away from its coast and Scheer to catch an isolated portion of the Grand Fleet – that the great naval battle of the war occurred almost by accident.'[37]

The clash of warships at Jutland, at the end of May 1916, is one of the most celebrated incidents of the First World War. Hundreds of books have been written on the subject and there seems to be no stemming the flood tide of new ones. Here was the big chance that Oliver and the other senior Admiralty figures had been waiting for, holding back on their use of Room 40's intelligence. The first indication that some move was planned by the German navy came from intercepts ordering the dispatch of a small flotilla of submarines. Initially there was nothing special in the sortie, but a couple of days after leaving port the U-boats had not shown up on any of the usual trade routes nor had they been spotted looking out for British warships. Submarines could remain on station for up to 10 days and their main mission on any voyage could begin only after they had arrived at their destination. 'In the absence of any signs of activity, it became obvious that they had been sent out on some particular service, in all probability connected with some operation by the German fleet.'[38]

But the lessons of the earlier clashes (described in Chapter 7) had not been learned. Indeed, the story that has passed down is that the arrogant dismissal among some senior commanders of the intelligence made available from Room 40 was even more marked than in the early days. William F. Clarke, who joined Room 40 in mid-1916, has left us a record of a small but significant incident that typifies that attitude. Admiral Henry Jackson had a particular dislike for Room 40. Clarke recalled that on the day that the German fleet sailed, Jackson came into Room 40 – one of his very few visits there – to ask the location of the call-sign used for the wireless set of the *Hochseeflotte* commander. He was told exactly what he asked for, namely that the call-sign was located in the harbour at Wilhelmshaven. What he did not ask was the location of the commander's call-sign when he had put to sea. The call-sign about which Jackson made his enquiry never left land. When the commander went to sea he adopted a new call-sign. But Jackson was not told this. His preconceptions shaped his question and thus, unwittingly, shaped the answer he got. He was in effect asking for confirmation of what he already supposed, namely that the *Hochseeflotte* had not left harbour. If Jackson had been a more regular and less grumpy visitor to Room 40 then a relationship could have developed that would have enabled the cryptographer to volunteer the extra information or to enquire if he wanted to know the location of the commander or of his shore-based call-sign. Instead, Jackson and Oliver based their orders to Jellicoe on their misconception that the *Hochseeflotte* was definitely not at sea and that the expected German raid would be limited to a smaller fleet. Jellicoe thus, foolishly, dawdled on the way (to keep coal in reserve for chase or flight later on) as he expected to meet only a few German ships. But this meant that he arrived too late to bring his big guns into play effectively. It also meant, once he discovered for himself that the German fleet was out in full battle array, that he mistrusted the value and reliability of later intelligence forwarded to him from Room 40. Important consequences flowed from Jackson's mistake.

Scheer sent ahead a 'scouting' squadron of some 40 vessels to draw any British ships onto the main German fleet. In all, over 250 ships put to sea. When Hipper's scouts and Beatty's battle cruiser squadron first met, Beatty was indeed drawn, unawares, towards the bigger, more powerful *Hochseeflotte*. But just as Hipper was drawing Beatty, so Beatty then started to draw the German fleets towards Jellicoe's even bigger ships – except that Jellicoe was dawdling, even taking time to stop and search some merchant ships. The battle truly took place in the fog of war, with both sides mistaking the enemy ships they glimpsed momentarily in the mist for isolated parts of the enemy fleet. The usual British inter-ship signalling problems and inability of the commanders to communicate with one another about intentions and orders ensured that the conflict did not turn into a great conflagration. However, three British warships – *Indefatigable, Queen Mary* and *Invincible* – were blown apart (the *Queen Mary* had been Hall's old ship until his appointment as Director of Naval Intelligence). The ships' demise was the result of shaving their armour plating to a minimum (in order to give them more speed) and the demands of upholding the navy's tradition of fast gunnery. This required keeping open flash doors that, if closed, could have stopped shell hits on the guns from spreading down to the arsenals. The workman blamed his tools: Beatty commented, 'There seems to be something wrong with our bloody ships today.' If Jellicoe had arrived earlier the battle may indeed have been more violent. Instead, it gave the German fleet the time to turn for home. The escape was successful due to more cock-ups. The Admiralty failed to pass on Room 40 intercepts to Jellicoe which would have allowed him to know which route the German ships were taking back to the Bight. Jellicoe was sent one intercepted message that should have alerted him to the German route home, but he did not really trust the intelligence. Later messages that would definitely have pointed him in the right direction – such as asking for airship reconnaissance – were not passed on. A Room 40 assessment at the end of the war suggested, 'Throughout this period of the battle, instances were multiplied of intelligence of vital importance to the British commander in chief, reaching the Admiralty but not being retransmitted … neither accurately nor fully was the available intelligence made known in the only quarter where it could be of use.'[39]

A post-war footnote is relevant here. After the war there was considerable controversy over Jutland. The full story of the battle could not be told without reference to the fact of Room 40's intelligence in general and also the grisly details of its partial supply to Jellicoe by the Admiralty chiefs in particular. Any account of the battle that did not include reference to the intelligence and its dissemination was guaranteed to make it look as if Jellicoe was mainly to blame for the indecisive nature of the clash. The Admiralty's censor, none other than William F. Clarke, opposed post-war publication of the details and content of the Room 40 signals *sent* to Jellicoe on several grounds, but mainly because their publication would lead to demands for the *unsent* messages to be published. This was allegedly a real concern because, while the general fact of Room 40's reading German naval wireless messages no longer needed to be kept secret, the unsent messages had been transmitted in a different code. It was vital, even in the 1920s, that the ability of British codebreakers to read messages sent in this type of code was kept secret. This story does not fit well with a number of facts. The HVB was replaced in May 1916 by the FFB. The HVB was the codebook with the lowest security level of the main set of German naval codebooks and there is no evidence that its successor was greatly superior in security techniques. Both codebooks were 'alphabetical' or one-part and it was not a secret during the war, let alone in the 1920s, that alphabetical codes could be broken. The FSB, which replaced the SKM, was not introduced until 1917. One possibility is that Clarke was referring to a new cipher technique, rather than a new codebook, but this is not clear. So, all in all, while Clarke's post-war justification for continued resistance to publishing these messages is not very convincing, it cannot be dismissed entirely. As well as this security justification for censorship, Clarke was quite candid that exposure of any of the intercepted intelligence would embarrass senior naval figures.

Returning to the aftermath of the Battle of Jutland, Jellicoe was soon aware of the partial nature of the intelligence and demanded that in future he be sent all raw intercepted messages so that he could make his own intelligence assessments. Oliver wrote to Churchill's replacement as the First Lord of the Admiralty, Arthur Balfour, to say that he had told Jellicoe that 'copies of messages will *not* be forwarded to him' though he was willing to send the commander-in-chief a daily summary for his personal use. Balfour wrote to Jellicoe in November backing his chief of staff. 'The principal advantage which the possession of the German naval codes gives us is that of security. We can be reasonably certain that no naval operation can be undertaken by the High Seas Fleet without our having information about it ... The possession of these codes being then of such great importance, every precaution should be taken to keep secret the fact that we have them.' The best way to do this was to minimise the use of wireless telegraphy to transmit messages based on intercepted German messages. 'If they have had their suspicions these have not been strong enough to compel a change of system. Of this [Admiralty] Board only the First and Second Sea Lords have official knowledge of it, and the War Committee itself has not been informed. We must be most careful not to relax our precautions ... I have had many anxious moments, but so far the secret seems to have been well kept. ... These precautions may seem excessive, but the value of the information we get may be so great in major operations that its loss would be a national misfortune. We cannot be too cautious.' Finally Balfour assured Jellicoe that 'whenever the Grand Fleet has been sent out, the information you get is the *best and fullest* which we possess' (emphasis in original).[40] Of course, this last claim was not true. Balfour was on safer ground when he said that the intercepts gave only clues as to what was afoot and that the idea of a German fleet operation had to be assembled from the 'cumulative effect of many small circumstances laboriously pieced together'.

Jellicoe was told not to discuss the daily summaries with any of his subordinate officers, to burn the summary after reading it and not refer to it in telegraphs, except, on very rare occasions, as the 'Japon Return'.[41] The great secret had to be maintained so that the navy would be ready next time the German fleet ventured forth. As it happened, all this did not really matter, at least as far as future major German naval operations were concerned, because there were no more attempts to goad the Royal Navy. The issue of the use of Room 40's intelligence mattered from now on more and more in the realm of *Kleinkrieg* and especially the submarine war, not in big clashes of capital ships. Unfortunately it took quite a while for this to be understood within the Admiralty and the navy.

Whatever the contemporary and post-war controversies, the key point about the Battle of Jutland was that the German ships turned for home as soon as Jellicoe's ships appeared. German propaganda was quick to paint the battle as a great victory for the Imperial navy and an unmitigated disaster for the Royal Navy. It was true that Britain suffered more casualties (6,954 compared with 3,058) and lost a greater tonnage of shipping (111,980 to 62,233 tons).[42] And, indeed, this view was widely accepted at first, both in Britain and abroad, in neutral countries where the great battles were eagerly followed for hints of who would be the likely winners of the war. At home,

Jellicoe was criticised for showing inadequate aggression and determination to engage with the enemy. The attitude persists. Jellicoe, in the words of a naval historian writing 90 years after the battle, was a worrier and 'great worriers are rarely great warriors'.[43] In Germany, Kaiser Wilhelm was ecstatic: 'The English have been beaten. The spell of Trafalgar has been broken. You have written a new chapter in world history.'[44]

Intercepts of German diplomatic messages between Berlin and Madrid illustrate what happened. Immediately after the Battle of Jutland, the German ambassador in Spain had been quick to report back to Germany: 'The Spanish press, including papers not specially friendly to Germany, recognise that Germany has had a great victory at sea … [with one paper declaring] the end of the 400-year supremacy of England.'[45] But the propaganda soon wore off as the implications of the fact that the German fleet fled the battle scene sunk in. The German ambassador lamented, as a Room 40 intercept revealed, that 'considerable harm has been caused by concealment of the loss of *Lutzow* and *Rostock*. The unofficial report [of the sinking] created a bad impression in German circles and, unfortunately, especially so in Spanish circles friendly to us. … The first impression of a great German victory has been entirely destroyed.'[46] Over time it became ever more obvious that the real outcome of the encounter was that the *Hochseeflotte* withdrew to its harbours. Scheer's aggressive strategy had failed. Apart from the odd sweep in home waters or maybe as far as the Norwegian coast, the *Hochseeflotte* never ventured to sea again. However badly the Admiralty may have handled Room 40's intelligence, however badly Jellicoe, Beatty and other commanders may have mucked up the operation, the outcome of the battle was a clear victory for the Allies. For the rest of the war the North Sea was free of the threat of the German *Hochseeflotte*. Simply getting the British fleet out every time German ships ventured out had proved sufficient in itself to stop further sorties even without a decisive and destructive engagement. The German Imperial navy had been swept from the surface waters of the North Sea. Once again German naval commanders concluded that only submarines could stand in Britain's way at sea. Within a month of the battle, Scheer told the Kaiser, 'even the most successful outcome of a fleet action in this war will not force England to make peace … [because of] the disadvantages of our military/geographical position and the enemy's great material superiority … a victorious end to the war within a reasonable time can only be achieved through the defeat of British economic life – that is by using the U-boats against British trade'.[47] Hindenburg and Ludendorff, the military high commanders, also backed a renewal of unrestricted submarine warfare, as did yet more influential German military figures. Germany's first big gamble – the knock-out attack on France – had failed. Now it was drawn to another big bet – that the USA would not be drawn into war if the submarines were once again sent out into the Atlantic.

Chapter 9

'For You the War is Over'

Captain Malcolm Hay joined the Gordon Highlanders at the start of the war and was among the first of the British Expeditionary Force to land in Belgium in August 1914. He and his men spent the first few days marching 'along pleasant country roads through a country of hedges and orchards, very like central and southern England', but also on tiring cobbled roads. On Sunday 23 August they marched to a peaceful rural scene where they were ordered to dig a trench. When some cavalry passed, heading rearwards, it dawned on Hay that their trench must now be the front line. After a day of fierce fighting, where they held off the advancing Germans, Hay received orders to 'retire'. On pulling back he learned that other units had suffered badly and the whole British army was retreating. During the retreat Hay and his men came back into contact with the Germans again, near a village called Bethancourt. A German machine gun began to play up and down another trench they had dug. 'The bullets began to spray too close to my left ear, and laying my glasses on the parapet I was about to sit down for a few minutes' rest, and indeed had got half-way to the sitting position, when the machine gun found its target. Recollection of what passed through my mind at that moment is very clear. I knew instantly what had happened. The blow might have come from a sledge-hammer, except that it seemed to carry with it an impression of speed. I saw for one instant in my mind's eye the battlefield at which I had been gazing through my glasses the whole day. Then the vision was hidden by a scarlet circle, and a voice said, "Mr. H. has got it".'[48]

Hay had been hit in the face and was helped back by his troops, but eventually had to be left behind when further retreat was necessary. He was expected to die but against the odds he survived, ending up as a prisoner in a Belgian hospital where he slowly recovered. In his account of his experiences Hay does not tell the reader the exact nature of his injuries directly, though it is clear that they were pretty serious. But he indirectly lets us know what happened when he records the later arrival of a wounded French soldier, Jean. 'His wound in the head was on the left side, almost exactly in the same place as my own – the bullet had made the same furrow, all the symptoms were identical, the right leg dragging, the right arm hanging, the slow elephantine movement; but there was a difference ...

between the two points of impact. In the case of Jean the impact of the bullet was a hair's-breadth more to the front of the head, only the difference of perhaps a tenth of a millimetre. And so it was that poor Jean had not only lost the power of motion on the right side, but also speech, memory and understanding.' Fortunately for Hay, while he did indeed have much trouble in moving, his powers of speech and thought were unimpaired. As his health improved he was transferred to a prisoner-of-war camp in Germany where he met brutal Germans and kind Germans. On a long train journey to the camp he witnessed Germany's massing of men and materials for the front. Hay later wrote, 'Most impressive was this glimpse of Germany at war. It is difficult to convey to those who have not seen Germany in a state of war. Men who have been at the front see little of this power which is behind the machine against which they are fighting.' Eventually, in January 1915, Hay was one of a number of badly injured officers and men exchanged for German prisoners on the Dutch/German border. His injuries made it impossible for him to make further contributions to the war effort, so it was safe to send him home. As he was about to leave the prison camp in Würzburg he was told by one German, 'For you the war is over.'

***

The territory of northwestern Europe, from the Netherlands to northern France, is marked by a series of frontiers, tide marks left behind when incursions of war and rebellion into these lands receded. Going south from the province of Holland, the first frontier to be crossed is a religious one, between the Protestant north and the Catholic south. The next frontier on the journey south is the political border between the Netherlands and Belgium. This border has some highly unusual aspects. There are some small enclaves of Belgian territory entirely enclosed within the Netherlands, rather like splattered paint blotches. Even today a Dutch police officer cannot arrest a suspect who flees – or just steps – into part of 'Belgium'. The largest enclave, Bar-le-Duc, proved rather useful to Allied intelligence during the First World War. A wireless transmitter was erected in what was sovereign Belgian territory and used to transmit intelligence gathered in France and Belgium to the Allied military authorities (until the Germans learned how to feed in disinformation). Further south comes the linguistic border between Dutch (in its Flemish dialect) and French (with its local Walloon usages such as 'septante' and 'nonante' in place of the 'soixante-dix' and 'quatre-vingt-dix' of French French). This boundary is the oldest and stretches back to the time of the Roman Empire which brought the Romance language into the lowlands of northwestern Europe. It has moved very little in the last two thousand years (one modern exception being when Brussels in the 19th century became a Francophone enclave in Flemish territory). A short way further south there is another political boundary, that between Belgium and France, though the situation is actually a bit less regular than implied, for the language boundary crosses into the far northern corner of France where there are about 100,000 Dutch speakers.

In late 1914 a new frontier was carved into the soil of the French borderlands – the trench systems that divided Germany's armies from those of the Allies. After Germany's attempt to knock out the French army was defeated on the Marne in September 1914, the British and German armies launched a series of attempts to outflank each other to the northwest, eventually reaching the sea near Dunkirk. An order on 15 September to the British Expeditionary Force, BEF, said, 'The commander-in-chief wishes the line now held by the Army to be strongly entrenched, and it is his intention to assume a general offensive at the earliest opportunity.' The second part of the order was not put into effect until after August 1918, but the first part was fully implemented by 14 October and the trench systems ran from the shores of the Channel to the Swiss border. The German army effectively created a massive linear fortress, enclosing the Belgian and French territory which they had occupied, and to which the Allied armies laid siege for the next four years.

There was an immediate consequence. As Denniston recalled, 'When the Armies settled down to trench warfare, the number of messages intercepted, and the number of stations heard, gradually diminished until about April 1915 when [army] work had practically ceased.' All the same, the German army's wireless sets remained in place not far behind the trenches. One day after a successful German attack on the French army, a message from the German HQ was sent out by wireless congratulating all the units involved in the assault. Each station replied in turn, in the traditional manner, with its own call-sign acknowledging receipt of the message. But this was an unusual break in the near overall silence in the ether on the Western Front from mid-1915. The two wireless stations that did remain in regular use were thought to be armoured trains that could not readily link up to the telephone and telegraph networks which increasingly provided for German military communications from November 1914 onwards.

We have seen that excessive secrecy was a problem in the Royal Navy when it came to exploiting the produce of Room 40's work. In part this was possible because of the central control exercised by the Admiralty in London, linked by telegraph and wireless to ships across the globe. This centralised control of all wireless intelligence was hard to replicate on land. The commander-in-chief of the BEF in northern France had considerable freedom of action. He was able to decide what forces to use where and when. He also had control of his own intelligence division in northern France which handled interception, codebreaking, translation, assessment and dissemination within the BEF. Colonel MacDonogh, head of the intelligence division at the War Office in London, received copies of translations of decrypts made in France, but had to request copies of the original German version of the deciphered messages (needed for his cryptographers and intelligence analysts in London to get the most out of the intercepts). In November 1914 an instruction was issued to Anderson, head of MI1(b) 'that, in view of the importance and secrecy of the messages which pass through your hands, no one should have copies of these messages ... The fewer the people who see these messages in view of the recent press indiscretions the better.' As we shall see, MI1(b) gave technical support to the BEF's own codebreaking unit, but in general, with the decline in German military wireless traffic, the unit was at a bit of a loss as to what it could now do.

Battlefield communications, or the lack of them, helped impose the stalemate of trench warfare. Out on the front lines, landlines were laid to provide for telephone and telegraph communications between the commanders and the commanded. Both sides dug in many tens of thousands of miles of wire (ie, bare metal) and cable (ie, sheaved metal) behind the lines. They also tried, unsuccessfully, to lay out communications lines in the wake of attacking troops. These complex networks were essential so that commanders could issue orders, follow progress, find out where reserves were needed and direct them there. The trench war was primarily an artillery war (artillery, not the machine gun, gas, rifle bullet or bayonet, was the single largest killer of soldiers). Artillery could damage cables, unless they were laid six feet below the surface. The networks of links were 'meshed' so that if one link was damaged, communications could be switched to another link.

While cable communications were fine for those on the defensive, they were not much use for offensive operations. This did not matter so much to the German army after the onset of trench warfare as it had largely to sit tight and hold on to its occupation of northern France and Belgium, one of Europe's most important industrial regions. Except during the German attack at Verdun in 1916 and the 'Ludendorff offensive' of 1918, Germany would remain on the defensive in the west. But time and again the British and French attacked into a communications void, sending troops blindly into the killing zones. This problem of communications during an attack was one major reason why the state of military technology and tactics at the time favoured defence over attack. Commanders, ensconced safely some way from the front, could give middle-ranking and junior officers precise and detailed orders before a battle started, but once it began communications were immediately severed. It could take a human messenger or 'runner' hours to negotiate a passage through the battlefields and get back to HQ to report and receive new orders. But the situation had already changed by the time they reached HQ, let alone when the runner returned – if they returned. Once a battle had been launched it was effectively out of the control of commanders who could not know where to apply extra pressure or where to withdraw tactically, and so were left with pouring more and more troops in the vain hope that the forward momentum of fresh flesh could surge past a storm of steel.

Codes and ciphers were essential to all the means of communication devised for use on the front and in enemy territory. As a result, the interception and decryption of enemy messages became a key weapon of both sides. One military historian has written that the First World War marked the 'dawn of modern signals intelligence'. As we have seen, the use of wireless initially declined quite rapidly once the trenches had been dug. But before long wireless made new appearances on, around and above the battlefield. Air and ground 'forward observers' needed to communicate with artillery batteries telling them where to aim their guns. Special codes were for use with a technique known as 'earth telegraphy' (also called 'power-buzzer' or 'Morse-buzzer'). This system used a standard telegraph tapper key, a short length of wire, a metal rod and a battery to provide power. It could be taken forward with troops for an attack, or by ground observers, and used from anywhere without a wire back to HQ. It was light in weight, easy to use and needed only one person to carry and operate it. A short length of wire from the battery was attached to a rod which was plunged into the ground. The signals tapped out on the key were conducted by the earth and could be picked up by a similar rod connected to a receiver back at the command post. First introduced by the Allies, the German army became aware of the system in 1915 but did not make use of it themselves until late 1916. Depending on the soil and the underlying geology, transmissions could be detected over distances of two and a half miles, though often much less. But, like wireless, it was open to all to listen in to, so again specific codes were essential. Generally, the German army restricted its use to emergency SOS calls where no other means of communication was available, but it was also used for observer/artillery communication.

On the Allied side, communications for a long time depended on telephone and telegraph lines. British *Field Service Regulations* specified that orders should preferably be given in written form – by telegraph for example or by runner carrying a piece of paper – so that misunderstanding of orders could be minimised. The telephone, however, soon became the preferred means of communication between command posts. It allowed questioning and discussion, so misunderstanding of the situation could be minimised. But 'unfortunately, the mud, damp and shell fire made the laying and maintenance of telephone lines particularly difficult and the reliable communications seemingly offered by the telephone often failed at critical moments … [All the same] because the telephone seemed to offer an answer to all the army's communication needs, other forms of communication were ignored, shelved or dropped and the undue reliance on the telephone began to produce real problems'. These 'real problems' were caused by the ability of the German signals corps to intercept British telephone conversations from late 1915. The German army developed a listening device, the Moritz, which was widely used. It was able to intercept and amplify very weak signals.[49] Each German listening post was staffed by a sergeant-major, two interpreters, two Morse operators and two 'linesmen'. The system involved, somewhere or other, making a direct contact with an Allied telephone wire. This then gave access to any calls on any wire connected to that wire. As a British intelligence report noted, 'Instructions issued by various formations, regarding the use of the telephone and the danger of interception of telephone messages, together with threats of disciplinary action if such instructions were disobeyed' and had little effect. While conversation is useful for communicating orders and reports with great understanding on both sides, it is hard to devise – and enforce use of – a coding system for spoken language, especially in developing or unusual situations. So, telephone conversations inevitably took place in plain language. The German army intercepted orders being sent to British units on the front line, heard returns on battalion strengths, listened as units moved in and out of the line, thus building up a picture of the British 'order of battle' and detecting planned assaults. Until the middle of 1916, indeed, this was the major source of intelligence for the German army. The first hint that the Germans were tapping telephone calls came from a prisoner-of-war in March 1916, but nothing was done to prevent the security breach.

The lack of telephone security allowed the German army to know when and where the Battle of the Somme would be launched. Later that portentous day, a German listening post was discovered in a dug-out by the advancing British troops. They found wiring in place and documents which showed that calls had been intercepted for some time, including details of conversations from telephone links far back from the front line, such as between division and corps headquarters. When the documents made their way back to the intelligence section, some of the officers there were in for a dreadful shock. 'One of the intelligence officers was able to recognize some of these notes as being conversations in which he himself had taken part, whilst others contained copies of orders issued by his Corps.' Renewed efforts to convince commanders and junior officers to use the telephone with great care slowly began to take effect and from late 1916 'the regular and uninterrupted stream of intercepted English gradually ceased, any signal successes being sporadic and due to local indiscretion or carelessness on our part'. Later on, a 'scrambler' telephone was introduced, the Fullerphone, which secured calls effectively.

The Somme was a turning point in the war in terms of wireless use. At the start of the battle the British army made more use of wireless than its German counterpart. During the battle, however, the German army started to introduce many more wireless sets, taking advantage of developments in lighter weight 'short wave' wireless technology. By December 1917 the position had been reversed and the German army was the more enthusiastic user of wireless communication.[50] Wireless sets were introduced further and further down the army's organisational hierarchy, to divisions, brigades, regiments and battalions. The driving military need was for communication between artillery units and forward observers on the ground and in the air, who would direct fire to where it was needed, as well as for better communication between commanders and frontline infantry units. Special codes were devised for air to ground or ground observer to artillery communications. So from late 1916 there was a steady growth in German wireless traffic on the Western Front, with a corresponding increase in the use of codes and ciphers.

***

From mid-1915, MI1(b) in London was left looking for a new role. On 11 January 1915 Anderson agreed that his unit should take over 'all duties connected with the supervision and attempted solution of suspected codes and ciphers within letters intercepted by the Postal Censorship'.[51] Major Haldane, who had been dealing with codes in intercepted letters, handed over some material and a memo on solutions that he had developed. As the war spread around the world new opportunities arose for MI1(b) to make a cryptographic contribution.

The British military's main focus was on the Western Front. Army leaders stoutly resisted pressure from politicians for opening a new front aimed at Turkey, which had joined the war on the side of Germany and Austria-Hungary in December 1914. Eventually a campaign was launched in March 1915 at Gallipoli in an attempt to knock Turkey out of the war. It was a disaster, leading to a withdrawal in December of the same year. Turkey was then the centre of the Ottoman Empire which included much of the Middle East and the Balkans among its wide-ranging imperial lands. But, like the Austro-Hungarian Empire, it was in long-term decline and the British were masters at playing off local rulers against distant and increasingly impotent imperial governments. At the same time, Germany's rulers saw the Middle East as a good place for fomenting *jihad* against the British Empire. This led to German involvement in the area and the resulting capture of some important German documents.

The first seizures seem to have taken place early in 1915 (or perhaps late in 1914). News reached MI1(b) of the capture of a Turkish spy along with his codebook in Egypt. The codebook was sent to London, but there was little expectation that it would stay in use for long, as soon afterwards some more information arrived. London was dismayed to hear that the authorities in Egypt, presumably eager to dissuade other potential spies with a well-publicised execution, put the spy on trial. The captured codebook was among the evidence reported in court and in the Egyptian press. However, a fortnight later photographic copies of the codebooks used by Enver Pasha, the Turkish war minister, and by the Grand Vizier of the Ottoman Empire, were delivered to MI1(b) in London. A week after that the cryptographers were also provided with information about the call-signs used by Turkish wireless stations to address one another. Then, on 29 January, a translation of the instructions for using Enver Pasha's codebook also made its way to Room 219. However, when MI1(b) asked the intelligence unit in Egypt if they had translated any messages using the captured codebooks and instructions, they received the disarming reply that no messages had been intercepted. All the same, the attention of MI1(b) was being steadily drawn away from the Western Front towards the wider war. And by capturing codebooks belonging to the Grand Vizier as well as the war minister, Pasha, it was being drawn outside strictly military cryptography and ushered into the mysterious world of diplomacy.

Another major step towards diplomatic cryptography – properly the concern of the Foreign Office, not the War Office – came in mid-February. A surviving MI1(b) file of 15 February 1915 notes, 'It is suggested that we should try to get hold of American code – an opportunity arising from the impending transmission of a [diplomatic] note to America which of necessity must go verbatim.' In other words, here was an opportunity too good to be missed. A diplomatic note, of which MI1(b) expected to see the plain text, was to be sent to Washington in code on international transatlantic telegraph cables from which a copy could be obtained. Clearly, if the trick could be pulled off, this would give the cryptographers an enormous step in working out the meaning of codewords in the American diplomatic codebook (see Chapter 10). Several American messages were intercepted and translated in an informal way.

So, looking for something to do, MI1(b) had its attention diverted from wireless to cable messages, from military to diplomatic. Britain was the global hub of the world's cable networks and most transatlantic traffic between the USA and Europe had to travel via Britain to get to Scandinavia and other parts of neutral Europe. When the war started, the legal constraints on intercepting telegrams were lifted and a strict censorship imposed. Private codes and ciphers were banned and all telegrams examined by the censor's office. Enemy telegrams were also banned, both for citizens and governments. Neutral governments, of course, could continue to use codes and ciphers. But there were now no legal constraints on British codebreakers preventing them subjecting the diplomatic messages of neutrals to close scrutiny. The official historian at GCHQ, the post-1945 successor to Room 40 and to Bletchley Park, wrote, 'There is no evidence on the reason for this switch to cable, though it may be relevant that Anderson had worked on such intercepts during the South African [ie, Boer] war.'

***

This chapter started with an account of how one soldier had experienced the start of the land war, how he was injured and how he was extremely lucky to survive. More luck came his way when he was sent back to Britain in an exchange programme. Captain Malcolm Hay was fairly wealthy so would be able to live comfortably. He had done his duty and sustained serious injury, so his illustrious family history could record another glorious chapter. Hay's grandfather, Lord James Hay, had been at Waterloo a century earlier. Lord James was the seventh Marquis of Tweeddale and an experienced soldier, having been *aide-de-camp* to Wellington at that epic battle. He was installed as the military governor of Paris following the defeat of Napoleon. His son, James Gordon Hay, lived in splendour at the family home at Seaton, near Aberdeen, but did not have children until quite late in life. He was 65 when his son, Malcolm Hay, was born. Malcolm's father died a couple of years later and his mother died when he was only 11 years of age.[52] He was brought up for much of the time by a part of the family that lived in France where he was well educated in modern and classical languages. At the age of 21 he inherited the family estate at Seaton where he lived the leisurely and seemingly unambitious life of the Scottish laird, walking the local hills, rooting around in local archives, getting involved in local politics. This seemed likely to be the pattern that his adult life would follow until, in 1914, the war started. Hay immediately volunteered, only to be wounded before the end of August and back home on his estate by the beginning of 1915.

After a few months' convalescence, Hay was itching to do something for the war effort. So he went to London and, hauling himself along on two sticks, turned up at the War Office, demanding to be given a job. Some acquaintances, seeing him on sticks, rushed to hide to avoid 'embarrassing' him. Hay was effectively bilingual in French and English, and had very good Italian as well as a 'reading' knowledge of German, Spanish, Greek and Latin. So, though he had difficulty getting around, he could surely make a contribution. In December 1915 he was appointed to MI1(b) where, as we have seen, some small initial efforts were being devoted to looking at diplomatic telegrams. But it was a limited effort and there was much more untapped diplomatic traffic passing through British-controlled cables which could be exploited. Hay's second wife later wrote that the injured soldier 'at once saw the possibilities and potential value of information available in the central control of the world wide cable service … He therefore protested at the waste of existing opportunities to procure valuable intelligence in this field, and eventually secured permission, on his own conditions, to re-organise and re-form the department.'[53] For Hay the war was just beginning.

Chapter 10

'The Pillars of Hercules Have Fallen'

One of the murkiest incidents in English history is that of Titus Oates and the 'Popish Plot' of 1678. An outcast and a misfit, Oates was nevertheless at the centre of a violent national panic over an alleged Catholic plot to murder King Charles II and place his brother, the Duke of York (later James II), on the throne. The allegations were lies and half-truths, but gained momentum in the febrile times. To question the validity of the plot was to provide unarguable evidence that one was part of it. Several innocent people were executed and old political scores were settled. Even Samuel Pepys, secretary to the Navy and its most formidable administrator, was sucked up into the whirlwind of fear, suspicion and violence because of his closeness to the Duke of York. Pepys was lucky to escape with his life.

Some of the evidence used to convict some of those who did suffer the agonies of execution – as traitors, by hanging, drawing and quartering – was made up of intercepted letters, one with passages in cipher. It was found in the possession of an English Jesuit priest, Edward Coleman. He had previously been secretary to the Duke of York and at the time of the uproar was secretary to the Duke's wife. As one writer commented, 'The only legitimate evidence against [Coleman] is that provided by his own correspondence; this is written for the most part, in language so obscure that it can be twisted as much or as little as the historian desires.'[54] The enciphered letters, from the Papal Nuncio, were not very convincing evidence of anything. Yet, in the temper of the times, with an economic downturn and high unemployment in London adding to the volatile emotions of the crowd, horror at the prospect of a reversion to Catholicism drove the frenzy of fear and suspicion. The fact that the letter was partially encrypted was obvious proof that there was something amiss. It has also been taken as such in many historical accounts of the furore surrounding Oates and the plot since then.

The incriminating letter had been written by the Papal Nuncio on 12 January 1675 and contained various passages where some of the plain language is replaced by a series of numbers. The key section reads: 'What you propose touching 51666279669961 which is, 66717576661676676 cannot be put in execution 566662516756665667 but with the 7776999166996167976669961 of all 5167917766629664996719 and only 667191776691 comprising 96669991516791947151416791 you may then consider if the terms wherein at present are 51679166545666646267919680204 it would be for the interest of the Duke to produce unto light an affair of this nature. That which I can with truth assure you, and whereof the Duke may be persuaded is that 66997766916564519167627664617199647671625167976664916162679632 04 will employ 6681272 and 5108126 and 516777626796646 for 5166919164916167626662679161669451646451665166812666799812O4.'

All attempts to break the cipher and reveal the contents by a House of Commons special committee of investigation were failures. Indeed, the cipher remained unbroken until 1934 when a retired army captain and landowner published a book entitled *The Jesuits and the Popish Plot*. The author had written other books on Catholic history, setting the record straight on a number of issues where the rough and tumble of the life and death struggle between adherents of Protestantism and Catholicism in Britain had led to a besmirching of the reputation of British Catholics. Of interest to our story is an appendix to the main text where the author provides a solution to the cipher that for over 250 years had defied decryption. The cipher, he pointed out, was in fact a straightforward substitution cipher (in effect a simple code) with 'code-groups' (codewords with numbers rather than letters) of two or three numbers replacing the plain language words. The author noted that only seven numbers were used and that the number 2 only ever appeared in the second place. He also pointed out, 'The number 8 or any two-figure group [codeword] containing that number, seems to have been used as an indication of change to another table, or rather code of three figures which was used for names of persons, places and words used frequently in the correspondence.' The 'cipher' was, he said, 'extremely simple' and was defeated by simple frequency analysis.

The newly decoded letter did not provide any conclusive evidence to the historical dispute. The Papal Nuncio was no doubt a very wily politician and knew how to write a letter without giving too much away. The section of the letter cited above, reads: 'What you propose touching the money which is in the castle [ie, Castel S. Angelo where the Pope was supposed to keep a stash of treasure] cannot be put into execution by the Pope [except] with the consent of all the cardinals, and then by means of a Bull; you may then consider if the conditions, where are at present the affairs of England, it would be for the interest of the Duke [of York] to bring to light an affair of this nature. That which I can with truth assure you, and whereof the Duke may be persuaded is that, should he happen one day to become the master of England, they will employ at Rome both money and credit to assist him to restore the Catholic religion in England.'[55] No doubt it would in fact have made little difference to the case against Coleman even if the letter had been decrypted. Still it must have been very satisfying for the author, a non-academic historian, to crack a code that had stymied so many for so long. He did, however, have an advantage. He had been beneficiary of an ideal opportunity to learn an awful lot about codes and ciphers, for he had spent nearly three years as the head of the War Office's decryption unit, MI1(b). He was none other than Captain Malcolm Hay – whom we first met in the previous chapter, being wounded in the retreat from Mons in August 1914 and then again at the beginning of 1916 as he dragged himself on two walking sticks along Whitehall to the War Office to demand a job.

***

The information available on MI1(b) in 1915 before Hay joined is extremely limited. He later wrote that 'before my appointment some progress had already been made by Messrs. Strachey and Pletts with the American diplomatic code. I am not able to say definitely how this code was first broken. I was told that some clear texts were obtained which facilitated solution. Until the beginning of 1916 the work of the War Office cryptographic section was limited to investigation, with intermittent success, of German [army] field ciphers, and to the reconstruction of the American Diplomatic codebooks.'[56] The US traffic was coded and then enciphered using substitution 'tables'. However, unlike the German naval codebooks, there were no miraculous deliveries of the US codebooks into British hands. A post-war intelligence account suggests, 'The work was entirely fresh to all members of the staff, there were no past records as guidance, and the problem of how to solve large codebooks had to be thought out *ab initio*.'[57] Actually, this is a somewhat misleading claim. As we saw in the previous chapter, and as mentioned above by Hay, the first steps were taken into 'reconstructing' the American codebooks when it was known that some known plain language text was to be transmitted in code. It is probable that the plain language text was 'planted'. A report noted, 'On 17 February the plain language text was received in MI1(b) and on the 22nd 'the same note [was] received in a five-figure code.' Unfortunately we have no details of the planted text.

Such planting is not unknown as a cryptographic technique (for example, it was used by the French cryptographic bureau during the Dreyfus Affair). Some diplomatic issue or question would be put to the local embassy which it is certain will have to be transmitted verbatim to the home country for a response. The codebreakers can then look for the planted text in the encoded/enciphered message. Careful construction of the planted text can help elicit useful information for breaking the code. We can be fairly certain that this is what occurred here. MI1(b)'s cryptographers were thus able to begin the reconstruction of the US diplomatic codebook. We will look at techniques for 'reconstructing' codebooks later (see Chapter 12), but for the time being we can just note that it is not an easy task, requiring intense concentration, considerable mental capacity and stubborn determination, but using this form of planting, MI1(b) started work on US codes. All or part of three different US codebooks were reconstructed by mid-1916 and several encipherment tables were also broken. Given the high volume of intercepted traffic available from telegraph cables, there was plenty of material that could now be decoded. In fact, with Strachey and Pletts successfully reconstructing codebooks and cipher tables, more members of staff were needed to handle the highly secret and rather repetitive task of decoding the intercepted messages using the reconstructed cipher tables and codebooks. Several more wounded officers joined the team to handle this task, but none was used to help with the codebreaking activities.[58]

The first surviving copy of a decoded US telegram dates from 3 May 1915 and is a report from the US ambassador in Berlin. Like all the surviving copies of MI1(b) decodes, it begins with the statement that 'MI1 has received the following reliable information'. These surviving decodes are obviously copies that were sent to people on the circulation list for such sensitive intelligence. The scant evidence suggests that several sections in military intelligence, the Navy Intelligence Department, the Foreign Office and the Prime Minister's office would have received at least some decoded messages.[59] The copies of the decodes that have survived (with a few exceptions such as the intercept of 3 May 1915) are held within Admiralty files, so they appear to have been the copies sent to Room 40 or to Hall as Director of Naval Intelligence. The only exception I have come across is a file of some of the earliest US decodes which are held in a War Office file.[60]

In the first surviving decode by MI1(b) of US diplomatic traffic, the US ambassador in Berlin, James W. Gerard, reports on the German reaction to a US diplomatic note on submarine warfare. He said that Kaiser Wilhelm 'spoke of the rather rough and uncourteous tone of our note as he considered it'. Gerard also reported that he had told Wilhelm that 'outside the three-mile limit [of territorial waters] the sea was free and no one could make it war territory; [and] that as for the British blockade, we had first to settle cases where lives of Americans were lost.[61] The full decode expands on these points and must have been quite reassuring to the Foreign Office in revealing America's fairly solid line with Germany. The USA was insisting on dealing first with the problem of Germany's submarines illegally killing US citizens (albeit sailing in ships flying enemy flags) before it would tackle Britain's own breach of international law with its blockade – even though, of course, the British blockade had preceded the submarine campaign. We will look at other US decodes later (see Chapter 14). Here we can note that MI1(b)'s move into diplomatic cryptanalysis had quickly offered some very useful intelligence material on managing relations with the USA – one of the central strategic issues facing the Allies in late 1915 and early 1916.

At what point Hay took charge is not known, but sometime in 1916, MI1(b) systematically widened the scope of its diplomatic cryptanalysis, probably under his direction. His second wife, writing in the 1970s, said that Hay 'at once' saw the value, if used properly, of MI8's censorship and negotiated with Colonel French for complete independence so long as he 'produced the goods'.[62] This seems like an exaggerated account for, as we have seen, Anderson had started to widen MI1(b)'s activities in early 1915. Hay's own narrative is only marginally more modest: 'In the spring of 1916 I began to realise the potential value of the enormous mass of encoded messages from all over the world which was accumulating in certain War Office cupboards. About this time I had an interview with the [Deputy] Cable Censor, Lord Arthur Browne, who arranged for copies of all diplomatic cables to be sent to my office. In 1916 information was badly wanted about what was going on in Greece and I decided to make a start with the Greek code. No one in this country had hitherto succeeded in breaking a diplomatic codebook without what we used to call 'a crib' [such as the diplomatic note of which a plain language copy was available when breaking one US diplomatic codebook]. The problem was undertaken and solved by Mr. John Fraser, who [later became] Professor of Celtic at Oxford.' Fraser joined MI1(b) in February 1916 and was to prove to be a prolific codebreaker and an accomplished linguist, having knowledge of some 21 languages at the end of the war. He broke or helped to break Greek, Spanish, Argentine, Uruguayan, Turkish, Swiss, Swedish, Norwegian, Brazilian, Dutch and Vatican codes before he left in 1919. The Greek codebook was his first major achievement. Hay recalled, 'The chief difficulty was the language; we had no means of knowing in what language the messages were written. The natural hypothesis was that they were written in Greek. After working for many weeks on this assumption Fraser concluded that the text must not be in Greek but in French. In June when I was home for a few days leave, Fraser sent me a telegram: "Pillars of Hercules have fallen.". The Greeks used a number of different codebooks, some in Greek, some in French. All these books were reconstructed.'[63]

The diverse and intensely divisive patchwork of states in the Balkans and southeastern Europe was to be a focus of much diplomacy by both sides during the war. Each alliance sought to turn the neutrals into allies, or at least into 'benevolent neutrals', clearly favouring one side. Greece had emerged exhausted from the Balkan wars of 1912 and 1913 and was distracted by deepening internal political antagonisms, leading to the assassination of the king in 1913. It wanted to keep out of the European war, but pressures from different domestic political factions favouring one side or the other, as well as bullying and cajoling from the belligerents, economic dislocation and continued regional tensions (especially with Turkey, Germany's ally in the war, and Bulgaria, which was also moving towards supporting the Central Powers) all combined to make life for Greece as a neutral very hard indeed. Step by step, the various currents of opinion within Greece coalesced into two factions. One, led by the prime minister, feared that Bulgaria and Turkey would claim Greek territory if the Central Powers won, so favoured an accord with them to avoid this fate. The other faction, led by the king, feared upsetting the Allies more than Germany, Austria and Turkey.

In 1915, the Serbian army had been forced out of Serbia by Austrian forces and the Allies approached Greece asking for the expelled Serb troops to be evacuated to Salonika. By September 1915 the king had agreed to the Allied request, but when this decision became public it led to the collapse of the government which had a pro-German prime minister. In early November the new government declared itself to be a 'benevolent neutral' favouring the Allies. Details of the intense political and diplomatic negotiations that led to this development were revealed to MI1(b) by its breaking of the Greek codebooks. The intercepts provided what was claimed to be excellent intelligence. It is not really possible to say whether the intercepts allowed Britain to modify its diplomatic stance and nudge Greece towards a benevolent stance, but this is quite possibly the case. Certainly, Fraser's reconstruction of the Greek codebook was timely. According to a MI1(b) document, 'The solving of the code in which [very long Greek] messages were sent proved of the very highest importance.'[64]

By the autumn of 1916, MI1(b) had ten cryptographic staff, though it is impossible to be certain whether they all worked on diplomatic codes. In July 1916 a new section was split off from MI1(b) to handle intercept intelligence about German air raids on Britain (see Chapter 17) and it is possible that the figure of ten cryptographers may include some who went to work for that new section, MI1(e), which initially had a staff of just four officers. MI1(b) moved to 5 Cork Street as it expanded. A tall, well-built, no-nonsense, non-commissioned officer stood guard and made sure that no one wandered into the building by mistake. However, central London street life could at times impinge on the codebreakers. At one stage a letter to the police was considered appropriate. 'One of my sub-Sections located at 5, Cork Street complains constantly of the nuisance caused by the large number of itinerant musicians constantly parading that street. This sub-Section is now engaged on important work for which quiet is essential. If you could see your way to prohibiting street noise in the immediate vicinity … I should be extremely grateful.'[65]

The odd problem that did arise often came from an unexpected quarter. In March 1917, HM Procurator General, at the Treasury, sparked off a security alert. He wrote to MI1(b) that he 'begs to enquire whether there would be any objection to his incorporating in an Affidavit to be used in the Prize Court, in proceedings which are pending for the condemnation of a number of cargoes belonging to Messrs. K. and E. Neumond, the substance of a Secret Service report relating to disposal in Germany of the cargo of the S/V *Prinz Waldemar* which was collusively captured, and where cargo was released to this firm'. Colonel MacDonogh was 'horrified and angry' at the letter. 'I propose to send Colonel French to the office of the Procurator General to explain that this information was obtained from Secret Service sources and cannot possibly be used and that it is imperative that it should be expunged from their records.' An inquiry into how the leak occurred pinned it on the Foreign Office when R. H. L. Campbell, the private secretary to Lord Hardinge, Permanent Under-Secretary, was on leave and someone sent a precis to the Procurator General of an intercept that had been circulated to Campbell who was responsible for distribution within the Foreign Office.[66]

***

Back in the Admiralty Old Buildings, Room 40 was also expanding its sphere of operations into diplomatic codebreaking. But it was not a move that was co-ordinated with MI1(b). The two organisations' activities did in fact turn out to be complementary, but that was by chance. The frosty relations between Room 40 and MI1(b) endured throughout 1915 and into 1916 and each organisation went about its business like two tribes in parallel valleys aware of each other's existence, but having no contact. All the same, changes were occurring that would end that isolation. Room 40's diplomatic work slipped out of the control of Sir Alfred Ewing and came within the oversight of Blinker Hall, the head of naval intelligence. It was Hall, the navy career officer, who provided the driving force behind the shift of attention from purely naval intelligence into systematic diplomatic codebreaking, not Ewing, the career academic administrator. Hall also restored relations with MI1(b), not Ewing.

In an internal account of Room 40 written at the end of the war the author Frank Birch comments acidly that although Britain had constrained Germany's communications with the outside world for the first two years of the war, the fruits of this activity were left to wither on the branch. Any future 'historian', he notes, 'will wonder whether any cause save the most crass habitude prevented the full utilisation of the favourable situation in which the Allies found themselves'. Between August 1914 and May 1915 some 170 German diplomatic telegrams were transmitted as neutral traffic via cables that passed through Britain on their way to the Americas, containing information about negotiations with the US government and about German sabotage and espionage efforts in the Americas. 'Owing to the deficient co-ordination of British intelligence none of these telegrams ever reached a deciphering bureau. ... Had there existed the slightest liaison between the various sections of the Intelligence Department or had a central body existed capable of co-ordinating the works of these sections, all messages sent must have been compromised. ... A strange medley of causes prevented any of these telegrams from arriving in an English deciphering bureau. The main cause was that the various intelligence services departments were compelled to work in "watertight" compartments, a radically false system by which deciphering departments, censorship, press reading departments etc., had no knowledge of each other's intention, and received no news of each other's activities, or of the problems on which they were engaged, and which they were capable of assisting each other to solve. The system was deliberately adopted, but it is difficult to see what ends it could serve, except to paralyse the individual sections and workers.'[67]

This changed only after Hall (who is not necessarily a reliable witness) was approached by a censor clerk who thought, incorrectly as it turned out, that a lot of information was leaking from Britain to Germany. Hall went to talk to Colonel Cockerill, head of the censorship office, to tell him that he thought all mail should be opened and examined. Hall was 'fairly certain that once I had secured Colonel Cockerill's interest and approval that I should be able to lay my hands on the necessary money and staff'. Hall's new system of controls showed that in fact there was no leakage of information, but it did uncover details of how Germany was trying to buy supplies abroad, naming the companies it was working with, the routes used and details of false information designed to hide the transactions. 'In a little while we were understanding how and where the Germans were ordering vast quantities of contraband stuff. It was a momentous discovery. Indeed, I do not think it is too much to say that our little censorship was the first real move in the new blockade. ... Everything worked smoothly. The staff did not talk. And I do not think that anyone of us was aware that the law was being quietly and systematically broken.'[68] This led to the setting up of the War Trade Intelligence Department and steady tightening of the blockade.

Another important factor that nudged Room 40 towards diplomatic surveillance was the amount of wireless traffic between Berlin and Madrid. When examined it turned out that these were often diplomatic messages from and to military and naval attachés. More striking was the fact that some of these diplomatic messages were coded in the *Verkehrsbuch* (VB) codebook – which had been recovered in late 1914. Madrid was of great importance to Germany. Here was its most important European embassy and also its centre for communications, espionage and trade with the rest of the world. We will look at Germany's communications with Spain, and with the wider world via Madrid, later (see Chapter 13). This wireless link was to be a prolific source of intercepts and intelligence.

At this point a small diversion and a short step backwards is necessary to review some events in Persia in early 1915. Germany and its new ally, Turkey, wanted to stimulate disaffection in the British Empire among its millions of Muslim subjects. Early in 1915 the highest religious figure in Constantinople, the capital of the Islamic Ottoman Empire, declared a *jihad* on the rule by foreign infidels over Muslims. Turkey would attack the Russians in the Caucasus and assault the British in Egypt and Suez, hoping to raise a popular rebellion and sever Britain's lifeline to its Empire through the Suez Canal (and also to secure the recovery of Egypt as a subject territory of the Ottoman Empire). German diplomatic/military/sabotage/espionage teams were to be infiltrated into Persia and Afghanistan.[69] Arthur Zimmermann, Under-Secretary for Foreign Affairs in Berlin, was in overall charge of planning for *jihad* in the east. He was author of the so-called Zimmermann Plan. He chose a fit, young, brash Foreign Office staff member and intelligence officer, Wilhelm Wassmuss, to lead a team whose job would be to stir up anti-British rebellion first in Persia and then in Afghanistan.

Britain underestimated Turkey's military strength, both at Gallipoli in 1914/15 and at Kut in Mesopotamia in 1916 where a besieged force had to surrender to avoid starvation. On the other hand, Germany overestimated the chances of *jihad*. The Turkish offensive in the Caucasus, allied with a call for revolt among Russia's many Muslims, was a disaster. The attack in mountainous terrain in midwinter led to the loss of 75,000 out of 90,000 troops, many simply frozen to death. A planned rebellion in India was betrayed and crushed before it could start. Interception of messages played a key role here, as did British control of communications, which helped by preventing information getting to the rebels about arms supplies being sent to India. Also, the Turkish attack on Egypt was repulsed and the expected uprising of Egyptians did not take place (as they had no more wish to be subjects of the Ottoman Empire than they did to be part of the British Empire). At first, British and Indian troops failed to take advantage of these setbacks for Turkey. But eventually there was a sustained military effort by Britain in the Middle East aimed at carving out new fiefdoms for the Empire. We will return to codebreaking operations in that imperial adventure later (see Chapter 17).

Almost immediately Wassmuss's plans started to go awry. He fell out with his colleagues and abandoned them and started his own guerrilla war in Persia against the British – earning him the title of 'the German Lawrence'. He had been in Persia before the war, knew local languages and some of the tribes.[70] Wassmuss's campaign almost came to an early end in March 1915 when he was captured by British-funded local forces near Bushire (Bushehr). He escaped and for the rest of the war caused fairly minor damage to British interests, raiding British-owned banks, committing sabotage and even holding a few British citizens as hostages. However, when he fled from capture in Bushire, Wassmuss was forced to leave behind two German companions, all their arms and ammunition, large quantities of propaganda material (aimed at stirring up revolt in India) and various other papers. These documents were sent back to India House in London where the Indian Civil Service (which governed British-controlled southern Persia) was based and found their way into a basement storeroom. The legend, put about by Hall himself, is that he had a chance meeting with a young naval officer not long back from Persia who recounted various daring ventures, including the story of Wassmuss's capture and his escape. Hall's attention was grabbed by the mention of the documents.[71] So he made enquiries as to their whereabouts. When the documents were brought to his office ('within hours'), it was discovered that they included a copy of a German diplomatic codebook known as 13040. This code was used, in part, for the famous Zimmermann telegram which brought America into the war (see Chapters 14 and 15).

This at least has been the standard story until recent times. However, nothing is entirely clear about this episode – not even how Wassmuss was arrested and how he escaped, for example. This lack of clarity extends to the codebook, for an alternative story exists. A British civil servant, C. J. Edmonds, based in Persia at the time, later wrote an article entitled 'The Persian Gulf Prelude to the Zimmermann Telegram', which appeared in the *Journal of the Royal Central Asian Society* in 1960. According to this account, shortly after Wassmuss's escape, the German consul in Bushire was arrested by British troops. 'Two dictionary ciphers' were discovered 'wrapped up in several pairs of long woollen underpants'.[72] Some writers have suggested that Wassmuss deposited his codebook(s) with the consul before his arrest and thus these are the same codebooks. Others point to the repeated concern Wassmuss expressed for his lost papers, suggesting therefore that they must have contained important documents such as codebooks and not just propaganda material. Yet others argue that Wassmuss was unlikely to be carrying any diplomatic codebooks anyway. Support for the Wassmuss connection comes from the diary of one of his abandoned colleagues, Dr Niedermayer. He claimed that 'after Wassmuss's narrow escape from capture the British had found his baggage … all his papers, including his code'.[73]

Whatever the precise details, historians now generally accept that the two codebooks captured from the German consul in Bushire were known as 89734 and 3512, and came from a quite different 'family' of codes to 13040.[74] Denniston has left us with the brief comment that 'one day in April [1915, Hall] produced a fresh line of goods – treasure trove in Persia it was said'.[75] Clearly, there could be some confusion between the incidents, or they may all be separate and real happenings. At this stage we cannot really tell. Hall later admitted that he invented the capture of 13040 codebook as a cover story when these matters were first made public shortly after the war (as a result of claims in 1926 made in US courts for damages caused by German saboteurs in the USA). Current opinion is that the Wassmuss story is a blind and that the two codebooks were taken from the consul and that they were codebooks 89734 and 3512. In any event, when Room 40 turned to diplomatic codebreaking it had a useful start with the captured codebooks.

***

A short account of the history of the 'political' or diplomatic section of Room 40 was written by George Young.[76] He was a Foreign Office diplomat, an expert on the Near East, who was serving in Lisbon when the war started. He resigned his post to seek 'active employment' and somehow came to the notice of Hall. He was seconded to Room 40 when it became clear that the VB codebook was being used by Germany's military attachés at embassies in neutral countries and for communications between Berlin and Madrid. (Young was, however, not happy with an office job and still longed for action, so he left Room 40 in 1917, gaining a commission in the Royal Marines.)[77] A letter dated 28 September 1916 from the Admiralty to Ewing informed him that their Lordships approved the 'proposal that Mr George Young ... should be definitely reorganised as supervising under you the branch of your special work dealt with in Room 47 OB, together with the Ladies Section. ... The work of this Section should be, as is the case of Room 40, be kept in touch with the Intelligence and Operations divisions, and the DID [Director of Naval Intelligence] is to be consulted with regard to it in the same manner as hitherto. The intelligence division is to continue to be the connecting link between this Section and the Foreign Office.'[78] This last point is important as it gave Hall a degree of control over the new section's work, and which he used to lever Ewing out of the picture. Young recalled that 'the political work of Room 40 began as overtime and sparetime work'. The pressure of naval work restricted the effort that could be put into the Madrid-Berlin traffic, but where it could be tackled it proved to offer valuable insights into German activities in Spain and elsewhere. 'Sir Alfred Ewing gave me leave to organise the political work as a separate branch ... the results subsequently reached in the political region were very largely made possible by the partial separation from the naval work.'[79] Young's second point is significant as he is saying that the diplomatic codebreaking was due to the new section being separated from Ewing's control. Through his role as the 'connecting link' with the Foreign Office, Hall took ever greater charge of the new section, edging it away from Ewing. The two men did not get on. Oliver later recalled that Hall 'was always trying to boss Sir A. Ewing and he would not put up with it, he was not that sort of man, and when he [joined] the First Lord had promised him a free hand.'[80] However, slowly Hall took control of Room 40's diplomatic work. His behaviour has been presented as an uninvited intrusion by Hall into affairs that were properly the concern of the Foreign Office. But, as we have seen, Hall was specifically appointed as the connecting link between the new diplomatic section and the Foreign Office.

Young recorded that it was only when a separate system of 'files, registrations and indexes etc' for diplomatic work was set up that real progress began to be made. The new section consisted of Young, Benjamin Faudel-Phillips, Nigel de Grey and Montgomery (the belligerent Ulster clergyman). Faudel-Phillips was a 'city' man with family connections to London's financial centre. Both his father and his grandfather had been Lord Mayor and that became his nickname. De Grey had studied languages and tried to join the Foreign Office as a diplomat. Though his German and French were good, he did not reach the required standard in Italian and was turned down. He found instead a job with the publishing company William Heinemann. In August 1915 he joined the RNVR and was appointed as an observer in the Royal Naval Air Service in Belgium. Somehow or other he ended up in Room 40. Hall, who had taken charge of finding recruits for Room 40, apparently thought highly of him and had him added to the diplomatic section. Montgomery we have already met as antagonist of Herbert Morrah (see Chapter 7) over his support for Home Rule in his native Ireland. Montgomery at one stage told Hall that 'he was not one of those [clergymen] who believed that clerics should not take part in war and that his only regret was that he could not get to sea'.[81] No doubt Montgomery's move to a different room meant fewer spats over the issue of Ireland's self-determination and more peace and quiet in Room 40 itself. We should note that Faudel-Phillips, de Grey and Montgomery (as well as Dillwyn Knox who joined later) were all excellent cryptographers and their move denuded Room 40's naval sections of some of their best staff members.

The new section, based in Room 45, started life in possession of the VB, knowledge of the cipher systems used with it, and two German Foreign Office codebooks, 89734 and 3512. These two codebooks turned out to be very similar to one another. They were in fact re-shufflings of the same sets of printed pages. The individual code-groups were made up from the three-number page number and a two-number entry number (with 100 entries on each page). The pages were printed in double-sided pairs, so that there were four pages on a single sheet. These sheets could be changed in order, but the entries on each sheet stayed the same. It was then discovered that several other codebooks were also re-shufflings of the same sets of pages. This meant that when a new code in this family was introduced, and once one code-group had been worked out, it revealed the meaning of all the other code-groups on the same sheet – some 400 meanings in all.

Three such codebooks were 'reconstructed' (see Chapter 12) through logical analysis during 1915 and 1916. As a British intelligence report observed, 'A large quantity of very secret negotiations travelled in codebooks easy to reconstruct. The only methods of ciphering or 'keying' these books were sent in telegrams that at some stage passed over British wires and were easily decipherable. Nor was it until 1918 that the wireless messages to Madrid proved any serous difficulty to anyone who cared to read them.'[82] According to Young, 'These gave immediate admission to the very secret wireless correspondence between the [German naval ministry] and the Madrid naval attaché, the semi-secret wireless correspondence between Berlin Foreign Office and Madrid and Lisbon and occasionally North and South America. ... [the VB was] an integral and indispensable part of the general diplomatic correspondence with Madrid. From the beginning it has been in the hands of Lieutenant Faudel-Phillips who can best report on its technique of "sliders" and "keys" and on the knock-outs it has administered to various German coups.' The sliders and keys refer to the encipherment technique, employing a 'subtractor' cipher, used with the coded messages. Alastair Denniston solved the cipher and a significant amount of intelligence about German activities in the Middle East was revealed. The British gained knowledge of strategic agreements between Germany and Turkey, approaches to the Afghan government, and the hoped-for uprising in Persia. From then on 'German political and military dispositions both Persian and Afghan were known with a few hours in London'.[83] Regrettably, there is no hint that Faudel-Phillips, who took over in charge of the section when Young left in 1917, ever put pen to paper to leave us such an account. The codebreakers set about decoding the considerable accumulation of material that had been gathering. But there weren't enough people to cope with the task. Young recorded that 'the deficiency of staff being to some extent made good by labour saving devices, such as the "pianola" a mechanical means for making troublesome group transpositions'.[84] We will return to this machinery in Chapter 12.

**

Room 40's naval section found itself stretched in this period. Early in 1916, the AFB *Allgemeines Funkspruchbuch* replaced the HVB. This time no copy of the codebook was delivered into Room 40's eager hands. But the expert cryptographers knew enough about the old codebook and German telegraphic habits to 'reconstruct' the new book from scratch. All the same, this took time and messages were only partially decipherable. A copy of the codebook was eventually recovered from the crashed Zeppelin L-32 on 27 September 1916. Room 40 could then decode entire messages again. Downed Zeppelins were a handy source of cipher keys too, with ciphers being recovered from L-32 on 24 September 1916 and L-48 on 17 June 1917.[85] Sunken U-boats also provided useful material, such as U-109 in 1918.[86] A major change occurred in May 1917 when the FFB, *Flottenfunkspruchbuch* replaced the main naval signal book, the SKM. FFB was a two-part code, the only one introduced by the German navy during the war. The introduction of the new codebook was accompanied by the German navy's first complete change of call-signs, by the introduction of daily key changes and a new system of map grid squares 'disguised by a transposition code'. However, by then Room 40's knowledge meant it could break the new codebook and the daily keys. As a British intelligence report noted, 'The Germans succeeded [on 1 May 1916], for the first and last time throughout the war, in changing their codebooks and call-signs simultaneously. Most of the call-signs could be guessed immediately, at least, in so far as the type of vessel or area to which they belonged. A few, however, baffled analysis for some considerable time.' In the face of these difficulties Room 40's output in terms of naval intercepts reached its peak in the second half of 1917, in the months after the new codebook and security measures had been introduced.

A number of factors helped the reconstruction of the new codebook from scratch, such as the fact that submarines were compelled to use 'spelling-group' codewords to spell out the names of steamers they sank and whose names had not got a specific codeword. This gave a way into the system (see Chapter 12). The FFB was also compromised by wireless operations in the Baltic in 1917 where the old SKM codebook was kept in operation in parallel with the new FFB in the North Sea. FFB was difficult to decipher and was broken on the principle that because the codebook had too many entries, then only a few were used, so when the key-finder has found the first two numbers in cipher he could easily guess the last one (in the case of FFB which had three-number code-groups) or two (for ciphers with four letters or numbers in codewords/code-groups). 'It was indeed on this principle alone that the keys on the successor to the SKM, the FFB, were originally solved.'[87] 'The key used for ciphering the code was first known as Gamma Alpha, and from 21 April 1918 as Gamma F.'

The intercepts also showed Room 40 that British naval codes were being broken by the German navy's codebreaking unit at Neumuenster. But, more importantly, they confirmed that Room 40's activities remained unknown to the Germans. As a British intelligence report noted, 'The very serious error was made by the German authorities of using and publishing freely to the fleet by wireless signals the results of Neumuenster's researches. Thus the English and Russian authorities could often be aware of the failure of their efforts to secure secrecy by the use of a code. The climax was reached in 1917 when decipherings of the English [naval] code were sent unenciphered alongside the equivalent [code-group] in the German codebook which had then only lately come into force: Not only was it evident to the English authorities that great progress had been made in the decipherment of one of their codes, but also the sense of certain yet unresolved meanings of German code-groups could be ascertained on this side merely by looking them up in an English decode-book. The apparent failure on the English side to act on intelligence received must have lulled the German Admiralty into a false sense of security'.[88]

***

By accident Room 40's and MI1(b)'s diplomatic work meshed quite well at this stage and there was little overlap. This was fortunate as there was still no communication between them, let alone co-operation. However, as MI1(b) had concentrated on cables it was picking up the traffic of neutrals (given that Germany was cut off from the cable network). Room 40 did not source its intercepts from cables, but from German, allied and some neutral wireless transmissions. Some overlap was to develop when it came to traffic from the USA, Sweden and Spain (the latter using wireless for some diplomatic communications), but this was a bit later on and by then Ewing had been fully edged out and replaced by Hall. But on the whole MI1(b)'s concentration on cables and neutrals complemented Room 40's focus on wireless and Germany. We will look at the fruits of this naval and military foray into the world of diplomatic surveillance in subsequent chapters. At this stage it must have appeared to the codebreakers that they had Germany well penned in. It was cut off from the world's cable network and all its wireless transmissions could be intercepted and, by and large, decoded. But this complacent attitude was to be shaken by the discovery of two separate channels of communication that Germany had found to circumvent Britain's communications stranglehold.

Somehow or other, it was discovered that German messages were being included within Swedish diplomatic telegraphic traffic passing through London on its way between Stockholm and Washington. This was first reported to the Foreign Office in May 1915. British diplomats, presumably without thinking about the possibilities of interception, delivered a protest to Sweden. The Swedish government was appropriately embarrassed and promised that no more German messages, pretending to be Swedish diplomatic messages, would be sent on the Stockholm to Washington route. What they did not add was that instead the German messages would be sent as Swedish messages via Madrid to Buenos Aires and then forwarded to Washington. So, the Foreign Office reaction in immediately complaining to Sweden had simply shifted the link, not stopped it from working. And had pushed it out of sight.

Exactly what happened between May 1915 and September 1916 is unknown. But for all that time the German Foreign Office was sending its messages over the Swedish routeing (via London) without anyone being alerted to the fact. The intercepted cable traffic, including that of Sweden, must have gone to MI1(b). Why it got no further is one of the great mysteries of the whole story. It is surely relevant that Hall (see below) took over control of Room 40 in mid-1916. In September of that year Room 40 received an intercepted coded letter (probably seized during a search made by a blockade-enforcing ship) sent from the German minister in Mexico to the Chancellor, Bethmann-Hollweg, recommending that the Swedish Chargé d'Affaires in Mexico City should be awarded a German honour. 'He arranges the conditions for the official telegraphic traffic with your Excellency. In this connection he is obliged every time, often late at night, personally to go to the telegraph office to hand in the [German] dispatches,' the German minister explained.[89] Hall later recalled, 'It was clear that steps would have to be taken to have all Swedish Foreign Office cipher telegrams brought to us for examination ... In many cases it was found that after a few Swedish [code-]groups, our old friend 13040 would appear. Our excitement, moreover, may be imagined when through this means we discovered the route by which Bernstorff [the German ambassador in Washington] was communicating with his government ... In this way we found ourselves in full possession ... of the enemy's every move in the diplomatic game of the moment'.[90]

The route between Stockholm via Spain and the Swedish embassies in South America was dubbed the 'Swedish Roundabout'. The messages were sent in German code, so to a seasoned eye it would soon be obvious that there was something amiss if the traffic was studied closely. This time there was no protest. Hall was firmly of the view that a communications link, once uncovered, should not be broken but observed. 'Once across it, let it run,' he said.[91] Thus, from 14 September 1916, Germany's supposedly secret communications link with the world at large was exposed to Room 40's scrutiny and telegrams, including messages sent in the German Foreign Office code known by the number 13040 were decoded.

Code 13040 was frequently used for communications between Germany and its representatives in North and South America. It was never captured and Room 40's diplomatic section had to reconstruct it from scratch (despite Hall's claim that it was captured from Wassmuss in Persia). One of the new recruits, de Grey, who had soon been found to have a 'great talent' for cryptography, was put on 'research' work looking at messages sent in code 13040 that had been accumulating.[92] De Grey soon reconstructed enough of the 13040 codebook so that the general sense of messages was clear. Very soon after the Swedish Roundabout had been discovered it was supplying good intelligence on the communications between Berlin and the German ambassador in Washington. The intercepts also produced many messages about buying goods and setting up lines of credit to pay for them.[93] Hall recalled, 'We knew from the ambassador's admirably clear dispatches the points of greatest importance in [President] Wilson's fluctuating policy.'[94]

Within a few days of coming across this leak, Room 40 discovered (perhaps from intelligence picked up by British agents in the USA) that Germany had yet another hidden outlet. This time it was with the help of the USA and on the orders of President Wilson. The German Foreign Office would take coded telegrams to the US embassy in Berlin, where they would be transmitted to the State Department in Washington – via Copenhagen, London and the transatlantic cables – before being handed over to the German embassy. According to the former official historian at GCHQ (the modern successor of Room 40 and MI1(b)), 'This practice is generally considered to have begun on 2 June 1915 when the German ambassador in Washington, Count von Bernstorff, agreed it with President Wilson to facilitate negotiation during the crisis following the sinking of the *Lusitania* by a German submarine and it is not clear why MI1(b) had not already spotted it.'[95] As the furore receded, the link was closed.

It was re-opened in September 1916. A decrypt of an intercepted American message from the US ambassador in Berlin to the State Department in Washington revealed what was afoot. Wilson was at this point pursuing peace proposals and getting negative responses from the Allies. But in Germany he found an apparently more positive attitude. The US ambassador in Berlin reported back to Washington, 'Germany is anxious to make peace. I can state on the best authority that if the President [of the USA] will make an offer of mediation in general terms … that Germany will accept in general terms immediately and state her readiness to send delegates to a peace conference. Today [German foreign minister] von Jagow will ask me to forward a cipher message to Bernstorff through the State Dept. … Of course the utmost secrecy is desirable for if any hint is given that the suggestion came from Berlin and not as the spontaneous act of the [US] President the whole matter will fail and be denied. I desire to know whether the message may be forwarded for delivery to Bernstorff.'[96] We will look at the messages intercepted by Room 40 dealing with the USA's peace feelers in Chapter 14. Here we need note, first, that the channel was opened to Germany with the express approval of the US president for use in connection with the peace talks and, second, that the US ambassador's report would have been intercepted by MI1(b) and must thus have been passed on to Room 40. No doubt after the Swedish discovery, Hall and Hay had come to an agreement to look out for any other German circumventions of the communications blockade.

***

It became increasingly obvious that Room 40 and MI1(b) needed to communicate more than they had done since the autumn of 1914. Some neutral cable messages might well contain information about matters that were also discussed in German messages, so co-ordination was vital both to improve cryptographic success and to ensure the best evaluation of the intelligence uncovered. For example, Room 40 received letters and messages seized by the blockade enforcing ships from neutral vessels which might reveal the names and addresses of agents or companies willing to supply goods in South America or Spain or the USA. It would then be vital to work with MI1(b) to check that any cable telegrams between neutral countries sent to these addresses and companies were intercepted wherever possible.

In October 1916, Ewing effectively left Room 40 to become Principal of Edinburgh University. This was not Ewing's choice. He would have preferred to remain where he was, but the official view of his contribution had soured. As a post-war internal account put it, 'The officer in charge of Room 40 from October 1914 to [October 1916] was a civilian – Professor Ewing. He would not regard his section as part of the Intelligence Division and its work was severely handicapped in consequence.'[97] Having gained control over Room 45, the political/diplomatic section of Room 40, Hall chafed at Ewing's unwillingness, or inability, to turn the intelligence bonanza into a tool of aggression in the war, rather than just fashioning it as a purely defensive shield.[98] Nigel de Grey, who was to become a key figure in Room 40 (and in GC&CS in the Second World War), recalled that Hall mistrusted Ewing and 'made a compact with the "research party" that if ever we dug out anything of importance we were to take it direct to him without showing it to Ewing, who he saw as a "chatter-box" (rightly)'.[99] Oliver recalled how the irritation that existed between Hall and Ewing eventually exploded into a row and the First Lord of the Admiralty appointed Oliver and the Secretary to the Admiralty, Sir Graham Greene, to hold an 'enquiry' and 'we spent a long afternoon restoring peace'. The peace did not hold and in May 1916 Ewing was approached with the offer of the principalship of Edinburgh University. This was a significant offer, the capstone to an outstanding academic career, and in normal circumstances he would have jumped at the opportunity.

However, Ewing was reluctant to let go of his 'baby' and told the university that he was busy on 'secret war work' which he could not possibly afford to give up. In October 1916 the offer was repeated, this time in an interview with Balfour, then First Lord of Admiralty, who obviously made it clear that Ewing was no longer needed full time in Room 40. It was functioning so well that he could combine his current job with the university position. This time Ewing recognised that he was being sacked and accepted the job in Edinburgh. He was supposed to retain his title of Director of Naval Education and some supervisory role in Room 40, but this was a face-saving gesture. When Hall was awarded a knighthood in October 1917, Ewing graciously wrote to him to say that he was 'glad to see that your work as Head of the Intelligence Division is receiving special recognition. Anyone who knows how good it has been will feel, as I do, that the recognition is well deserved. I hope that my baby prospers.'[100]

It is not coincidental that Ewing departed at the time when the importance of diplomatic traffic grew. It had not been part of his organisation's original brief but now it was coming to dominate interest in its output. The great stalemate on land and at sea meant that neutrals were coming under increasing pressure as the belligerents sought ways to break the deadlock. Nor is it coincidental that shortly after Ewing departed, Room 40 and MI1(b) started to communicate with one another once again. In fact, Hall and Hay in MI1(b) were already talking and co-operating before Ewing left the Admiralty. The archives show, for example, that in August 1915 Hall gave MI1(b) information about a German cipher and in May 1916 he sent the Director of Military Intelligence translations of correspondence between the German ambassador, Count Bernstorff, in Washington and the Imperial German Chancellor, Bethmann-Hollweg, in Berlin.[101]

Hay, in charge of MI1(b), respected Hall, realising that he was intent on exploiting wireless interception for all its worth in the struggle against Germany. Hay no doubt recognised a kindred spirit in their shared determination to help the Allies win the war. Yet Hay, who was a man who liked to get his own way, also recognised that Hall had a streak of ruthlessness about him that he, Hay, lacked. Hall would stop at nothing to achieve his tactical goals of gaining information, as well as deceiving and misinforming both the enemy and, if necessary, his colleagues. Hall delighted in subterfuge and sleight of hand in his dealings with the Germans. He respected few rules at home either. All the same, he worked well with Hay, realising that gathering more intelligence was more important than empire-building and inter-departmental sniping. When MI1(b) moved to Cork Street in Piccadilly in mid-1917, Hay had a private telephone line installed to connect him with Hall's office at the Admiralty.

The archives contain some correspondence between the two units, with the earliest dating from 15 October 1916, discussing technical issues about Greek and Spanish codebooks. A letter sent in Ewing's name in September 1916, shortly before his sacking, illustrates that he was being forced to overcome his antipathy to co-operation by the needs of his own staff. 'Enclosed is an example of a kind of message we occasionally get. It looks like it might be giving a bearing from a Directional station. There are no calls. Do you recognize it as military?' he asked MI1(b).[102] Some letters to and from Denniston and Lord Lytton in Room 40 to Crocker in MI1(b) bear witness to the intensifying level of co-operation. In December 1916 Denniston wrote, 'I am very glad this opportunity of avoiding duplication of work has arisen and hope it may be carried through successfully.' On 13 February 1917 Denniston wrote to Crocker, 'Herewith some more Spanish work and one small Chi [a type of military cipher message]. Touching the

Turkish question I wonder if Strachey would like to see some intercepts of a year ago when Constantinople and Berlin were only joined by W/T. As there is now an expert in this language something might in time be made of them which would throw light on subsequent events.'[103] On 21 March 1917, Crocker wrote to Lytton, 'Many thanks for the two telegrams you have just sent over. I suggest that the missing words in the second telegram are "three hundred". Very few messages in this code are received here but I will see that copies of everything I get are sent over to you.' On 24 March, Denniston was informed, 'I have complained to the Censors about the gaps in the serial numbers of the Chilean telegrams and hope they will retrieve those missing. The Greek telegrams you kindly sent over are proving most useful in providing examples of some of the rarer varieties. I am sending you all the Bulgarian stuff we have ... With regard to the Swedish telegrams, we are not entirely convinced there is really more than one code. When we get a little bit further I will let you know.'[104] With Hall in place, co-operation between the two units improved dramatically. There were still tensions, but the two teams were able to get together to ensure that they complemented each other rather than engaging unawares on the same codes and ciphers.

The year 1917 saw a dramatic expansion of MI1(b). Codes were broken belonging to Argentina, Brazil, Denmark, Italy, Japan, the Netherlands, Norway, Persia, Sweden, Uruguay and the Vatican. By the end of 1917, 43 members of staff out of a total head count of 50 worked on diplomatic codes. Room 40 also expanded its diplomatic section, but to no more than ten people. Once the USA joined the war and Argentina and Brazil broke off relations with Germany in mid-1917 there was less diplomatic interception done by Room 40. Only the Berlin-Madrid wireless link then remained a fruitful source of diplomatic traffic for Room 40. The Foreign Office too began to appreciate the sort of intelligence it was receiving from intercepts. A letter to the War Office of 23 August 1917 noted that 'it would be of the greatest use if we could collect gradually the personal factors of Allied and Neutral Diplomatists all over the world, especially of course of Ambassadors, Ministers and Chargé d'Affaires. Do you think it would be possible to initiate the collection of such exceedingly valuable information?'[105] Diplomatic interception was establishing itself as a central part of the war effort, just as had already happened with military and naval interception.

Chapter 11

Inside Room 40

'**A** visitor entering the rooms grouped around [Blinker Hall's] office at the Admiralty or being granted the rare privilege of passing through the door marked "No admittance" which led to the cluster of rooms in the old building, known as Room 40, was at once struck by a change of atmosphere. On his way through the long, bleak corridors he had passed some elderly messengers, leisurely delivering papers to rooms from which there came no sound but the scratching of pens, and had caught a glimpse of some solemn-looking officers, talking in whispers, and he now found himself in an atmosphere vibrating with excitement, expectation, urgency, friendship, and high spirits ... There was much to astonish a visitor to those rooms, and some excuse for his believing that he was a victim of hoax. In Room 40 he would be introduced to a number of officers in RNVR uniform, and some, over military age, not in uniform, and told that in real life they were Fellows of Colleges at Oxford and Cambridge, Professors with a galaxy of academic distinctions, a Director of the Bank of England, a famous music critic, a well-known actor, a publisher, an ex-President of the Oxford Union, an art expert, a world-famous dress-designer. Perhaps his greatest surprise would be when he was introduced to a Professor of Divinity and a Roman Catholic priest in clerical garb. ... If he was lucky, Hall himself would come in like a tornado, and in his inimitable staccato way tell his staff, eagerly awaiting his return, what he had been doing. ... A visitor entering the watchkeeper's room, in 1916, about 11.30am, would either have seen three or four men, very tired and drawn, who had for the last eight hours been straining their brains to discover the cipher key, which changed at midnight, and had been defeated, or he would have seen these same men looking very cheerful and waiting to tell their reliefs, with a little pardonable pride, that they had nothing to worry about for the rest of the day. If he had entered one of the adjacent rooms, occupied by the men wrestling with unbroken ciphers, he would have seen two or three sphinx-like figures, who had perhaps been torturing the medley of figures or letters in front of them for several months, but had never relaxed their efforts, though it had often seemed that no progress was possible.'[106]

This account of an imaginary visitor's likely reactions on entering Room 40 was written by Captain William 'Bubbles' James in his biography of

Blinker Hall. Interestingly, one of the very few other accounts from the inside of Room 40 is also set around the same device. This time, however, the visitor is not male, as James assumes his imaginary visitor would be, but a young girl. She ends up in Room 40 by some fantastic imaginings and then proceeds to meet the weird and wonderful denizens of the cryptanalytic world. Is it coincidence that both writers, in telling us about a place that was carefully guarded to prevent visitors getting inside, should choose this method rather than a more straightforward narrative? Does this tell us something about the barely suppressed desire of those in on a secret to tell the world about it, the urge to break out of the adopted silence about their work? For the insiders, of course, such accounts are evocative of what for most of them must have been a strange interlude in their normal academic or business or military lives and we must pick up clues from these writings. However, our picture must remain a partial one, as noted in a post-war internal account of the role of intelligence in the naval war against Germany: 'So much is missing. Of the hurried consultations, the notes or slips of paper, the one hundred little details that are so vital to [the secret service] side of this subject, there remains no trace.'[107]

Birch's privately published booklet (with a very limited print run) is entitled *Alice in I.D. 25*[108] and tells the story of a young girl walking along Whitehall with her nurse, when a slip of paper suddenly falls from an upper window to land at her feet. She picks it up and starts to read it: 'Ballybunnion – Short begins – vd – sn – dd – um – um – v.v.v. – depresses key – fierce x's and wipers.' As she reads the text she starts to feel herself getting smaller and smaller, then a White Rabbit appears dressed in 'Sunday best – spats, spectacles and a little back coat, and he kept doing up and undoing its buttons with nervousness. "Dear me, dear me," Alice heard him say as he passed her, "it's past ten. I shall be late for the DIND".' The DIND, of course, is a slight misabbreviation of Director of Naval Intelligence Division, Captain Blinker Hall. The While Rabbit may represent Frank Adcock, a Cambridge ancient historian who played a significant role in both the First and Second World Wars in identifying suitable academic recruits for Room 40 and 25 years later at Bletchley Park (where he brought in Alan Turing).

Alice follows the White Rabbit hoping to see this DIND, only to fall into a hole and tumbles for some time down a twisting and turning tube before falling into 'a sort of cage of golden wire'. She looks around and sees a large room full of big creatures, all fast asleep. As she falls into the basket someone picks her up and asks where she came from and what was her 'time-group', to which she has no answer. The creature says in that case she must be either 'N.S.L. or Baltic'. At that everyone in the room wakes up and 'howled in chorus, "We *don't* do Baltic. We *won't* do Baltic. We *have* never done Baltic. It's a tradition." ' Birch was in charge of the Baltic section of Room 40 from

1917 and maybe reflecting some of the attitudes he met when running that area of naval codebreaking. It was only in the middle years that Room 40 started looking at German naval wireless traffic in the Baltic, having not considered it relevant to the centre of attention in the North Sea.

We need to handle Birch's ramblings with care. Clearly he has exaggerated for comic effect. Also his pen portrays only a handful of the inhabitants of Room 40. It seems likely that Birch wrote only about people who he was pretty sure would not be upset by his caricatures. Two of those mentioned by name in *Alice in ID25*, Morrah and Knox, certainly gave their help to the project (we have already seen part of Birch's tale, as applied to Herbert Morrah, the quietly determined Home Ruler, and the strenuously anti-Home Rule clergyman, Rev. Montgomery, in Chapter 7). So, as long as we allow for a suitable degree of over-egging of the pudding by Birch, the booklet gives us a unique glimpse of some of the characters inside Room 40. No doubt there are many in-jokes which pass over our heads, not having any intimate knowledge of the organisation. The tea party of the better known Alice story is replaced by a 'key party' and when a key arrives some of them jump up and demand their beds because 'they go to bed for the next 48 hours'. 'The Little Man' is probably Denniston who was indeed short of stature; the Dormouse may be Nigel de Grey, Grumbling Willow could be historian Leonard Willoughby and the Chief Clerk is probably William F. Clarke (who also left us with some pen portraits of Room 40 staff – see below). As Alice wanders around she comes across an open door with a notice on it: 'This door must be kept shut.' One creature she meets is described as 'like something between a Labour Member [of Parliament] and Sir Francis Drake. He kept on turning out his pockets and poking into dark corners and he is counting beds, having found that one is missing.' Here it is difficult to know who this is or understand the joke about counting beds.

Captain William 'Bubbles' James, who replaced Herbert Hope as the senior naval officer in Room 40, makes several non-appearances in *Alice in I.D. 25*. Quite a few times Alice asks questions to which she is told she will have to ask James, whose 'hours are 7 to 10 and 10 to 7', yet he is apparently never there despite it seeming as if he should be there twenty-fours a day. It eventually transpires that he is actually present from seven minutes to ten until ten in the morning and from ten minutes to seven until seven in the evening. The joke here is that James did not spend too much time at his desk in Room 40. The creature poking into dark corners and counting beds underlines the point by telling Alice, 'Nice chap, Captain James, knows 'is place. Mind you, I 'ave known owners as couldn't leave you alone, but 'e ain't there more'n'e's wanted. 'E leaves it to me.'

James's 'Bubbles' nickname was due to a portrait of him as a baby, blowing bubbles, having been widely used for the advertising of Pears soap. He was cast in a very different mould from his predecessor, Hope, and set about the job in his own fashion, putting the eccentric academics and wealthy gentlemen into naval uniforms – sometimes to almost comic effect as in the case of the classically unmilitary body and demeanour of Dillwyn Knox (see below). James saw his task as more an administrative one than being, like Hope, a part of the team analysing the decoded intercepts. For this sort of task James had no feel. Hope's paternalism was blown overboard and replaced by a 'brisk and breezy quarterdeck manner'. The term 'breezy' is indeed the most common description of James's approach to his colleagues and is obviously a euphemism. His first few weeks left not a few of Room 40's cryptographers feeling a little bruised. If it took time for the codebreakers to adjust to the new captain of their ship, it also took James a while to get used to his most unusual of naval 'crews'. If James did not become part of a working team, he did give Room 40 more weight and authority among the Admiralty's top officers who saw James as one of their own. Gradually Room 40 adopted more responsibilities, even drafting intelligence signals sent to the fleet, something that was previously the jealously guarded preserve of Oliver, the chief of staff.

One of the characters who drew a lot of attention, more indeed than any other person, in Birch's tale was 'Dilly' Knox, widely said to be the most gifted of Room 40's bunch of codebreakers. Birch had first met Dilly in 1910 when they were both at Cambridge (where John Maynard Keynes was also a friend of Dilly's). Dilly is teased unmercifully in Birch's tale, but he must have enjoyed it as he contributed the verses which are included in the booklet. Alfred Dillwyn Knox was the second oldest of four brothers, all of whom went on to become well known in their own fields (their two sisters, however, are less well known). One brother, Ronnie, also became a First World War codebreaker, joining Room 40 briefly. After the war he became a Catholic priest and, as Monsignor Ronald Knox, was immensely famous in religious and theological circles as a writer on Catholicism and as translator of the New Testament. Another brother, Wilfred, was an Anglo-Catholic priest and a social worker in the East End of London. The oldest of the four, Edmund, went on to become editor of *Punch*. The boys' father had been a bishop of Manchester, but clearly did not or could not imprint his views on his offspring, Dillwyn becoming an atheist. Dilly stayed with Room 40's successor organisation after the war and was still working on German codes and ciphers up until his death in 1943. He played a key role in the breaking of the German *Enigma* cipher machines in the Second World War. Details of some of his achievements in that war remain secret even today, allegedly because they would give away information about cryptographic methods that are still relevant. In 2009 the author of a biography of Dilly (who worked with him at Bletchley Park) was allowed to see the relevant file to refresh her memory, but was told which sections of the file she could not mention. She claims that there is nothing in the file which needs to remain secret. So, the fact that some information about Dilly's work is still secret could tell us something either about Dilly or about the obsessive secrecy of Britain's modern-day eavesdroppers.

But in 1916, when he joined the staff of Room 40, he was a lanky, socially awkward intellectual with an interest in some of the obscurer aspects of ancient languages and poetry. Dilly was far and away the most eccentric of the brothers. Birch describes him in *Alice in I.D. 25* as 'Dilly the Dodo'. Alice, he writes, 'thought he was the queerest bird she ever had seen. He was so long and lean, and he had outgrown his clothes, and his face was like a pang of hunger. ... Alice thought him a very hard man to please ... he handed her a sheet of very dirty paper on which a spider with inky feet appeared to have been crawling ... [Dilly the Dodo] began fumbling in his pockets. "What's the matter?" asked Alice. "I've lost my spectacles," cried the Dodo angrily, as he turned up the chairs and table. "Where are my spectacles?" and he glared angrily at the secretary. "I expect they are in *that*," jerked the secretary pointing to a tobacco-pouch on the table.' Dilly the Dodo, it turns out, keeps his glasses in the tobacco-pouch, so that when he finds them, he knows where his tobacco is, namely in his glasses case. However, when the glasses case is actually opened it contains a ham sandwich. Dilly the Dodo observes, ' "Now this serves to remind me that I'm hungry." Poor Alice was now completely bewildered, but she managed to ask, "Can't you remember when you're hungry?" [to which Dilly the Dodo replies] "I'm always hungry," he gobbled, "but I can't always remember it." ' A while later Alice observes that Dilly the Dodo 'who had been stuffing silently all the time, suddenly jumped up and doddered past her crying, "I must go to Room 40 and find fault with things." '

Knox targets himself in one of the verses which he wrote for *Alice in I.D. 25*:

> The sailor in Room 53,
> has never, it's true, been to sea.
> But though not in a boat
> he has yet served afloat –
> in a bath in the Admiralty.

He had indeed persuaded the authorities to install a bath in his room and he claimed that it was in the hot steaming tub that he did his deepest thinking. Knox did not look too impressive, however, in the military uniform which he, and the other codebreakers, were required to wear after 'Bubbles' James took over. His brothers, Ronnie and Wilfred, were one day walking along Whitehall when they saw 'Erm' (as they nicknamed him in recognition of his persistently hesitant speech) 'coming out of the Admiralty, all dressed up, as Wilfred put it, like Lord Nelson. Both were too overcome to ask him what he had done with his telescope.'[109] One of Knox's biographers (and his niece) put it thus: 'Dilly himself conspicuously failed to look naval, long thin wrists stretched out from the cuffs of a uniform that hung on him like a sack. His work was presented, as it had been in his Eton days, in inky scribbles on sheets of dirty paper, frequently mislaid. … [But] there was a certain art, a certain flair with which Dilly was born, for the shadow patterns of groups of letters, no matter in what language, revealing themselves, like a secret dance, only to the patient watcher.' Knox was at that 'borderland where the mind, prowling among misty forms and concepts, suddenly perceives analogies with what it already knows and moves into the light'.[110]

In 1908, Dilly had taken on the task of completing an edition of the 'mimes' of Herodas, a second/third century BC Greek poet, recorded on a battered bunch of papyrus dating from about AD 100. The academic who started the edition died and the young Dilly was the obvious person to finish the job. He set about the task with gusto. 'He intended to be not only linguist, palaeographer and papyrologist but to understand the whole world of the ordinary Greek people depicted by Herodas.'[111] The verses, or 'mimes', that he translated could be rather rum, concerning 'the pander [pimp] who sues for assault because a girl has been stolen from the brothel; the mother with a delinquent son; the woman whose slave has proved an unsatisfactory lover, and wants him whipped, but doesn't want anyone else to see him naked; the woman who complains about servants, visits the temple, can't wait to see the expert leatherworker in the sex shop … The mimes provided an intensely difficult game in which nearly all the rules were missing, but Dilly intended to win.'[112] Probing the seedy verses about the daily lives of ancient Greeks would seem to be rather a different task from studying the operations of the German navy's small vessels or the ponderous diplomatic telegrams emanating from the German Foreign Office. But Dilly's focus was on the intellectual excitement of solving the translation/cryptographic puzzle, not the content of the messages, whether titillating or terrifying. In his academic work he would have to deal with fragments of writing on fraying pieces of papyrus, filling in the gaps from insight and intuition – not so different from his task as a cryptographer. Once during his years as a codebreaker he managed to reconstruct a Hungarian codebook, without having bothered to learn any Hungarian, simply from logical analysis of the patterns of the encoded messages.

Dilly was in the office, where he virtually lived, when a bunch of test messages were picked up in the German flag officers' code (which replaced the VB in some uses). The code was fairly new and largely unknown, but Knox reckoned that he could recognise several different spelling-group codewords used for spelling 'en', one of the most common German word endings (featuring in the infinitive form of verbs and in many plurals). One message drew his attention as there seemed a rather well-ordered and

Above: Whitehall's Admiralty House, home of Room 40, in 1915. *Getty Images*

Above: Morse code 'tapper' key for use with telegraph and wireless communications. *Author's collection*

Above: Marconi's first wireless system. *Author's collection*

Right: Alfred Ewing, founder of Room 40. *Getty Images*

Opposite: A young Winston Churchill, the First Lord of the Admiralty, in 1916. *Getty Images*

Below: A Room 40 working document – a partially reconstructed 13040 codebook. *National Archives*

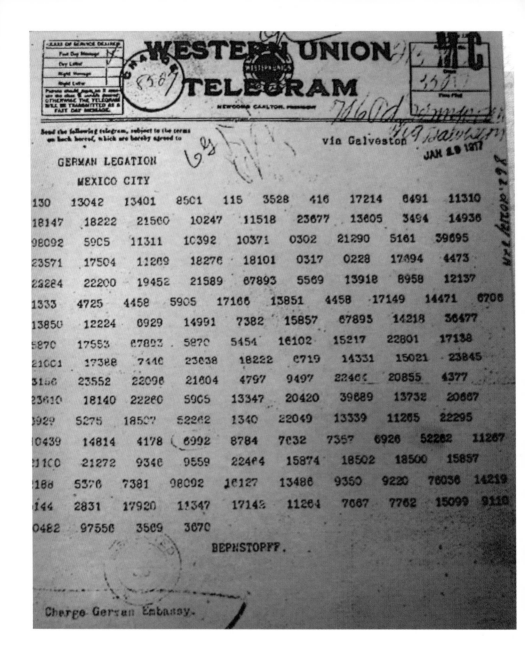

The intercepted copy of the 'Zimmerman Telegram', the publication of which brought the US into the First World War. *Author's collection*

Geheim!

TITEL A 20   № 151   1

Signalbuch

der

Kaiserlichen Marine.

(Entwurf.)

Herausgegeben vom Admiralstab der Marine.

Berlin 1913.

The title page to the Signalbuch der Kaiserlichen Marine (SKM) codebook, found on board the Magdeburg. *National Archives*

Zahlen-Signal	Buchstaben-Signal	Bedeutung
		A
500 01	A Ü B	a
02	A Ü C	á
03	A Ü D	Ab, ab-
04	A Ü E	abändern -ung (dahin, daß) [s. Reiseplan]
05	A Ü F	abgeändert (dahin, daß) [s. Befehl, Bestimmung, Operationsbefehl]
06	A Ü G	in Abänderung (des Befehls Nr. n)
07	A Ü H	Abänderungsvorschlag
08	A Ü I	abberufen -ung (aus von)
09	A Ü J	abbestellen -ung [s. Kohlen]
500 10	A Ü K	abbilden -ung
11	A Ü L	Abbitte tun (bei)
12	A Ü M	abblasen [s. Dampf]
13	A Ü N	abblenden
14	A Ü O	abgeblendet sein
15	A Ü Ö	Abblenden aufhören [s. Übung]
16	A Ü P	abblenden mit Ausnahme der Anterlaterne
17	A Ü Q	abblenden mit Ausnahme der Dampfer- und Seitenlaternen
18	A Ü R	abblenden mit Ausnahme der Seitenlaternen
19	A Ü S	besser abblenden
500 20	A Ü T	besser abblenden an B. B.
21	A Ü U	besser abblenden am Bug
22	A Ü Ü	besser abblenden am Heck
23	A Ü V	besser abblenden an St. B.
24	A Ü W	mit Beginn der Dunkelheit abblenden
25	A Ü X	abblenden nach Vorgang des Flaggschiffes (oder von ...)
26	A Ü Y	abbrechen, Abbruch
27	A Ü Z	Abbruch tun [s. Handel]
28	A Ü α	abbrennen [z. Blaufeuer, Fackelfeuer, Feuer]
29	A Ü γ	abbringen [s. abschleppen]
500 30	A B Ö	abbüßen -ung
31	A B C	nach Abbüßung der Strafe
32	A B D	abdämmen
33	A B E	Abdampf, abdampfen
34	A B F	Abdampfleitung
35	A B G	abdanken -ung
36	A B H	abdichten -ung
37	A B I	abdrängen -ung (von)
38	A B J	bin (ist) abgedrängt
39	A B K	werde abgedrängt [z. Unterstützung]
500 40	A B L	abdrehen [z. Torpedobootsangriff]
41	A B M	abziehen nach B. B.
42	A B N	abziehen nach St. B.
43	A B O	Abdruck, abdrucken
44	A B Ö	Abend -lich, abends
45	A B P	gestern Abend
46	A B Q	heute Abend
47	A B R	jeden Abend
48	A B S	keinen Abend
49	A B T	im Laufe des Abends
500 50	A B U	morgen Abend
51	A B Ü	übermorgen Abend
52	A B V	—
500 53	A B W	—
500 54	A B X	vorgestern Abend
55	A B Y	Abendbrot [s. Mannschaft]
56	A B Z	Abendbrot machen
57	A B α	nach dem Abendbrot
58	A B γ	vor dem Abendbrot
59	A C Ö	Abendmahl
500 60	A C B	Abendwache
61	A C D	auf der Abendwache
62	A C E	aber
63	A C F	aberkennen -ung
64	A C G	abermalig, abermals
65	A C H	abfahren, Abfahrt (nach) [vgl. abgehen, Abreise]
66	A C I	abgefahren (nach)
67	A C J	Abfahrtshafen
68	A C K	Abfahrtszeit und Reiseziel den Behörden falsch angeben
69	A C L	Abfahrtszeit und Reiseziel verheimlichen
500 70	A C M	Abfall, abfallen, abfällig
71	A C N	abfangen
72	A C O	suchen Sie abzufangen
73	A C Ö	abfassen -ung
74	A C P	abgefaßt
75	A C Q	abfertigen -ung [s. Depeschenbuch]
76	A C R	abfeuern -ung
77	A C S	abfinden -ung
78	A C T	abflauen
79	A C U	abfließen, Abfluß
500 80	A C Ü	abführen -ung
81	A C V	Abgabe [s. Nebelpositionssignal]
82	A C W	zur Abgabe bereit halten
83	A C X	Abgangsbesteck
84	A C Y	Abgangsmeldung
85	A C Z	Abgangsrohr
86	A C α	abgeben
87	A C γ	abgegeben
88	A D Ö	kann (können) abgeben (an)
89	A D B	abgeben (am), Abgang [vgl. abreisen] [s. Ablösungstransport, Dampfer, Post]
500 90	A D C	bin (ist, sind) abgegangen (am, nach) [s. Telegramm]
91	A D E	wann sind Sie (ist er) abgegangen (nach)
92	A D F	weiter abgeben (von)
93	A D G	abgelegen
94	A D H	Abgeneigt -heit (gegen)
95	A D I	Abgeordneter, Abgeordnet- n-
96	A D J	Abgesandter
97	A D K	abgesehen (von)
98	A D L	abgrenzen -ung (durch)
99	A D M	Abgrund
501 00	A D N	abhalten -ung (von) [s. Musterung, Schießübung, Torpedoschießen]
01	A D O	abhanden kommen
02	A D Ö	Abhang
03	A D P	abhängen (von)
04	A D Q	(es) hängt davon ab (ob)
05	A D R	—
06	A D S	—
07	A D T	—

A sample page of the Signalbuch der Kaiserlichen Marine (SKM) codebook. *National Archives*

Geheim.

TITEL A 57

Verkehrsbuch.

(V. B.)

3. Auflage.

Berlin 1908.
Gedruckt in der Reichsdruckerei.

The title page to the Verkehrsbuch (VB) codebook. *National Archives*

I. Interpunktion, Hilfszeichen und grammatikalische Umbildungen.

Interpunktion.

00 Setze Anführungsstriche oben
01 Setze Anführungsstriche unten
02 Setze einen Apostroph
03 Setze ein Ausrufungszeichen
04 Setze einen Bindestrich
05 Setze einen Bruchstrich
06 Setze einen Doppelpunkt
07 Setze ein Fragezeichen
08 Setze ein Komma
09 Setze einen Punkt
10 Setze ein Semikolon

Hilfszeichen.

11 Es beginnt ein neuer Absatz
12 Ende des buchstabierten Ausdrucks
13 Die folg. Zahl ist als Dezimale zu lesen (0...)
14 Anfang e. eingeklammerten Wortverbindung
15 Ende e. eingeklammerten Wortverbindung
16 Klammere die folgende Bedeutung ein
17 Die folg. Bedeutung ist als Frage zu lesen
18 Bilde d. verneinende Form der folg. Bedeutung
19 Streiche den letzten Buchstaben
20 Streiche die beiden letzten Buchstaben
21 Streiche von der folg. Bedeutg.:
22 – desgl. – das erste Wort
23 – desgl. – das zweite Wort
24 – desgl. – das dritte Wort
25 – desgl. – die beiden ersten Wörter
26 – desgl. – die drei ersten Wörter
27 – desgl. – das letzte Wort
28 – desgl. – das vorletzte Wort
29 – desgl. – die beiden letzten Wörter

Grammatikalische Umbildungen.

30 Bilde das Hauptwort der folgenden Bedeutung
31 – desgl. – mit Endung er
32 – desgl. – mit Endung heit
33 – desgl. – mit Endung ien
34 – desgl. – mit Endung keit
35 – desgl. – mit Endung ung
36 Bilde d. Nominativ der Einzahl der folg. Bedeutg.
37 – desgl. – Genitiv – desgl. –

38 Bilde den Dativ der Einzahl der folg. Bedeutg.
39 – desgl. – Akkusativ – desgl. –
40 Bilde d. Nominativ der Mehrzahl d. folg. Bedeutg.
41 – desgl. – Genitiv – desgl. –
42 – desgl. – Dativ – desgl. –
43 – desgl. – Akkusativ – desgl. –
44 Bilde das Eigenschaftswort der folg. Bedeutg.
45 – desgl. – mit Endung e
46 – desgl. – mit Endung em
47 – desgl. – mit Endung en
48 – desgl. – mit Endung er
49 – desgl. – mit Endung es
50 Bilde den Komparativ der folg. Bedeutg.
51 – desgl. – mit Endung e
52 – desgl. – mit Endung em
53 – desgl. – mit Endung en
54 – desgl. – mit Endung er
55 – desgl. – mit Endung es
56 Bilde den Superlativ der folg. Bedeutg.
57 – desgl. – mit Endung e
58 – desgl. – mit Endung em
59 – desgl. – mit Endung en
60 – desgl. – mit Endung er
61 – desgl. – mit Endung es
62 Bilde den Infinitiv der folg. Bedeutg.
63 – desgl. – mit zu
64 Bilde d. Indikativ des Präsens der folg. Bedeutg.
65 Bilde d. Konjunktiv des Präsens der folg. Bedeutg.
66 Bilde d. Indikativ des Imperfekts d. folg. Bedeutg.
67 Bilde d. Konjunktiv des Imperfekts d. folg. Bedtg.
68 Bilde den Imperativ der folg. Bedeutg.
69 Bilde das Partizip des Präsens der folg. Bedeutg.
70 – desgl. – mit Endung e
71 – desgl. – mit Endung em
72 – desgl. – mit Endung en
73 – desgl. – mit Endung er
74 – desgl. – mit Endung es
75 Bilde d. Partizip der Vergangenheit d. folg. Bedtg.
76 – desgl. – mit Endung e
77 – desgl. – mit Endung em
78 – desgl. – mit Endung en
79 – desgl. – mit Endung er
80 – desgl. – mit Endung es

A sample page of the Verkehrsbuch (VB) codebook. *National Archives* unusually high number of 'ens' in a very short message. When Knox scribbled his blotchy ink marks onto a scrap of paper he noted a pattern:

——·— ——en —·————en —·—-en
————·—-en — ————— —-en

and detected a poetic metre in it. He suspected a poetic form known as 'dactyls'. Dilly took the scrap of paper to the room where the professors, who in normal life were experts in German literature, were now tackling German navalese. Leonard Willoughby (possibly Birch's Grumbling Willow) very quickly worked out that it was a fragment of verse by the great German poet, Schiller:

> Ehret die Frauen; sie flechten und weben
> Himmliche Rosen im redliche Leben
> (Give reverence to women; they plait and weave
> Heavenly roses in this earthly life).

Knox and his fellow codebreakers were rewarded with the recovery of nine or ten new codewords. The flag officers' code was broken by the middle of 1917 and played a role in undermining the submarine attacks that had been restarted in full force at the end of January that year (see Chapter 16).

Dilly was the classic socially inept academic. One biographer wrote of his rather cold, utilitarian personality which elevated intellectual pleasure above human relations. 'Dilly had eaten cold porridge at Aston [public school], because the pleasure of eating consisted of the pleasure of filling your belly, so now [at Cambridge] he declared that one should drink only to get drunk, and that women (to whom he was always timidly and scrupulously polite) existed only for sex. True pleasure came from solving problems.'[113] However, at the end of 1917 he was given a new secretary, Olive Roddam, from a wealthy Northumberland landowning background. As Roddam worked in the room equipped with a bath, Knox had to finish with his soaking before she arrived in the morning. From someone used to the all-male environment of the common rooms at Cambridge this was an unsettling intrusion into a settled way of life. It was probably the first time he had been in such close contact, for hours each working day, with a woman. He was overwhelmed and immediately after the war Knox and Roddam were married – to the surprise of everyone from friends and colleagues to family members on both sides. Their marriage took place a couple of weeks after that of Frank Birch and Vera Gage, daughter of Henry Charles, fifth Viscount Gage. The Knoxes and Gages at first attempted to live in the same house, but this was soon abandoned, Dilly and Olive moving to rural High Wycombe. Dilly so much enjoyed the intellectual challenge of codebreaking that he stayed on after the war and was still codebreaking in 1939. However, he was rather ill by then, suffering from stomach cancer which was diagnosed in 1938. He spent his last few months working from his bed at home, dying at home in 1943.

***

Another member of Room 40's staff, William F. Clarke, was closely associated with Frank Birch, helping him at the end of the war to compile a history of the naval war with Germany based on intercepts and other intelligence. In fact we owe to Clarke a considerable amount of the historical material on Room 40, both in terms of his authorship and his gathering of documents from others, much of it acquired after the Second World War. Clarke was a 33-year-old barrister in 1915. 'I had always had a sneaking desire for the sea … When war broke out I used all my ingenuity to get into the Naval service, all in vain for a time at least; I was too old. However, my brother, eleven years older, was also trying and got accepted, dropping ten years of his age which nearly made us twins. I pursued the same tactics, secured an interview, went through an amusing medical only to hear that my defective eyesight disqualified me' for active service.[114] This imperfection did not prevent him being of use to the navy and Clarke became a paymaster, handing out cash to about a thousand servicemen each week. 'Later I took over the job of supervising all the disciplinary work, for which my eight years at the Bar had fitted me.' In early 1915 he was summoned, unexpectedly, to see the Director of Naval Intelligence, Blinker Hall. 'I was then told that I would be transferred to HMS President for duty outside the Admiralty. What this meant I had not the faintest idea. Early in March I reported for duty. Then at last my eyes were opened; our task was cryptography, of which I had never heard.' Clarke was told to work alongside Captain Hope, handling the decoded intelligence.

In an account, slightly reminiscent of Birch's version, Clarke described the kerfuffle whenever there was a change in cipher key. 'When it changed the experts were called in, retired to the other room whence they emerged after a short or long interval with the solution to the amazement of us, ordinary folk.' For the non-experts, the night watch in particular was fairly relaxed. 'In 1916 one generally slept half the night, only one of us remaining to deal with traffic.' This arrangement, however, did not suit all. 'Some fellow watchkeepers like Fremantle were either too fussy or too noisy to allow anyone to sleep in the adjoining room.' This was in early 1916 when the key changed infrequently, but after Jutland a new key was introduced every twenty-four hours. From then on it was the job of the night watch to break the new key. Each watch had one cipher expert and if they were on the night shift, breaking the new cipher was their task. Clarke recalled that 'in normal conditions, coming on at 10am we found the night watch had already solved the problem unless one had the ill fortune to relieve the so-called Gentlemen's Watch, Norton, Lord Monkbretton and Morrah'. All the same, 'the work was quite easy for anyone with reasonable common sense and a good knowledge of German; things were to be very different in later years when new codebooks were frequently introduced, reciphering tables lasted but a short time and became more complicated and the volumes increased enormously'.

Clarke has left us short comments on many of his colleagues. It is social chit chat and gossip about one's colleagues, all too often only giving us a name and a note of when they had died. The comments tend to be either dismissive or fawning. For example, he records of our old acquaintance Herbert Morrah that he had 'quite inexplicably from what we know of him and his capabilities, been President of the Union [at Oxford]', but Lord Lytton, as Clarke later takes pains to point out, a civilian lord of the Admiralty and Viceroy of India, is 'a most charming and modest personality and a very good cryptographer who solved the hardest problems we ever had to tackle'.

Clarke certainly fawned over Rotter. 'The great success that we achieved, in spite of the idiosyncrasies of his chief [ie, Ewing], was due to his indomitable patience … Captain Hope is the greatest member of staff … To him, more than to anyone else, the credit of [Room 40's] achievement must be assigned. Modest, retiring, he exercised a control over all its operations with unfailing skill and understanding.' Elsewhere Clarke wrote of Hope that he was, 'the hub of Room 40. Was mainly responsible for its success. Our beloved chief … Left us in 1917 much to the country's loss and did most valuable work in the Adriatic. Came back in 1939.' However, 'Bubbles' James, Hope's replacement, was obviously inferior. 'He was a very different type to Hope, very pushing, very self-confident. He had been a remarkable success as a commander at sea but he came to a job which required other qualifications which, in my opinion, he did not possess. But luckily by then everything was so organised that we required little but a figurehead and for that he was admirably suited.' Even his success in persuading the Admiralty to increase staffing levels to cope with more intercepts is cast in an unfavourable light, Clarke suggesting that James's motive was to gain influence and power by having a bigger organisation. James wrote a biography of Blinker Hall in 1955 and during his researches he saw Clarke's papers, thus reading these comments on himself and others. He observed that Clarke 'seemed to dislike a lot of people'.[115]

Clarke leaves us with two snippets on George Young (see Chapter 9). First, he informs us that Young 'made a claim to Inventions Board for devising a system of solving German FO ciphers'; unfortunately there seem to be no more records of this (unless it refers to the machine devised to guess codewords in two-part or 'hatted' codes, see next chapter). Second, he coldly states, 'there died the other day Sir George Young and got published a note making the remarkable and quite false claim that he was sent to the Admiralty "to reorganise Room 40". He was in it, it is true, for some time but he was never employed on its most important work.' This last comment seems rather unfair as Young set up Room 40's political/diplomatic section. There is no doubt that this section – in the decoding of the Zimmermann telegram, the breaking of numerous German Foreign Office codes and ciphers, and the development of machines to guess codewords – did some of Room 40's most important work and Young surely deserves some credit for its success.

Sir Alfred Ewing was very definitely at the top of Clarke's list of people he disliked. When acting as the Admiralty censor in the 1930s he objected to some of Ewing's claims about Room 40 in a book he wanted to publish (see Chapter 19). Clarke wrote to the Attorney General, 'It may be observed that the statement about deciphering is quite untrue. Sir Alfred Ewing, as far as I know, never solved any cryptographical problems himself – he only hindered others.' In another document he wrote that Ewing 'had been titular Head of Room 40 on its inception in 1914 … and was technically over Captain Hope. In fact, ie, in actuality he never was, he never really understood the problems and wasted much valuable time of his subordinates than can be imagined.'

Clarke's memory provides us with a peculiar mix. Edward Bullough, a professor of Italian, it is noted, is married to the daughter of Eleanora Duse, but we are told nothing of Bullough's cryptographic service. Duse was a famous actress, then about 60 years of age, who had been the most notable of the many lovers of the Italian poet, war propagandist and ideological fount of Italian fascism, Gabriele D'Annunzio.[116] Other famous or wealthy people whom Clarke admired included Lieutenant-Commander F. C. Tiarks RNVR, a city broker, who 'had been in the navy for a few years. Ran our D.F. [direction-finding] section – interspersed with his purchase of Anglo-Persian shares. Shocked Admiralty messenger who came from 1st Lord to summon him, by looking at his watch and saying he would come in three-quarters of an hour.' An unpaid member of the team was Ralph Vaughan-Williams, the composer. William F. Clarke's only comment was that he was the son of Lord Justice Vaughan-Williams, 'whom WFC knew'. Lt J. Beazley RNVR, was a Fellow of Christchurch Oxford. 'Great authority on ancient pottery. Called 'kingo' as dealt with the German 'Ingo' code. One of the few employed in Room 40 who did not advertise the fact in Who's Who.' Lieutenant Benjamin Faudel-Phillips RNVR, was the son of a former Lord Mayor of London. According to Clarke he was a 'Serocold "find" … He succeeded Young as head of Diplomatic section. Wealthy, generous and popular. Entertained members of Room 40 OB at his lovely house, Balls Park.' Mr Harold E. Boulton was known as 'Daddy', says Clarke, adding, 'as far as I know no particular but a charming character. I think he died some time ago.' R. P. Keigurn, a schoolmaster in Room 40, was a 'good cricketer'.

Fortunately Clarke left us with a few comments on some of the women who worked in Room 40, some as cryptographers such as Miss Hannam, who knew French and German and had served in France at GHQ on German field codes, and Miss Haylar, who worked on 'current Italian non-alphabetical' codes. Denniston, recommending that they be kept on after the war, later commented that 'Re: Hannam, Watkins, Spurling, Marreco, Anderson, Haylar: 'The services of these ladies are invaluable. They are experienced in the working out of all kinds of codes.'[117] June Spurling joined MI1(b) in 1918, having been transferred from GHQ in France where she had worked on German field codes. Unfortunately there is no hint about how she got to France to do codebreaking work in the first place, but she must have been very good to have earned the transfer. Also she was one of the handful of cryptographers kept on at the end of the war when only the very best were offered a post (see Chapter 19). Clarke tells us little about the women's cryptographic skills but was keen to list their social pedigree. Miss Joan Harvey was the daughter of a secretary of the Bank of England, 'Returned for WW2'. Miss R. M. Welsford was a university graduate who 'in 1939 insisted on coming back uninvited'. Miss Violet Hudson was the 'daughter of soap magnate'. She acted as Clarke's secretary and 'used to arrive at unearthly hours in the morning. Very nice child.' Miss Catherine Henderson was 'daughter of "Billie Willie" Admiral Henderson, later one of the organisers of the convoy system'. And Mrs Margaret Bayley, who joined only in November 1917, was the 'wife of city doctor. Her love affairs with W. L. Fraser and Russell Clarke caused some trouble. Called "the Golliwog".' By 1916 there were twenty women working in Room 40. The secretaries and typists were kept in hand by Ebba Hambro, wife of Sir Everard Hambro, the merchant banker. Lady Hambro amazed some of her more staid male contemporaries when she smoked a cigar at a social function.

There were less fortunate colleagues too. Lt K. Marlowe, son of Marlowe of the *Daily Mail*, 'committed suicide when off duty'. G. H. M. Haggard was 'a regular naval officer who had lost his leg as a result of a misfire. Strange creature [who] went to Cambridge after the war and married a girl who was in the family way to save her name.' Captain Ralph George Barnes of the Canadian Engineers was a tubist from 5/12/17 to 4/3/19. Clarke's only observation was, 'one-eyed, called The Ghost'. Major James Dubuisson was an 'Army cavalry officer who had lost his legs. Charming fellow.' Fremantle, a Royal Naval officer 'of a famous family … was for some time my fellow on the night watch and he created some amusement by asking for the day off as he was to be divorced'. With these short glimpses into the people of Room 40, we come to the end of what Clarke's recollections can tell us about what it was like to be inside Room 40. In his words, 'So much for personalities. I am afraid my memory may have led me into a few errors, but it is the best I can do after these long years.'

***

According to an internal assessment written at the end of the First World War, 'Recruits [to Room 40] were chosen rather on the grounds of military incapacity than for aptitude at research and in the main, the lack of foresight at the beginning of the war – the failure to obtain the services of a sufficient number of suitable men – embarrassed and curtailed the efficiency of the section throughout. Almost to the last, there was an inner body of some half-a-dozen officers attempting the impossible. They were experts and as such solved all the enemy codes and ciphers; they were intelligence officers engaged in continuous research for supplying the operations division with a summary of the daily situation; and until 1917, the whole routine of watchkeeping, copying and circulating signals as they arrived fell on their shoulders'.[118] Another assessment noted, 'The very greatest difficulty was experienced throughout in finding individuals with the necessary "flair" for cryptography. This was equally true of the purely military as well as of the diplomatic side of the work. Really expert cryptographers can never be found ready made: only experience can make "expert" the individual who possesses the necessary mental qualifications and aptitude for the work. In the majority of cases it was found that the most likely source of technical experts lies amongst those trained in scientific and linguistic work. For the work of decoding messages and amplifying diplomatic codebooks already solved, the personnel was mainly drawn, irrespective of sex, from the members of the Universities possessing high linguistic qualifications.' An aptitude test was devised in 1918.[119]

In addition to Birch's and Clarke's sharp pens, there are also a few documents which shed light on some of the cryptographic work of individual codebreakers. These come from CVs compiled at the end of the war by those wanting, or wanted, to stay on in the post-war cryptographic successor to Room 40 and MI1(b). These CVs show us how the codebreakers moved from one job to another, expanding all the time their ability to cope with a wide range of codes, ciphers and languages. The selection of those asked to compile their CVs is obviously biased towards those with the greatest range of experience – we are dealing here with some of the half-a-dozen or so star cryptographers of Room 40 and MI1(b) – but they can usefully illustrate the sort of work that a cryptographer would do over a period of several years.

The most detailed account of cryptographic activities comes from the clerical warrior, William Montgomery. As we have seen, Montgomery was no mild, peaceful clergyman. His CV also shows that he was not into humility. Like most new recruits, his first spell of duty in Room 40, beginning in April 1916, was on the watch, decoding naval messages in SKM and VB. In September 1916 he was transferred to the political/diplomatic section, dealing with cable messages sent to and from Washington, Mexico, Argentina, Brazil, Chile, Peru, and minor South and Central American states. He worked on code 13040 and claimed a significant contribution to decoding the Zimmermann telegram which brought the USA into the war (see Chapter 15), arguing that his 'careful linguistic work' was so convincing that the German Foreign Office thought that the telegram must have been stolen rather than intercepted and decoded. Montgomery also informs us, 'Half a dozen other ciphers were dealt with by this sub-section including the "hat" (arbitrarily constructed) [ie, 'two-part' codes, see Chapter 12] cipher 7500, to the early stages of which I made some useful contribution. At this time I discovered independently the "sliders" used to disguise messages passed on from Washington to Buenos Aires and vice versa, and (later) the "slider" used to disguise VB messages sent to the German forces in East Africa.' Montgomery is here referring to a numerical 'subtractor' cipher key technique use to 'disguise' or encipher the coded messages.

From March 1917 he was back on naval work: 'I was practically in charge of the sub-section dealing with American ciphers.' The code then in use, 26040, had daily changing keys 'which had to be discovered from the message itself. This was regularly done with success.' He worked as well on 'odd' or occasional ciphers including a 'multiple alphabet cipher with certain curious features used by the Germans in Morocco', a complicated multiple alphabet cipher used by a German agent in India and many others. Also, 'by recognising the connection of certain messages submitted to us by the Americans with the old HVB, I was able to supply evidence which secured the condemnation in the American Prize courts of a vessel which had acted as a supply ship to the *Dresden*'. In decoding a Buenos Aires message he 'conjectured the phrase "spurlos versenkt" [sunk without trace] (not then in our reconstruction of the codebook) which was afterwards so useful for propaganda purposes'. Montgomery is here referring to intercepted messages dealing with the sinking of Argentine ships. The intercepts revealed that German diplomats decided that complaints from the Argentines would not arise if ships were sunk without trace. The intercepted telegrams were carefully leaked to the press. The callous sentiments behind the phrase were a propaganda defeat for the Germans, reverberating around the world of shipping nations.

'Later when the American material stopped owing to the publication of certain telegrams' – ie, the Zimmermann telegram – Montgomery was 'entrusted' with going back to American cables from before the first decipher. 'If prompt use was to be made of the valuable material which it contained, it was impossible to wait till the whole was decoded. A rapid survey and selection had to be made dealing with newspaper and political intrigues, supply ships, firms deserving to be blacklisted, dangerous persons, agents, etc. The Americans, to whom the results were generally communicated, made a special acknowledgement of their value.' From February 1918, Montgomery was in charge of Room 228. The first cipher he tackled there was a 'hatted' or 'two-part' cipher (see Chapter 12) used for communications between Berlin and Madrid, 'in which their most important material was sent out'. He recorded that 'the cipher was already in a workable stage, but as it was not very advanced, and as there was a considerable amount of daily material, I had little time for any other research … I did however during this time discover a dictionary-code used in Morocco, build up to a workable point the 'Delmar' cipher, of which the beginnings were given to us by the French, get out a Spanish alphabet cipher, etc. besides keeping up the general direction of the work on the old American material … In conjunction with Miss Robertson, the very efficient head of the lady decoders in Room 229, I worked up from an early stage another "hat" cipher containing much important political material, which it was thought at the time might be wanted for publication. This involved constant overtime work for six months.' This work would undoubtedly have brought Montgomery into contact with the machine techniques used to 'reconstruct' the 'hatted' codes by guessing codewords at a far more rapid rate than could be done by human codebreakers (see Chapter 12). 'I also at various times, by orders of the late Director of Naval Intelligence, prepared dossiers of cipher material on various subjects. The most important of these was commended by him as "good staff work". I have a considerable facility in acquiring a working knowledge of a language, eg, I can read Dutch without having studied it, and lately got up enough Polish for certain practical purposes.'[120] This is truly a formidable list of achievements.

Another codebreaker who left us with a good account of his work was Mr C. Somers-Cocks. He joined in June 1916 and worked on the watch until 'transferred by Sir A. Ewing to political side; assisted for two months in getting current messages out in cipher 9972 and its variants, of which a portion had been made out … and also Madrid messages 89934 … Beginning of 1917 Washington, South and Central America, 13040, 5950 and their variants (which had been partially made out) until the messages stopped about the end of the year. Examined American messages in commercial code, then "back numbers" of same ciphers. About April 1918 current messages in 92700 (Arab or Persian cipher) variant of 13040, made up a more complete edition of this for sending abroad.' He later worked on 6400, an incomplete 'hatted' code, and a code known as 'Delmar' as well as others, including German-Bulgarian codes and ciphers. Little else is known about him except comments left by Clarke, who observes a couple of times that he was 'celebrated for his spats'.[121] Another cryptographer with a long record of achievements was John Fraser of MI1(b), later Professor of Celtic at Oxford. He joined in February 1916 and made an immediate contribution by breaking the French-language Greek codebooks (see Chapter 10). He was familiar with 21 languages and broke or helped to break Greek, Spanish, Argentine, Uruguayan, Turkish (Army Field Code), Swiss,

Swedish, Norwegian, Brazilian, Romanian, Dutch and Vatican codes and ciphers.

Lieutenant John Hooper was a modern languages teacher at the Royal Navy School, Osborne, who joined Room 40 on 17 November 1917. As with all new recruits he started as one of the people keeping the watch, working on German naval codes. His work, 'consisting in deciphering messages from the German High Sea Fleet and "getting out" the daily key'. Denniston gave him his highest accolade: 'very sound'. Despite his obvious skill he had to be returned to Osborne in January 1918. 'The authorities at the RN College Osborne having refused to release me for work in ID25 I resigned my appointment there, but as a term's notice was necessary, I was compelled to proceed for one term to the RN College Dartmouth to which I had previously been lent.' He returned to Room 40 in April and from then until June resumed watchkeeping duties there. He also handled German political/diplomatic ciphers and the translation and summarising of plain language wireless news. From June until July 1918 he did 'research work in connection with the new German naval cipher'. Then he was appointed as an Intelligence Officer, keeping the Operations Division supplied with information about the distribution and movements of the German High Seas Fleet. After the war ended he stayed on and acted through December 1918 as an interpreter at Scapa Flow where the German fleet was ordered to be laid up. In January 1919 he worked on the compilation of a daily 'Summary of Wireless News', derived from reading and summarising all *en clair* messages from all parts of Europe. 'The knowledge of contemporary political events thus acquired should be of considerable assistance in cryptographic work. When time permitted I have also been engaged during this period in familiarising myself with the various German diplomatic ciphers eg German FO book, 'Satzbuch', naval cipher between Madrid and Berlin, Austrian cipher, etc.'[122]

A few surviving documents have allowed us to gain a few impressions of what it must have been like inside Room 40 and we have made mainly brief acquaintance with the foibles, pedigree, personal charm or otherwise, injuries, date of death and even cryptographic skill of a few of its inhabitants. There were many more members of staff of both Room 40 and MI1(b) about whom we have no more than a record of their name on a 'tea-list' or in a staff address book. Often, where names occur on more than one list, there are spelling differences, so that it is not always possible to be precise about exactly who was and was not a member. It is even less clear when it comes to assessing who did what and how well. Apart from the handful of end-of-war CVs, we have only a few hints. In the next chapter we will look at some of the techniques used to 'reconstruct' codes as mentioned in this and previous chapters.

Chapter 12

Codebreakers

From mid-1916 the volume of German army wireless traffic started to grow significantly as wireless sets became lighter and more commonly available. New codes and ciphers were developed, often for specific purposes. Special very short codes, for example, were devised for battlefield spotter aircraft directing artillery fire (such as just a map grid reference and a command to shell it). In the early years of the war the German army commonly used transposition ciphers (see Chapter 4) to keep communications secret on and around the battlefield. But from the middle period of the war the German army increasingly used codes, rather than ciphers. This was partly due to a desire for greater security, and partly to the need for a less complex means of communication for those under shell fire or during infantry, tank and aircraft attack. Well-designed codes were quicker to use, less prone to error, made messages much shorter (by replacing a phrase of several words with a single codeword) and, if used properly, could afford greater security. The instructions from a German army codebook, *Schluesselheft* ('key book') reminded users, 'In front line positions the coding of messages is rendered more difficult by the battle conditions (hostile fire, exposure to weather, moral[e] influences). Experience shows that the troops are inclined to use "clear" without considering that this may often have serious tactical consequences. This must be avoided in all circumstances.'[123] According to a British intelligence report, 'From the evidence now available, it seems clear that during March 1917, the Germans realised the value of the information which could be obtained by us from their wireless signals and messages. At this period a radical change was made in the system of aeroplane and field station calls, so as to make it much more difficult to obtain information from them, while at the same time the use of a cipher for wireless messages was abandoned in favour of codes.'[124] So, from the middle of the war, the army's field cryptographic units and MI1(b) were faced with the new challenge of breaking codes without having captured a copy of the codebook.

Coincidentally, in the middle period of the war, some of the captured German naval codebooks that had been in service since the war started, or even earlier, were replaced (see Chapter 10). Room 40 was suddenly blinded to the plain language meaning of the new codewords. Some of these new codebooks were later captured (downed Zeppelins were a good source), but not all of them. The messages sent in such codes could only be read if the codebook was 'reconstructed' by intellectual effort. In later chapters we will also see the vital importance of German Foreign Office diplomatic codebooks. Some of these German codebooks were captured (such as those acquired in Persia when a German consul was arrested) but others were literally a blank book as far as the British codebreakers were concerned, and, like those facing MI1(b) and the army field cryptographic units, had to be reconstructed from scratch.

So, from the middle of the war, in the British army, navy and diplomatic cryptographic sections, the art of reconstructing a codebook more or less purely from intercepted, coded messages became an increasingly important skill. Unfortunately we have no good narrative accounts of the codebreakers working on their mundane daily messages. What we do have are a few working documents, including a couple of training manuals, that detail the techniques of codebook reconstruction. From these archival documents I have compiled a brief account of how the task was undertaken. The techniques are applicable whether the codebook was military, naval or diplomatic code, but the examples are mainly drawn from army documents.[125]

The biggest difference between an army field cipher and a diplomatic cipher was the number of codewords each contained. An air-to-ground communications code would have only a couple of hundred codewords, an army field cipher probably had around 2,000, but there would be at least 10,000 in a diplomatic code. Air-to-ground codes might have only two letters in a codeword, while field codes needed codewords with three or four letters (or numbers), and diplomatic codes used code-groups generally (but not always) made up of five numbers. Field codes may be easier to break as the smaller number of codewords means that each codeword is likely to reappear more frequently. However, this may be offset by more frequent changes of codebook (smaller ones being easier to update). A good secure codebook would ensure that all codewords were used and that all were used a roughly similar number of times. But in real life codes did display noticeable differences in the frequency of use of codewords. The codebreakers discovered that they needed to know the meanings of about 20 per cent of the codewords in a code to be able to decode messages effectively and to know about 50 per cent to be able to decode nearly all messages.[126] For field codes with about 2,000 codewords the codebreakers would concentrate on working out the meaning of codewords until they had gathered about 300 meanings. Then they would turn to attempting to decode all the messages they had accumulated.[127] This would provide a lot more useful solutions and allow more messages to be decoded.

Codebreaking required persistence, much repetitive and tedious work, and a few brief glorious moments of insight and intuition. As one of the codebreakers concluded, 'It is necessary to dig deeply as well as widely in the process of code solution, and one message, if worried as a dog worries a bone, will sometimes yield more marrow than several pages discursively scanned.'[128] The War Office concluded that 'research of this kind requires an active, well-trained and scholarly mind; not mathematical, but classical ... When once you have got together two or three men of the right class, they will soon map out the work [for] themselves.'[129] The universities were the obvious places to find such people. They had to be recommended by colleagues for their skills, as it was impossible to find individuals from society at large, there being no simple, single, straightforward means of identifying suitable people (though the army did use a specially designed crossword puzzle to identify likely candidates). As one military historian has concluded, 'The emphasis on classics as the school of thought, on learning through practice rather than theory, on the man of the right kind, were all characteristic of the culture of the British elite. ... Whereas codebreakers at least purported to view their own success as stemming from hard work and common sense, outsiders viewed them virtually as magicians. Cryptanalysts certainly tested the limits of military tolerance.'[130]

However, while Room 40 or MI1(b) could adopt such a strict outlook, the army's field cryptographic units had to be less choosy and to pick from the soldiers sent out to serve those who looked as if they might make a useful codebreaker. One military officer later described the cryptographers he had to liaise with in northern France: 'A rummier set of fellows I never came across in all my born days. It was not in the smallest degree possible to teach these wonderful fellows a scrap of discipline. You had to treat them as geniuses, and to expect from them the most erratic behaviour. ... They were men of all ages, one of them had been a schoolmaster, another was a stockbroker, a third was a designer of ladies' hats – a very rum bird – and the fourth was a solicitor's clerk. They lived together in a dirty little rabbit hutch, smoking pipes all day and all night, the hut being frightfully untidy, like themselves, and I don't think they looked upon washing or shaving as part of their day's serious work. But they were amazingly brilliant fellows – both as linguists and as mathematicians. As soon as a new code came along they pounced upon it like vultures on their prey, and stuffing their pipes with tobacco, and muttering new letters over and over again as they felt in their pockets for a match, they would wrestle with that new problem until they had made it clear as daylight.'[131]

***

The codebreakers would seem to have an impossible task. They are presented with a page of jumbled, apparently meaningless numbers or letters and have to derive some information with no idea of the meaning. In fact this is an exaggeration for no Allied codebreaker was ever confronted with an utterly new phenomenon. There was always some background information with which to make a start. The codebreakers had gathered a vast amount of knowledge of the German army or navy units ranged against them, their communication networks and the internal structure and content of their messages. This background knowledge gave the first insights into a 'blank' codebook, identifying codewords for names of army units or locations from their place in a message.

The codebreakers were also aided by errors of all sorts. A British intelligence report observed, 'Experience shows that no cipher or code can be completely "Fool-proof". This is especially true of field ciphers and codes, owing to the very large number of people to whom the enciphering and encoding are entrusted, very few of whom have had any previous experience of the work. Regulations and instructions, however detailed they may be, and however carefully worded, are bound to fail somewhat in practice.'[132] Many more mistakes were made whenever a new code or cipher system was introduced. This was useful as it undermined the effectiveness of frequent changes of code. In fact the high number of mistakes when a code or cipher was changed was often critical to the codebreakers, providing the initial clues when confronted with a new code.

In March 1918, the German army introduced what could have been a very effective system. It consisted of a brand-new codebook (using three-letter codewords), *Schluesselheft*, 'key book', for the whole army on the Western Front. The encoded messages were enciphered using a system based on a grid of squares and a keyword. Each army wireless unit had its own keyword and all units were to change all keywords daily. But a message sent in both old and new systems helped the Allied codebreakers to start the recovery of the new codebook revealing details of its structure. Also, the German operators, probably trying to recover the time taken using an unfamiliar codebook, did not bother to encipher the coded messages and about half of messages in the early days were sent un-enciphered.[133] As one British intelligence officer concluded, 'Mistakes have never been completely eliminated. Whether they can be so eliminated by means of an efficient system of control remains to be proved. Numerous as the mistakes are, they can generally be traced to lack of discipline and care on the part of the encoder.'[134]

Another factor which helped the codebreakers is something inherent in the nature of codes. Codes direct the user towards building messages constructed from the stereotyped language of the codewords for phrases. This is then accentuated by individual users who resort to a subset of familiar phrases remembered from the full range of those provided by the codebook.

So the same codewords appeared frequently and often in some sort of order or relationship. Even where the code explicitly provided several codewords for a very common single plain entry, such as *punkt*, full stop, operators would restrict themselves to using just two or three of the options provided. The British codebreakers also noticed that German operators plumped for pronounceable codewords, for example KAD rather than DKA.

However, the codebreakers could not depend entirely on errors. As one expert put it at the time, 'The would-be solver must possess a thorough knowledge of the language employed, not only from the point of view of vocabulary but also from that of a knowledge of all the peculiarities of its grammar, syntax and idiom and the peculiar phraseology, diplomatic, commercial or military, in which the messages are likely to be couched ... a highly trained visual memory which will help him to remember the look of a code-group, to recognize it on its reappearance, and to remember where he has seen it before, what its sequences were, and what theory, if any, he had formed about it each time it occurred. ... [the codebreaker] must possess the faculty of keeping anything from a dozen to twenty theories in his mind in order to build up a chain of coincidence and reasoning until each link fits into its place and forms a coherent whole.'[135]

***

The theory has it that once a cipher key has been broken, all messages enciphered with that key can be broken, but working out the meaning of one codeword in an unknown code does not help solve the meaning of other codewords. Practical experience with German codes soon disabused the codebreakers of this asserted security advantage of codes. 'It is astounding to anybody who has not actually worked on the solution how the discovery of one code[word] will lead to that of numerous others. One apparently insignificant word discovered in a practice message, and applied to other messages from different parts of the front, may yield between ten and twenty-five other codewords.'[136] The art of 'reconstructing' a code is based on close analysis of the relations implicit in adjacent strings of codewords.

All the messages and records applicable to the new code were gathered together and typed out so that the maximum amount of material could be 'brought under the eye' at any one time. The codebreakers' main tool was an index which they compiled, recording every time a codeword was used in any message sent in a particular code. When the meaning of a codeword was determined that too was added to the index. Very quickly the index would build up a record of the frequency with which various codewords were used. Obviously, the more messages intercepted in any particular code, the more accurate the index.

Table 12.1

Sample army field message

Sample message based on an army battalion's morning report, taken from an Allied training document:

An Division 105 punkt Abend Meldung 18-2-17 punkt (1) von 10 Uhr 25 Morgens bis 3 Uhr 30 Nachmittag 40 Schuesse schweren Kalibers auf Kartenpunkt M2 Planquadrat 5209 punkt (2) Fiendliche Flieger Taetigkeit gering komma 5 Flieger ueber Abschnitt 7A punkt (3) Wetter gut komma sicht klar punkt (4 bis 7) nichts punkt (8) 2 Unter-offiziere und 7 Mann schwer verwundet komma 10 Mann leicht verwundet punkt (9 bit 10) nichts punkt Gezeichnet Bataillon II/316 [end-of-message-codeword]

To Division 105 fullstop Morning report 18-2-17 fullstop (1) from 10am to 3 hours 30pm 40 shots of heavy calibre on map point M2 gridsquare 5209 fullstop (2) Enemy aircraft activity low comma 5 aircraft over Section 7A fullstop (3) Weather good comma visibility good fullstop (4 to 7) nothing to report fullstop (8) 2 non-commissioned officers and 7 men seriously wounded comma 10 men lightly wounded fullstop (9 to 10) nothing to report fullstop Signed Battalion II/316 [end-of-message-codeword]

The first step was to identify certain codewords from their position in the message. Messages usually started with sequences too, such as 'message number, date and addressing information' and ended with sequences such as 'fullstop, sender's-name, end-of-message-codeword'. The German for 'to' – *an* – commonly appeared at the start of the name of the person or unit to whom a message was sent. There were various types of opening and addressing used by different operators or units and it took time to build up the full range of possibilities. Existing knowledge was useful here, for example, knowing how particular units used letters or numbers to spell out names and addresses, or knowing how different users such as divisional commands or wireless administrative units formatted their messages. If a unit always started its messages 'to commander 4th division', or '5th division', etc, when the code was changed it was likely that the codewords for 'to', 'commander' and 'division' would remain in place in new messages (unless a systematic restructuring of the format of messages accompanied the new code). In the example message in Table 12.1 some of the start-of-message ('To Division 105') and end-of-message ('Signed Battalion II/316 end-of-message-codeword') material could soon be identified The codebreakers also learned that comparison of initial and final codewords often showed that the same codewords occurred at the beginning of some messages and at the end of others, leading the codebreakers to conclude that 'this will point fairly conclusively to the fact that these groups represent the units or persons sending or receiving the message'.[137]

The next step was to start looking at the text of the message, trying to identify codewords representing very common phrases, words, spelling-groups, numbers, punctuation marks and grammatical signs. Frequently used words would be searched for in recognisable combinations or places. *Punkt* (full stop) was the most commonly used codeword, appearing at the end of sentences, in formatted reports, and appearing with numbers and names, as in the example message. *Komma* (comma) was also very frequent, often appearing with numbers, but not at the end of sentences. The example message shows a typical formatting of a regular situation report with specific items being mentioned in specific order in every message (probably sent in identical format by several different units).

The sequences in which codewords appeared took on overriding significance. Numbers were particularly important in this sort of analysis. Those in the example message, with its repetitive formatting, are easily uncovered. But there were many other ways of identifying numbers and their values. *Bis* (to) could not end a message and was nearly always between two groups of numbers, such as 'four to five'. *Und* (and) was frequently used with numbers on each side, but could not begin a message and was sometimes followed by *bis*. *Uhr* (hour) sometimes occurred among numbers, but at other times was preceded, but not followed, by numbers (distinguishing it from *bis*). Other useful plain meanings, such as *von* (from), *zwischen* (between), are similarly restricted in their ordering. Such words and numbers were often used together in sequences, such as 'from 8 hours 40 to 10 hours 45 and between 11 hours 10 and 12 hours 20'. Numbers also appeared in addressing information – close attention to the parts of the message saying 'to 5th division' or 'to 9th division' not only revealed some codewords but also identified certain codewords as numbers.

This initial assessment of a new code would reveal several sequences of codewords that probably represented numbers or the words frequently used in conjunction with them (*Uhr, von, bis, Division, Bataillon* and so forth). Further logical analysis can help work out the plain values codewords representing numbers. For example, in specifying times of the day, the number before 'to' or 'between' will be lower in numeric value (in most situations) than the numeric value of the number that comes after it. The numeric value of a number preceding 'hour' must be between '1' and '12' and if there are two numbers in front of it, then the first must be '1' and the second must be '0', '1' or '2'. It should be pointed out that clock times in many codes were given using 12 different codewords to prevent this particular type of analysis. All the same, from long practice it was realised that if there were any numbers after 'hour' then there were 'practically certainly' '5', '10', '15', '20', '30', '40' or '50' and by far the most frequent was '30'. If there were two codewords, then the first ranged from '1' to '5' and the second invariably represented '5'.

Standard reports might reveal codewords for numbers quite readily. For example, in the sequence, *20 bis 30 Schuesse* (20 to 30 shots), the numeric value of the first number was almost invariably lower than the second. The example message also shows how formatted reports often gave section numbers in sequence, ie, starting with 1, then 2, and so on, and used in conjunction with surrounding brackets or other grammatical symbols, so giving a conspicuous set of codewords that unravels the plain meaning of several numbers. Weather reports where observers sent in returns of readings of atmospheric pressure, temperature, wind, humidity and conditions contained lots of formatted numbers often within specific ranges (so that atmospheric pressure would range from about 950 to 1040 millibars). Casualty reports could also be put to use. At one stage when the Italian army was reeling from a German attack in northern Italy, the German army transmitted information about the numbers of Italian soldiers captured. These numbers were correlated with numbers of losses known to the Allies and the codewords for several numbers worked out.

Having accumulated this mass of logical relations between sequences of codewords and any assistance offered by past knowledge of division names and the like, the cryptographers could then use logical reasoning, experience and intuition to work out what actual numbers were represented by what codewords. Knowledge of, say, the army divisions known to be in an area could give some numbers away. For example, if two codeword sequences – RQD-RIM-MFR and ADR-MFR-SXG – were found in two messages next to another codeword that is thought to mean 'division' and it is known that divisions 245 and 356 are in the area, it can be guessed that RQD = 2, RIM = 4, ADR = 3, MFR = 5 and SXG = 6, even though there is only one codeword in common.

By this stage the codebreaker has worked out a number of codewords that represent certain known numbers, identified codewords that represent unknown numbers, and identified several basic words such as *punkt, komma, und, von, bis, zwischen, uhr* and so forth. The next step requires from the cryptographer agile leaps of the mind based on a deep understanding of German military (or diplomatic) speak and an appreciation of the subconscious logic of language. 'It is at this stage of solution that the faculty mentioned above of being able to keep a dozen or 20 groups in one's mind at a time, with their sequences and context whenever known, and any theories that may have been formed about them when first encountered, will be most invaluable.'[138]

***

Very few codes can provide sufficient codewords to cover all situations. In such cases 'spelling-group' codewords would have to be used to spell out the word in syllables or (if unavoidable) letter by letter. For example, a code might spell out syllables with three-letter 'spelling-group' codewords, so that AWN-ZNH-KDR spelled out *El-ber-feld* (a place-name) with AWN being the spelling-group codeword for *el*, ZNH for *ber* and KDR for *feld*. These same codewords would reappear in different strings depending on the word being spelled out. So, *Felderwirtschaft* (crop rotation), could be KDR-BUL-SOM-MFZ-PYQ, representing respectively *Feld- er-wirt-sch-aft*. Or, *bereit* (ready) would be ZNH-JGY, representing respectively, *ber-eit*. The codebreakers learned to spot spelling-group codewords in coded messages by the same sort of analysis of codeword combinations as we saw used to identify numbers. It was found, for example, that when the same codewords often appeared in sequences of two, three or four, though not always in the same order, they were most likely to be numbers. But if sequences appeared in exactly the same order, it was almost certain that they would be codewords for spelling-groups.

Table 12.2

Codewords for spelling-groups

Note: three-letter codeword used for this example.

Plain	Codeword	Plain	Codeword
A	WIM	ber	ZNH
B	EDN	…	
C	MBU	el	AWN
…		…	
Z	GYT	feld	KDR
Ab	RFN	…	
Abt	TIL	ge	XAM
Abn	PQV	geb	RZE
Abt	EBQ	gebr	KCH

Once a few spelling-group codewords were broken, decoding became a sort of giant crossword puzzle. Context, frequency and background knowledge provided the clues. Spelling was supposed to be used solely for those few words within a message that could not be expressed by the use of the codewords provided. If used with abandon, spelling-groups became a highly vulnerable part of any codebook. But, as with so many rules that needed to be obeyed if the system was to be kept secure, this one was regularly broken. Operators often found it easier to spell words out rather than search for them in the codebook. The excessive use of spelling-groups was most common when codes were changed. Certainly when the German army first started to move from ciphers to codes there were inevitably many hiccups as the operators adjusted themselves to a quite different procedure. According to an intelligence report, 'To the person who has been accustomed to encipher his messages, the search for code-groups representing words may seem tedious. He will therefore prefer to spell out his message.'[139] The German cipher authorities, who had to rely on local commanders to enforce rules out in the field, were powerless to prevent this practice.

The codebreakers often depended on some inspiration to start the reconstruction of spelling-group codewords. Note that in the following examples, for ease of reading, I have used a single letter to represent the spelling-group codewords rather than three letters – so that in the first example X stands for a codeword of, say, XHW, Q for a codeword of QVU, and so on. An intelligence report noted, 'It would, for instance, be fairly simple to spot the translation of the sequence [of codewords] X Q V P Q V as L-o-n-d-o-n, of W B Z Z B D L B as C-a-r-r-a-n-z-a, of L J C F Q C F M as T-h-o-u-r-o-u-t, of X Q S S Y A Y Z Y as Z-o-n-n-e-b-e-k-e, of M D Q Q H Y A D Q Q M I Q Y Z as D-r-o-o-g-e-b-r-o-o-d-h-o-e-k, etc. etc., if these were likely to be referred to in the text.' Carranza was the Italian army's psychopathic chief of staff, Thourout, Zonnebeke and Droogebroodhoek (literally 'dry-bread-corner') are place-names.[140]

A glance at a German dictionary will show that many words begin with common groups of letters – *sch, schr* and *vor*, most notably. There are also many common word endings, such as *eck, lich* and *keit*. Indeed, the German word *Schrecklichkeit* (beastliness) combines *schr, eck, lich,* and *keit*. There are also many frequent pairings of letters in plain language German words, such as *au, ei, eu, ie*. Close study of words thus became important in working out the meanings of these types of codes. One German army field code seemed to the codebreakers to make frequent use of spelling-group codewords to spell out commonly used abbreviations (rather than using specific codewords for them). Sequences of codewords such as B W R W B and others were quite frequent. At first it was thought that these sequences must be words such as *neuen, neben, stets,* etc (new, beside, always). But then longer sequences were identified such as W B W R W B W, etc. One anonymous codebreaker had the hunch that W meant either *punkt* (full stop) or *bindestrich* (hyphen) and B R B stood for an abbreviation and meant either *r i r* (reserve infantry regiment) or *k t k* (*kampf truppen kommander* – battle troops commander). As was observed shortly after, 'This was a very slender thread with which to unravel a whole code, but in codes it must be remembered that "*c'est le premier pas qui coûte*" [it is the first step that counts] and upon this slender foundation the whole code was eventually reconstructed.'

All the occurrences of the *punkt/bindestrich* codeword were identified and the message texts were broken into blocks separated by this codeword. This, it was hoped, would indicate sentences or some other self-contained passages. These chunks of codewords were then analysed, as described above, to identify likely features such as numbers, common words (*Uhr, und, bis,* etc), names and spelling-group codewords. If several different wireless stations sent in short coded messages with the same stereotyped messages – such as *25 Schuesse auf Abschnitt* (25 rounds on section) or *Waehrend der Abend Stunden Flieger Taetigkeit gering* (during the evening hours little aircraft activity) – it became possible to start cracking the spelling system.

This process was aided by a serious failing in the code system. A number of commonly used spelling-groups – such as *in, an, ich, ist, es, da, ein, acht, und* – could form individual words on their own, or they could be used as part of a longer word. A single codeword, for example, represented *acht* when used to mean 'eight' as well as when used as a spelling-group in longer words (such as *Acht-ung*, attention. *Acht-en*, respect, etc.). Its meaning was first revealed using the techniques to work out logically the numerical value of codewords identified as numbers. From this start, the word *W-acht-me-ist-er* (sergeant) was then worked out. Others such as *Es-t-am-in-et, L-am-p-e,* and *Fl-an-der-n* followed. Having already worked out the spelling-group codewords for *k* and *t*, strings of letters such as *-kt——* or *-—-kt* were revealed. The codebreaker with a good knowledge of German and of military communications would soon conclude that these words were *taktisch* (tactical) and *kontakt* (contact). 'One of the most interesting words which helped in beginning to get out the spelling words in a new code was a sequence of groups in the order Q W X Q W X W. This turned out to be *B-a-r-b-a-r-a*, useful as the codename of a certain unit. The fact that the same word was spelt out in a succeeding message as *B-ar-b-ar-a* gave us [as well] the group for *ar*. Having got a possible *s* in the word *P-o-s-t* in another part of the code, we were soon able to identify another group as *S-a-tz-b-u-ch* (sentence/clause [code]book). From this point on all was plain sailing.'[141]

The spelling-groups *el, ber* and *feld* were recovered when a codebreaker was trying to complete the decode of the two-word sequence: W-*lue*-N-A and W-*ie*,-Z (I have again substituted a single-letter codeword again, A, Z and K respectively for this example to replace the full codewords, AWN, ZNH, KDR as given in an earlier example). Noting that the two words both started with the same spelling-group codeword W, the codebreaker hazarded a guess that this might well be *sch* and that the meaning of the words then might be *Sch-lue-ss-el Sch-ie-ber* (key slider, used by operators to work out cipher settings). This gave the meanings of rare codewords A and Z, respectively *el* and *ber*, as well as the more common ones for *sch* and *ss*. From *el* and *ber* the codebreaker went on to guess that the codeword sequence A, Z, K was *El-ber-feld*. This gave the meaning of another codeword, that for *feld* (field). This then helped work out the meaning of other codewords.

Table 12.3

Common spelling-groups

Ab	bis	des	er	gegen	mit	unter
Am	da	die	es	im	nach	vor
An	dem	durch	fuer	in	uber	wie
Auf	der	ein		ist	um	zu
Aus	bei					

The crossword-like skill could reach dizzying heights. It could even defeat instances where alternative codewords were available for commonly used plain meanings such as vowels whose repeated appearances would soon show up in frequency analysis. For example, in one code two different codewords, X and W, could both be used for *a*. So when presented with two sequences X K K X Q X T and X K K W Q W T the codebreaker guessed that the word was *apparat* (apparatus), helped no doubt by the knowledge that the unit sending the message was connected with the signals service and frequently had to mention machines and apparatus, but it was nonetheless an astonishing guess. Similarly, one codebreaker was presented with a partially decoded word, —*st*—*a-ast* and guessed that it would be *Justizpalast* (court of justice). Once a few spelling-groups had been filled in, more and more codewords fell to the players of this gigantic crossword puzzle. As one codebreakers' training book observed, 'When one clue seems likely to be a fruitful one, everybody should work at it until it either proves to be the right one or is definitely discarded as leading nowhere.'[142] One military historian concluded, 'Successful codebreakers combine the pedantry of the grammarian with the logic of the linguistic philosopher and the flair of a chess grandmaster.'[143]

***

Various techniques were developed to make codebreaking more difficult, such as 'dummy' codewords. These had no plain language meaning. They were intended to hide frequency counts and also to break up the relationships between codewords. Properly used, dummy codewords could disrupt this form of analysis. But this required well-designed cryptographic systems and tight discipline over their use. Instead, many operators simply chose to insert dummy codewords into messages with great regularity – such as every fifth codeword – or they simply used far too many. 'It is a mistake to think that excessive use of dummy groups will hinder solution ... Even if there is no regularity in their position in the message, their excessive use betrays their presence and does not hinder solution.'[144] Some operators even copied whole columns of codewords out as dummies. 'These hindered us for some time, but, as soon as we found out what was the matter, we derived great benefit from this practice' as the order of codewords and the structure of the codebook was revealed.

A US intelligence report from the Western Front in 1918 concluded: 'No code ought to be insoluble, given a sufficient quantity of material, a proper method of work, the necessary qualities in the would-be solvers, and sufficient time between changes of the codebook to admit of the reduction reaching such a stage as to yield information even if only fragmentary. In code as distinct from cipher a certain length of time must elapse before complete or even partial reduction is possible. The time taken is directly proportionate to the amount of material to work on, to the amount of outside information or of analogy with previous codes available, and to the number and experience of those engaged on it. ... A code is not solved in a day, nor even in a week, not even by a miracle. Complete reduction of a code can only be attained when every [codeword] existing in it has been used in messages. Nevertheless it is often possible ... to obtain a certain amount of very valuable information, even when only about a hundred groups are solved.'[145]

***

Codes could be made much more secure if they were 'two-part' systems with alphabetical listing of plain words/phrases etc, alongside a random or 'unsystematic' allocation of codeword (see Chapter 4). This type of code was considerably more difficult to reconstruct than 'one-part' codes which had both plain entries and codewords in alphabetical order (thus being 'systematic'). A two-part code was also sometimes known as a 'hatted' code in British cryptographic jargon – as if the allocation of codewords to plain meaning was done by picking the entries out of a hat. The German name was *Lotteriechiffre* (lottery cipher). These were 'the most confidential class of German diplomatic codes'. When first introduced it took some time for the British codebreakers to work out their nature. It 'was ascertained by means of messages duplicated in readable codes and discovered by the system of registration and cross-referencing [ie, indexing] and the preliminary work done by Fleet Paymaster Rotter on code 64, that these codes were unsystematic ... so each group had to be separately resolved [and had no connection] other than its context to other groups'.[146]

The only means of reconstructing such a code was by logical analysis and repeated trial and error. No doubt there were many inspired guesses such as those we have seen above, but most of the time they were wrong guesses, discovered to be wrong only after a lot of effort, then starting again, systematically analysing an unsystematic code. Given enough messages to work on, an expert cryptanalyst could perhaps work out the meanings of about five codewords of a hatted code in a day. But the diplomatic codebooks contained 10,000 or more codewords and it was essential to have worked out at least 2,000 codewords before messages could be read with good effect, and preferably to have 5,000. But, as the life of a diplomatic code was on average about 18 months before it was replaced, this could hardly make for any practicable dent into the code's security. A naval intelligence report observed, 'A wholly new codebook of 10,000 code-groups, all of them in effective use, is impossible to [re]construct; but suppose 2,000 to be in fairly constant use and that there are plenty of alternatives for each sense, it would need perhaps an average of 300 mentions of each code-group before the book was effectively compromised. German W/T traffic was about 1,200 code-groups a day; and a non-alphabetic codebook could theoretically have remained in force for two to three months before complete compromise could occur.'[147]

We have seen above that a lot of the rules that flow from the way language is structured mean that only certain types of codeword can follow or precede others. These rules can be built into logical equations: 'If A follows D and F comes before T, then A and F must be numbers and A must be greater than F.' The codebreakers were the sort of people who could juggle in their minds such comparatively complex strings of logical conditions and spot sequences that did or did not fit the rules. But even for brilliant mathematicians and linguists the number of such conditions that could be handled soon became too complex, even with the aid of scribbling on scraps of paper. This was the limiting factor – the time it took for the brightest brains of British universities to plod through trial and error assessment of guesses until either a condition was not met and the assumption had to be discarded or all conditions were met and a codeword solved. Today such operations are of course performed for us by electronic computers. But a century ago there were far fewer means of processing such logical operations.

It is now fairly well known that the world's first electronic computer, Colossus, was conceived at Bletchley Park to help decipher German messages during the Second World War. However, this story has become rather confused as Colossus was not employed to break the German *Enigma* cipher settings (or keys) but those of a far more secret and complex cipher machine, the *Geheimschreiber* or 'secret writer' (though many accounts still conflate Colossus and *Enigma*). There were other codebreaking machines developed at Bletchley Park, including the Bombe which was indeed used to break the *Enigma* cipher settings. It was an electro-mechanical machine, while Colossus was electronic, as were several other codebreaking machines with such names as Proteus, Dragon and Aquarius. Though much of the story has only recently been told, it has generally been assumed that the use of codebreaking machinery only began with the Second World War, though it is known that some elementary machines were used in the inter-war period (using electromagnetic telephone relays) to work on Japanese codes.[148] One important technical point is to note the difference between *codebreaking* and *decoding* machinery. The latter we met in Chapter 10 dealing with Room 40's first forays into diplomatic codebreaking, where a 'pianola' or punched card machine was used to *decode* messages once the cipher and code were already known. A *codebreaking* machine helped with the process of working out or reconstructing – 'breaking' – the code itself. The Second World War Bombe and Colossus machines were codebreaking machines.

Just a few hints have now been uncovered in Room 40 files at the National Archives to show that *codebreaking* machinery was actually first employed during the First World War. According to one document, on the history of Room 40's political/diplomatic section, 'It was not realised that this form [ie, hatted] code required special treatment until May 1916 when leave was granted to set up a special staff of educated women to work machinery by which the guessing process could be accelerated. By this method the [number of] guessed [code-]groups rose at once to twenty daily and by the law of increasing returns grew mechanically to a maximum of 100 per day by which time the cipher [actually a code] was approximately readable. In fact the reading of messages in such codes, which resemble those used by our Foreign Office, proved to be merely a matter of tedious drudgery for one or two experts and the staff of ladies trained by Miss Robertson.'[149] Their task was described as 'grinding groups out of the hat machine'.

This is the most important discovery from Room 40 files released over the last few decades. Unfortunately, there are very few other details, and no other references to these machines in any other documents that I have seen. There are a few references in some documents to 'machinery' (for example a reference to the 'machinery set up' by Ewing) but these are figurative uses, in the sense of 'the machinery of government' or the 'civil service machine'.[150] The hard machinery used by the codebreakers would have been a 'punched-card' machine. Punched-card machines had become fairly common in administrative, commercial and, to a lesser extent, scientific applications and could indeed handle repeated, elementary logical processing steps within limits. The job the 'hat machine' had to do was a complex one, working out possible codeword meanings. Such a machine might have to check all occurrences of that particular codeword in all messages received to ensure that it met the appropriate logical rules about its appearance in sequences with other codewords. The punched-card machine was thus being used as a prototype computer, performing logical processes that could be also be carried out by humans with pen and paper, but on quite a different timescale. This machine radically accelerated the process of codebreaking. Suddenly it was possible to reconstruct hatted codes in a practicable timescale. This revelation brings the birth of mechanised codebreaking forward to 1916.

The first hatted code to confront Room 40 came into use in March 1915, code number 6400. Rotter started work and this was carried out, 'on the ordinary lines' (ie, without the aid of a machine), over the winter of 1915/16, but progress was slow. From May 1916, code 6400 became the first hatted code to be worked on with the aid of the codebreaking machine and the code was soon readable. When the German Foreign Office took the code out of use, in the winter of 1916/17, Room 40 and its machines had worked out half of the 10,000 codewords. Codebook 6400 was followed by 5300. Material sent in the code began to accumulate in the autumn of 1916, messages being sent between Berlin and Greece and also Berlin and Madrid. The German operators did not make the mistake this time of transmitting messages in both old and new codes, so the early stages were hard work. The code was used with a 'subtractor' cipher adding to the difficulty of breaking it. According to Young, the combination of code and cipher was so difficult to break that it would have remained unreadable had it not been for the earlier break of 6400. Other hatted codes included 53, 39, 42, 2700, 7600, 9751, 6937, 9972 and 9572, though several of these were variations of each other.[151] Another important hatted code was number 7500 (see Chapters 13 and 14). Young reckoned that some 13,000 German code-groups had been correctly guessed by the diplomatic section in the first year and a half of its life. Each word involved an average of three guesses. 'This implies a missing word competition for a year and a half with an average of 70 guesses daily.'

The women and their machinery, housed in Room 229, also dealt with neutral messages. By 1918 they were handling German, Austrian (with Room 57), Turkish, Bulgarian, Spanish (with Room 47) and other codes. American codes were the province of the team working in Room 54. Room 47 was set up under Lord Lytton to tackle items such as intercepted mail from neutral countries that were suspected of being in code or cipher. Within 18 months Hall and Young had turned the unit into a sophisticated, partly-mechanised, diplomatic codebreaking unit. Room 40's diplomatic work uncovered German espionage and sabotage plans. The machine breaking of Code 64 'made it possible to defeat German intrigues in Spain, Portugal, Ireland and Morocco, including a series of risings in the latter country; and to keep His Majesty's Government in touch with their diplomatic activities in north America and southwest Europe'.

A fearsome new weapon was unveiled in the middle of 1916 on the battlefields of northwest Europe – the tank. Around the same time another new tool of war was also first deployed – mechanised cryptanalysis. Both tank and decrypting machine are symbols of the intensified prosecution of the war by the Allies and their determination to find ways round the stalemate of the war on all fronts. Ironically, it is possible that the codebreakers of the time did not see this machine as a great advance, merely as a drudge that saved a bigger drudge. Some indeed saw such machines as a drawback. One First World War cryptographer, in the inter-war period, observed, 'Quite early on tabulating machines had been brought into use and while in certain circumstances they were of great use, they did, in my opinion, a great deal of harm as many idle people thought they relieved them of personal indexing; this, I think, led to failure to solve many of the hand codes as contrasted with machine types.'[152] It is also noticeable that no one added their experience of working with machines to the CVs discussed in the previous chapter, yet from his work it is certain that Montgomery must have been closely connected and probably Nigel de Grey too. The CVs were designed to show how essential their authors were to the post-war successor to Room 40 and MI1(b), how intelligent and skilful they were at devising means of breaking codes by the dedicated application of their brain power. To be associated with the simplistic mechanistic plodding of machinery was hardly conducive to achieving this aim.

In an address to the British Association in 1931, Ewing said, 'More and more does mechanical production take the place of human effort, not only in manufactures, but in all our tasks … Almost automatically the machine delivers a stream of articles in the creation of which the workman has had little part. He has lost the joy of craftsmanship, the old satisfaction in something accomplished through the conscientious exercise of care and skill.'[153] One wonders if Ewing was here thinking in part at least of the machinery which started to change the workshop codebreaking unit which he had set up into a faceless bureaucratic section of a bigger operation in which the individual counted for little, managing machines that mindlessly churned out codeword meanings instead of sweating over them like some gigantic crossword puzzle. It is, of course, also quite possible that he was just an old man expressing surprise and disappointment at the way the world he had helped to make had turned out, having perhaps entirely forgotten Room 40's early contribution to the mechanisation of codebreaking and information processing, if indeed he knew of it at all. Today, in the light of the remarkable invention of the ultimate plodding but fast machine – the electronic computer – we attach more credit to those who conceive and build such machines.

Chapter 13

The Spanish Interception

In the late 1560s, Queen Elizabeth I's position on the throne of England was threatened by the arrival on English soil of Mary, Queen of Scots, chased out of Scotland after a rebellion by Scottish nobles. Mary, in some eyes, had a more legitimate claim to the English throne than Elizabeth. She was also a Catholic. Mary represented a serious threat to both Elizabeth's life and to England's Protestantism. All the same, Elizabeth would not countenance anything more than keeping Mary under house arrest, even though she became a focus of discontent for English Catholics and less favoured magnates, as well as attracting support from the Vatican, France and Spain – all embittered enemies of Protestant England.

By 1585, England's relations with Spain – the greatest maritime imperial power the world had ever seen – had deteriorated to a state of open war with Spain's widespread colonies in the Americas and the Far East. Mary welcomed the prospect that Elizabeth's navy might be defeated by a much superior maritime force. There had already been some plots to unseat Elizabeth and replace her with Mary (eg, the Ridolfi Plot in 1571/72 and the Throckmorton Plot in 1582). So in 1585, as international relations deteriorated, the security conditions under which Mary was held were tightened to minimise the chances of her communicating with Catholic conspirators and Spanish invaders. An austere Puritan, Sir Amias Paulet, was appointed Mary's new warden and delighted in being her direct daily antagonist. He worked hard at his task of preventing Mary from communicating with the outside world and declared, 'I cannot imagine how it may be possible for them to convey a piece of paper as big as my finger.'[154]

Elizabeth's foreign affairs secretary and 'intelligence chief', Francis Walsingham, did not intend to remain a passive gatherer of intelligence, but set out to entrap Mary.[155] He used a renegade priest to open up an apparently secret communications channel for Mary but had her letters diverted to his own codebreaker, Thomas Phelippes, the son of a London customs officer. Phelippes was described by Mary as 'of low stature, slender in every way, dark yellow hair on the head [marked] in the face with small pocks, of short sight, thirty years of age by appearance'. His special skills were first employed in Paris in 1578 where he helped the English ambassador to decipher some intercepted correspondence. Phelippes was a gifted linguist, with an excellent command of French, Italian and Latin, though his Spanish was somewhat less fluent. His skill uncovered a plot to assassinate Elizabeth ahead of a Spanish invasion of England to which Mary gave not just support, but also offered advice on how to ensure that she would end up taking the throne. Phelippes deciphered the incriminating letter and passed the plain language copy to Walsingham, recommending him to arrest Babington, Mary's correspondent in the plot, immediately. But Walsingham wanted to wait. He did not yet know the names of the other plotters. He wanted the communications channel to serve up more intelligence. He told Phelippes to forge a postscript to Mary's letter asking Babington the names of the other plotters. This ruse was not successful and the plot was launched. However, it never got off the ground and the plotters went on the run, soon to be caught and executed.

Walsingham was not a nice man. Torture was a standard tool of interrogation (if threats of it did not encourage co-operation). Bribery, blackmail, intimidation, arrest and imprisonment, enticing of crime and barbaric punishments were his day-to-day practices. Double-agents provided him with some of his most important coups, such as the tricking of Mary into providing evidence of her support for plots to kill Elizabeth. This is Walsingham's most renowned piece of skulduggery. But of greater importance perhaps in strategic terms was his providing Elizabeth and her naval commanders with priceless advance intelligence of the coming of the Spanish Armada. Walsingham had set up a wide network of agents across Europe to report on any information that might help build up a picture of Spanish plans and allies. He also planned all sorts of operations aimed at disrupting the enemy's preparations. One involved challenging the authenticity of Spanish bills for loans in Genoa where ships were built and supplies acquired. In those days, long before the telegraph (let alone computerised finance), validating the bills could slow down for months the financing of Spain's purchases of materials for building its fleet and its armaments. Such tactics successfully delayed the sailing of the 'Enterprise on England' from 1587 to 1588. When the Armada did sail, its approach to English waters was observed by a screen of fishing boats and land-based observers who reported to the naval commanders on the size, composition and speed of the fleet. A central theme of English history is the story of how the Armada passed up the Channel, enduring one clash with the waiting English fleet, stopped overnight off the coast of Flanders (where it was supposed to pick up troops for the invasion of England) and was attacked by English fireboats, then scattered as it ran for safety up the east coast, around the north of Scotland, only to be struck by storms and wreckings on the coasts of Ireland. Of the 130 Spanish ships and 15,000 men that set out, only 35 ships and 6,000 men returned. Spain's position as the leading maritime power was damaged for at least a decade, while English (and Dutch) maritime trade flourished.

***

William Reginald 'Blinker' Hall has often been compared with Walsingham. Both were extremely energetic intelligence chiefs and consummate plotters. Both were ruthless men determined to make use of the intelligence they gathered to attack and confuse the enemy. But both were also good administrators. Walsingham set up an almost recognisably modern intelligence organisation with interception of communications as well as spies, a specialist codebreaking unit, and a 'special operations' branch. Hall turned Ewing's cryptographic unit into an intelligence centre, integrating it with the Naval Intelligence Division to very good effect. Hall was born in 1870. His father was a Royal Navy officer and became the very first Director of Naval Intelligence.[156] The family link with the navy stretched back to the end of the 18th century, so it was little surprise that Hall found himself joining the navy – as was the fashion – at the age of 14. He was promoted to sub-lieutenant by the time he was 20. Family connections and hard work earned Hall useful promotions, getting his first command in 1901 and becoming a captain in 1905. He developed a reputation for running a smart, efficient and disciplined ship, but he also showed a progressive side to his character, opening the first cinemas, bookshops and chapels to appear in navy ships (all of which became accepted features). He could be ruthless with suspected malingerers, who were soon transferred, but took a paternalistic interest in his crew, earning their loyalty.

His ship's gunnery was exemplary. As fast firing was viewed as the pinnacle of naval excellence, Hall was doing the right thing for an ambitious officer. In 1913 he was rewarded with command, under Admiral David Beatty, of one of the navy's brand-new massive battle cruisers, *Queen Mary*. Within a couple of months of the war starting, however, a stomach illness prevented Hall from continuing in a sea command. This happened just as Henry Oliver was promoted to be the navy's chief of staff. Hall filled the empty position, being appointed Director of Naval Intelligence in November 1914. If Hall had remained captain of his ship, then in all likelihood he would have been one of those killed at Jutland when the *Queen Mary* exploded because the bomb-proof doors and hatches between the gun turrets and shell stores were kept open to ensure speed of firing.

Some of Hall's exploits have been frequently recounted in books over the past few decades, often based on his own unpublished 'autobiography'. This was written with the help of a ghost writer who recorded in a letter to Hall how he saw his job: 'You may not have realised yet how much embroidery there will have to be. I shall of course supply this, but equally of course only after I have got the framework from you.'[157] Most of these events are pretty much generally outside the scope of this book, but there is some material about codebreaking. What is not certain is how much of the detail is true and how much made up. One story that is not sourced to Hall himself, however, is his alleged role in planting the idea on Admiral von Spee that there were no British warships at the Falkland Islands in late 1914. This lured Spee to the island where a powerful British squadron had just arrived. Hall left us a few hints as to how information was at times planted. Hall did claim that one navy agent was employed to go to lunch with neutral diplomats at a 'gentleman's club' in St James's and quietly pass on snippets of useful information. According to Hall disinformation was passed on by 'men who in more normal times would have laughed at the idea that they could ever be of any conceivable use to a branch of our Intelligence service'.

Hall claimed to have planted on the Germans, 'some time' after the spring of 1915, a false British codebook, due to be used only in a national emergency, the Secret Emergency War Code. It was taken to Rotterdam by British agents and sold to the German consulate for £500. The seed was allowed to germinate in late 1916 when the war was going though a bad phase for the British army and a diversion was needed. Messages were sent out in the Secret Emergency War Code relaying orders about a planned British invasion of Belgium. Not all such intriguing worked entirely as planned. When Hall had disinformation earlier spread to Germany about British plans for an invasion of Belgium, the Netherlands or Germany in late 1914, it led to German defensive measures and troop movements on the North Sea coasts that were detected by British military (ie, army) intelligence. They knew nothing of Hall's games and suspected a potential German invasion of Britain was being planned.

One incident that is reasonably well documented illustrates Hall's ruthlessness and his willingness to abuse his position in pursuit of his personal views. During 1916, Room 40's wireless interception stations picked up a total of thirty-two German wireless messages, most of them between Berlin and Washington, concerning German support for nationalists in Ireland. The war had put a stop to all political developments in Ireland, especially any discussions of Home Rule. The obstacles to any durable solution were pretty formidable even before the war; now they seemed even greater. But some currents within Irish nationalism saw in the conflict an opportunity to accelerate independence through an armed rising. Britain's resources were stretched and the government's attention distracted, so if it gained popular support a rising could be effective. However, one nationalist leader, Sir Roger Casement (son of a Protestant father and Catholic mother), doubted that an Irish revolt could succeed unless it could count on the support of the Germans. He negotiated for arms and ammunition and a treaty was drawn up in 1915 promising material support. The Germans too were unconvinced of the prospects for the uprising and as 1916 drew on they scaled back their support, promising 100,000 rifles, but in the end actually only dispatching 20,000 (and they were captured Russian rifles in poor condition). Room 40 intercepted messages from early 1916 which gave details of these plans. Some messages between the German ambassador in Washington and the Foreign Office in Berlin related that the rising was due for 23 April, Easter Saturday. It also said that arms would be dispatched from Germany and gave the codewords that would be used to start or to cancel the operation. The rifles and ammunition were due for delivery, by a converted German steamer disguised as a Dutch boat, to a remote Irish bay on Good Friday.

Casement, who was in Germany, also had to be conveyed to Ireland by a German submarine, along with two colleagues. The ship carrying the arms set sail on 9 April from Luebeck. On 15 April, Room 40 intercepted a message from Nauen enquiring 'whether German auxiliary cruiser vessel, which is to bring weapons to Ireland has actually …'.[158] The message was garbled but its meaning was clear. A submarine with Casement and colleagues as passengers set sail on 12 April, but it was damaged and sent a wireless message saying that it had to return to port. This gave Room 40 an indication that Casement was on his way. He left Germany again, in U-19, on 15 April. The arms-carrying ship arrived at Tralee Bay on 20 April but made no contact and sailed off to wait. Here it was met by British warships. The German commander scuttled the ship as it was being escorted to harbour. Casement landed at Tralee Bay on 22 April, but was arrested within hours. The rising took place but failed to capture widespread support and was brutally crushed by the British army. Casement and many other rebels were condemned to death.

There is a coda to the story involving Hall, though not Room 40. A widespread campaign took place in Britain and America for Casement's death sentence to be commuted, with several US newspapers backing his case. Casement had been a British consul in Africa and South America for nearly 20 years. During this period he campaigned against the abuse of native labourers and on his return to Ireland in 1911 he became sympathetic to Irish nationalism. He was well known in the USA as a campaigner for human rights. His supporters also claimed that he had returned to Ireland in the U-boat in order to counsel his compatriots against the revolt, though this is doubtful.[159] As the campaign gathered force it looked possible that he might escape the noose. This angered Hall who saw Casement as a traitor, plotting with the enemy while so many died dreadfully in the trenches and at sea. Hall had the means at hand to sway opinion against Casement. In the words of William 'Bubbles' James, 'for some years Casement had been addicted to unnatural vices and had recorded his experiences in a diary'. The diary was among the papers seized when Casement was arrested. According to James, Hall saw to it that Casement's homosexuality did not remain secret. 'Typewritten copies of pages of the diaries and photographic reproductions of specimen pages were circulated in London clubs and the House of Commons, and were seen by journalists who were known to be sympathetic to Casement and by signatories of the appeal for Casement's reprieve, whilst the appeal was pending.' The US ambassador in London, Walter Hines Page, when shown the copies, said, 'Forgive me, but I have a luncheon engagement today and if I read any more, my host and his guests will think that I have been taken suddenly ill. One needs a strong stomach to eat anything after reading this.'[160] After the story was made public, support for Casement drained away and he was duly executed. The weak-stomached US ambassador in London said of Hall that he was 'a clear case of genius. All other secret service men are amateurs by comparison.' Hall's proclivity to leak secret intelligence for political purposes resurfaced in the post-war period when he was a 'die-hard' right-wing Tory MP.

***

Since Walsingham's times England had become part of Great Britain and Great Britain had become the centre of a world empire. Spain had lost its American and eastern empires, and was no longer a significant power, but a backward, troubled nation. In the First World War, it was Germany that was Hall's target, not Spain. But Spain's role as the major neutral European country and its development as a hub of German wireless and cable communications ensured that it became a focus of operations both for Room 40 and for Hall's adventures. Each side in the war wanted Spain's support in one way or another, so they cajoled and bullied the Spanish government. Each side saw Spain as a vital theatre for espionage, counter-espionage, sabotage, overt and covert propaganda, so tensions were imported. The country was pulled apart. Internal dissensions intensified and became increasingly intertwined with disputes over Spanish policy towards the contending alliances, leading to constant political crises and culminating in revolution in 1917.[161] As one historian has written, 'The Spanish governing classes struggled in vain to keep the country free from the conflict. The official neutrality of the state did not save its political system.'[162] In some respects the war was good for neutral Spain. Short supplies of Welsh coal meant that domestic coalfields were developed. Mineral mining and steel manufacture were also stimulated. Short supplies and high prices paid by desperate buyers in other countries meant that profits boomed. But inflation took off and overall industrial production went down as owners extracted high profits on goods in short supply. Some regions did better than others, with some suffering from increased industrial militancy. Parliamentary government became ever more precarious. Between 1914 and 1918, 65 Spanish ships were sunk by German submarines, adding to the nation's woes.

Spain already faced severe internal political schisms, persistent economic woes and a prolonged, messy colonial war in Morocco. In 1912 the prime minister had been assassinated and in 1913 an attempt was made to kill the king. Some Spanish factions, especially the king, his court and the army, and conservative 'Carlists', were pro-German. Some others, such as the 'liberals' (representing business interests), tended to favour the Allies. But even those who sympathised with one side or another wanted to remain neutral. The working and peasant classes were desperate to improve their standard of life. Others wanted to modernise the creaking system of governance in Spain. Some were absorbed by the struggle between the church and secularism, or by regional versus national sentiments. Yet others dreamed of a renewed Spanish Empire. None saw involvement in the war as a good way forward for promoting their cause. One exception to this general rule was Conde (Count) de Romanones, leader of the liberals and, from late 1915 to 1917, prime minister. A political progressive, he was really interested in modernising Spain's economy and political system. He was thus naturally closer to parliamentary democracies such as Britain and France than to monarchical states such as Germany and Austria. Romanones was also a major shareholder in mining industries of Morocco and coalfields in Spain. The output of these extractive industries went to France and supported the Allied war effort, so he had an interest in supporting the Allies. He thought that global economic realities meant that the Allies were likely to win. His policy was to be as helpful as possible to the Allies, but to keep that secret from public opinion and to pretend that he was pursing a policy of strict neutrality. This made him the object of hate in the German embassy in Madrid and in Berlin at the Foreign Office. Germany helped sustain a vicious campaign against Romanones, aiding his many enemies in Madrid's court, military and political circles. The period of Romanones's premiership roughly coincided with months when Germany was reconsidering the introduction of unrestricted submarine warfare during 1916 and early 1917. Room 40's intercepts illustrate how this wider issue slowly entangled itself with Spanish politics. Eventually, in early 1917, Romanones came close to breaking off Spanish relations with Germany, but instead the prime minister fell to a coalition of otherwise incompatible internal forces, encouraged by German money and propaganda.

Romanones tried to let the Allies know that he was on their side, but they received his message coolly, concerned that the instability of Spanish politics could easily lead to a new government at any time. The Allies wanted some dramatic concrete action, such as the seizure of all German merchant ships sitting out the war in Spanish ports. Romanones's diplomatic sympathy offered no such immediate practical help. In the words of one Spanish historian, 'The relative passivity of the Western Powers contrasted with the ruthless determination and forceful methods of Germany and her friends to ensure that Spain never abandoned the position it had adopted at the outbreak of the war.'[163] During 1916, Germany toughened its attitude to Spain, engaging in sabotage and propaganda, attacking the interests of the Allies and Romanones's administration. Some 70,000 Germans lived in Spain. But Germany's most useful tools were its supporters among the court, military and Catholic circles. On 27 January 1916 intercepts revealed that 'representatives of all those institutions assembled at the German embassy in Madrid to celebrate the Kaiser's birthday and express their sympathy for Germany at that critical time'.[164] The conservative Carlists and army officers were encouraged to rebel or to disobey orders if Spain took any action in favour of the Allies.[165]

Germany set up local propaganda bureaux in important neutral countries that could source pro-German press material. The German Foreign Office had a *Zentralstelle fuer Auslandsdienst*, Central Office for Overseas Service, run by Matthias Erzberger, which distributed books, pamphlets, films, poetry, and photos as well as funding newspapers and magazines. Plenty of German money was paid to sympathisers and to pro-neutrals, so long as they were against the government. Germany even funded Spain's anarcho-syndicalists, hoping a militant working-class audience would be influenced by propaganda against pro-Allied 'capitalists', accusing them of being responsible for the 'orgy' of exports which was the 'real cause' of their impoverishment. As 1916 drew on, a publicity campaign was launched to prepare public opinion for the reintroduction of unrestricted submarine warfare. The attacks on Romanones intensified in December 1916, shortly before the fateful decision was taken by the Kaiser and his closest policymakers to risk renewed submarine attacks.

The Spanish section in Room 40 was led by Lord Herschell, a friend of the Spanish king and familiar with courtly circles across Europe. The bulk of the transcripts, stored in the National Archives, of naval and diplomatic decodes from Room 40, from 1915 onwards, are printed on to pre-prepared forms. It is clear from the files that several carbon copies could be made and the printing is well-defined and clear, not like most typewriter output. Also, the typing is faultless, with no re-typing. These have the feel of a machine-printed document or of a power-assisted typewriter, but this is speculation. The contrast of these multi-typed decodes with the handwritten ones in a bound ship's log book (containing the messages cited in Chapter 1) shows the rapid expansion and modernisation that Room 40 underwent during early years of the war. The prepared forms are pre-printed in red ink, with 'Most Secret' in large type in the middle of the top of the page. More red printed sections at the top of the page allow for entry of information such as time, cipher, wavelength, addressing information and a Room 40 number for the message. Below this information (which was often not fully filled in) the lines of the message are typed in blue ink between feint red lines printed on the page. The fact that several copies could be made indicates that this was the way in which Room 40 distributed its intelligence to the few senior naval officers or diplomats allowed to see its output. Interestingly, the transcripts are verbatim translations without significant comment, background or interpretation. There are occasional references to previous messages or technical comments, but that is about all. There was also no attempt to hide the fact that it is a transcript of an enemy wireless message. This contrasts with the way in which MI1(b) used to prefix its transcripts with the message that the information came from 'a reliable source' and did not refer to ciphers or wireless signal wavelengths.

The intercepts revealed the full extent of German activities in Spain. One very useful feature of the intercepts was the way they gave details of German spies and agents. For example, in May 1916, the military attaché in Madrid was informed that 'Agent Lago has been despatched … to Paris with fresh instructions. He has been told to communicate with you only in the case of utmost urgency. In this event he will telegram from France as arranged with his sister-in-law in Madrid, Madame de Ilanos, who will bring the report in clear to be forwarded by telegram to Berlin.'[166] In June 1916, the German embassy in Madrid was informed of an agent, Arnold, on his way to Spain to organise the destruction of ships transporting iron ore from Spain to Britain. A perplexed embassy queried in reply that the ores were always carried on neutral Spanish ships, so did the agent's instructions mean that the ban on attacking neutral ships had been lifted?[167] Another example, from 4 October 1916, revealed to the British that a German agent, known as South III, was considered 'quite reliable [and] he has been since May in Spain where he directs an intelligence service in France. He is 1.79 metres in height, slender (brown-haired and brown-eyed), 24 years of age and speaks the Berne dialect. You should instruct him to come here [Berlin] if possible for fresh instructions, via Holland, as he is compromised in Switzerland and Italy.'[168] The intercepts often gave details such as the address of family or espionage contacts in Spain or other countries.

The intercepts also revealed details of sabotage planned to be carried out in France and Portugal by agents from Spain. On 31 May 1916, Room 40 decoded a message from the General Political Staff of the Foreign Office in Berlin sent to the German military attaché in Madrid. It reported the arrival in Spain of an agent instructed to organise 'further undertakings' against Portuguese factories, French hydro-electric plants, French roads in the Pyrenees and iron ore shipments from Spain to Britain. 'You should apply for such moneys as are required for these enterprises; [agent] A will travel further after three or four weeks.'[169] Madrid enquired of Berlin, 'Please give further particulars as to the water-works in the Pyrenees whose destruction would be most important and whose surroundings make such an undertaking possible.'[170]

A plan to equip a group of North Africans with boats and arms in order to raid Morocco was also uncovered by the intercepts. Plenty of warning of the raid and its personnel was given. In June 1916, an intercept revealed that a German agent (of unknown nationality) had been sent to Morocco. The local station master who was supposed to introduce him to people interested in insurrection proved not to be of much use. Of his contacts 'some of them were entirely unknown, some of them quite unusable and some of them unwilling to accept the Agent's proposals'. The mission soon ended as the agent was arrested after fourteen days.[171] An intercept revealed that the Germans had 'given up on' another local agent, Muley Hafid, who had taken money but done little to fulfil his promises. Instead Abd El Malei and Raisuli were recruited to lead an action planned for October to land a party on the North African coast and damage French interests. Details of the financing and other agents were also revealed.[172] The plot's ups and downs were traced over the months. On 7 October 1916, the embassy in Madrid reported to Berlin that 'all is ready'. The decode revealed that the raiders had plenty of rifles, but were short of cartridges. They also needed to be sent a copy of cipher 604 for communication with Madrid.[173] Three weeks later another intercept revealed that seven men, four machine guns, 1,000 rifles, plus ammunition and 50,000 francs were about to be sent to North Africa, but, 'We have got the impression from Hiba's communication that the enterprise has been betrayed … In order to mislead the French, we suggest that without betraying the present change of plan, a message should quietly be sent to Hiba to inform him that the enterprise has been postponed until a better season, when a landing will be made at Arksis.'[174]

Portugal began the war in turmoil, with the ruling classes divided over which side to support. A military coup in January 1915 put a pro-German ruler in charge, but he was ousted by a democratic rebellion in May 1915. Fearful that if it did not ally with France and Britain, it would lose its colonies in Africa in a post-war peace settlement, the new government veered towards the Allies. In February 1916 the government seized German and Austrian ships that had taken refuge in Portuguese ports at the beginning of the war, so in retaliation Germany and Austria declared war on Portugal in March 1916. In early June 1916 a message from Graf (Count) Ratibor, the German ambassador in Madrid, to Berlin proposed a form of extreme sabotage. 'In order to close the Spanish-Portuguese frontier and make communications difficult between Portugal and the Allies, I suggest contaminating at the frontier with cholera bacillus rivers flowing through Portugal. Professor Kleine of the Cameroons considers the plan to be perfectly feasible. It is necessary to have two glass phials of pure culture, which please send when a safe opportunity occurs.'[175] The idea was quickly dismissed by the Foreign Office in Berlin, though poison plots were undertaken by the Germans to damage the trade supplying ponies from South America to Britain. Another intercept on 11 October 1916 indicated how Germany intended to prosecute its war with Portugal, a country so far away and so difficult to get at. 'It is intended to produce a National rising of elements which are discontented with the present condition of affairs against the Republican government, which is dependent on England.' Germany was to have no official connection, but would fund the rebels. 'I propose,' said Ratibor, 'to begin with 200,000 pesetas and consider myself authorised to grant, apart from this sum, bonuses for the destruction of factories, etc.'[176] As it turned out, German manipulation was no more successful in prompting rebellion in Portugal than it was in North Africa.

The intercepts also revealed regular German intelligence reports from observers in Spain. A typical example comes from 6 October 1916, when it was reported that 116 steamers left Huelva with an average cargo of 2,700 tons of copper ore pyrites: 58 of the ships were British, 29 Spanish and they were mainly destined for Britain and France.[177] Such intelligence reports were intended for onward transmission to German U-boats who would then attack the shipping if possible.

Room 40 was also able to pick out useful information about German plans for acquiring and transporting supplies, discovering the names of companies set up to buy or ship goods anonymously and about the routes they used. There was also plentiful information about German financing of Spanish supporters and some deserving impecunious Germans stranded in Spain without income. One message, on 25 May 1916, revealed that Berlin was in the process of setting up a line of credit for six million pesetas with Spanish banks to be guaranteed by Deutsche Bank.[178] In October the Berlin government was demanding economies and care with spending as it was proving difficult to acquire pesetas.[179]

This sort of information, about sabotage plots, agents, purchasing, transportation and financing, could be used to take counter-action – arresting spies, thwarting purchases of supplies and seizing goods en route. But in the political and diplomatic arena measuring the effectiveness of intelligence is extremely hard. Whether things would have turned out any differently in the political sphere without Room 40's access to these detailed intercepts is uncertain. The reports of the political situation submitted by the German embassy in Madrid tend on the whole to be hyper-pessimistic, occasionally hyper-optimistic, and seldom realistic. Clearly the people behind these telegrams are intensely wound up, only too ready to burst into a long moan or complaint. It is also clear from German messages that they often misunderstood the situation, having a strong tendency to take anything other than whole-hearted support as an expression of outright opposition. In these reports, whatever happened in Spain was caused by either Allied or German manipulation. Thus, when railway strikes broke out in Spain in mid-1916, the German ambassador reported back to Berlin that they had been instigated by the British, who were supposed to want a political crisis which would allow them to present an ultimatum to the Spanish government demanding more concrete support for the Allies.[180] No doubt Allied intelligence agencies also interpreted the intercepts according to their own prejudices, but at least they were presented with unequivocal evidence of the German view of the political situation in Spain. An intercept of 12 September 1916 made the German position clear. The 'danger lies in the personality of Romanones. His removal however from the Spanish ministry by regular means is all but impossible. The clipping of his wings would have to be done through the king, but with the utmost prudence, as otherwise consequences are to be feared.'[181]

As the German high command moved steadily towards the resumption of unrestricted submarine warfare in the Atlantic, the opportunities for direct conflict with Spain grew. Anyway, Germany's restrictions on sinking of neutrals did not apply in the Mediterranean, so Spanish ships were already at risk. The propaganda war became more vital. An intercept from September 1916 reported how Ratibor believed that 'the enemy's propaganda is succeeding in convincing wider circles of the inevitability of our defeat. In consequence there is a great depression and even partial defection in circles friendly to us … The success is generally attributed to the abandonment by us of the submarine campaign.' Previously friendly merchants were reported to be shunning German clients. 'Military circles, which formerly spoke openly of refusing to act against Germany, now say that they will do what they are told in a case of conflict.'[182] Ratibor reported to Berlin in early October that Romanones was making every effort to influence national sympathies against Germany's submarines because of their effect on trade. Germany needed to blame the Allies for leaving it with no choice but to sink neutral ships. The sinking of Spanish ships was the fault of the British and the greedy ship owners. The situation facing Germany was different from that facing the Allies. They could still trade across the seas and oceans. Spanish ships could, for example, sail to Britain with Spanish fruit, but not for Germany in the north or to its allies in the Mediterranean. So Germany saw it as only fair that it should be able to prevent ships, any ships, from delivering oranges and other fruit to its enemies. And, if the threat to Spanish trade with the Allies led to terror and fear among the population, so much the better. 'Public opinion is much alarmed. Our campaign in favour of neutrality is prospering,' telegraphed a momentarily euphoric Ratibor.[183]

The fruit trade was critical for the economic survival of many small farmers and fruit trading and processing businesses as well as shippers. The Spanish government tried to persuade the Germans to allow safe passage to Spanish fruit ships sailing to Britain. Germany's response was to offer immunity from submarine attack to these ships en route to Britain – but only on condition that Britain permitted an equal number of fruit ships to sail to Germany.[184] If Spain wanted its special protection, then it would have to persuade the British government to allow a breach in the blockade of Germany. No doubt the German government knew that the British would not agree to such an arrangement, but it thought that it had neatly pushed onto the Spanish the task of approaching the British for permission to allow ships to take fruit to Germany and at the same time thrust the responsibility for final refusal of safety to Spanish fruit ships onto the British. The negotiations dragged on. The Spanish put off an approach to the British, while the Germans nagged on at them to demand British acquiescence.[185] At one point Ratibor, passing on an enquiry from the Spanish, asked Berlin whether 'onions will count as fruit for the purposes of safe conduct, but not raisins, almonds or dried figs?'[186] Berlin was not in the mood for expansive gestures. 'In consequence of the war on commerce which England began ... Spain must see in our concession regarding fruit-ships an act of exceptional friendship and of consideration for its poorest classes. It is impossible to go further out of consideration for our own people.'[187]

As the year ended a momentous decision was taken by the German military high command (which had become the effective government of Germany) that unrestricted submarine warfare would be reintroduced at the end of January 1917. The beginning of 1917 was fateful for Spain too. Romanones offered the king his resignation as prime minister, but the king refused to accept. This was a manoeuvre, designed to strengthen Romanones's position as the choice of the king on his re-appointment. On 11 January the German naval attaché in Madrid sent a report – using a private code that could not be read by the German ambassador, but which could be read by the British – to Henning von Holtzendorff, chief of the *Admiralstab*. Holtzendorff was one of the strongest proponents of using submarines to attack neutral and enemy shipping. The attaché told him that 'the ministerial crisis is treated by the [Spanish] press as a farce ... The result of this is that we cannot in any early future expect a ministerial change. A distinct cooling off is noticeable among our partisans.'[188]

The German concerns about Romanones's bias in favour of the Allies reached a crescendo around this time. The German Foreign Office feared the consequences of neutral reaction when the decision on submarine warfare became known. Romanones, complained Ratibor to Berlin, was 'allowing a steadily growing quantity of war material and raw material to be exported [to

Britain] to compensate for exports [to Germany] which he has embargoed'.[189] The fear was that the announcement of unrestricted submarine warfare would give Romanones the opportunity to abandon Spanish neutrality. As long as he remained prime minister they would remain fearful. However, Ratibor was reluctant to use force to overthrow the Spanish premier. 'So much has been gained by the wrecking of prestige of Romanones that the taking of any violent measures might be too much risk.'[190] Romanones's premiership was to stagger on, pressed in on all sides by conflicting domestic and external interests, until June when an unholy alliance of leftist workers and rightist army officers, clerics and Carlists led to his final downfall. He was replaced by a series of short-lived administrations that were inclined to be rather more sympathetic to the German position than he had been.

Before leaving Spain on the eve of the renewed campaign of unrestricted submarine warfare, it is worth noting some intercepts relating to cryptographic matters. A note added by Room 40 to a message, number 1016, sent on 22 May 1915 from Madrid to Berlin, read 'Telegram 1060 is a fictitious telegram,' adding that telegrams 1061 and 1079 were also fictitious. 'These refer to messages to be sent in [cipher] 064, a partly readable cipher, containing false news and intended to deceive the French who are supposed, probably erroneously, to be able to read it.'[191] The intercept revealed that the Germans had become aware that the French knew that instructions had been sent to the German naval attaché in Madrid to set in motion plans to prepare to destroy German merchant ships stuck in Spanish ports since the start of the war (for fear of Romanones giving into Allied demands to seize them). Also the French appeared to know something about the 'Cartagena affair' (referring to a visit of submarine U-35 to the Spanish port) and about some of Germany's intrigues in Morocco. At first it was feared that the cipher – which had been in use continuously since April 1915 – had been compromised.

In an attempt to fool the French, and trick them into some pointless action or put them off the scent, the German embassy sent the fictitious messages to Berlin hoping that the French would intercept them. On 29 May, Room 40 intercepted a message from Berlin with a sternly worded reply to Madrid's report of a possible compromise. 'If the French government,' spluttered the German Foreign Office, 'has obtained a knowledge of your ciphers it can only be through treachery or through insufficient precautions. Your excellency will receive three new keys, which are to be employed in turn. ... Your excellency should keep the new keys in your personal charge, in your pocketbook or purse, and on the despatch or receipt of telegrams should supervise the ciphering yourself or through your deputy, and then resume possession of the keys. All telegrams received by you should be burnt immediately after deciphering. Ciphered secret correspondence should be kept in your personal charge.' The intercepted message then gave the three new keys: 'Key number

11: 371, 107, 416, 923, 514, 235. Key number 12: 237, 916, 721, 184, 352, 618, 531. Key number 13: 614, 247, 814, 324, 657, 347, 506, 134.'[192] These were keys for use with a 'slider' as a 'subtractor' cipher. The sender of the message was right – the breach of security was due to a lack of sufficient precautions. But he was wrong about the sort of precautions that were missing. And he was crassly mistaken in sending out the new keys by wireless. Room 40 was no doubt saved a lot of effort by that error.[193]

Madrid replied in equally terse vein: 'In the opinion of my informant the leakage has taken place in Berlin.'[194] Ratibor also said that the compromise must have occurred in Paris because the information was known there at the same time or even before the German officials in Madrid had been informed. 'We must in my opinion consider the auxiliary personnel concerned with general papers and to whom the secret papers are not accessible, but who, owing to their temporary employment in the office, are in a position to get an insight into what is going on and obtain possession of bits of messages … The fragmentary and partially false information of the French secret services strengthens the suspicion that the traitor is a subordinate and is himself an incompletely informed person.' All the same, even though the ambassador did not think that the cipher itself had been compromised, he proposed some changes to the way the 'Schieber' or 'slider' was used to encipher the most sensitive of coded messages by reversing the order of the numbers on each of the three sliding pieces. The telegram even went on to explain that this meant that 'the first row would read 457, the second row 665 and so on'. A code wording at the beginning of a message would indicate this reverse technique was employed on a particular message. The intercepted message also (helpfully for Room 40) provided the proposed code wording: 'Is Considered Secret'. This angry conversation, and the showering around of details of cipher keys, must have been particularly amusing to Room 40. Not only did the codebreakers get access to useful cipher material, they were also able to watch German Foreign Office officials get themselves into a completely unnecessary panic about the possible compromise of the cipher to the French. Room 40 commented on one transcript that the German belief that the French had broken the cipher was mistaken. There was another cipher scare concerning the French just a few months later, in October 1916. The embassy in Madrid reported that a French agent 'informs me definitely that particulars have been obtained from Berlin which enable them to get knowledge of our cipher communications', although apparently the then-current cipher used between Madrid and Berlin was not yet compromised.[195] But this concern did not stem the flow of secret messages or the supply of code and cipher details over the airwaves. Over the next week or two several more messages were decoded by Room 40, giving details of ciphers.

Chapter 14

'Most Secret, Decipher Yourself'

In his secret history of the German naval war, written immediately after the war and based on intercepts and other intelligence, Frank Birch posed a rhetorical question. How, he asked, did it happen that 'the United States, genuinely the most disinterested participant and undeniably moved to defend the highest principles, yet entered the war at the moment when, her trade endangered, neutrality ceased to pay and emerged from it the only profiteer among the belligerents?' In November 1917, just after the Bolshevik revolution, one of its leaders, Leon Trotsky, provided his own answer to Birch's question. 'The United States began to intervene in the war after three years, under the influence of the sober calculations of the American Stock Exchange. America could not tolerate the victory of one coalition over the other. America is interested in weakening both coalitions and in the consolidation of the hegemony of American capital. Apart from that, American industry is interested in the war ... Exports go almost entirely to the Allied countries. When in January Germany came out for unrestricted submarine warfare, all railway stations and harbours in the United States were overloaded with the output of the war industries. Transport was disorganised and New York witnessed food riots such as we ourselves have seen here. The finance capitalists sent an ultimatum to Wilson: to secure the sale of the output of war industries within the country. Wilson accepted the ultimatum, and hence the preparations for war and war itself.'[196]

The First World War was a battle between empires. The USA saw itself as a non-imperial country despite having its own imperial holdings. It had taken the states of Texas, New Mexico, Arizona, Louisiana and California from Mexico between 1845 and 1848. Then, in 1898, it purchased Cuba and the Philippines from the declining imperial power of Spain. It also started its own minor colonial wars, with military incursions into Mexico, in both 1914 and 1916. The invasions were prompted by the desire of Woodrow Wilson, the US president, 'to teach South American republics to elect good men'.[197] In 1916, Wilson ordered General John Pershing to lead a punitive expedition into the territory of its southern neighbour. In true Western tradition the Yankee troopers were charged with hunting down a violent outlaw, the Mexican revolutionary leader, Pancho Villa, who was responsible for ransacking the US town of Columbus, New Mexico. Unlike the films, however, this real-life incursion was a flop. Villa and his forces faded into the lushly vegetated and intensely mountainous Mexican landscape. Even Villa's domestic political opponent, President Carranza, was pushed close to retaliating against the invading US forces. They were quietly brought back home in early 1917 as German-US relations went into free fall. The poor performance of US troops in Mexico was one reason why the German high command was not overly concerned at the prospect of America joining the Allies and was consciously willing to risk war with the USA. In July 1916, Room 40 intercepted a message from the German ambassador in Washington to Berlin, assessing the US performance in Mexico. 'It becomes clearer and clearer that the American government has drawn back from a rupture because her military resources are not sufficient to face a war with Mexico.'[198] Obviously, a country that was unable and/or unwilling to risk war against a state such as Mexico constituted only a minor worry for Germany.

The US president, Woodrow Wilson, was an Anglophile, taking bicycling vacations in the Cumbrian Lake District before he was elected president. But Wilson was determined to keep America out of the Europeans' war. He was appalled by the war and saw it as a disastrous imperial adventure. He faced an election in 1916 and appreciated that his chances of success depended on being seen as the man who would keep America out of the conflict. Anyway, even if Wilson had wanted to declare war it is most unlikely that he would have found either public or congressional support. A war in Europe, most Americans felt, need not affect them very much. America was protected by the great wastes of the Atlantic and Pacific Oceans. Yet, America had become too big a country for it to remain untouched by the rest of the world. It was faced with the rise of Japanese power and influence in the Pacific and East Asia. The prospect of a military rapprochement between Mexico and Japan – which could bring the aggressive Asian state to the borders of the USA – added to Wilson's woes. And the war could not be wholly ignored. There were areas of policy where, whatever decisions the USA made, it would upset one side or other. If the USA denied loans to the Allies, then it would lead to their bankruptcy and military defeat. If the USA gave the Allies loans, which were then spent on arms and ammunition and so forth in America, then it would damage Germany and its partners. Wilson's legalistic neutrality reflected an asymmetry that benefited the Allies (whose outlook was dominated by another asymmetry – German occupation of Belgium and parts of France). Germany's arguments were ignored by Wilson, infuriating the German military. They saw their soldiers being bled to death by Allied supplies from the supposedly neutral America.

By late 1916, the German high command had convinced itself that the resumption of unrestricted submarine warfare was the only way it could now win the war. The apocalyptic battles of Verdun and the Somme had shown that armed assault, however gargantuan, could not break well-emplaced armies. The great clash of the fleets at Jutland, with only a few minutes of actual firing during the long hours of chase and manoeuvre, ensured that the German navy could not again risk a meeting of the fleets. The German response was born out of frustration. The army had conquered enemy territory, but the German nation was being bled to death in a ghastly struggle to hold on to those conquests. It could have solved the problem by retreating from Belgian and French territory, but then the German people would demand to know why they had lost so many young men for a pointless military adventure. The solution was sought in the submarine. Although Germany had called off its earlier half-hearted attempts at submarine warfare in the Atlantic (but not in the Mediterranean), it had built many more submarines and it seemed as if the country had sufficient numbers of raiders to make a submarine blockade of Britain a reality. The civilians within German policymaking circles worried that renewed submarine warfare would bring the USA into the conflict against Germany. The military countered that the USA, with its pathetic little army, could well enter the war, yet that would not matter because Britain would be knocked out within a few months. Both Ludendorff and Hindenburg were sure that they had to act soon and that the longer they delayed, the greater the chances of Germany's defeat.[199]

Thanks to intercepts of US diplomatic communications by MI1(b) and of German communications by Room 40, the British government was able to watch the developing diplomatic struggle between Germany and the USA. One of only very few hints as to the circulation of Room 40's diplomatic intelligence within the British government comes from a diary entry made in early 1916 by Maurice Hankey, the Cabinet Secretary (and a key figure in British policymaking). Significantly, after the war Hankey marked the entry as not suitable for inclusion when his diary was being edited for publication as a book. He wrote, 'I saw Captain Hall again first thing this morning. He showed me more of Colonel House's telegrams sent from Berlin ... I found that Hall has not shown these telegrams to the First Lord [Balfour]. This information is of course priceless.'[200] Colonel House was Wilson's personal envoy, sent to seek out conditions for peace. Unfortunately, we have no hard evidence of how the British inner circles of policymaking used – or did not use – this priceless intelligence, except in the case of the Zimmermann telegram. We do know, however, from the files of intercepts that full, detailed transcripts of the diplomatic rumblings were available.

***

The US ambassador to the court of St James, Walter Hines Page, was a firm supporter of the Allies and repeatedly argued for US involvement on the side of liberal parliamentary democracies against the autocratic regimes of Germany and Austria (the autocratic member of the Allies, Russia, was conveniently not mentioned). A dispatch, intercepted by MI1(b), of 25 January 1916, is typical of many of his reports. He argued that a 'draw' – that is, with Germany remaining in possession of its 1914 conquests – would not bring about a stable peace, as both sides would remain armed and in a state of readiness for renewed war. Great Britain, he predicted, would have to withdraw from the Pacific, leaving the USA alone to deal with an increasingly aggressive Japan. 'Permanent peace depends on the two great English-speaking nations ... we [in the USA] are the larger in white population and potentially the stronger of these nations and peace cannot be obtained without our active sympathy with the smaller empire which is spending its resources fighting the assault of a military monarchy on a free Government. If we accept the forthcoming blockade, as England accepted our weaker blockade of the Confederate states [in the US Civil War], we shall save the world from the aggressive ambitions, both of Germany and Japan.'[201] During the American Civil War, Britain had stepped back from trying to breach the Unionist blockade of Confederate ports despite generally backing the southern states in the war. Now was the time to return the favour. Many such missives were sent to Wilson from Page during 1916, but Wilson was not listening; indeed, he may well not have bothered even reading the dispatches. As historian and diplomat, George F. Kennan, wrote, 'Wilson was largely his own Secretary of State insofar as the formulation of policy in major questions, [and] he shared with many other American statesmen a disinclination to use the network of America's diplomatic missions as a vital and intimate agency of policy.'[202] For advice on war diplomacy, Wilson preferred to rely on his personal envoy, Colonel Edward House, an old buddy.

The messages from the US ambassador in Berlin, James Gerard, have a different tone. The German Chancellor, Bethmann-Hollweg, in an interview in March 1916, had told Gerard that peace could only come about under certain conditions. 'Germany must have back all of her Colonies and an indemnity for the surrender of northern France. About the Belgians he was vague but Germany would probably consent to give up most of it ... [but before that was possible] he said he hoped America would do something against the English blockade and so create a better impression in Germany. The Chancellor seemed in favour of good relations with America and for a reasonable submarine war but he will have great trouble.'[203] In fact, there was very little prospect that Bethmann-Hollweg could have persuaded the German military high command to relinquish its grip on northern France. He could not have delivered such a peace. But again, there is doubt here too about whether Wilson took any notice of Gerard's words. Wilson thus failed to hear the messages being sent by both the Allies and the Central Powers.

In May, Gerard's report of a talk over lunch with the Kaiser was intercepted by MI1(b). Wilhelm had been in an angry mood and started by asking the US ambassador, 'Do you come like a Roman pro-consul bringing peace in one hand and war in the other?' Gerard replied that any differences between the two countries could be sorted out. At this the Kaiser 'began a speech' and accused the USA of a 'rough and uncourteous tone'. He took objection to Wilson's description of Germany's method of warfare as 'barbarous'. As 'Kaiser and Head of the Church in his country he had endeavoured to carry on war in a knightly manner ... [but] the opponents of Germany had used weapons and means which had compelled him to resort to similar means ... [the British starvation blockade] justified any methods of submarine war and that before he would permit his wife and little grandchildren to die of hunger he would utterly destroy England and the whole English royal family.'[204] If Wilson appreciated the extent of the Kaiser's frustration with the British blockade he did nothing to show it. The intercepts revealed the two countries were talking to one another, but it also became clear that they were not listening to what the other was saying, each having their own incompatible agenda. An interesting side note comes from another MI1(b) intercept which revealed that, behind the scenes, Germany's position was winning support from the Vatican, according to US sources. The 'Vatican states that America can stop the war in twenty-four hours if it would act as it professes with complete neutrality and stay all trade with the Allies. This would seem to confirm the opinion frequently stated that the Vatican sympathises' with the German position.[205] This intercept was not the only one to show the Vatican promoted a peace which would allow Germany to retain its conquests.

A long intercepted message sent in September 1916 from the German Chancellor, Theobold von Bethmann-Hollweg, to the urbane and Americanophile German ambassador in Washington, Count Johann von Bernstorff, illustrates the evolving discussions in Berlin. Despite victorious battles with the Russian army, 'It is, however, still doubtful if we shall succeed here [in Central and Eastern Europe] in attaining a success which would terminate the war in the course of this year; we must therefore reckon for the present with a longer duration of the war. In connection with this the Imperial Navy promises itself by a ruthless resumption of the avoided submarine [warfare] in view of the economic position of England a rapid success which will make the arch-enemy England in a few months more inclined to thought of peace. For this reason the High Command of the Army has had to include a ruthless submarine warfare in its measures, (with a view) among other things also to relieve the position on the Somme ... the whole situation would, however, be changed were the President [of the USA] ... to make a proposal for peace ... [but this must happen soon if Britain was not to] improve her military and economic position at our expense.'[206]

Although influential circles in Berlin were determined to resume full submarine warfare, the German ambassador in Washington, Bernstorff, was keen to avoid war with the United States, which he thought would be a disaster for Germany. He could see that the German military high command failed to understand the potential of America if roused to war. Bernstorff worked hard to avoid a breach in relations. He argued against military and commercial sabotage operations carried out in the USA and Canada by German agents, organised and paid for through the German embassy. But he was ignored and a number of bombs were set off in US factories. The military attachés had their own codebooks, which were different from the diplomatic codebooks used by the ambassador, so they could communicate with Berlin about their planned operations without letting Bernstorff in on the secrets (though of course intercepts revealed much about these sabotage operations to the British). He had no control over these operations, but it fell to him to explain and defend the actions to American officials, politicians and the public. Just as Woodrow Wilson turned a deaf ear to his ambassador in London pleading for support for the Allies, so the German high command was in no mood to listen to its own ambassador's case for restraint. It saw its only option as more aggression.

Bernstorff's popularity with the diplomatic and fashionable circles of Washington and New York made the military commanders contemptuous of him. Late in 1916 the British press published a photograph of Bernstorff in a swimming costume, his arms around two women in similar garb. The photo was probably acquired and circulated by British intelligence in an attempt to belittle Bernstorff's reputation in the USA and thus undermine his attempts to achieve a deal with the USA. The public humiliation was taken up by Bernstorff's many enemies in Berlin.[207] But for the time being, his favour among the Americans served the purpose of keeping the USA from getting too close to the Allies while Germany built up the number of U-boats in its submarine fleet. In the meantime Bernstorff would have to string the Americans out. 'Germany is anxious to make peace,' said an intercept of 25 September 1916 from Gerard in Berlin to Wilson in Washington. 'I can state on the best authority that if the President will make an offer of mediation in general terms ... that Germany will accept in general terms immediately.'[208] But this was only a bluff. By the end of 1916 the Allied blockade was beginning to bite. Though not tight enough to damage the German war machine, the blockade combined with inflation, harvest failure and an excessive spending on armaments to push the German economy into crisis and to set off a collapse in civilian morale. Germany became more insistent that America do something soon to relieve the blockade. The pleas were followed by threats. Bethmann-Hollweg told Colonel House and Gerard on 22 November, 'If his suggestion that Germany wanted peace should be continually ignored, Germany would be forced in response to adopt hard measures, but this would not be Germany's fault ... What do these matters in Belgium matter compared to the hecatomb of [German] lives lost on the Somme since last July?'[209]

The foreign minister, Gottlieb von Jagow, a firm opponent of unrestricted submarine warfare, was sacked in November 1916. His replacement was the first non-aristocrat ever appointed to the post, Arthur Zimmermann. Wilson, mis-advised by Colonel House, thought the change of personnel actually signalled signs of compromise in Berlin. According to the historian Barbara Tuchman, House and Wilson 'believed they saw in the promotion of Under-Secretary Arthur Zimmermann the signal of an upsurge in liberal forces that would open the way to peace and the salvation of the world. ... [Zimmermann] was a big, ruddy, good-humoured, square-headed bachelor of fifty years with blue eyes, reddish blond hair, and bushy moustache, the very epitome of the German middle class, although his middle-class origin he had contrived partially to remedy by an approved duelling scar on his cheek.'[210] In fact Zimmermann got the job only because he backed the military and he only kept the job as long as the military command were prepared to have him there. He saw that power in Germany was moving towards the anti-liberal forces. So, Zimmermann cast in his lot with them, hoping for personal promotion. He did initially express fears about the consequences of adopting unrestricted submarine warfare, but soon moulded himself to the dominant mood.

Gerard, as an intercept revealed, reported how Zimmermann had angrily demanded American action against the British blockade. Zimmermann told Gerard that if America should join the war against Germany 'there will be half-a-million trained Germans in America who will join the Irish and start a revolution'. Gerard reported that at first he thought Zimmermann must be joking, but soon realised that he was truly in earnest. Gerard responded that in that case 'there are half-a-million lampposts to hang them on'. Gerard was advised by the Germans to go home and speak to Wilson directly to convince him of the need for a change in US policy. Wilson put off making any serious peace moves until late in the year, after the election was out of the way, and did not hear Germany's increasingly shrill tone. Bernstorff, under pressure from the military, begged Wilson to respond to Germany's expression of support for a declaration of peace 'in general terms' to stave off the final adoption of unrestricted submarine warfare. Safely re-elected, Wilson finally asked the belligerents for declarations of peace on 18 December. But by then it was too late: the German decision had been made (though it was not formally approved by the Kaiser until early January 1917).

Nine days after Wilson's proposal, Bernstorff met Colonel House and asked him for a favour. To help him communicate in detail about Germany's response to Wilson's initiative, Bernstorff said it would be useful to have access once again to the US diplomatic telegraph channel. Bernstorff told

House that he was reluctant to put his proposals through the State Department because the secretary of state, Robert Lansing, was biased towards the Allies and was prone to leak information to the disadvantage of Germany. It had already been made plain that Germany would have to disown the peace initiative if it became public. But if a secret channel could be used to Berlin, Bernstorff would facilitate direct communication between the Kaiser and the president. Wilson agreed to allow the channel to be used – but only for communications about the peace initiative. Lansing objected strenuously. He would have to suffer the indignity of having German messages coming in and out of his department in a code which he could not read. He would be cut out of the discussions between Bernstorff and House/Wilson. It was true that, as Bernstorff complained, Lansing was biased towards the Allies. He continued his resistance even after the principle of opening the channel was approved by Wilson. He had to be personally ordered by House, in the president's name, each time the channel was used. At one point Bernstorff even had to complain directly to House about the obstacles presented by Lansing. Germany, he threatened, would not be able to pursue the peace initiative 'if the State Department takes this attitude'.[211] This was, of course, not the only communications route open to Germany. The Swedish Roundabout could get messages to the Americas and in some cases this route was used. But it was slow – taking as long as a week or two. The State Department channel by contrast could carry messages between the Foreign Office in Berlin and the German embassy in Washington within two or three days.

Wilson had laid down the condition that the route only be used for messages related to the peace initiative. But by then the German military leadership had already decided that it was ready to risk certain war with the USA. The Kaiser went along with the high command and the decision was formally approved to resume full submarine war, including attacks on neutral ships, commencing on 1 February 1917. The newly re-opened US communications channel would be very handy for sending out instructions to German embassies to prepare for this dramatic step and its implicit intensification of the war – rather than messages about the peace proposals it was supposed to carry.

***

In mid-January 1917, German Foreign Secretary Arthur Zimmermann drafted – or had drafted for him – a telegram that was to be sent to Bernstorff in the Washington embassy. It was not the first time Zimmermann had had to draft a very important diplomatic telegram. In the crisis days of July 1914, in the absence of the then Foreign Secretary, von Jagow, Zimmermann had the job of drafting the telegram sent to Austria promising Germany's full support in whatever action Austria took over the assassination of the archduke in Sarajevo.[212] This promise of unqualified backing is often blamed for propelling the world into the war – though of course Zimmermann did not decide the policy. The same was true in 1917. Though he gave support to the reintroduction of unrestricted submarine warfare, he did not make the decision. His telegram to Washington would again be expressing his masters' orders. It was a long telegram – when coded it had 856 codewords in all. In it Zimmermann informed Bernstorff of the decision to resume unrestricted submarine warfare. He was not to tell Wilson until the day the campaign was launched so as to ensure the maximum shock. Drafting this telegram was Zimmermann's main task, one set him by his superiors. But he also decided, apparently on his own initiative, to draw up a second telegram. This is the message which has become known to history as the Zimmermann telegram. It was addressed to the German minister in Mexico. It instructed him, in the event of war starting between Germany and the USA, to approach the Mexican president with an offer of an alliance, making joint war on the USA with the objective of recovering for Mexico its lost territories of New Mexico, Arizona and Texas. It also suggested that the Mexicans should attempt to bring Japan into the alliance.

On the surface it must have seemed like a good idea. Germany had friendly relations with Mexico. Mexico had friendly relations with Japan. Both Mexico and Japan had frictions with the USA. If this triangle could be exploited, then the USA would have its attention drawn away from Germany's renewed submarine warfare in the Atlantic and towards its southern border and eastern coast. But it must be emphasised that this Mexican adventure was an afterthought.[213] One historian concluded that the idea of an alliance with Mexico 'was more likely intended for use in the political struggle between government and military in Germany rather than as a serious treaty proposal to Mexico'.[214] But the idea fitted in with the mood in German military circles, which already thought of the USA as an enemy. Approval was gained only informally from the military high command for this second telegram. The military commanders probably had no interest in, or hopes for, the initiative. It is possible that the Chancellor, Bethmann-Hollweg, was not even told about the proposal for a belligerent alliance being sent to another nation state. All eyes were focused on preparations for unrestricted submarine warfare.

The draft of this second telegram went through several stages, passing up and down through ranks of interested officials in the German Foreign Office. The Zimmermann telegram – only 150 codewords in all – would be tacked onto the end of the first telegram. This was a much longer telegram, with some 850 codewords. A general comment is necessary here. Much has been written about the sending, interception and decoding of the Zimmermann telegram. It now seems that much of what has been published is misleading, with much of the blame being due to Blinker Hall. One of the two men who decrypted the Zimmermann telegram, Nigel de Grey (see next chapter), later wrote, 'Many of the statements made by Admiral Hall are incorrect. Some were I think wilfully so.'[215] Hall threw out quite a few bits of misinformation – with the good intention of protecting the real source – and these snippets have been widely repeated, building a legend similar to that created around the origins of Room 40. In recent years, however, new documents have been released in Britain and research by historians in Britain, Germany and the USA has brought other information to light. The present view of events differs in several ways, some significant and some minor, from the previous standard accounts (provided by writers such as Barbara Tuchman and Patrick Beesly).

Having drafted his messages, Zimmermann had to make some technical decisions about how he would get them to the addressees and what codebook(s) to use. The first plan was to deliver the two telegrams by submarine. The U-35 was conceived as a blockade buster, a freight-carrying submarine rather than an attack vessel. It had already visited the USA twice, the second time as recently as 2 November 1916, partly to transport goods, but also as a propaganda exercise. Its westbound cargo was designed to show off Germany as a powerful and compassionate nation, carrying 750 tons of dyestuffs and medication for use against poliomyelitis. It also delivered a new diplomatic codebook, number 0075, for use by the embassy in Washington. A third voyage for the submarine was scheduled for mid-January. However, the imminent announcement of submarine warfare made that rather awkward and the trip was cancelled. The sub-sea freighter was sent off to the shipyards to be converted into an offensive submarine. Wireless was not a practicable idea as any messages could be intercepted. Contrary to the legend, the Zimmermann telegram was not sent by wireless, nor the Swedish Roundabout route. Instead, a single copy only was sent and that was via the US State Department channel. The US channel would get both of the telegrams to Washington and from there the Mexican telegram could be forwarded on commercial telegraph lines without interference by the British.

The second technical matter was the choice of codebook or codebooks. There were several different codebooks used by the German Foreign Office, but the ones that interest us here are codebooks 13040 (sometimes known as 13042) and 7500. While 13040 had been in use for some time, 7500 was comparatively new. Indeed, as we have just seen, it was delivered to the German embassy in the USA by U-35 only in November 1916. As soon as it arrived in Washington it was brought into use for secret communications between Bernstorff and Berlin. And it was immediately worked on by Room 40 using the techniques described earlier (see Chapter 12) to 'reconstruct' a blank code. The first of the two telegrams – that advising Bernstorff of the renewal of unrestricted submarine warfare – was considered the most sensitive. If the date were leaked, it would undermine the shock effect. It might even allow for diplomatic and military counter-measures. As 13040 had been in use by the German Foreign Office for communications with the Americas since 1907 and as the new codebook had finally been delivered to the USA, it made obvious sense to send this telegram in the newer, and thus more secure, code. But the German minister in Mexico City did not have a copy of 7500. So, communications between Mexico and Washington had to use 13040 codebook. This meant that Zimmermann's two telegrams – combined and sent as a single 'message' of just over 1,000 codewords for the leg between Berlin and Washington – would be sent over the US channel coded in 7500. Once in Washington, Bernstorff would have to decode the long message, discovering it contained one part for him and another part to be forwarded to Mexico. The forwarded message, however, would have to be coded in 13040. The instruction to Bernstorff to use this codebook was included within the overall long telegram. Once these decisions had been taken, the telegram was ready for transmission.

The coded message was transmitted (it is not clear whether this was done telegraphically or by courier) from the German Foreign Office to the American ambassador in Berlin on 16 January at 3pm with the request that he should telegraph it to the US State Department for forwarding to the Imperial embassy in Washington. When Gerard received the message he asked what it contained. He was told that it concerned Wilson's peace initiative.[216] Gerard then immediately sent it on to the American legation in Copenhagen who transmitted it to Britain for forwarding onto one of the transatlantic cables. It was soon in America and the Central Telegraph Office in Washington had sent it on to the State Department by 7.50pm. Lansing objected to the unusually long telegram and declined to pass it on to the German embassy until he received a direct instruction from the president. Colonel House explained to a frustrated Lansing that the German government was talking to the President 'unofficially through me' and that, therefore, the message must go through.[217]

The State Department then forwarded it on 19 January to the German Imperial embassy. There seven clerical officers were set to work, each decoding a portion of the 1,000 codewords of the combined messages using copies of the newly received 7500 codebook. Once that had been done, two of them then re-encoded the message to be sent on to Mexico in 13040. It used code-groups with four or five numbers. As the telegraph companies charged each number in a message as a word it was common practice to encipher such messages into codewords (as several letters counted as one word). Perhaps to avoid the delay of a further stage of coding work, this was not done for this telegram. It was taken to a Western Union office in

Washington and sent on from there to Mexico City, arriving the same day. Because the message had not been enciphered into letters it was rather costly at just over $85 (estimated to be about $1,300 in 2005 prices).[218] A message acknowledging receipt of the telegram in Mexico was sent, on 20 January, back to Berlin via the same route, arriving there on the 27th. The copies of both telegrams held in the embassy in Washington were burnt. It was expected that the declaration of unrestricted submarine warfare would at least lead to a break in diplomatic relations between Germany and the USA, and perhaps to war. So, many secret documents were destroyed to ensure no trace of incriminating or embarrassing information was left behind.

Chapter 15

'97556 = Zimmermann'

A map published in 1898 by the *Bureau International des Administrations Télégraphiques* in Berne shows the world's main submarine telegraph routes at the end of the 19th century. It is immediately obvious that the densest concentration of cables is around the coasts of northwestern Europe and the Atlantic. Cables spread out from these areas, mainly jumping from one point on the coast to another along the shores of the great continents of Africa, the Americas, south and east Asia, the south Asian islands and Australasia. Apart from the dense clump of northern transatlantic links, a couple of lonely cables cross the Atlantic, two from Spain and one from West Africa, to Pernambuco in Brazil.[219] The map is part of an assessment of the strategic significance of global cable networks drawn up in the latter half of the 19th century and now held in the National Archives. Another submarine cable, laid after publication of this map, eventually linked western Canada, across the vast wastes of the Pacific to Australasia, completing a multi-threaded chain of cables around the globe. This link completed the strategic requirement of a network where communications could not be severed as alternative routes would be available if one link were cut. The 'topology', or structure, of the network reflected the interplay of three key factors: geography, economics and politics. The transoceanic crossings took the shortest practicable distance between lands. This obviously put Britain and Ireland at a substantial advantage when it came to the choice of landing places for transatlantic cables. But it was economic and political history which determined that Britain would be the centre of a global web of cables, the result of it being the first industrialised nation and the core of a global empire. The telegraph network made the global empire of the late 19th and early 20th centuries possible. British companies owned the great majority of these submarine cables, and even where cables were owned by companies or state authorities of other countries, their international link was usually to a point where it could connect with the British-owned network.

Other countries bridled at British domination of global telecommunications.[220] France and Germany ensured that they had their own transatlantic cables to avoid dependence on British-managed cables. France geographically was reasonably well placed for transatlantic links, but Germany, if it wanted to avoid using cables going through Britain, the Netherlands, Belgium or France, had to thread its cables leaving Germany just north of the Dutch border and then running down the North Sea and through the English Channel to gain access to the Atlantic. These German cables, as we saw in Chapter 1, were cut on the first day of war. The USA, too, wanted to control its own physical cable connections between the Americas and Europe, and was determined to wrest control of transatlantic cables from Britain. The US government permitted higher prices to be charged for telegrams landing on American soil on a foreign-owned cable. British companies could not compete and most transatlantic cables came wholly under American ownership. But the American cables still paid homage to economics. They still chose the shortest routes across the deep ocean floor. With the exception of one cable from Brest to Cape Cod, all the other transatlantic cables made landfall on Nova Scotia (acquired for the British Empire in 1713) before using shorter submarine cable links laid just off-shore linking to Boston or New York and thus to the US overland network.

The densest collection of cable landings on the European side was at Valentia in the far southwest of Ireland. From Valentia telegraph traffic was transmitted via landlines to the east coast of Ireland where it was carried further by another short submarine cable to either north or south Wales. Some cables missed out Ireland and landed on the southwestern limits of the British mainland in Cornwall. All these cables were linked from their landing points through to the central telegraph exchange in London, either to connect to the British telegraph network or for onward transit to other European countries ranging from Scandinavia, the Baltic, northern Germany, the Netherlands, Belgium, France and Spain, or beyond Europe, via the global network, round Africa or through the Suez Canal. Even USA-owned submarine transatlantic cables, put in precisely to overcome the British monopoly of transatlantic transmission capacity, had to connect to the British network in London if they were to be of any use for onward transmission of messages. For the US diplomatic service to send a cable from, say, Copenhagen to Washington it would travel first on the Danish domestic network to a landing point on the Danish west coast. There a submarine cable would carry traffic to Newbiggin, about 10 miles north of Newcastle upon Tyne. From Newbiggin landlines would carry traffic to London where it would be copied for transmission on whichever transatlantic cable was chosen.

As Zimmermann's telegram passed through London a copy was made by the Censorship staff at the central telegraph exchange. This copy was telegraphed, on a direct line, to the Admiralty's own telegraph office. A copy of the incoming telegram was then sent by pneumatic tube to Room 40. The coded copy of the long telegram was thus received in Room 40 very early in the morning of 17 January, well before it had arrived at the German embassy in Washington. The officer receiving the telegram would make some notes on its time and date and probably classify it according to various characteristics; he might too perform some basic decoding work on simple parts of the message. A former official historian at GCHQ, Room 40's modern successor organisation, Peter Freeman, suggested in a paper written after his retirement that the clerical staff sorting out the incoming messages would have been trained sufficiently to have undertaken some analysis of the long message and to have spotted that it actually contained two messages, one of 850 codewords and the other of 150. It fell to two young codebreakers, Nigel de Grey and Dilly Knox, who were manning the night watch in the political/diplomatic section, to begin work on the two messages.[221]

At the end of the war Nigel de Grey recorded how he had 'begun work in [Room 40] in September 1915 under Sir Alfred Ewing. Was first instructed in the codes and ciphers used between Berlin and Madrid.' Some writers have suggested that he worked almost exclusively on 13040 code from the time that he joined the codebreaking team. However, it seems more likely (from de Grey's own account) that, though he was initially assigned to the political/diplomatic section, he worked on diplomatic ciphers in VB code. Also he was not kept in the political section permanently, for he tells us that he 'Was then drafted to Room 40 where I did the usual Watchkeeping work, three-letter and four-letter Naval Signals, VB to the Naval and as used to America.'[222] Blinker Hall, however, later recorded that de Grey showed considerable aptitude for cryptographic work so he was taken off watchkeeping duties and was moved into 'research', ie, the political/diplomatic section. According to Hall, 'There had been a pile of unciphered stuff to work upon, but nothing else. Yet by this time de Grey was rapidly reaching the stage where he could understand at any rate the general sense of nearly all dispatches sent in the 13040 code.'[223] De Grey's own account covers a wider range of topics, but with less detail. 'In spare time [I] worked also the [German Foreign Office] ciphers and codes as used to the Near East and generally wherever despatches or other material came to hand from other parts of the world. Shortly after the change of four letter [code]book in 1916 was drafted to work out the new book. When that was solved was returned to watchkeeping but in spare time worked alone on [German Foreign Office] code used to Washington and the South American states [ie, 13040]. When this was solved it was discovered that constant traffic was maintained by cable through London between America and Berlin under cloak of Swedish [Foreign Office] and I then was instructed to form a small section for dealing entirely with American matters [plus the Far East]. In all during this period some five or six analogous ciphers [were] solved; and one new [code]book was worked out in conjunction with Paymaster

Rotter [presumably 7500].'[224] De Grey did not stay on at the end of the war, returning to publishing; however, in 1939 he was recalled to Bletchley Park, where he soon became deputy director responsible for day-to-day running of operations, security and machine cryptography.

In the introduction to this book I quoted de Grey's account of this meeting. Here we can indulge in Hall's rather more colourful account (thanks no doubt to his ghost writer's fine embroidery work). 'I am not likely to forget that Wednesday morning, 17 January 1917. There was the usual docket of papers to be gone through on my arrival at the office, and Claud Serocold and I were still at work on them when at about half-past ten de Grey comes in. He seemed excited. "D.I.D.," he began, "D'you want to bring America into the war?"

"Yes, my boy," I answered. "Why?"

"I've got something here which – well, it's a rather astonishing message which will do the trick *if* we could use it. It isn't very clear, I'm afraid, but I'm sure I've got most of the important parts right. It's from the German Foreign Office to Bernstorff." I must have read through that imperfectly decoded message three or four times without speaking a word. I gave it to Claud, and he too read it in silence.'

The partially decoded message read: 'Most secret, decipher yourself. We propose to begin on the 1st of February unrestricted submarine warfare. In doing so however we shall endeavour to keep America neutral ...? If we should not (succeed in doing so) we propose (to Mexico) an alliance upon the following basis: (joint) conduct of the war; (joint) conduct of peace. (... an obscure passage ...). Your Excellency should for the present inform the President secretly (that we expect) war with the USA (possibly) (... Japan) and at the same time to negotiate between us and Japan ... (Indecipherable sentence meaning please tell the President) that ... our submarines ... will compel England to make peace in a few months. Acknowledge receipt. Zimmermann.'[225] The sections in brackets are marked as such on the archive copy of the files on the Zimmermann telegram affair and indicate guesses as to a meaning. Elsewhere there are wholly indecipherable parts indicated by '...'. As can be seen, the general intent of Germany to seek Mexico as a partner in war and peace is easily discernible in the partly decoded text. But it is not clear that Germany is encouraging war on the USA nor, crucially, is the passage promising Mexican acquisition of US territory in return.

There is a document which reveals that it was de Grey who actually recounted this story to Strauss when he was compiling information for Hall's autobiography. Strauss recorded that he had had 'an entrancing evening last night ... Dinner at 8 and talked to 2am. Kelly, Mrs. K (who retired for one of the stories which will NOT appear in our book). I found I knew everybody there, Nigel de Grey, Lawrence, AEW Mason.' Strauss then notes the conversation as recounted by de Grey to him that evening, including the first exchanges recorded in the Hall/Strauss account quoted above. Before we get too attached to the idea that this charming account is wholly reliable it is worth noting the next paragraph in Hall/Strauss's story.' "A cablegram," [Hall] said at last, "sent, I suppose, through Stockholm? And will it go to Buenos Aires and thence up to Washington?" De Grey nodded. "And they'll probably use other routes as well?" [asked Hall]. De Grey replied, "Almost certainly they will." ' Hall adds the observation: 'At least two other routes were used.'[226] As we now know, this whole second bit of dialogue and the assertion that 'at least' two other routes were also used were pure invention. They do not feature in the notes made by Strauss after his dinner with de Grey et al. Hall and Strauss were working on the biography in the early 1930s. The other important item of disinformation spread by Hall was that a copy of the 13040 codebook had been captured in Persia (from Wassmuss – see Chapter 10). As we have seen, 13040 was actually 'reconstructed', largely by de Grey. Hall later explained, 'It was the official explanation which we had decided to give the American Government … it would be much better from our point of view for the Germans to suppose that a copy of their 13040 codebook had come into our hands than that we were able to read their most secret dispatches.'[227]

De Grey's own account of those days is worth noting: 'The telegram was sorted first to Knox whose business it was to fill in any known [code-]groups. His knowledge of German was at that time too slender for him to tackle any difficult passages in telegrams (and German diplomatic telegrams can be very ponderous) so that the procedure was that if the telegrams appeared from what could be read to have any interest he brought them to me for further study. We could at once read enough groups for Knox to see that the telegram was important. Together he and I worked all morning upon it. With our crude methods and lack of staff no elaborate indexing of groups had been developed – only constantly recurring groups were noted in the working copies of the code as our fancy dictated. Work therefore was slow and laborious but by about midday we had got a skeleton version, sweating with excitement because neither of us doubted the importance of what we had in our hands. Was not the American-German situation our daily bread? As soon as I felt sufficiently secure in our version, even with all its gaps, I took it down to Admiral Hall … I was young and excited (so incidentally was Dilly Knox) and I ran all the way to his room, found Serocold alone and Blinker free. I burst out breathlessly, "Do you want America in the war, Sir?" "Yes, why?" said Blinker. "I've got a telegram that will bring them in if you give it to them." As may be seen I had all the confidence of my years. Then came the job of convincing a man who knew no German with a half readable text. And Blinker was no sort of fool. But he was patient with me and was convinced.'[228]

Though Hall added the imaginary part of the conversation about the use of different routes, Strauss's dinner notes also offer a few interesting details that did not make it into Hall's account for some reason or other. He wrote that the partially decoded 'telegram was "shadowy" and de Grey had to do some explaining; you wanted to know exactly how it could be used … You said you must think things over by yourself.'[229] It was vital that any use of the telegram did not expose the fact that the British were intercepting and decoding German diplomatic communications. Hall also considered it essential not to admit to the US authorities that the telegram had been intercepted from traffic between the US embassy in Copenhagen and the State Department in Washington. Assessing the way the telegram might be exploited took Hall into unusual waters. 'It was the most anxious time, and from my point of view, a peculiar time, for to the study of the enemy movements, which was our primary duty, was added the necessity for an intensive study of American politics.'[230] Hall knew from the intercepted telegrams that unrestricted submarine warfare was soon to be resumed and that there was a good chance that this alone would bring the USA into the war. Also, the decode of the message in 7500 was only partial: open to question, indeed. Hall told de Grey, and later Montgomery, to work on the partial decode and they did add a few code-groups to their reconstruction, but did not get very much further. Hall also decided to sit on the information, locking all papers up in his safe and telling de Grey that no one else must be told about the telegram. 'At that moment, nothing was to be done except to take all possible precautions to keep the news to our three selves.'[231]

The decoding work was slow as the message containing the two telegrams was coded in 7500 which was a fairly new codebook and was 'hatted', ie, it was a two-part codebook with random allocation of code-groups to plain entries.[232] It had code-groups made up of four numbers, though it was also possible to use a fifth number in a code-group to signify the definite article or other grammatical inflexions. Room 40 had worked out some of the basic code-groups, but not much else. According to de Grey, '7500 had been too recently introduced for Commander Rotter to have progressed far in its solution. It should be remembered that he worked alone or nearly alone on a 10,000 group code which was "hatted". It was only in use to Washington and we had but few messages in it.'[233] The draft decode taken by de Grey to Hall did not include the names of the states that Germany offered to the Mexicans. This was because at least some of them had to be spelled out using code-groups representing one or two letters. So, for example, 'Arizona' was represented by four code-groups representing the plain language letter combinations, 'AR', 'IZ', 'ON' plus a single letter code-group representing 'A'. These had not been solved. De Grey also recalled that the partial decode revealed that 'an alliance was being proposed with a country the code-group

(0979) for which was not positively identified but which might be Mexico. Negotiations were also mentioned.'[234].

In Chapter 12 we looked at the invention of machine methods by Room 40's political/diplomatic branch to help speed up the reconstruction of hatted codes, where each codeword had to be separately resolved having no connection 'other than its context' within the coded message to the other codewords.[235] There is no hint in the files whether the codebreaking machine was used on 7500, though it seems quite possible that it would have been. However, against this we must balance De Grey's account, cited above, which emphasises that the methods were unsystematic and that Rotter worked alone or 'nearly' alone, and that there was no significant indexing (which was possibly a key to successful use of machines) and so on. Some questions thus remain. Was machinery used? Was it unsuccessful in the given time? Or, if it was not used, why not? Or has its role been conveniently shoved aside?

***

On 5 February, Hall went to see Lord Hardinge, Permanent Under-Secretary at the Foreign Office to request a meeting with Balfour, the Foreign Secretary.[236] The same day he sent a telegram to the British naval attaché in New York saying that it was 'essential to try and get copies of all telegrams from German Embassy Washington to German minister Mexico since January 18th. If procurable wire in original to me.'[237] Hall and Strauss have left us with an off-beat account of how the telegram was acquired through some good luck and some bad luck. The story concerns a British printer living in Mexico who was arrested for forging Mexican paper money and faced the death penalty. The good honest printer was said to be a victim of a malevolent employee. A friend of the printer (in later accounts it is said to be his brother) knew a British diplomat, presumably Hohler, in Mexico City who was able to secure the printer's release. His friend (or brother) worked in the Western Union telegraph office in Mexico City and in return for saving the printer's life was only too happy to hand over some copies of telegrams. In all probability this is another legend, perhaps with a grain of truth, perhaps not. The British diplomat, Tom Hohler, later claimed that he had already made contact with a telegraph office employee (having considered and rejected theft as a means of acquisition). Most probably the telegram was acquired for cash or under pressure of blackmail.

When the copy of the telegram arrived in London it changed the entire situation. The message between Washington and Mexico was coded in 13040 and the codebreakers had already managed to reconstruct about 50 per cent of this codebook. It used three, four or five numbers to make up its code-groups, of which there were some 11,000 available for use. The basic code-groups were made up of two or three numbers representing the page number, and two numbers representing the entry number on a page (see Table 15.1). The book was printed on double-sided sheets with four pages on each. These sheets could be shuffled into different order and the pages then numbered, so it has been described as a 'quasi-one part' system, with alphabetical plain entries assigned to code-groups in ascending numerical order on each page, but with the some shuffling of pages. There was also scope for some limited shuffling of entries within each page (but not across pages). There were several different code-groups for punctuation characters such as *punkt* and *komma*, each being given a code-group on every page. The code-groups with just four numbers were reserved for numbers, dates, frequent phrases and grammar. A small additional complexity was that some pages were given two page numbers, either of which could be used.

Table 15.1

Partially reconstructed 13040 codebook

15 – tyrann	40 – 300	65 – TT	90
16 – tyrannisier-en-t	41	66 – TU	91 – 299
17 – TZ	42 – U	67 – TUE	92 – truppentransport
18	43 – U	68 –	93
19	44 – U	69 – tuechtig	94 – TS
20	45 – U	70 – trotz	95 – TSCH
21	46 – U	71 – trotzdem	96
22	47 – U	72	97
23	48 – UA	73	98
24	49 – UB	74 – TRU	99

Notes
1. The two- or three-figure page number would precede the two-figure entry number to make a four- or five-figure code-group.
2. Blank entries are where Room 40 had not discovered the plain language meaning.
3. There are several repeats of plain language letter 'U' (42-47) as an attempt to minimise code-groups showing frequently used characters; however, this is partially undermined by using consecutive code-groups. Codebook 13040 was the parent of several other codebooks (such as codebook numbers 5950, 26040, 4401, 4631, 2970 and 'Arab' ('used chiefly in Persia').[ccxxxvii]

The plain text of the message became clear, revealing the offer of the three US states to Mexico. Montgomery left us with a short comment on his central role in the decoding of the telegram in 13040. He claimed that the codebook, 'had lately been discovered and brought to a workable point by Lt Cdr de Grey, but it was still in an early stage, and I believe that Lt Cdr de Grey would endorse the claim that my ['my' written in handwriting on top of 'the' in the typed original] careful linguistic work contributed to the result when the famous Zimmermann telegram to Mexico (in this cipher [sic]) was published, the decode was so accurate that the Germans thought it had been stolen and did not venture to disavow it'.[239]

The full text of the telegram in English is: 'Foreign Office telegram 16 January No. 1. Most Secret, decipher yourself. We intend to begin on 1 February unrestricted submarine warfare. We shall endeavour in spite of this to keep the United States of America neutral. In the event of this not succeeding we make Mexico a proposal of an alliance on the following terms: make war together, make peace together. Generous financial support and an undertaking on our part that Mexico is to reconquer the lost territory in Texas, New Mexico and Arizona. The settlement in detail is left to you. You will inform the President of the above most secretly as soon as the outbreak of war with the USA is certain, and add the suggestion that he should on his own initiative invite Japan to immediate adherence and at the same time mediate between Japan and ourselves. Please call the President's attention to the fact that the ruthless employment of our submarines now offers the prospect of compelling England in a few months to make peace. Acknowledge receipt. Zimmermann.'

The text of the telegram in German is: 'Auswaertiges Amt telegraphiert Januar 16: No. 1. Ganz geheim selbst zu entziffern. Wir beabsichtigenam ersten Februar uneingeschraenkt U-Boot Krieg zu beginnen. Es wird versucht werden, Vereinigte Staaten von Amerika trotzdem neutral zu erhalten. Fuer den Fall, dass dies nicht gelingen sollte, schlagen wir Mexiko auf folgender Grundlage Buendnis vor. Gemeinsam Krieg fuehren, Geimeinsam Friedensschluss fuehren. Reichliche finanzielle Unterstuetzung und Einverstaendnis unsererseits, dass Mexiko in Texas, Neu Mexico, Arizona frueher verlorenes Gebiet zurueck erobert. Regelung im einzelnen Eurem Hochwohlgeborenen ueberlassen. Sie wollen Vorstehendes dem Praesidenten streng geheim eroeffnen, sobald Kriegsausbruch mit Vereinigten Staaten feststeht und Anregung hinzufuegen, Japan von sich aus zu sofortiger. Beitretung einzuladen und gleichzeitig zwischen uns und Japan zu vermitteln. Bitte den Praesidenten darauf hinweisen, dass ruecksichtlose Anwendung unserer U-Boote jetzt Aussicht bietet, England in wenigen Monaten zum Frieden zu zwingen. Empfang bestaetigen. Zimmermann.'

With the telegram fully decoded, Hall could now get to work using it. De Grey later wrote, 'I remember his saying to me, "Our first job will be to convince the Americans that it's true – how are we to do that? Who would they believe. I've been thinking and the only person I think they would believe is Balfour." '[240] The former First Lord of the Admiralty (following Churchill in 1915) was appointed Foreign Secretary when Lloyd George became Prime Minister at the end of 1916. Thus, Balfour already had an intimate knowledge of Room 40's naval work including Room 40. Now, as Foreign Secretary, he was a recipient of diplomatic intelligence from Room 40 and MI1(b).

This point is of some importance as Hall has been accused of keeping this vital intelligence away from the politicians who were properly the people who should have seen it. But here it seems that in fact Hall decided very early on to go to the appropriate politician, Balfour. As we have seen, Hall had been appointed to liaise between Room 40's diplomatic section and the Foreign Office. Yet, it has to be emphasised that he was already running Room 40's political/diplomatic section as if it were his own department, not keeping Ewing informed about what was going on. Dilly Knox, writing in 1927, recalled that the 'material came from Hall; [the] messages [were] sent to Hall [and] action taken on messages by Hall'. The Room 40 staff working on diplomatic material were 'In so working on 13040 [cable intercepts] as against material coming from wireless they were acting without Ewing's knowledge and their activities were concealed from him. … [intercept] material provided by Hall was worked on and returned to Hall by a staff appointed by Ewing; the staff was lent to or, more accurately, stolen by Hall.'[241] Now, with full control of Room 40 and with the decoded message, Hall had in his hands the potentially most explosive intercepted telegram of the entire war.

Chapter 16

On Timing and Treachery

The last week or so of January was a sort of limbo. The British and German inner circles knew that submarine warfare was about to break out, but the Americans and other neutrals did not. Telegrams with instructions on how to inform neutral governments had gone out to German ambassadors and ministers, but as with the American government, those other countries were not to be informed until the last moment. Then they would be told: 'Neutral ships will sail in the blockade areas at their own peril.'[242] Any armed merchant ships even outside the area would be treated as 'belligerent'. Bernstorff made a final plea to Berlin to change its mind. 'To begin the submarine war without first negotiating on the above proposals would in my opinion place us utterly in the wrong ... injury to Wilson's feelings would make the avoidance of a breach quite impossible.'[243]

On 31 January the American ambassador in Berlin, James Gerard, reported to Washington about an interview with Zimmermann who had informed him of the resumption of unrestricted submarine warfare. Zimmermann said, 'it was their last chance as Germany could not hold out a year on the food question ... he realized that it was a very serious step and would probably bring the whole world into the war, but that Germany had this weapon and must use it no matter what the difficulties were'. The ambassador said, 'there is no doubt but that Germany believes that Americans are a fat, rich race without sense of honour and ready to stand anything in order to keep out of the war ... the Germans think and newspapers have stated that the US Government's peace moves are inspired by fear only'.[244] The reaction of America was indeed restrained, limited to the breaking off of relations. Fear and uncertainty kept a lot of neutral ships in port, waiting to see how serious things would become before daring to sail, but Trotsky's claim of food riots in New York (see Chapter 14) was a groundless exaggeration. German expectations that the USA would join the war were proved wrong.

On 5 February, Zimmermann sent another telegram to Mexico, this time via the Swedish Roundabout. It instructed the German minister to present the proposal for a joint alliance with the USA to the Mexican president without delay. The telegram was intercepted by Room 40 in London on 8 February. It was coded in 13040 and was fully decrypted by 10 February. The decoding cleared away any doubts that the plain language meaning of code-group 0979 was indeed Mexico (see Chapter 15).[245] The message read in part, 'Provided there is no danger of secret being betrayed to USA you are desired without further delay to broach the question of an alliance to the President. The definite conclusion of an alliance, however, is dependent on the outbreak of war between Germany and the USA. The President might even now, on his own account, sound out Japan. If the President declines from fear of subsequent revenge [by the USA] you are empowered to offer him a definite alliance after conclusion of peace provided Mexico succeeds in drawing Japan into the alliance.'[246]

**

With America showing little sign that the submarine attacks would push it into war, Hall decided the time had come to act. On the same day that the copy of the telegram from Mexico arrived in London, Hall showed a copy of the decode to Edward Bell, the contact for military and intelligence matters in the US embassy in London. He asked Bell not to do anything until Balfour had decided what he wanted to do. The following day, 20 February, Hall, holding a copy of the fully decoded message, met Balfour, Hardinge and his private secretary, Campbell. Balfour decided that Hall should handle arrangements with the US embassy and then Balfour would formally hand it over to the ambassador, Walter Page. Balfour is recorded as having said, 'I think Captain Hall may be left to clinch this problem. He knows the ropes better than anyone.'[247]

Page was presented with a translated copy of the decoded telegram and other background papers at the US embassy on 23 February. The State Department was informed the next day, but Secretary of State Robert Lansing was away and Page's memo was received by his assistant secretary, Polk. He informed Wilson. He decided to wait until Lansing returned to Washington which was not until the following Tuesday, 27 February, before deciding what to do. On the 26th, however, Gaunt, the British intelligence agent in New York, heard about the telegram from US contacts and telegraphed Hall asking if he had any more information. Hall replied the next day, 'Do not use till [Wilson] announces it, premature exposure fatal. Alone I did it.'[248] Hall's self-congratulatory message rather underplays the role of de Grey and others in the decoding, and of Hohler (and unknown individual(s) in a Mexico City telegraph office), as well as that of senior officials and politicians. One writer, formerly the official historian at GCHQ, says that Hall's actions were approved at the 'highest quarters', this being a two-word codeword for the Prime Minister, Lloyd George. On 1 March, Hall sent another telegram to Gaunt in New York: 'It is imperative that knowledge of this affair shall never be traced to British source.'[249]

When Wilson and Lansing met on 27 February, Lansing, not surprisingly, pointed out that the telegram proposing war on the USA had been transmitted over a US State Department channel. A shaken Wilson exclaimed, 'Good Lord! Good Lord!' The two men agreed that the telegram should be made public, but not before a copy had been acquired in the USA. They also agreed that it should not be published officially. That would make it look as if the government was trying to herd the American people into war or to put pressure on Congress. A copy of the telegram was acquired, despite initial resistance, from Western Union. It was slightly edited by Lansing and then handed over to a news agency on 28 February. The next day, 1 March, the story appeared in the US newspapers. Whilst there was much outrage, there was also a loud, nagging voice of doubt as to its authenticity. It just appeared all too much like a British propaganda exercise. Pro-German newspapers and senators denounced it. *The Fatherland* newspaper declared that it was a 'brazen forgery planted by British agents ... obviously faked'. Randolph Hearst instructed his newspaper editors to treat it as a forgery, this even after Wilson had vouched for its authenticity. And several senators loudly voiced similar doubts. A motion was put down asking the government to reveal the source of the telegram. Lansing replied, 'The Government is in possession of evidence which established the fact that the note referred to is authentic, and it is in the possession of the USA, and that the evidence was procured by this Government during the past week, but that it is in my opinion incompatible with the public interest at the present time, [to provide] any further information.'[250] It looked as if the release of the telegram might backfire.

But the growing wave of opinion which viewed the telegram as a forgery dissipated entirely on 3 March when, to the amazement of all involved, Zimmermann acknowledged that the telegram was indeed genuine. William Bayard Hale, a Hearst newspaper correspondent in Berlin and a German agent (having received $15,000 for propaganda work) tried to prevent him making the admission, but Zimmermann said, 'I cannot deny it, it is true.' Lansing, in his memoirs written in 1935, observed, 'From the time that the telegram was published, or at least from the time that its authenticity was admitted by its author, the United States' entry into the war was assured.'[251] The story shifted from 'Germany against Britain' to 'Germany against America'. The papers called Zimmermann's proposal the 'Prussian Invasion Plot'. Pro-Germanism, neutralism and pacifism all lost their influence as the realisation dawned on the American public that Germany had mooted a declaration of war on the USA. Americans adjusted to the realisation that they would be going to war. Wilson, however, was still reluctant to take the step into the abyss. On 18 March, German submarines sank three American merchant ships with heavy loss of life. Wilson's hopes that the German submarines would be cautious were dashed. The next day, the Russian Tsarist government was toppled by revolution. The Allies no longer counted an autocratic monarchy among their number, removing one of the factors that had held America back from earlier participation. The US conspiracy theorists' pendulum swung from an irrational belief in the telegram's lack of authenticity to the other extreme, with one senator proclaiming that the telegram contained unpublished sections about setting up German submarine bases in Mexico and amassing German reservists in Mexico to 'attack all along the border'. Lansing denied this, but the omniscient senator insisted, 'that the denial was diplomatic but he believed that his information to be absolutely correct'.[252]

On 20 March, Wilson's cabinet voted unanimously in favour of war. The following day Wilson called a meeting of Congress for 2 April, two weeks earlier than had been planned. Even at the last moment, on the eve of the Congressional meeting, Wilson cried out, 'If there is any alternative, for God's sake, let's take it.' At a packed joint meeting of both houses the next day Wilson said that the German government 'means to stir up enemies against us at our very doors, the intercepted note to the German minister at Mexico is eloquent evidence. We accept this challenge of hostile purpose.' Wilson confided to a colleague that he was sure that 'Germany would be beaten and so badly beaten that there would be a dictated peace … At the end of the war there will be no bystanders with sufficient power to influence the terms.'

Table 16.1

Zimmermann telegram timetable

28/8/16	Hindenburg and Ludendorff take control of German high command
22/11/16	Foreign minister, von Jagow, is replaced by Arthur Zimmermann
9/1/17	Formal agreement of Kaiser and Chancellor to resumption of unrestricted submarine warfare at Pless, Silesia
13/1/17	Zimmermann drafts telegram to Mexico
16/1/17	Telegram sent in 7500 from Berlin to Washington (via US diplomatic channel)
17/1/17	Telegram arrives in Room 40 and is partially decoded
19/1/17	Telegram arrives at German embassy in Washington, sent on to Mexico in 13040

19/1/17	Zimmermann telegram arrives in Mexico City and is decoded by German minister Eckardt's secretary, Magnus
20/1/17	Eckardt in Mexico sends acknowledgement of receipt to Washington in 13040
21/1/17	German embassy forwards acknowledgement of receipt from Eckardt US State Department, coded in 7500
23/1/17	State Department forwards Eckardt's acknowledgement of receipt to US embassy in Copenhagen
26/1/17	Eckardt's acknowledgement of receipt arrives in Berlin
31/1/17	Germany resumes unrestricted submarine warfare
3/2/17	American government breaks off diplomatic relations with Germany
5/2/17	Second telegram sent to Eckardt in Mexico (via Swedish Roundabout) to propose alliance to Mexico immediately, even without war with the USA
5/2/17	Hall approaches Hardinge of Foreign Office
9/2/17	Bernstorff leaves New York by ship for Halifax, Nova Scotia
16/2/17	Bernstorff arrives at Halifax, but is not allowed to leave.
19/2/17	Room 40 receives copy of telegram in 13040 from Mexico
19/2/17	Hall claims that he shows decode to Edward Bell, but asked him to wait until Balfour had decided what to do with the telegram
20/2/17	Balfour gives approval for copy of telegram to be given to USA; Hall is given the job of working out how to arrange the handover
22/2/17	Hall fully reveals telegram to Page and gives him a copy
23/2/17	Balfour hands copy to Page
24/2/17	Wilson receives full copy of telegram
27/2/17	Wilson decides to publish telegram

27/2/17	Bernstorff's ship home allowed to depart from Halifax
1/3/17	Story of telegram appears in US newspapers
3/3/17	Zimmermann acknowledges that the telegram is genuine
18/3/17	3 US merchant ships sunk by German submarines
19/3/17	Russian revolution begins
6/4/17	USA declares war on Germany
14/4/17	Carranza declares Mexico will remain neutral
27/4/17	Hall promoted to Rear Admiral
5/8/17	Zimmermann sacked
10/17	Hall is knighted

Table 16.2

Changes to the Zimmermann telegram between sending and publication in the USA

1. British remove original serial numbers from published text
2. Bernstorff in Washington adds opening sentence to Mexico telegram
3. US officials add 'signed' and date (19/1/17)
4. US Secretary of State paraphrases the text leaving slight differences in every sentence

The US reaction to the offer of US territory to Mexico was painted by Zimmermann as validation of his sending the telegram in the first place. He said, rather obscurely, that taking into account US behaviour towards Germany and other facts 'which everyone knows, ... it is obvious that the consideration on our part was not frivolous as to what defensive measures we should take, if we were attacked by the United States. It was not only right, it was the duty of the leaders of the state, to make provisions for an eventual armed conflict with the United States.'[253] Never mind that those provisions brought about that very conflict.

The publication of the Zimmermann telegram and the entry of the USA into the war must have been greeted with undisguised joy by those in the know at Room 40 and upper circles of the British government. There followed, for the codebreakers involved, what must have been an immensely enjoyable series of intercepts documenting German attempts to destroy any more embarrassing material and to pin down the source of the leak of the Zimmermann telegram. Initially the blame was cast on 'treachery' within the German embassy in Washington. Zimmermann told the Reichstag that he had absolutely no idea of how the Americans got hold of the telegram which had been sent in an 'absolutely secret code'. In an official statement it was claimed: 'It is not known in what manner the American government was made acquainted with these instructions, which were sent to Mexico by a secret route; but the act of treachery – one may assume it to have been such – appears to have been perpetrated on US territory.'[254]

The possibility that the message might have come to the attention of the USA as it passed through two US embassies and the State Department does not seem to have arisen, perhaps because the code was believed to be totally secure (or maybe German intelligence assessed US cryptographic capabilities at that time as wholly inadequate to the task). With Bernstorff's return to Germany, the search for the culprit focused on Mexico. The German minister in Mexico City, Eckardt, reported how the telegram had been 'deciphered in accordance with my special directions, by Magnus [his personal secretary]. [It], as in the case of everything of a politically secret nature, [was] kept from the knowledge of the Chancery officials … [the] originals were burnt and ashes scattered … [and were] kept in an absolutely secure steel safe … up to the time they were burned'. Hall later wrote that Magnus was one of many odd people in the German ministry in Mexico. He was a 'grossly fat, good-natured secretary … [who] had continued to pester the British minister with invitations to dinner after the war had been declared and thought it churlish of him to refuse. Poor simple Magnus! He was stabbed in the stomach one day outside his Legation and his fat saved him, but it did not save him from some anxious hours later on', when the Zimmermann telegram was exposed.[255]

Berlin was not satisfied. On 29 March a message to Eckardt warned him, 'Various indications suggest that the treachery was committed in Mexico.' Eckardt responded, 'Greater caution than is always exercised here would be impossible. The text of telegrams which have arrived is read to me at night in my dwelling house by Magnus in a low voice. My servant, who does not speak German, sleeps in an annexe. Apart from this, the text is never anywhere but in Magnus's hands or the steel safe, the method of opening which is only known to him and myself.' He pointed the finger of blame at the Washington embassy where 'even secret telegrams were known to the whole chancery' and two copies were regularly made of all telegrams for embassy records. Eckardt concluded, 'Please inform me at once, as soon as we are exculpated, as we doubtless shall be.' He received such an assurance on 4 April.[256]

An investigation by a cipher expert, Dr Goeppert, decided from the outset that 'betrayal had resulted from American not British action … possibly by the treachery or carelessness of some member of the Chancery staff in

Washington'.[257] Thus three assumptions – that the British were not involved, that the Washington-Mexico message was not involved, and that the 13040 code had not been compromised – led the Germans away from the truth. It is possible that behind these assumptions lay an unwillingness to face up to the consequences. If 13040 had been broken, then communications with Mexico would be impossible. It was not practicable to get a new codebook out, at least not without long delays and the danger of compromise. If the existing code was compromised, then all communications were at risk. No one wanted to face up to this uncomfortable truth. Hall later observed, 'The Germans actually thought that there had been leakage between Bernstorff and Mexico, which is what I wanted. Right to the end of the war, I do not think that the Germans suspected that we knew as much as we did about their intelligence service.'[258]

Meanwhile an interesting correspondence was going on in Germany between the Foreign Office, the army and the navy over the security of ciphers. The army's cryptographic section reckoned that Foreign Office codes were not secure, though the diplomats disagreed. 'Your Honour's assertion that almost all cipher telegrams can be deciphered is untenable. If the matter were so easy, the German wireless stations would probably not fail to decipher Russian, English and French wireless messages. To my knowledge the German wireless stations have only succeeded in partially deciphering the Italian wireless messages; this may be explained by the fact that they had material supplied by the Austro-Hungarian army to serve as basis. Without such an aid, the decipherment of an unsystematic cipher [ie, a two-part or 'hatted' cipher *Lotteriechiffre*], is out of the question … [especially as they are also enciphered,] decipherment of these wireless messages is impossible even for the most clever specialists. It can only result if the entire cipher is betrayed or essential parts and keys come to the knowledge of a foreign government.' The report also dismissed rumours picked up in the Netherlands that a lot of German codes had been broken. A dozen false messages were handed to the source who was supposed to be able to get them to the Allies, but no signs had been seen at all that the messages had caused any response by the Allies. So, 'this shows the value of such reports'.[259] As far as the Foreign Office was concerned, the only cause of the leak can have been human betrayal.

But the army was not impressed by this line of reasoning. 'The art of decipherment has developed into a science during the war,' wrote one army official. He asked the Foreign Office to think again. 'Under the chief of field telegraphy there is an office which is exclusively occupied with the decipherment of foreign systems and which has succeeded in breaking all field and naval systems now in use as well as several diplomatic systems. Even unsystematic [codes] with changing encipherment have been solved by this office without aid from other sources.' A few days later it was reported that 'with respect to the so-called *Lotteriechiffre* employed for some important matters, investigation showed that this did involve greater difficulty in solution but nonetheless would only assure adequate security if certain defects were eliminated and if a number of codes were available for use at the same time'.

But the diplomats were not having it. In August a memo insisted, 'The Foreign Office adheres, first and last, to the point of view that its new *Lotteriechiffres*, especially when re-enciphered, can only be regarded as not absolutely secure if betrayal or careless use of the ciphers or of the enciphered correspondence occurs.' In September, with the row still rumbling on, the army reported that it had taken four weeks for two of its cryptanalysts to reconstruct enough of such a code so that 'almost every telegram could be solved for practical purposes'.[260] At that point, sadly, the archive file of the correspondence ends.

***

Before concluding this chapter, and the story of the Zimmermann telegram, we need to step back slightly to observe the reaction of the neutrals when the German decision to resume unrestricted submarine warfare was announced to them by German diplomatic note on 31 January 1917, the very same day that the submarines started their campaign. Reports from US ambassadors in various capitals, sent to Washington over cables passing via London, informed MI1(b) of the panic in neutral countries. The fear was not just that their shipping and essential trade were at risk, but that there might be a ratcheting up of the war generally, dragging them further into the conflict. Spain held back from reacting publicly because it wanted to know what the USA was likely to do. 'Spain desires to take identical action with the USA if that is possible,' reported the ambassador in Madrid. Switzerland too wanted to know the US reaction. 'The Swiss Government is anxious to know what attitude the Government at Washington intends to take about the German Note. Switzerland fears that her commerce with the United States and that her imports and exports will be ruined. Her position is precarious.' The Swiss newspapers 'appeal to President Wilson who has expressed himself with so much force against the violations of rights and the horrors of human massacres'. The American ambassador in Copenhagen reported, 'Great depression has been caused in Denmark by the German Note. The [Stock] Exchange has been closed indefinitely ... The King said emphatically that the only hope for little nations lay in the United States. He did not think that anyone could doubt the grave situation caused by the German Note.' In Norway there was 'consternation' and desperate attempts were made to persuade Britain and the USA to give protection to Norwegian vessels (which by 'voluntary' agreement reported to the Scottish port of Kirkwall for inspection by the Royal Navy).[261]

The USA informed neutral governments on 3 April that it would be breaking off diplomatic relations with Germany and invited them to follow suit. Several South and Central American countries declined to do so,[262] and naturally enough Germany's near neighbours were even less eager to take such a serious step. The ambassador in The Hague reported that the Dutch foreign minister said that he was 'very pleased with the action of the President and that he could not say how it could have been otherwise'. The Netherlands, however, would wait and see what happened before taking any action itself. 'He stated that Holland's position was very different to that of the USA ... the people are greatly alarmed and the Foreign Office is uneasy. The Germans are strongly entrenched along the Dutch frontier.' Norway too appreciated the President's call for joint action, but 'the foreign minister confidentially called attention to the difficulty of executing such a policy by reason of Norway's especially exposed position'. Denmark also said it was 'in no position to make an active partner or to join in the action of the USA as regards Germany'.[263]

Not everyone expressed outrage and fear at the threat from the submarines. The US ambassador to the Vatican reported that the Pope was expected to declare, 'Germany's attitude was not unexpected in well-informed circles since England is attempting Germany's political destruction ... the President holds in his hands the decision of peace or war, since it is in his power to forbid the exportation from America of money, food and munitions ... such a course would conform with perfect neutrality'.[264] It would also, of course, have allowed Germany to gain from its war of aggression by holding on to Belgian and French territory.

In April, as we have seen, the USA entered the war. European neutrals were bitterly disappointed that the USA, previously the most vociferous defender of the rights of neutrals, had overnight become the most enthusiastic promoter of ever tighter controls on neutrals now that it was a belligerent. The blockade could now be made much tighter and the USA did its utmost to ensure as few leaks as possible. The neutrals had to make significant concessions to the Allies to survive. But they also had to come to terms with Germany and insisted on some compromise in return for continuing to supply it. 'Shortly after the commencement of [unrestricted submarine warfare], Germany needed to conclude agreements with the major European neutrals – Denmark, the Netherlands and the Scandinavian countries – that allowed them to maintain their trade (including wood and food) with Britain.'[265] Faced with all these conflicting pressures the neutrals must have felt as if they had fallen between the hammer and anvil.

Chapter 17

Applied Intelligence

The winter of 1916/17 was the critical period of the war. All participants made determined efforts to break the stalemate. Talk was of 'total war', of mobilising the whole of society for the war effort. All sides had suffered severe shortages of shells and other armaments in 1914 and early 1915. The stalemate gave them time to boost production and reorganise their economies for more intense war.[266] But this brought the social cohesion of the combatant societies into question. In the words of one historian, 'Once stalemate set in on the battlefield in 1914, the First World War became as much as anything a contest over which belligerent's home front would collapse first.'[267] The locus of power shifted within governments as hardliners rose to the top. In Britain, France and Italy the politicians established dominance over the military, partly because of the gross failure of the generals to achieve anything other than mass slaughter.[268] By the end of the year Herbert Henry Asquith had been replaced as Prime Minister by Dafydd (David) Lloyd George, once the radical *bête noire* of British politics. He had made his name as an opponent of the Boer War, bravely risking his life in front of a violent pro-war mob in Birmingham. But age and several years at the heart of the British government had turned the fiery radical into an equally fiery partisan of the British Empire. Lloyd George – the 'Welsh Wizard' – had made his way into power entirely through his exceptional abilities. He had everything against him in his background. He was from a remote rural part of Wales. His mother tongue was Welsh, not English – though this did not stop him from becoming a silver-tongued orator in his second language. In the all too typical opinion of one military leader, Lloyd George was 'an underbred swine'.[269] By rights he should never have been able to rise to more than being an exceptionally able but woefully under-employed and increasingly frustrated backbench MP.

Early in the war, Lloyd George had taken on the job of improving the supply of arms and ammunition. By mid-1916 the armaments industry had been transformed and there were plenty of shells for the bloody attacks on the Somme.[270] Yet Asquith's direction of the war was lackadaisical and, after the Somme and Jutland, the military and navy were at a loss to offer a way in which the war could be won. If anyone could wrest control of the direction of the war from the military it was Lloyd George. An intercept, decoded by Room 40, of a report from Walter Page, the US ambassador in London, to President Wilson expressed a common view: 'Mr Page considers that Mr Lloyd George is decidedly not a spent force but the most active and inspiring mind that he knows in England with a most energetic and vivid imagination.'[271] In late 1916 Lloyd George took over as Prime Minister, promising to bring fresh ideas and determination to the management of the war. Lloyd George's wartime government has been described as an elected dictatorship, given its wide-ranging powers.

If Britain became an elected dictatorship, during 1916 in Germany it was a military dictatorship that progressively took power, reducing the civil government to a cipher (in the sense of an empty symbol). The dictators were the victors of the Battle of Tannenberg in August 1914, where a Russian army had been enveloped and destroyed by a German army commanded by Paul von Hindenburg and Eric Ludendorff. In August 1916 the former chief of staff, Eric von Falkenhayn, was demoted to a field command in the Balkans and the duo took control. Hindenburg was the dictatorship's public face. His main duties during the war, apart from threatening to resign any time the Kaiser or civilians challenged military views, seem to have been hunting and having his portrait painted. On seeing one new portrait he demanded that the painter re-work the picture, 'Otherwise posterity will believe that I had run around with missing buttons.'[272] The hard work of determining policy and seeing that it was carried out was the task of Ludendorff, a notably ill-tempered, misanthropic and mentally fragile army leader (at a time when such attributes were not in short supply among the top military commanders and monarchs of Europe).

Hindenburg and Ludendorff did not come to power through a sharp, sudden military coup. They achieved domination by steadily increasing their power at the expense of Germany's already limited civil authorities. Germany's parliament, the Reichstag, had little effective power and when the Kaiser and the Chancellor Bethmann-Hollweg gave in to the military, parliamentarians lacked the means and common purpose needed to re-assert civil power. Kaiser Wilhelm found that his imperial powers were worthless in the face of military insubordination. He had on one occasion to remind Ludendorff that he was talking to his Emperor, but the irascible commander stormed out – an unheard-of insult to the dignity of the monarch. Wilhelm became little more than an embarrassing and unwanted court jester to the military dictators. As we have seen, from August 1916 the military command set about forcing through the decision to launch unrestricted submarine warfare and to accept the likelihood of war with the United States.

Ludendorff wanted all-out mobilisation of human and material resources in what became known as the Hindenburg Programme. The army commanders were determined, as one historian put it, to 'overhaul the labour law, cull out those suitable for military service, tighten labour and production controls, and dictate priority usage of raw materials, oil and coal'.[273] The enforced labour law was passed. Universities and technical colleges were closed. 'The whole German nation must live only in the service of the Fatherland,' said Hindenburg. The whole of Germany was to become a 'single munitions factory'. Germany's technological advances during the war were in the realm of gas, flame-throwers, high-quality trench systems, steel-cored bullets and incendiary bullets. But in four important areas Germany fell behind: aircraft, motorised transport, tanks and cryptology.[274] Democratic reform was also pushed aside. 'The war does not in any way justify democratisation and parliamentarianism,' said Ludendorff. 'A policy of concessions to the spirit of the age is dangerous.'[275]

By the beginning of 1917 the Great War was beginning to look like a struggle between parliamentary states controlled by the civil power on the one hand, and monarchical/military states on the other. The non-parliamentary nations showed most signs of social fracture. The two ageing empires of Austria and Turkey were crumbling from within under the strain of war. That the same trend affected both 'sides' was emphasised by the collapse of the Russian monarchy – in the form of an emphatically incompetent and blinkered Tsar – and the heralding of a brief period, beginning in February/March 1917, when the locus of power shifted uneasily between the pro-war provisional government and the anti-war 'soviets' or soldiers' and workers' councils. In April, as we have seen, another parliamentary nation, the United States joined the war, bringing a fresh population, a rapidly expanding economy and an aggressive determination to win.

***

Meanwhile, during the first few months of 1917 the nation that came under most immediate military threat was Britain. Unrestricted submarine warfare had started again on 31 January. The first couple of weeks were something of an anti-climax. Neutral ships stayed in port, waiting to see what would happen, though British shipping continued to ply the seas. In January the U-boats had sunk 181 ships. In February the figure rose to 259 and continued to rise as spring drew on. The German naval attaché in Madrid sent a message to the *Admiralstab* in Berlin announcing, 'the arrival of shipwrecked people in Spanish harbours is the best propaganda against proceeding to the blockade area'.[276] In April he passed on a report from Mallorca: 'On account of shipwrecked persons who have arrived here from the French sailing-vessel *Andre*, panic has increased amongst the crew of the *SS Agios Georgios*; they refuse to sail.' Kaiser Wilhelm sent a personal message to the king of Spain, intercepted by Room 40, explaining that the British blockade was illegal because it was not close to German shores, it was 'only a "danger zone" bristling with mines'. Neutrals had accepted that blockade and followed British rules about where they could sail. So he 'felt sure that in the same way they would not risk facing the new German peril ... [he] expressed himself entirely satisfied with the results of the submarine war, which every day would become more intense, and was confident that it would contribute powerfully towards peace, which had always been the desire of Germany ... [the Kaiser] laid stress on the great importance in the future of submarines, which he regards as an evolution in the naval art which would reduce the naval power of British domination'.[277] The German advocates of the U-boat war estimated that sinking about 800,000 tons of shipping a month would bring Britain to her knees. The naval chief of staff, Admiral Holtzendorff, said, 'We may reckon that in five months, shipping to and from England will be reduced by 39 per cent ... England will not be able to stand that.' So it seemed as if success was close to hand. The collapse of the Russian monarchy augured well for the Eastern Front, and the German army was holding its own on the Western Front. Surely Britain would soon be prepared to sacrifice Belgium and northern France for peace.

The German submarine assault was helped by the British Admiralty. It was determined not to use convoys to protect ships. Another major problem was the watertight compartments which separated Room 40 from other sections of Naval Intelligence Division. We saw in Chapter 3 that the *Verkehrsbuch* (VB) naval codebook, which was used for communications to and from the U-boats, was recovered as early as November 1914. According to a post-war document produced by Room 40, 'Yet it was not until the summer of 1916 that a little information was allowed to trickle through from the section which dealt with enemy submarine signals to the officer [in another section] responsible for tracking enemy submarines, and it was not until the autumn of the following year that this officer was allowed access to the record of the cryptographic section ... The system entailed an enormous waste of time and loss of efficiency. The activities of several sections ... covered the same ground ... The compartments differed only as to the sources from which each obtained its information ... [and] resulted in very incomplete and patchy knowledge on important matters, which if the information had been properly pooled, would have been [better understood]. Many items of intelligence which to each Section severally might appear insignificant or unintelligible, would have become lucid and have been recognised as of the first importance, if the fragments divided among various compartments had been pieced together ... a secret is not worth having at all unless proper use is going to be made of it.'[278]

The author of this document, Frank Birch, went on to blame the preconceived notions of espionage and intelligence that were common both in society at large and among senior naval commanders. 'For brevity we might simply refer the reader to the works of Mr. William Le Quex [whose pre-war novels featuring German spies and invasions of Britain were best-sellers]. The atmosphere is melodramatic. The ingredients are spies, adventurers, dark alleys, passwords and crime. An Intelligence Officer, like the "Secret Service Agents" of romance, is something between a bandit and a detective. He is conceived as a sinister figure, in a slouch hat and cloak, armed to the teeth – a desperate fellow with a shady past and a lurid future. Such was the popular view. But it was only an exaggeration of the official conception. The object of intelligence was to conduct an underhand warfare. Instead of fighting your enemy in the field or at sea, you circulated false bank notes in his country. You blew up his factories and bridges. You slipped incriminating documents into the coat pockets of his most trusted officials. You sold him spurious information and set booby-traps of all descriptions in his path. Perhaps the most astounding instance to be cited was the bright suggestion from the German embassy in Spain that the Portuguese rivers should be poisoned at their source! Now it would be wrong to deny a certain shilling-shocker element in Secret Service work, at any rate in the early stages of the war ... however, the opportunities for such methods became very rare and the results obtained out of all proportion to the risks. Agents supplied little more than the back-stairs gossip and, for the rest, activities of the kind subsided into petty chicanery and propaganda.' As long as senior naval officers held this sort of attitude it was impossible to integrate intelligence effectively into operations and policymaking. Hall's great contribution was to reorganise Room 40 and to unify it with naval intelligence generally.

Even as the number of sinkings rose dramatically, the navy's top commanders fiercely resisted organising convoys. This was despite the fact that convoys had proved successful for troop-carrying ships, for cross-Channel colliers and in the Mediterranean (where the submarine war had continued unaffected by the tussle between Germany and America). But the Admiralty wanted its ships to undertake aggressive action, searching out and destroying submarines, not to act as mere escorts for traders. The scattering of merchant ships, the navy's top commanders asserted, provided the best cover for the many, reducing their chances of coming across a submarine. The anti-submarine commander, Admiral Alexander Duff, led investigations into all and any solutions – including training circus sea lions to detect submarines.

The prime killing zone for the submarines was in the southern and western approaches to the British Isles. In the worst two weeks – 'the black fortnight' of April 1917 – nearly 400,000 tons of British shipping were sunk. Some 373 ships were sunk in that one month, exceeding the rate of replacement.[279] But, although technology was improving (depth charges becoming available, for example), active search and destroy tactics remained pretty ineffective.[280] In the first four months of the submarine campaign British warships managed to sink between one and five U-boats per month. Over the same period 30 new submarines came into service.And they were larger vessels, better armed, capable of sailing further, submerging for longer periods and diving more deeply.The new vessels sailed out some 300 miles into the Atlantic to await ships approaching landfall. In mid-1917 the Royal Navy was managing to sink about eight submarines a month on average, a lot more than the beginning of the year, but still a wholly inadequate number.

Table 17.1

Gross tonnage of merchant shipping losses, January–December 1917[cclxxx]

	British	Worldwide
January	153,666	368,201
February	313,486	540,006
March	353,478	593,841
April	545,282	881,207
May	353,289	596,629
June	417,925	687,505
July	364,858	557,988
August	329,810	511,730
September	196,212	351,748
October	276,132	458,558
November	173,560	289,212
December	253,087	399,111
Total	**3,729,786**	**6,235,878**

In February 1917 the Secretary to the British cabinet, Maurice Hankey, wrote a paper for Lloyd George putting the case for 'scientifically organised convoys'. He based his argument on information supplied by a junior naval officer who disagreed with his superiors. His data disproved the Admiralty's arguments about there being too many merchant ships for the navy to cope with and other excuses. Lloyd George, though already favourable to the idea of convoys, was still establishing his power and did not feel able at that time to overrule the Admiralty. Hankey's memo was intended to unblock the bar on action and the naval commanders reluctantly agreed to organise some experiments with convoys. These proceeded with extreme slowness. Meanwhile, sinkings rose week by week, reaching potentially critical levels. When the USA joined the war in April it meant that many more ships became available, and the US admiral William S. Sims was in favour of using them for convoys. The dreadful figures for sinkings in April helped concentrate minds at the top of the British government. The Cabinet authorised Lloyd George to review the anti-submarine war to ensure that it was being properly organised, in effect at last giving him political backing for overruling the reluctant admirals. He suddenly announced that on 30 April he would make a personal visit to the Admiralty to discuss the matter: this seemingly insignificant gesture was in fact a quite unprecedented move and in itself was a challenge to the Admiralty.

Their Lordships were furnished in the Admiralty Boardroom with a dial connected to a wind vane on the roof of the building, which showed them at any time from which direction the wind was coming. This was vital intelligence in the age of sail. However, First Sea Lord John Jellicoe did not need his weathercock to see which way the political wind was blowing. By the time Lloyd George turned up for the meeting, the Admiralty had already started to shift its position. Two days earlier Duff sent a memo to Jellicoe recommending the general introduction of convoys. The navy did not like retreating and to this day naval historians persist in painting this as a voluntary move, not one forced by Lloyd George. The first North Atlantic convoy sailed on 10 May and from June there were regular convoys every eight days. From August regular homebound convoys were arranged. Even so, it took some months for convoys to become general practice. But it was immediately seen that the Admiralty's 'scattering is safest' reasoning was faulty. In fact that approach had made it easier for the U-boats to alight upon isolated merchants. Simply by concentrating the ships, the chances of a submarine happening to share the same spot in the vast reaches of the oceans was reduced (and the submarines obviously could not spend too much time at juicy spots where ships were funnelled into narrow channels). Of the 5,090 ships that sailed in convoys in 1917, only 63 were sunk.

But the success of the convoys did not rest purely on the probabilities of a random encounter between predator and prey in the vast stretches of the ocean. Wireless intelligence enabled convoys to be routed away from locations where submarines were known to be – wireless intelligence derived from direction-finding and decoding of messages. But this could only happen, of course, once the watertight compartments had been broken through. As Birch concludes, as far as combating the submarine menace, 'Room 40 only became of real value when its material was handed over directly to the Convoy Section, to Carrington's Chart, to E1 and was sent out to all commands'.[282] In May 1917, Room 40 became part of the Naval Intelligence Division. The officer in charge of tracking U-boats within the Intelligence Division, Fleet Paymaster E. W. Thring, was then allowed access to wireless interception intelligence, responsible for tracking U-boats.

With more submarines at sea and with the *Admiralstab* attempting to control the submarines out on patrol, the quantity of wireless traffic increased. U-boats coming from and to the German Bight ports continued to announce their presence. The naval transmitter at Norddeich continued to broadcast intelligence on British shipping and British minefields that had been reported by U-boats. And longer voyages resulted in more reports from the distant submarines as well as more orders being sent out from the naval command. There were more frequent changes of cipher key, but this did not present a problem and new ciphers were usually broken within a few hours of the first intercept landing on the desks of Room 40. There were limits on the accuracy of the intelligence. It was not possible to state exactly where the submarines were at any one time, the direction-finding system giving an accuracy of about 20 miles in home waters and up to 50 miles in distant Atlantic ones. Room 40 could tell the Admiralty roughly where submarines were lurking, pointing out the likely areas of attack and enemy strength in those areas. Even when Room 40 learned, as it often did, the location of a U-boat, there was very little chance that the navy could intercept and destroy the vessel. However, the important point is that Room 40's intelligence was accurate enough to route convoys safely away from areas known to hold prowling U-boats. It was not refined enough to support the offensive 'search and destroy' tactics so close to the Admiralty's heart, but this did not matter. Despite this, large numbers of naval ships were kept on such missions almost until the end of the war.

Germany's gamble had failed. Britain was not knocked out of the war. America had joined the war. As for German threats that not a single American soldier would reach Europe, these were proved utterly empty. In fact, not a single American soldier was lost to enemy submarines. By the end of 1917 there were 100,000 American troops on European soil and many more were on their way. Germany could still take comfort from having almost knocked Italy out of the war in October 1917 and from the Bolshevik revolution which brought the hopes of Russia's imminent retirement from the war.

We saw above how it was necessary to break through the 'watertight compartments' imposed on the intelligence division of the navy and over use of intercepts. Having discovered that there were real advantages to be had from sharing and using that intelligence, senior naval officers in specialist areas and remote theatres worked with Hall and his naval intelligence department to identify more ways that their work could help win the war. A memo from July 1917 illustrates the new attitude. 'It is proposed that positions of enemy submarines in the southern part of the North Sea, determined by directive wireless telegraphy and plotted in the Admiralty should be passed to the air stations interested, as is already done in the case of Zeppelin positions similarly ascertained.'[283] Special sections were set up to handle air raids, minesweeping, U-boats, direction-finding, the Bight, the Baltic, Austrian codes and so on.

The most important development, though, was the widening of the number of people allowed to see the fruits of Room 40's work, through the circulation of the War Diaries (daily summaries of intelligence from intercepts) and other forms. The intercepts were no longer passed on in their unedited, unannotated raw form, but were edited and explained, creating 'reasoned assessments'.[284] Various forms of dissemination were devised for different recipients, such as 'War Diaries, "Navintell" telegrams, intelligence by wireless to Dover, Portsmouth and Air Exchanges'.[285] Under Ewing's stewardship Room 40 had no typists or secretaries, something which Hall soon rectified. The staff levels were increased. By May 1918 there were 74 men and 33 women working for Room 40. Seven new wireless interception sites opened up and 12 additional stations were put into operation at existing sites. Most important, as we have seen, under Blinker Hall it had begun its transformation from a decryption bureau into an intelligence centre. And, as we shall see below, Room 40 started interception and codebreaking operations in the Mediterranean. One organisational point is worth noting: in May 1917, Room 40 was officially incorporated within the Naval Intelligence Division, as ID 25. This represented an important step in Room 40's transition into an effective part of an intelligence centre. The ID 25 name is sometimes used in contemporary documents, but the Room 40 label has refused to go away.

***

The integration of Room 40's output of naval intelligence with convoys was only one of the ways in which British intelligence and military leaders started to use wireless intelligence to gain an advantage in the war. Captain Round, Marconi's wireless receiver engineer and developer of the direction-finding networks, had 'reappeared with proposals for intercepting signals in wave-lengths not [previously] taken by any of the stations'.[286] The new and more sensitive receivers meant that signals could be picked up from further afield, even from as far as 'transcaucasia' in the region to the east of the Black Sea, where Russia's empire butted up against its Ottoman counterpart.[287] So, during 1917 the quantity of German naval messages intercepted increased significantly owing to improvements in wireless receiver technology. The volume of traffic intercepted reached its maximum towards the end of the year.

It was also possible to pick up German naval wireless messages from the Baltic. Up until August 1916, all wireless messages intercepted from the Baltic had been 'put aside and destroyed' as they were not seen as having any relevance to British naval operations. As Frank Birch observed in a post-war internal document, 'When the reader reflects that Kiel was the training base of all new units of the German fleet and that the enemy talked far more garrulously by wireless telegraphy in those waters than in the North Sea he will form some idea of the amount of intelligence which had been wasted for two years of the war.'[288] The Baltic theatre was divided into two spheres of operation, the Eastern Baltic and the Western, which included the tortuous entrance to the Baltic via the Sound, between Denmark and Sweden. In the Eastern Baltic the Germany navy effectively had dominance over its Russian counterpart. But the German navy remained essentially no more than the German army's 'right wing', supporting it in its operations. The Western Baltic proved to be of more direct significance to Room 40. The German coasts east of Denmark served as the training grounds for the entire German navy, including submarines, torpedo boats and minesweepers as well as warships. The submarine school at Kiel alone had at any one time between two and three thousand officers and ratings undergoing training or waiting for an assignment. 'In the latter days of the war, the organisation of the [submarine] school assumed huge proportions,' wrote Birch. The Eastern Baltic was also where all new ships and submarines came for trialling, so again Room 40 could monitor the ships and submarines likely to be available soon for operations in the North Sea. Room 40 could watch the German navy developing its tactics. 'Once a year, at dates varying between January and March, all Battle Squadrons, accompanied by cruisers and destroyers, came to the Baltic simultaneously for battle practice.'

Room 40 had to think about the naval war in the Mediterranean too. Although there were Italian and French naval forces active there, they had limited resources. And they did not trust or co-operate with each other, concentrating on limited tasks that concerned their own direct military interests. France focused on supplying North Africa and Salonika, where it had troops. Italy was interested almost exclusively in the Adriatic. As a result, many of the general naval duties, such as protecting merchant ships, as well as supplying Allied forces in the Middle East, were the responsibility of the Royal Navy.

According to a post-war internal history, 'The importance of intelligence concerning the more remote theatres of the war was not realised until late, indeed too late. Mediterranean intelligence was thus allowed to continue for some time on the simple pre-war system ... The interception of enemy signals, was confined almost entirely to H. M. Ships [because the Allies were not trustworthy enough and were liable to indiscretions] ... it was subsequently discovered that the French and Italians had been in possession and use of an Austrian codebook – of which a copy had lain untouched for two years at the British Admiralty – until it went out of use, but [the French and Italians] failed to work out its successor, a comparatively simple task afterwards accomplished ... Nor had they any success with the submarine ciphers in use in those waters, a cipher which was a mere variation on the same codebook with periodical changes and easy of elucidation.'[289] In the spring of 1917, Blinker Hall made a tour of the Mediterranean, visiting Rome, Malta and Alexandria to assess how interception and codebreaking operations could be improved. He reported, 'I think the time has come when every effort must be made to assist our joint naval operations in the Mediterranean. The sinkings there are ... a matter of grave concern.'[290]

Hall thus sent one of his best cryptanalysts and most effective administrators, Nigel de Grey, with some seven or eight cryptographers plus several wireless engineers, to Italy. De Grey and his team set up an improved interception and cryptanalytic unit there and spread the benefits of Room 40's growing expertise. De Grey recalled at the end of the war that he had been working on US codes, but, 'When research on that was then no longer necessary I was given the Austrian Naval ciphers as used in the Adriatic to solve. On the solution of the particular cipher as used by German and Austrian submarines when in the Adriatic I was sent to Malta and Italy to arrange for the establishment of an advanced post for dealing with such messages on the spot. The Otranto wireless telegraphy intercepting station was erected and an officer installed ... for doing this work. I then returned to England having in Paris arranged with the *Etat Major* of the ministry of marine to attack the general fleet cipher of the Austrian navy in collaboration – this entailed working out a new book and took about six weeks before messages were readable. On their becoming so I was instructed to form two centres in Italy: one at Brindisi and another at Rome. This was done and I was appointed head of the Naval Intelligence Division to Rome where both ID 25 work and general Naval Intelligence was carried on. The Brindisi Centre was subsequently absorbed by Rome and worked with varying success until the armistice. The staff consisted of nine officers, four lady clerks and fifteen ratings, myself and the personnel of Numana wireless telegraphy station, which came under my command. The mission intercepted and manned all its owned communications through as far as Brindisi, working side by side with the Italian Ministry of Marine who had invited our co-operation and asked us to put the benefit of our experience of cryptology, [direction-finding] and general organisation at their disposal. We organised all the [direction-finding] communications for the Adriatic and for the Italians and communicated all results to ... Brindisi. Although much of the work that I did while at Rome was not precisely ID 25, ie, cryptographical work, ... it arose entirely from the solution of the Austrian Naval codes and was the logical development.'[291]

***

At the War Office, MI1(b)'s attention was diverted to the eastern Mediterranean when Allied troops were sent to Greece. It was also drawn towards interception and codebreaking in the Middle East, where British and Indian troops had been engaged since the start of the war, with mixed results.[292] The British army was involved in military operations all across the region, from the Caucasus, Persia (Iran), Mesopotamia (Iraq), to Palestine and Syria. According to one military historian, the Middle East formed the 'most complex task of intelligence in the entire First World War ... This theatre was vast and the needs for intelligence exceptionally precise. The Turks had small forces fighting the British but large reserves in Anatolia and the unexpected arrival of merely 20,000 Turkish soldiers could overthrow the balance of arms in Iraq or Palestine.'[293]

The Middle East was the seat of intense political and diplomatic competition, with the Ottoman Empire, the Russian Empire, the British Empire, the French Empire and the German Empire all meddling and conflicting. Britain had already gained sway over Ottoman lands in Egypt and the Gulf coast route between Suez and India. In 1915, an Indian army force was sent to take Baghdad, but the expedition ended in disaster when it had to surrender, having incurred 10,000 casualties, at Kut el-Amara. An additional 25,000 casualties resulted from fruitless rescue attempts. The losses at Kut and at Gallipoli signalled the end of belief in the invincibility of 'Western' troops. The setback in Mesopotamia prompted fresh thinking. In February 1916, control of forces in the Middle East passed from India to London. During the winter of 1917, Lloyd George convinced other policymakers of the strategic importance of the Middle East. An indecisive end to the war would leave Germany and its Ottoman ally in control of large parts of the Middle East. The security of the British Empire depended, he argued, on preventing German influence in the region, just as the security of the British homeland depended on preventing German control of the Channel ports. The German threat in the Middle East was seen as justifying further expansion of the Empire. The capture of German East Africa in the early months of the war had already established a continuous run of British-controlled territory between Cape Town and Cairo. The prize for the British was to link this African corridor directly with India. 'As of 1917, Palestine was the key missing link.'[294]

After the surrender at Kut, the British army ceased military operations in Mesopotamia and devoted time to building up forces and capabilities. The Middle East cryptographic unit of the War Office became a fairly important codebreaking operation and was born in 1916. 'Although wireless activity on the Western Front had entirely died down by the end of 1915, it was realised that where his land communications were bad the enemy would still be using his wireless.'[295] This drew MI1(b)'s attention to the southern Mediterranean and the Middle East – and specifically to Salonika, Egypt and, later on, Mesopotamia, where interception stations were set up.[296] By August 1916, the

Egyptian interception unit was taking in so much material that it started to become impractical to send it all back to London for decoding work. So 'one of the senior members of the cryptographical section' was dispatched to Egypt to set up a local unit there, handling intercepts from Egypt and Salonika. Initially the interception and codebreaking staff were managed as one unit, but, for unstated reasons, this did not work too well. Things improved in 1917 when the codebreakers were placed under the General Staff and they managed to decode most of the material that was intercepted, and only small numbers of messages still had to be sent on to London.

The British intercepted German service messages, Flying Corps messages, local purchasing orders as well as 'messages dealing with the activities of German intrigues with Persia … German intrigues with tribes in Arabia, the Anizah, Shammar, and Dilam and especially Ajaim of the Muntafik'. German and Turkish army tactical messages were common only during operations or when telegraph wires were interrupted, though there were daily reports to the German chief of staff back in Germany.[297] The most important intercepts were those which helped the British get a view of the Turkish 'order of battle', the names and details of the army units ranged against them. Intercepts also gave details of the discussions of strategy and operational planning conducted between senior Turkish and German commanders out at the various fronts (Mesopotamia, Palestine, Syria, the Caucasus) and capital cities. These intercepts allowed British commanders to plan counter operations.

Both the British and the Germans sent new commanders to the Middle East in 1916/17 as they realised the region's strategic importance. The new German commander was Erich von Falkenhayn, chief of staff of the German army until mid-1916 (when he was replaced by Ludendorff). He was then sent to the Romanian front, taking Bucharest in December 1916. From there he went to the Middle East to command the small German contingent of troops and provide military expertise to the Turkish commanders. As Falkenhayn had always been a determined 'Westerner', insisting on the crucial importance of the Western Front for the outcome of the war, his new mission signalled German recognition of the potentially decisive role of the Middle East. The new British commander, General Edmund Allenby, also came from the Western Front and imported some of its mass attack techniques. A post-war intelligence account notes that Allenby's successes were based, in part at least, on intercepts. 'In the near East wireless was largely employed in operations [by German and Turkish military units] and to the successful interception and solution of wireless signals much of General Allenby's success is said to have been due.'[298]

Another important factor was that Turkey was distracted by the prizes on offer in the disintegrating Russian Empire in the Caucasus (former Ottoman lands). This strategic view was evident in the intercepts which ordered a weakening of the defences of Turkish positions in the Middle East. Early in 1917, British and Indian troops recaptured Kut el-Amara, 'lost in humiliating circumstances' a year earlier, and then went on to take Baghdad. The commander, General Frederick Maude, had already planned his operation when intercepts informed him about Turkish debates on whether to reinforce their troops in Baghdad. The intercepts revealed that if they were to send more troops, it would take a few weeks before they could be got there. This intelligence confirmed Maude in his opinion that it was right to push on immediately towards Baghdad. Meanwhile, in Palestine, a British attack on Gaza in late March 1917 had been successful, but a stupid error led to the withdrawal of British troops. An intercepted message of 3 April 1917 revealed that Turkish intelligence believed that British 'positions have been withdrawn south of Ghasa to the lines of communication Rasel Markab'.[299] A new battle, between 17–19 April, was a Turkish success. Allenby arrived in July and spent his time carefully building up his forces, refusing to be hurried by calls for immediate successes. He finally launched the attack on Gaza on 27 October, but it was only a feint. The main attack swung round the defensive forces on the right, attacking Beersheba.[300] Again, it was intercept intelligence that confirmed to the British commander that his troops could strike at an unexpected point. Intercept evidence 'revealed the enemy's reaction to the British breakthrough, its plans for counter-attack – and the weak spot in its line. This was precisely where [Allenby] threw his reserve'.[301] A key part of the overall British campaign was gaining support from the 'Arab Revolt'. British diplomats promised Arab leaders independence (a promise that was broken). They did not contribute vast numbers of fighters, but played an important role in sabotaging (with the involvement of T. E. Lawrence) telegraph wires and Turkish troop-carrying trains. Intercepts gave the British an oversight of German and Turkish attempts to persuade and cajole rebels and potential rebels into supporting them and not the British.[302]

The codebreakers had to contend with 'double transposition' ciphers (see Chapter 4) and numerical 'subtractor' keys used on encoded messages. Initially the codebreakers were aided by a spectacularly bad piece of German operating procedure. The cipher key was changed irregularly every five days to five weeks. But there were only five keys in use and they were used over and over again. This practice was abandoned in May 1917 and a new set of keys was introduced, all of different lengths and used for just eight days. The codebreakers then developed several methods, known by names such as the 'perfect rectangle', the 'semi-perfect rectangle' and 'anagramming' to break these new cipher keys, but it should be noted that they were aided in the beginning by the retransmission of some messages in old and new keys.[303] The setbacks for Turkey and Germany in the Middle East in 1917 offered some relief to the Allies at a bleak time, as did the failure of the submarine war against Britain.

***

The First World War saw the birth of war in the air. Battlefield aircraft fought each other, directed artillery fire, bombed and strafed the enemy. Naval aircraft attacked enemy ships and submarines. Most shocking of all was the terror bombing from airships and aircraft of cities and their populations, aimed at damaging morale. As a post-war British intelligence assessment put it: 'It is difficult to account for the extraordinary widespread interest taken in Count Zeppelin's invention by the German public during the few years preceding the war. More than any other weapon possessed by the Army or Navy, it engaged the enthusiastic attention not only of practically the whole German people but also of the military and naval authorities who appear to have pinned their faith to the rigid airship rather than the heavier-than-air machine.'[304] Initially the naval airships were used for scouting so that the German navy need not risk engaging in action unless it was in superior force. However, cloud and poor visibility – not uncommon in the North Sea – limited their usefulness. 'In the meantime the Zeppelin had made her debut as a raider, a role she was to play with ever-increasing frequency and which was ultimately to become the chief end of her existence.'[305]

The German aircraft and airships organised a sustained campaign of bombing British cities. In response the War Office organised a system of defending British air space. This air war is now often called the 'First Battle of Britain'. This label is not misplaced. There were many similarities with the battle in Britain's skies in 1940. As in so many ways, the First World War version was a pre-cursor to the Second World War. But there were also differences. The greatest aid to winning the 1940 battle was radar, which allowed defending fighters to get into the air and meet the raiders. But radar was not available in the First World War. Instead it was wireless intelligence that gave the defenders advance notice of an air attack. It was impossible to keep defending aircraft aloft all the time in case of an attack, so such advance knowledge was critical. The solution came in a fine meshing of wireless direction-finding, wireless interception and decoding, and sophisticated communications and control systems.

The German air forces made the same frequent and systematic use of wireless before and during air raids as their ships and submarines did at sea. In fact it was German wireless traffic that announced a raid in the offing. Raids were invariably preceded by the transmission of a weather report from Bruges. Then, once the airships had taken off, they started sending messages, confirming to the British codebreakers that they were on their way. The rule was for Zeppelins, immediately after launch, to send by wireless a standard report, 'Naval Airship [number] taking off for distant scouting course [bearing]. Only HVB on board.'[306] The last part of the message was intended to ensure that crews complied with an order that they were only to take the commercially oriented HVB (the *Handelschiffsverkehrsbuch* – the merchant ships' codebook). To the benefit of the British codebreakers, airship crews repeatedly broke this rule and retrieved from crashed Zeppelins such prizes as the FFB (successor to the SKM) as well as the AFB (which succeeded the HVB). A third useful indicator of approaching Zeppelins was the system they used for locating themselves over the North Sea (dead reckoning not being feasible for an airship high up in the atmosphere). The Zeppelins would send a wireless signal so that German direction-finding stations could locate their position. This information would then be transmitted to the airship so that it could determine an approach route to its target. By listening out for the Zeppelins the British direction-finding stations could also take bearings on the airships. As seen earlier (Chapter 7) the British stations could give a more accurate triangulation of an airship's position than the Germans could supply to their own airships given that the British stations were spread between 49 and 57 degrees of latitude, whereas German stations were limited to a spread between 51 and 55 degrees of latitude. The British air defenders thus had a better idea of the position of the raiders than the raiders themselves.

This sort of information meant that British forces had time to prepare for airship raids (and to a lesser extent for aircraft raids too).[307] As one historian has concluded, 'Throughout the first Battle of Britain, wireless sources provided virtually the only operational intelligence available to British air defence. This material was of first rate quality.'[308] A special intelligence section was created within the War Office to handle all the intelligence about air raids (and the navy had a duplicate system) as it was recognised that the cryptanalytic tasks were specific to the bombing offensive and that it was best to bring all sources of intelligence together. The new section, known as MI1(e), was formed in mid-1916. Initially it had four cryptographer officers, two collating the Zeppelin messages and two breaking the cipher keys which changed daily.

The section developed into a sophisticated intelligence gathering and dissemination organisation. The individual wireless interception stations were connected 'by direct lines to the War Office telegraph room, and thence by pneumatic tubes to the main plotting centres in Room 417. This was the nerve centre of the organisation and was [the Director of Military Intelligence's] responsibility. As plots of raiding aircraft came through, warning was passed out via GHQ's Home Forces at Horse Guards, to all Home Commands. Four plotting tables were maintained and bearings were usually received within about 90 seconds of the original transmission.

Plotting officers wore headphones and microphones connected to Home Forces and Admiralty, and they talked as they plotted. The plotting maps covered England and Scotland. There was a hole in the map at each [direction-finding] site with a cord passing through it and a degree protractor printed round each [direction-finding site]. When a plot was made from two or more [direction-finding] bearings, a light was switched on below the map and the appropriate map square could be read out. Different Zeppelins were tracked on the various plotting tables and a master map was maintained to follow the whole raid. An example of the work done was to pick up the German daily weather reports to Zeppelins from Bruges. As Zeppelin raids increased, this traffic of weather reports plus the number of Zeppelins active and their movements during the forenoon indicated the likelihood of a raid the same night. Flying very slowly, at some 30 knots or so, and emitting a stream of [wireless] messages, the approaching Zeppelins gave ample warning to the War Office MI1(e) to organise duties and reliefs before nightfall.'[309] 'On one famous occasion,' reported a MI1(e) officer, 'in bad weather the interception service learned from the Zeppelin transmissions that the bombing fleet tho' over the east coast was badly off track and hopelessly lost. The AA guns and searchlights around London were silenced as a calculated risk,' so that the airships could not use them as a means of working out their position. One third of the attacking force was destroyed by British attacks or by accident in the stormy weather.[310]

German military engineers responded by building Zeppelins that could go higher and higher, out of reach of heavier-than-air fighter aircraft. This 'was the sole means of defence possessed by the Zeppelin ... Every change made in the construction of Zeppelins was henceforward to be in favour of increased size and greater powers of climbing, to the sacrifice of everything else, crew, space, offensive and defensive armament and even in the desire to reduce weight, the margin of safety provided in the strength of structural materials.' The largest Zeppelin had a capacity of two million cubic feet and was too unwieldy to land and manoeuvre close to ground, and anyway the great height meant greater navigational problems. As engineers sought to get away from the defenders they overlooked the role of wireless intelligence and intelligence handling. Many German officers suspected that the British must have had spies in Germany who kept them informed about the launching of air raids by airships or Zeppelins. Not only could they never find any of these spies, but they could not understand how it was possible for them to get their information to Britain quickly enough for them to intercept the approaching raiders. One suggestion put forward was the possibility of a secret submarine telegraph cable running from near Wilhelmshaven to Denmark where the spies' reports could be forwarded to Britain.

For all its sophistication, the British air defence system was of limited effectiveness. 'At best wireless interception might define the number of incoming airships and show that each would enter a given twenty-five mile long section of the coast in a twenty minute period, but it could not define their altitudes and could only approximately estimate speed and direction. Signals intelligence could not even meet this standard for aircraft – it could only warn that raids had been launched at a specific moment from a given place'.[311] Despite the deaths, injuries and heartbreak it caused, the air war on Britain remained a comparatively minor nuisance. It was strategically irrelevant and a waste of resources for the Germans. But, integrated with wireless intelligence, it prodded the British towards adopting a precedent that was of inestimable value just over 20 years later.

***

With the failure of the submarine campaign to knock Britain out of the war, and with its failure to prevent US troops from starting to arrive in Europe, Germany's second great gamble had failed. The submarine campaign was not called off but limped on, carefully watched over by Room 40, right up until the end of the war. As with the air war, it remained a death-dealing nuisance to the Allies. But it did not threaten defeat. Germany's military leaders needed to find a new way of bringing the war to an end. They flatly ruled out peace negotiations. So they had to look for a military solution. The situation cannot have looked that bleak. Russia, under Bolshevik leadership, had withdrawn from the imperialist war. The foreign affairs commissar, Leon Trotsky, imagined that his historic role would be to publish the secret war aims agreements of the Allies, issue a few proclamations calling for worldwide revolution and then shut up shop.[312] In fact his first task was to negotiate terms of disengagement with Germany – after all it was only Russia which had declared an end to the war. Trotsky and Lenin tried to drag out negotiations, expecting German troops would follow the Bolshevik lead and start their own socialist revolution, or at the very least that they would refuse to fire on Russian soldiers. Just after taking power, Lenin proclaimed to the Congress of Soviets that once 'the German proletariat realises that we are ready to consider all offers of peace, revolution will break out in Germany'.[313] By January 1918 he began to realise that world revolution was no longer imminent, so he then sought to prolong the talks while the Bolsheviks secured control at home. By March 1918, Germany's leaders had lost patience and moved forward, occupying large parts of Russia and its empire. The revolutionaries, realising that their bluff had been called, hurriedly agreed the treaty of Brest-Litovsk, giving Germany control of some 1.25 million square miles of territory, 56 million people, one-third of Russia's railways, three-quarters of its iron production and nine-tenths of its coal output. Military leaders and right wing elements who fantasised about populating a greater Germany were delighted with their gains. War could still pay. But there were downsides too. Germany had to keep a million soldiers in the occupied territories to control the population and exploit local resources. This meant that the great dividend which had been promised by the defeat of Russia – the release of sufficient troops from the Eastern Front to alter the balance of forces on the Western Front – was sacrificed.

The only option open to the military command seemed to be yet another big gamble. A final mass effort would break the Allied line on the Western Front in the British sector and force Britain out of the war. The troops moved to the Western Front brought with them a tactical lesson learned on the Eastern front. First pioneered by Russian troops under General Brusilov in 1916, the Germans had adopted and adapted the new form of attack, using groups of 'stormtroopers' and follow-up troops to burst their way deep into enemy lines.[314] Ludendorff's offensive, planned to start in March 1918, was to be on a gargantuan scale. Millions of men had to be trained in the new tactics. Millions of shells had to be transported to the attack points, as did hundreds of artillery pieces. All these preparations could not be hidden from the Allies. The fact that an offensive was coming was obvious, but British intelligence and army commanders were misled about where on the Allied line the attack would take place. German military intelligence tried to hoodwink the Allies into believing that the troops being amassed in northwest Europe were in fact to be used elsewhere, such as Italy or the Balkans. This idea was spread among the diplomatic communities of neutral European countries, but was never taken seriously by the Allies. In fact the anxious vehemence with which the rumours were pressed on them made them suspect that a deception campaign was underway. More successfully, dummy wireless signals were used to give the impression that an army was being transferred to the opposite part of the French line. In fact the attack was to take place on the British line at the point where it made contact with the French troops (as this was likely to be a weak point with difficult communications and confused command between the two Allies). The amount of German wireless traffic increased significantly, overwhelming the Allied field interception and cryptanalytic units. Up until the end of 1917, British intelligence had a very good record of the German army's 'order of battle'. But from the beginning of 1918 they lost sight of which unit was being moved where. They picked up such a mass of hints of an attack at different places along the line that it was difficult to know where it might take place. Only in mid-February did it appear likely that the target was the British sector. And just before the attack the German army organised a complete change of code and cipher systems. In the last few days before the attack British commanders, on the section of the front that was to be the focus of the assault, discounted intelligence of the imminent offensive from prisoners. They also were incompetent in arranging defences, pushing far too many troops forward to the front line. This proved to be a disaster, given the new German stormtrooper tactics, but it should not have been done in any case.

At first the German offensive was a roaring success, capturing many square miles of territory in a few days, so much in contrast to the hard pounding needed under the old tactics to gain a few square yards. The Kaiser cracked open bottles of champagne to toast the reversal of fortunes. Victory seemed in reach. But the attack petered out as its supply lines became too stretched and the Allies started to organise themselves. Ludendorff lost sight of his objectives. He started switching the focus of attack, thus blunting it. And, crucially, German soldiers stopped fighting to gorge themselves on captured supplies of food and wine. After years of minimal rations, they preferred the opportunity to indulge themselves rather than fight. Even teams of baton-wielding *feldpolizei* (military police) were unable to rouse the revellers to pick up their weapons and fight on. The soldiers also realised that the propaganda they had been fed about the poor conditions on the Allied side were lies. This was the first major sign of the collapse of morale in the German army.[315] When the battle was finally called off, the German army had suffered some 250,000 casualties – killed, wounded or captured. The British suffered some 236,000 and the French 75,000. Germany could no longer replace its losses, while US troops were arriving at a rate of 125,000 a month and in May, at the end of the offensive, there were already some 670,000 fresh US troops in northern France. The full extent of the losses was hidden from the Kaiser, the Chancellor, German troops and the German public by Ludendorff whose propaganda puffed on about great German gains. But the fact that the offensive was a failure could not be suppressed. The submarine assault had not ended the war. The blockade was biting. Rations were again reduced. 'The entire army had anticipated an overwhelming victory from the March offensive, and when this did not occur morale sunk.'[316] Ludendorff, however, did not learn the lessons. He blamed inadequate efforts by his subordinate commanders, by his troops and by civilians on the home front. 'In some places,' he said, 'wages are so high that there is no longer any incentive to work. On the contrary, disinclination to work, love of pleasure and high living are on the increase. Workmen often lounge about all day.'[317]

Chapter 18

War, Revolution and Peace

In early 1917 the Russian Empire collapsed under the strain of war, unleashing the Russian Revolution. In late 1917 the Bolsheviks seized power, signing a peace treaty with the Germans in March 1918. The British military attaché in Moscow during the talks leading up to the signing of the treaty had access to intercepts of telegraph messages sent back and forth between the Russian negotiators in Brest-Litovsk (where the German military headquarters was located) and the Bolshevik government in Petrograd. The telegrams were copied by political opponents of the Bolsheviks at the telegraph office and passed to British diplomats. The telegraph line had been put in with the agreement of the Germans as it crossed territory controlled by them, so no doubt the German army and Foreign Office negotiators also had access to the Bolshevik communications. One diplomatic historian notes that some of the information used by codebreakers to crack the Russian messages came from a source high up in the Bolshevik leadership, none other than Trotsky's deputy until January 1918, Zalkind. He 'had the reputation in western circles of being a nervous and irascible man, of violent anti-western sentiments. None of the foreigners appear to have been personally drawn to him in any way. In some quarters he was denounced as a likely German agent. On the other hand, a curious unsigned intelligence report … would seem to indicate that Zalkind had been, intentionally or otherwise, the main source of Allied knowledge about Soviet' cryptographic operations.[318]

Blinker Hall was worried about the fate of the pre-revolution Russian codebreakers and of the big secret. One of the Bolshevik's first acts had been to publish secret war aims treaties signed by the Allies. This open diplomacy was a shock and there was a serious worry that it might lead to embarrassing revelations about British codebreaking activities. In return for the delivery of the SKM codebook to the Royal Navy at the start of the war, Room 40 and the Naval Intelligence Division had disclosed all intelligence that was picked up that might be of interest to Russia's armed forces. Back in April 1917, following the first stage of the revolution, Hall had written to his Russian colleague suggesting that he burn 'all documents and papers concerned with our mutual work. Should the situation improve I can replace everything.' By the time the Bolsheviks seized power in the autumn, Hall's fears were for his colleagues' safety – and, no doubt, their usefulness if they were to become part of Room 40. He was particularly concerned that they might fall into German hands and even proposed that they should all sail in Russian ships through the Baltic to the Sound, where they would be met by British warships. 'Arrangements could be made to have forces distract the enemy and assist vessels through Sound to England.'[319] Perhaps because this sounds more like a suicide cruise than a serious plan, it did not get implemented. However, at least one member of the Tsarist codebreaking team was brought out of Russia, with the help of British secret services. He joined Room 40 in June 1918. Ernst Fetterlein became a key asset as Room 40's successor turned its attention to its former ally and he was soon engaged in breaking Soviet ciphers, becoming an important codebreaker in the post-war organisation that brought together both Room 40 and MI1(b).

In 1918 it was Germany that appeared most likely to undergo a communist revolution. Ludendorff thought repression of the German population was justified because he imagined that its will to fight was being undermined by agitators and militants. In reality it was his own domestic policies that directed German workers – and soldiers and sailors – into the radical camp. In the words of one historian, 'Whatever the problem, he insisted on giving priority to narrow military considerations.'[320] Civilian morale sank lower and lower. Germany's allies too were faltering under the pressure of war. After the failure of the March 1918 western offensive, German military morale also started to collapse. By the end of July the tables were turned and Allied armies were on the offensive. When British, Canadian and Australian troops, along with 600 tanks, launched an attack on 8 August it was the beginning of the end for the German occupation of Belgium and northern France. The British army (with dominion troops playing the key role), the French army and the American army attacked repeatedly, each time grabbing a bit more territory from the German troops. During both the German and Allied offensives there was a significant increase in the use of wireless by the German army. 'The enemy has generally made great use of his wireless during the last two months, very high activity having been noticed following our attacks. As a result of our offensive of 8 August there was a considerable disorganisation of his wireless system: several messages were sent in clear and there were repeated requests for repetitions of messages etc. Activity ceased altogether at 11.00hrs evidently owing to the compulsory withdrawal of his stations. Prior to the enemy's attack of 11 July his wireless activity was slight along the Marne, but was considerable in the sector northwest of Chateau-Thierry, where there was much lateral communication. During the battle the activity of medium wave stations working for the higher formations was slight compared with their activity during the offensive of 27th May.'[321] One noticeable feature was the increasing use of wireless communications to high-powered anti-aircraft gun batteries to counter Allied aircraft. But it was to no avail. In August Ludendorff wobbled, in September he cracked. He demanded an immediate peace. The politicians to whom he turned to get him instantaneous peace pointed out that it would take some time. They began to make contact with President Wilson, who it was assumed would demand a less onerous peace than the bitter French and greedy British. Meanwhile the Allied offensive continued pushing the German army back towards the German border. At sea the submarine war also carried on. On 4 October, a U-boat sank a passenger vessel with the loss of 292 lives. On the 10th another ship was sunk with the loss of 176 out of 720 passengers on board. Wilson demanded an immediate stop to the sinking of passenger ships. Ludendorff, who now started to insist that he had never asked for peace, opposed giving in to Wilson's demands, as did the new navy chief, Scheer. But on 20 October the Kaiser finally found the will to overrule Ludendorff and called off the submarine attacks on passenger vessels. An angry Scheer recalled all submarines to base. The submarine ports at Ostend and Zeebrugge were closed as Allied armies pushed their advance. The submarine war was over.

Admiral von Scheer, however, was hatching another idea for the use of his submarines. In the words of one German historian, 'Among the naval commanders the idea still held force that the navy had to demonstrate and justify its future existence. Now this could only be done through a last decisive battle with the British.'[322] Scheer did not inform the *Admiralstab*, the Kaiser or the Chancellor about his plans. On 22 October he started preparations for such a final naval sortie with as many German ships as were available, including the entire fleet of U-boats. But rumours of the operation reached the German crews who mutinied. In Cuxhaven, Kiel and Wilhelmshaven, ships' crews took control of their vessels, snatched down the imperial flag and raised the red flag. In Kiel, thousands of armed sailors marched in the streets and formed workers' and soldiers' councils in imitation of the Russian 'soviets'. The fever spread to other naval and then commercial ports, such as Hamburg and Bremen, and finally to inner Germany, to Cologne, Hanover, Frankfurt, Dresden, Munich and eventually to Berlin itself. Mutiny threatened to turn into revolution.

Room 40 picked up hints of the planned final battle. On 22 October, intercepted messages showed that all German submarines were ordered to concentrate in the middle of the North Sea, but no one in the Naval Intelligence Division could be sure what this implied. Then overnight on 23/24 October there was an unusually high number of messages – and they were sent in an unknown cipher. It seems that Room 40 was unable to break this cipher so the content remained a mystery, but the unusual flurry of messages put it on alert. And it was still watching those submarines, noting that otherwise there was little naval activity. On the 28th some messages were decoded showing that five submarines had been ordered to start patrolling in the North Sea and also that a squadron of warships had been ordered to take on coal. These were sure signs of a sortie in the offing. An assessment sent to Beatty, then commander-in-chief of the Grand Fleet, stated, 'Dispositions of enemy submarines combined with position of their large minefield recently laid and now clear constitutes fairly decisive evidence of his desire to draw the Grand Fleet out,' but it was thought 'unlikely that the enemy will risk fleet action until Armistice negotiations are settled one way or another'.[323] In fact, at this time, the German fleet had been gathering in Schillig Roads prior to launching the sortie. Senior British naval commanders already suspected (and, in not a few cases, hoped) that Scheer would launch a final attack. This intelligence allowed them to confirm by 28 October that such a sortie was likely. All the same they still underestimated the extent of the German plans to draw the British Grand Fleet into a massive battle.

On the 29th wireless messages revealed that the *Hochseeflotte* was beginning to assemble in Schillig Roads. Early on 30 October the Naval Intelligence Division expected the sortie to begin that day, informing the admiral in charge of the Grand Fleet, David Beatty. But just after 8.30am, Room 40 learned that the fleet was to remain at anchor for the time being. Early in the afternoon more messages showed that the sortie had been postponed until the next day. Room 40's first guess was that this was probably due to foggy weather in the German Bight. But then messages to submarines were intercepted informing them that all operations up to 5 November had been cancelled and they could leave their current positions. On 31 October more decodes showed that minesweeping and other operations had also been cancelled and one squadron of warships had been sent to the Baltic. For a few days nothing out of the ordinary appeared in the airwaves, though an expected change in the cipher key did not take place. Otherwise minesweeping and similar operations by small boats resumed and continued as normal, as they had not been infected by the revolutionary fever.

On 1 November, Room 40 intercepted several messages referring to courts martial and deserters. A message was decoded on 5 November instructing all ships that all cipher key documents were to be locked up immediately and that messages were only to be decoded by officers. Shortly afterwards a message sent to U-139 informed them that there had been a 'revolution' at Kiel and that a workers' and soldiers' council had been set up. Early in the morning of 6 November a message instructed all submarines to fire without warning on any ships displaying a red flag.

On 11 November the armistice came into force, but German naval wireless stations remained as garrulous as ever. A selection of intercepted messages from that day illustrates how the war ended in confusion and revolt for the German navy. At 13.40hrs, U-boat U-70 reported that it was off Emden, but 'says she will not proceed into Emden unless an assurance is given she will not be put under the red flag'. The workers' and soldiers' council gave the submarine permission to come in using the naval ensign. Meanwhile the *Admiralstab* sent out a message announcing: 'Armistice concluded. Therefore all acts of war are to cease and all warships are to [head for port] at full speed according to directions.' A short while later another message was sent in the name of workers' and soldiers' council announcing the formation of a new government. The next day a message related that the previous 'order dealing with treating the Red Flag as an enemy flag is cancelled. Make sure this is transmitted to all submarines in the neighbourhood. Secondly, proceed to your base.' Later that day another message from the workers' and soldiers' council at Augsburg was intercepted. 'With reference to wireless of this morning and a telephone order … we request that the Workers' and Soldiers' Council at Cuxhaven to have the 1,000 sailors armed and in good order ready at the station at 1 o'clock. The courier of the Imperial government will arrive there about 1pm with sufficient train accommodation to fetch the crews. We are hastening the execution (of this order) as the Imperial government of the Socialists in Berlin is in a perilous position.'[324] The 'German Revolution', and similar ructions in Austria and Hungary, sputtered on but never really threatened to take Germany and central Europe down the road to Bolshevism. The German army general staff, the police and the national bureaucracy survived the upheavals. Fear of Bolshevism and chaos restrained the radical government, its failure leading to the rise of right-wing *Freikorps* and other counter-revolutionary paramilitary organisations. The war to end all wars was over, though a new war was brewing in Russia where the Bolsheviks, now lacking widespread support, resorted to terror to prolong their rule, taking the exhausted nation into a civil war.

After the Armistice, Room 40's work dwindled, but MI1(b)'s expanded for a few months. The peace talks at Versailles presented MI1(b) with stiff new challenges. It had to increase the number of staff working on diplomatic codebreaking from 70 at the end of the war to 100. MI1(b) had concentrated on neutral countries, Room 40 on Germany and its allies. Now the former enemies were defeated, demoralised countries racked by internal discontents, the neutrals and former Allies were now the important target countries – it was the balance of forces between them which would determine the terms of the peace settlement. Germany simply had to accept the terms dictated to it.

According to one original document, Room 40 handled some 37,000 intercepted naval messages during the war, and sent out about 54,000 messages to the navy's Operations division between October 1914 and June 1918.[325] Another document claims, 'Some 200,000 signals' were dealt with.[326] It seems most likely that all these figures account only for German naval messages and exclude 'political/diplomatic' messages. The diplomatic section alone handled another 30,000 intercepted messages of which 90 per cent were decoded.[327] There are no comparable statistics for MI1(b)'s and MI1(e)'s throughput. For MI1(b) the number of diplomatic messages handled was probably not much lower than Room 40's diplomatic tally. Also army field units must have decoded many thousands of field messages. We do know that 'At the time of the Armistice the total number of diplomatic [code]books solved [by MI1(b)] was fifty-two ... Trench codes had been solved to a number of forty-eight; while of German and Turkish field ciphers a total of over 700 different keys, etc., had been dealt with.'[328] Thus, in all, many hundreds of thousands of messages must have been intercepted and decoded by British codebreakers across the many fronts on which the First World War was fought out. This was no bumbling amateur lash-up that just managed to muddle through. By the end of the war, it was a finely honed, professional operation that laid the basis for the achievements of British codebreakers in the Second World War.

Chapter 19

After the War

A memo preserved in the archives, dating from May 1918, is the first sign of planning for the post-war future of Room 40 and MI1(b). 'It will doubtless be necessary to devise some system to come into operation after the war for combining and amalgamating the information at present accruing from several separate services.'[329] The Admiralty argued, 'there can be no question that, having once instituted this form of research [ie, cryptographic work], it would be a grave mistake to let it drop'. Cryptography provided, it was claimed, the cheapest and most reliable intelligence about 'the intentions of other powers'.[330] Those politicians 'in the know', such as Foreign Secretary Lord Curzon, were enthusiastic about the opportunity to benefit from eavesdropping. Curzon commented in November 1919 that 'the deciphered telegrams of foreign governments are without doubt the most valuable source of our secret information respecting their policy and actions'.[331]

As we have seen, MI1(b) handled cable traffic and Room 40 dealt with wireless messages. These cryptographic bureaux passed their intelligence on, respectively, to the Director of Military Intelligence, DMI, or to the Director of Naval Intelligence, DNI. These individuals in turn decided to send intelligence on 'to whom they think fit'. The Foreign Office only got its intelligence 'at the discretion of the DNI and DMI'.[332] The contingencies and urgencies of war dictated that this was a tolerable practice, but it was not acceptable in peacetime. A new joint organisation seemed necessary, serving the military, navy and government. There were several problems to be overcome – getting political approval, changing the law to permit interception, finding funds and appointing the right people.

Wireless interception rapidly became less important. The British army actually closed down all its field interception units except for those in the Middle East.[333] It became clear that the bulk of post-war interception work would come from the diplomatic traffic of other governments. The military thus looked to the Foreign Office to take charge. The Foreign Office, however, was not particularly keen to take on any new responsibility. It was 'obviously impractical for reasons of secrecy apart from financial grounds for these [cryptographic organisations] to be provided out of ordinary Diplomatic and

Consular vote [ie, funds approved by Parliament] … the cost of this secret work might be met by including the Admiralty and War Office experts in the organisation of the proposed new Codes and Ciphers Department, thus concealing them from view'. The Government Code and Cipher School, GC&CS as it became known, formally created on 1 November 1919, is now best remembered for its Second World War codebreaking achievements.[334]

The first problem was to mould one organisation out of two units which had developed into maturity within two traditionally uncooperative departments of state, the Admiralty and the War Office. From late 1918 discussions were held between Blinker Hall as DNI and Colonel French as DMI about how to amalgamate the two operations. Some of the urgency went out of the efforts when Blinker Hall left the service in January 1919 and his energetic approach to the conduct of affairs was lost. The Admiralty then played an awkward game, insisting: 'We should only consent to pool our staff with that of the War Office on condition that Commander A. Denniston is placed in charge of the new department. I do not say this on account of any jealousy of the War Office, or any reluctance to accept a War Office man, but because no one who had not been trained in the conditions under which we have had to work could meet the requirements of the Admiralty in time of war.' Room 40 had had to tackle a new key every morning, sometimes two or three times a day. 'This has of necessity developed a particular kind of aptitude for the work, which depends for its success more on a study of the psychology of the persons sending out the messages and a sort of intuitive "*flaire*" for the kind of things they are saying than a careful study and analysis for which there is no time. In the War Office they have dealt with cables which are far more accurate than wireless. They have never had to work against time, and the aptitude they have developed is *different from* – I don't for one moment suggest it is inferior to – that which the conditions of our work have produced.'[335]

There were two candidates to head the new organisation, one from MI1(b) and one from Room 40: respectively, Malcolm Hay, the wounded soldier Scottish laird, and Alastair Denniston, the hockey-playing navy schoolmaster. Hay had got along fairly well with Hall, but with Denniston it was different. 'When together couldn't agree on anything,' commented a colleague.[336] A conference took place at the Admiralty on 5 August 1919 to decide who would be offered the job (neither Hay nor Denniston was present). It was reported that Hay was willing to serve as head, but refused to take a post as subordinate to anyone else. Furthermore, he was willing to have Denniston work under him, 'but he did not desire the services of that officer, nor did he consider his services were essential'. Denniston was a more astute player of the bureaucratic game. He had said that he was prepared to serve under Hay, 'at all events for a time'. Hay's own boss, the

Director of Military Intelligence, 'considered it intolerable that an officer should attempt to dictate his terms of service in such a manner and rather than accept such conditions he would prefer to see the organisation started completely afresh'. A War Office representative said that 'although he could not explain the reason it was nevertheless a fact that the workers at Cork Street [MI1(b)'s location] did not like Commander Denniston'.[337] The Admiralty gave its full backing to Denniston. He 'is not only the best man we have had, but he is the only one we have left with special genius for this work'.[338] The conference heard that while 'Hay was perhaps the cleverer of the two, Commander Denniston was the better administrator'. With the War Office not backing its man, its call for a fresh start was a weak case against an Admiralty which saw the opportunity to put its choice at the head of the new organisation. Denniston was offered the job at £1,000 per annum.[339]

One point is important here. The now redundant Hay ordered the burning of all papers relating to MI1(b) before he left and as a result very few documents about the military cryptographical effort during the First World War have survived. Indeed, those few documents that are now available in the National Archives are nearly all copies of MI1(b) files and decrypts that were sent to Room 40 as part of the circulation of material. Fortunately, Denniston, or his Admiralty superiors, approved the setting up of a historical section within the Naval Intelligence Division to write a history of the naval war based on intercepted messages and other intelligence material. The authors were Frank Birch and William F. Clarke. Essentially, it is thanks to Denniston, or whoever took the decision not to follow Hay's example and burn all papers, that we are today able to study the events of the secret war of 1914-1918.[340] It is worth noting that one of the recently released files relating to MI1(b) contains a 'tea and lunch account', giving details of how much money each member of staff owed for the month of October 1917. Most had run up a tally of a few shillings, but some were in debt by more than £1. The list was not preserved so that we might have some insight into the alimentary habits of codebreakers. A scrawled handwritten note, presumably from a recent pruning of files at GCHQ, states, 'The tea and luncheon lists should not be destroyed – they give MI1(b) staff names in October/November 1917.'[341] It is thanks to such belated thoughtfulness that we owe some of the few facts that we do know about this secretive unit.[342]

A selection was made from those members of staff who wanted to stay on. Of the fifty staff in the new organisation about half were cryptographers, the others being translators, typists and clerical staff. A few letters from those who sought employment give us a hint of the desperation of some, such as officers who had been injured and for whom the prospects of interesting and gainful employment were not very high. Lieutenant J. Patrick Curwen, who had returned home from the USA at the start of the war to join the army, enlisted in the Artists Rifles and was invalided home after being wounded in 1915. After recovering he applied for more foreign service and was assigned to HMS *Excellent* (a naval shore station). Here he was injured on duty – though not in action – and was again sent home, ending up in Room 40 in September 1917. In his letter of application asking to stay on he took no steps to puff up his interest in cryptography, merely remarking, 'I should very much like to remain in ID25 in peace time. I have no other prospects of work in view whatever.' He had been in the Baltic section, in September 1918 becoming its head, and as Russia moved into the centre of focus he had potentially valuable knowledge. However, Dennniston's judgement on him was that while he was a 'sound worker' his command of foreign languages was only 'fair'. Another supplicant was Captain E. D. Hanly who joined the Intelligence Division in November 1917. According to William F. Clarke, Hanly was 'a Guards officer who had been gassed, wounded and taken prisoner. Sent to Switzerland to recover. Nursed by daughter of Lord Denbigh whom he married. Rich father but his money in Argentina. This broke up the marriage. Being a RC [Roman Catholic] he could not remarry. Remained a very rich man.'[343] After joining Room 40 he worked initially as a 'tubist' but was soon engaged in cryptography, key recovery, research work and writing appreciations dealing with messages sent by airships, aeroplanes and submarines. He was fluent in Spanish, acquainted with technical German and a qualified interpreter in French. On his CV he noted, 'I have been employed in Room 40 in every capacity, and I am therefore acquainted with every branch.' He wrote, 'May I ask you to include me, temporarily, among those who wish to remain on. I was invalided out of the Army last January after eleven years service and I have so far been unable to fix up my future in any way. If the pay were even moderately good and the prospects the same I should like, if possible, to remain on.' Denniston had marked him down, however, as one of three cryptographers who should only be considered 'as first substitutes in the event of any refusals among the initial choices'. Neither Curwen nor Hanly made it on to Denniston's list.[344]

Nor did Herbert Morrah, the writer, Home Ruler and strange creature in Frank Birch's parody, *Alice in I.D. 25*. His application letter made clear his desire for promotion and more varied work: 'As my past service has involved the knowledge of German and my general Continental experience in several other countries goes beyond that knowledge: I have always hoped that the scope of Naval Intelligence work in the future would be such as to afford me further chances of employment and advancement and that the work of the past might be taken into account. Whilst quite willing to continue in the task allotted to me, I am rather anxious to learn that the arrangements contemplated will be under naval authority and under naval officers. A definite principle is at stake here, but apart from that, my experience here, leads me to regard the authority of the Intelligence Department as a great help and encouragement in doing my daily work.'[345] No doubt Denniston was not keen to have a man who set such conditions. He had to mould a joint team out of the best of two organisations and it would not be helpful to have people obsessed with their wartime team loyalties.

On the other hand, there were cryptographers who Denniston did want, but who had to be persuaded not to leave. Mr Sansom was the Japanese expert but he was unwilling to stay on permanently. Denniston noted that the Foreign Office 'have been making up his pay to his requirements, as his work is so essential'. He would try to persuade him to stay long enough to train a successor. Another much-wanted team member was Captain Brooke Hunt who had been second-in-charge at Cork Street under Hay. 'As such [he] is most essential to the permanent office, as he carries with him the experience of dealing with cables. He has a marked aptitude for cryptography as well as experience in constructional work.' He should thus be offered suitable pay.[346]

Denniston's preferred choices for the research team were E. Fetterlein (the Russian émigré), J. Fraser, J. Turner, Dilly Knox, Lt Fryer and Oliver Strachey, with Fetterlein and Fraser as the senior cryptographers. The cryptographic teams would be Miss Anderson and Miss Watkins (French and Italian); Montgomery, Hardisty, Captain Hunt and Earnshaw Smith (Central and Eastern Europe); Lt Rees and Miss Spurling (Scandinavia); Lt Aitken and Hugo R. Ford (Spain and South America); Captain Brooke Hunt and Lieutenant McGrath (USA); Sansom and A. N. Other (the Far East). There would also be an intelligence office consisting of Lt G. L. N. Hope, Lt J. Hooper, William F. Clarke, Jopson, and a technical expert, Lt Lambert RNVR (the wireless broadcaster A. J. Alan). Four translators, among them Miss Haylar and Miss Lunn, and several wireless operators and clerical assistants were also needed.

After leaving, Hall pursued a political career, building a reputation as a leader of the 'die-hard' right-winger MPs who hounded the wartime premier, Lloyd George and wanted a tough line against Bolsheviks. During the General Strike of 1926, Winston Churchill appointed him editor of the *London Gazette*, recognizing that his energy and fondness for underhand tactics were ideally suited to weakening the strike. He was also implicated in leaking intercepted Soviet communications – with the intention of embarrassing the government into expelling Russian diplomats. Ewing returned to quiet academia. In the late 1920s and 1930s both Hall and Ewing craved recognition for their wartime activities and both tried to write books on the subject, but both were prevented by GS&CS from publishing their stories. Ewing had to be threatened under the Official Secrets Act when he started to talk about Room 40 in lectures at Edinburgh.

Hay retired to his Scottish estate, becoming a recognised writer on Catholic history.After the Second World War he upset the Catholic hierarchy when he bitterly criticised the Pope's silence over the extermination of Jews in Europe by the Nazis. Perhaps initial doubts about the his beloved Catholic Church first arose when he saw the First World War intercepts showing the Pope had supported a 'peace' that would have rewarded German aggression. Despite his physical wounds, Hay was keen on keeping fit. His second wife later wrote, 'I believe the physical activity that had always given him most pleasure was walking and climbing among the hills or in deserts, and if he had not been wounded and disabled, it is quite likely he would have been a serious mountaineer. Only 10 years before he died, when already over 70, he climbed, twice in one week, the highest hill in Braemar. The descent was always for him the most difficult part.'[347] Hay died in 1967.A memorial tablet in the Library at King's College, Cambridge, reads, 'Scholar, Writer, Soldier, Friend of Generous Causes'. It should include 'Cryptographer'.

Denniston remained head of GC&CS, through various ups and downs, until 1941 when he was shunted aside to be in charge of diplomatic interception. His replacement at Bletchley Park was his deputy since 1919, Edward Travis, said to be 'definitely of the bulldog breed'.[348] Denniston was 'disappointed and extremely bitter'.[349] An old colleague commented that Denniston 'was head strong and didn't like criticism; after all he had carried the group through the 1930s, against criticism quite often, and now that war had actually occurred he wanted to be at the helm, in charge of the organisation he had created … the villain of the piece was really a man named Freeborn … he was power-hungry and realized that with [Denniston] out of the way he could manipulate to his heart's content'.[350] Interestingly, Freeborn was head of Bletchley Park's punched-card machine operations and under Denniston's regime had to fight to keep his section in existence. Denniston, it seems, lacked the initiative to push for the resources needed by people such as Alan Turing who wanted to use machines more extensively in codebreaking. Four senior codebreakers, in a move of sheer bureaucratic insolence, took their complaints about the lack of resources to the Prime Minister, Winston Churchill, who, of course, knew quite a lot about the value of codebreaking. The general view is that Denniston was poorly served by being shunted off to handle diplomatic interception, away from Bletchley Park. One note of caution is needed before accepting this standard judgement as we know very little about British diplomatic codebreaking in the Second World War. It is possible that Denniston and his colleagues achieved more than we have been allowed to know about. A final assessment will have to wait until all the files are released. After the Second World War, Denniston retired and took up teaching German. He was a supporter of the Liberal party, but lived in an illiberal rural area, writing to a friend, 'I live in a village almost feudal where the Tories rule the roost and the pub will hardly serve a "red" ie, any non-conservative ... I only wish that Winston had retired – he is not a great man but a leader in time of war and I have no wish for a third world war in my lifetime.'[351] Churchill was, of course, the politician who promoted Travis to take over Denniston's job in 1941. Despite their flaws, it is thanks to men such as Ewing, Hay, Hall, Denniston and Churchill – and the cryptographers and intelligence analysts they employed – that Britain found itself on the winning side in two world wars.

Epilogue

The secrecy covering Britain's military, naval and diplomatic codebreaking had been pretty well maintained throughout the First World War. 'Bubbles' James sent a letter to all Room 40 staff, most of whom were leaving the organisation, reminding them not to take the end of hostilities as a sign that their obligation to remain silent about their wartime activities had also ceased. 'I think that at this moment it may not be out of place to say one word of warning about the importance of retaining secrecy about our work. During the last four years the whole success and value of our work has depended on its secrecy and now that we have come victorious out of the war it might not seem so important to keep this work secret as heretofore. This is not the case and it is just as important now as it ever was for our work to be unknown to any except those who have worked here and the few naval officers who have had the entrée in connection with their work.'[352] But it was not the lower ranks that needed the advice.

There were problems with the Admiralty's official history which had been promised to an eager general public. Jellicoe was most upset when he saw a draft, as the chapter on Jutland did not mention 'certain telegrams' sent to him by the Admiralty. These were, of course, the telegrams that conveyed the contents of intercepted and decrypted German messages. Jellicoe thought that his actions during the battle would be seen in a different light if the official history gave details of the intelligence that lay behind his decision-making. The guardian of the secret, the Admiralty's censor, William F. Clarke, wrote in a memo that if Jellicoe's demands were met it would mean that 'the source of his secret information will be practically made public and the publication will probably invoke a storm of criticism. The critics will ask why if the Admiralty had this source of information at their disposal, better use was not made of it, and the Board of Admiralty will be subjected to constant embarrassment.' He also listed several other reasons for maintaining silence about Room 40: Jellicoe might then also ask for publication of the decrypted messages about which he was not informed (but which he had subsequently found out about); other commanders would ask for publication of telegrams affecting their decisions; the whole of the official history would have to be rewritten; and, 'the existence of the political [ie, diplomatic] side of our work may also come to light and certain matters, which for reasons of state, it is most undesirable to publish [presumably, the Zimmermann telegram affair]'.[353] The line was held, but pressure was bound to build up.

The first exposure of the secret of Room 40's activities came from none other than the First Sea Lord at the time of its inception, the volatile Jacky

Fisher. He claimed that the wireless station on the roof of the Admiralty building in central London had intercepted all German naval messages and that they had been promptly decoded within the building. The controversies over naval command led to the next leak. It emanated from a journalist, Filson Young, who was friendly to Admiral Beatty. In 1914, Young had managed to blag his way into an appointment as a RNVR lieutenant on Beatty's flagship in the 'battle cruiser' squadron. With no naval or marine experience Beatty put Young in his intelligence section, receiving and decoding signals from the Admiralty to pass them on to Beatty. Young stayed for six months, so was present at the Battle of Dogger Bank in December 1914 (see Chapter 7).

Young's lucid account of his time as an officer in the battle cruiser fleet was published in 1921. Although he did not name Room 40, Young made it clear that German wireless traffic had been intercepted and decrypted. 'How it came to be decoded and deciphered is a matter that it is, I am informed, even now undesirable to explain … The great point was that we read clearly all they said, whether it was in code or cipher. To decide from the mass of material thus obtained an intelligent knowledge of the doings of the German Fleet required another staff of experts to coordinate, study and digest – and this is where we lost some of the great advantages which this system should have given us. Obviously it should have been entirely in naval control; and it was not. It was the old story of personal jealousy interfering with public interest. A piece of grit got into the machine here with sad consequences. The result of analysis of the material by non-naval minds, and not the material itself, was given to the Intelligence Division' for passing on to Operations Division and the Grand Fleet.[354] Young's account, especially the bit about the problem being rooted in the role of non-naval personnel, clearly expresses the views he picked up from his conversations with Beatty about the value of the intelligence received from the Admiralty. Obviously it suited the navy to blame civilians, but in revealing the extent of British naval codebreaking Young caused consternation in GC&CS.

Then, in 1925, Balfour, who had been First Lord of the Admiralty from 1915 to 1916, mentioned in public for the first time the name of Room 40 in a lecture to honour Sir Alfred Ewing at Edinburgh University. A report of the lecture appeared in the press. Two years later Ewing himself revealed a few details of Room 40's work and its successes. Again, it was reported in the newspapers. Ewing said, 'The assumed stupidity of the British was the most valuable asset; it was not, apparently, till the war was over that the Germans became aware how completely the confidential channels of communication had been compromised.'[355] At Clarke's prompting, Ewing's reward was a letter threatening him with prosecution under the Official Secrets Act if he did not keep quiet. When Ewing proposed writing a book the idea was squashed at Clarke's prompting (with much denigration of Ewing).

In the late 1920s a new threat arose when Sir George Aston proposed to publish newspaper articles and a book on the British secret services during the war which included several references to Room 40. Clarke vented his rage in a report to the secretary of the Admiralty. 'As one of those who worked in Room 40 I do feel very keenly on the subject of any exposure of the successes or failures which can be attributed to that organisation by one who never had any connection with it and whose information with regard to it must be based on mere hearsay or a study of what others have written … [While] those who did the work have kept loyally secret … [but] publishers, not from patriotic motives but merely for their own gain or aggrandisement' wanted to expose the secret. The secretary to the Admiralty was not as alarmed as Clarke. 'I have now read two or three [articles by Aston] and I should certainly say that they are harmless, woolly and uninteresting in the extreme. I cannot help feeling that if you had read them you too will have come to the same conclusion … [Aston will] make articles on Naval War Secrets unsaleable for the future.' Aston's book, due to be published in 1930, was censored.

Nothing could be done, however, about the head of the US's First World War codebreaking organisation, Herbert Yardley, described by one acquaintance as 'a man of broad humour and unrestrained enthusiasms'.[356] Yardley's team at the State Department was closed down in 1929. The new Secretary of State, Henry L. Stimson, when informed of the unit's existence, stopped its activities, exclaiming: 'Gentlemen do not read each other's mail.'[357] Yardley's own business ventures collapsed with the onset of the Great Depression. Dissatisfied with his rewards for his secret work and short of money, in 1931, he published his own account of codebreaking during the war and after, exposing not only American secrets but also British ones. His frequently asserted justification was 'Now that the Black Chamber has been destroyed there is no valid reason for withholding its secrets.'[358]

When he learned of the book and of plans to publish it in Britain, Clarke commented that they had suppressed Ewing's book even though it contained nothing that was current. Modern codes and ciphers were much more advanced than those employed in Ewing's time, which were 'child's play' in comparison.[359] However, Yardley's book, he alleged, unveiled much newer, more current techniques and was a serious blow. In a chapter recounting a visit to Britain in 1918, Yardley reported, 'I spent most of my time in the British Military Cipher Bureau, studying their methods for the solution of different types of codes and ciphers, collecting pieces of exposition on those subjects.' As for Room 40, Hall had been very unhelpful to Yardley and limited himself to hinting at dark affairs. But Yardley did expose an uncomfortable fact. 'The British Censorship had a difficult task in the censorship of cables and their methods were necessarily very thorough. All cables that passed through their hands, all messages intercepted by their wireless stations, were not only carefully analysed but the addresses and signatures as well as any names mentioned in them were accurately indexed by name, subject-matter and source.' He also claimed, contrary to the legend then being created by the Admiralty, the 'Admiralty Cipher Bureau was not founded as a war measure. It had a long and dark history, backed by a ruthless and intelligent espionage. The power, tradition and intrigues of this bureau fired my imagination.'[360] Yardley's easy prose style meant that the book became a best-seller in the USA and Japan, with over 40,000 copies being sold worldwide (though only clocking up a 'disappointing' 700 in the first three months in Britain).[361]

In 1932 the publishing company Faber and Faber informed the Admiralty that they were intending to publish a book by a Mr Foy, called '*40 O.B. – How the War was Won*'. There looked to be nothing new in the book, but Clarke and the Admiralty were now convinced that the less said about Room 40 the better. A meeting was held with the publisher in May 1932 to dissuade him from going ahead, but the Admiralty's case was hardly compelling. The disarmingly honest publisher said that he was surprised at the Admiralty's stance as he thought that all the information had already been published elsewhere. Clarke, who had been a barrister, tried being heavy-handed. He delighted in recording that he had 'pointed out to [the publisher] that previous publication of such matters was not a defence'. The Director of Naval Intelligence added that the Admiralty did not want to draw attention to codebreaking because 'foreign powers had improved their ciphers and now thought that they were quite safe, as in many instances they were'.[362] Not surprisingly the publisher was not convinced by these arguments and insisted on going ahead, but offered to change any particular points of concern. The Admiralty had to settle for that and Clarke submitted a long list of changes (hoping, as he explained in a memo, that the cost of making so many changes might prompt the publisher into abandoning the book). But the Admiralty accepted the situation, though with bad feeling. Clarke later dismissed the author as having been no more than 'a shorthand typist' in the Naval Intelligence Division who had no knowledge of Room 40.

The next challenge came from someone who could not be accused of knowing very little about Room 40: Blinker Hall. Like Ewing and others, Hall craved recognition for his secret activities and eventually engaged a writer, Ralph Strauss, to turn his memories into a publishable text. Hall, however, faced more problems than writer's block. Although the draft chapters of his autobiography covered mainly his intelligence operations and gave little detail of codebreaking work, the Admiralty flatly refused permission for publication thanks to Clarke's pointing out the row that was certain to be generated by some of its revelations about the performance of senior naval commanders.[363] In 1949, when he wanted to write his own memoir of Room 40, Clarke wrote to Strauss, Hall's ghost writer. 'I do not know if you will remember me,' he started, referring Strauss back to the meetings where Hall's plans had been discussed. Clarke informed Strauss that it was one particular chapter of Hall's draft which had been the problem at the time. 'Its publication would have done a lot of harm to the reputations of several people.' Clarke explained, 'I was at that time chief censor at the Admiralty, with regard to certain matters which affected national security' but he insisted that he did not take the decision to suppress it; rather, he had just passed it on to higher officials at the Admiralty. In a later letter Clarke took care to inform Strauss, 'I always enjoy your critiques in the *Sunday Times* and my wife and I find them most useful in making out our library lists.' Now, however, Clarke wondered, 'what happened to the manuscript and whether it is still in existence'. The reason for his enquiry was that he had 'started to put down some record of my experience ... not for publication ... although [that] would do no harm ... [but] some record should be preserved, made by one who actually took part, rather than it be left to someone who might be compelled to rely on books like '*40 O.B.*' by Mr Foy who was only a drunken typist who knew nothing'.[364]

Clarke was rather torn between his head, which told him that it was pointless to suppress all mention of codebreaking, and his heart, which in all cases that came before him seemed to require full suppression for one good reason or other. One such reason may have been jealousy. It is clear that Clarke, for all his anger at anyone else trying to write about Room 40, harboured his own urge to put something down on paper to secure his reputation in history. This was combined with an equally powerful desire to control whatever could be said. He wrote a rather fawning letter to Sir Alfred Ewing (given his vituperative comments on Ewing in his writings on Room 40) in 1933 suggesting that Ewing and Hall should collaborate on a joint history. 'You would be doing the State great service. There could be no further revelations ... [Room 40 would] gain its proper place in the history of the war as the final word on the subject.' Significantly, he pointed out, it could be censored only by 'those who know the exact state of affairs at the present like Denniston and myself [who] are able to say what will do harm'.[365] The idea went nowhere and indeed was never practical given that Ewing and Hall had established their inability to work together.

Clarke does not come over as a very pleasant person from his writings in official records, whether they be his working documents or his historical accounts. However, we have to thank him for a significant part of what information we do have about what it was like inside Room 40. There is often something of a chasm between Clarke's declared interest in preserving some record and the often puffed up and uninformative passages he actually left us. Perhaps here we can sense the tearing at the soul of those who had to work inside Room 40 and MI1(b). They lived with the tension of holding their secrets and resisting telling the world about the wonderful things they had done to help win the war. The contribution in itself was not sufficient. There was a craving for recognition too. In none was the craving greater than in William F. Clarke, the barrister, intelligence officer, guardian of 'The Secret' and would-be historian. In one of his jottings, Clarke noted that in James's post-Second World War biography of Hall he had named for the first time several of Room 40's staff members, including Lady Hambro, Molyneaux, Birch, Desmond McCarty, Frank Tiarks, Lord Monkbretton, Gerald Lawrence, Quiggin, Lambert, Savory and Norton. 'A curious thing is that nearly always no mention has been made in their obituary notices of their work in Room 40 although the notices of others have often made unjustifiable [reference] to the honour … Some day I hope the true story will be told and I hope that the notes that I have made from time to time may help the author.'

Endnotes

1   HW3/177.
2   Gannon, *Colossus*.
Lloyd George, *War Memoirs I*, 32–33.
Baker, *Marconi Company*, 159.
Nickles, *Under the Wire*, 130–132.
Nickles, *Under the Wire*, 132.
Lloyd George, *War Memoirs I*, 45–46.
Nickles, *Under the Wire*, 133, has a different account: 'At 10.40pm (London time), as the British government, having heard nothing from Germany prepared to release a declaration of war, the Foreign Office rashly concluded that Germany had pre-emptively declared war on Britain: the Royal Navy had intercepted a wireless message from the German government warning German ships that hostilities with the British were imminent; British officials incorrectly interpreted this information as meaning that Germany had declared war.' A British note of war was sent to the German ambassador citing the supposed German declaration of war, but had to be withdrawn before it reached him once it was realised that the interpretation was incorrect. Nickles cites two secondary sources for the whole paragraph (Gregory, *Edge of Diplomacy*, 70, and Albertini, *Origins of the War*, 3, 500–502) and which may refer to this message but no indication of which and with no further details of the message. ADM137/4065 records intercepted message sent out several times on 4 August, translated by British codebreakers as 'Declaration of war between Germany and Great Britain is to expected hourly'. The German original has not been preserved. However, this message was sent in the 'VB' code and was also ciphered. The general weight of evidence suggests that this telegram could not have been decoded and deciphered before November 1914. All the messages recorded as having been intercepted on 4 August in ADM137/4065 are cited as having been coded with the VB or HVB code and then enciphered.
John Ferris, Before Room 40: The British Empire and Signals Intelligence 1898–1914, *Journal of Strategic Studies*, vol 12, no 4, 450, citing ADM144/27, but no indication is given of any record of these interceptions; the earliest recorded interceptions I have seen are in ADM137/4065.
Hew Strachan, *First World War*, 38.
CAB16/14; CAB16/189; CAB8/1; CAB16/32; Headrick, *Invisible Weapon*, 116–142.
Paice, *Tip and Run*.
Yates, *Graf Spee's Raiders*, 80.
3   R. Holland, The British Empire and the Great War, 114–121, in Brown and Louis, *British Empire*, vol 4.
ADM137/4.
Hezlet, *Electron*, 297; Keegan, *Intelligence in War*, 138, says that the wireless message was intercepted at the British wireless station at Suva, Fiji.
Dixon, Clash of Empires.

CAB16/14; CAB8/1; Headrick, *Invisible Weapon*, 85-111.

Barbara Tuchman, *Zimmermann Telegram*, 10-11.

Hezlet, *Electron*, 297, 83.

German communications to the east via Austria and Turkey and the Middle East were not interrupted, but this did not provide any routes to the wider world because of British control of the submarine telegraph cables (and Russia of telegraph landlines) needed to forward any messages from the Middle East.

Keegan, *Intelligence in War*, 161.

4   HW3/7.

Beesly, *Room 40*, 9.

Hezlet, *Electron*, 89.

Headrick, *Invisible Weapon*, 158.

Cited in Headrick, *Invisible Weapon*, 159-160, 170-171 (referring to: Alberto Santoni, Il Primo Ultra Secret: L'influenza delle decrittazioni Brittaniche sulle operazioni navali della Guerra 1914-1918 (Milan 1985); Alberto Santoni, The First Ultra Secret: The British Cryptanalysis in the Naval Operations of the First World War, in *Revue Internationale d'histoire militaire*, no. 63, 1985).

Santoni cites as evidence for his claim intercepted messages in ADM137/4065. This is the collection of German messages which we looked at in Chapter 1. Santoni's case is weakened significantly by a handwritten entry in the first double pages of the document stating that the messages were only deciphered in November 1914; this fits with the official Room 40 story as the main German codebooks were not obtained by the Admiralty until about mid-October and then the keys used for the cipher system on top of the coded messages had to be worked out, which took a couple of weeks (details of these codebooks are dealt with later in Chapters 3 and 4 of this book). Headrick cites Santoni as claiming that messages sent in enciphered VB code between German ships in the Mediterranean, the *Göben* and the *Breslau*, were deciphered and decoded by the British in August before the supposed date of the capture of the VB codebook. But the note mentioned above about the date from when these messages were decoded undermines this claim (also, as Headrick demonstrates, having misinterpreted the date of the decoding of the *Göben/Breslau* messages (see Chapter 1 of this book), it becomes necessary to invent reasons why the Royal Navy 'despite its overwhelming superiority in the Mediterranean and its knowledge of [the German ships'] intentions, was not able to stop' them, p. 160). As noted in Chapter 1, the bulk of the early intercepts were sourced from the Eastern Telegraph Co and it is almost certain that the ETC would have kept copies of transmitted messages and that these could have been asked for by British codebreakers in the run-up to the war or even after it started (when censorship was introduced by law and the government censors had access to all cable telegrams). However, it is also clear that German wireless messages were intercepted in increasing numbers in the month before the war started. Headrick records that Santoni gives a title for this document, 'Log of intercepted German signals in Verkehrsbuch (VB) code from various sources. March 1914-January 1915'. This is misleading, for though the bulk of messages in the document are in VB, there also messages in other codes: HVB, SKM ('marine signal code') and ABC (a widely used public codebook); also some at least of these messages, in whatever code, *were enciphered*. Santoni is thus suggesting that the British must have acquired (or worked out) at least the German VB codebook *and* how to break the various cipher keys used for this theory to stand up.

Peter Freeman, MI1(b) and the Origins of British Diplomatic Cryptanalysis in *Intelligence and National Security* vol 22, no 2, 206. Freeman, who styled himself as a 'retired civil servant' in this and other papers (on the 'Zimmermann telegram'), was in fact the official historian at GCHQ for several years.

Freeman, Origins, 224.

Freeman, Origins, 224.

John Ferris, Before 'Room 40':The British Empire and Signals Intelligence 1890-1914 in *Journal of Strategic Studies* vol 12, no 4, 435-42 is the source for the details of the India Office cryptanalytic operations.

Ferris, Before 'Room 40', 441.

Andrew, *Secret Service,* 10/11.

Andrew, *Secret Service,* 13/15.

Matthew Seligmann, *Naval Intelligence*; Seligmann, *Spies in Uniform*.

Andrew, *Secret Service*, 15.

Ferris, Before 'Room 40', 442-5.

5   Hall papers.

ADM137/4065.

Baker, *Marconi Company*, 159.

ADM137/4065.

Ewing, *Man of Room 40,* 173 gives 4 August as the date Ewing and Oliver lunched together; Kahn, *Codebreakers*, 266, also has it that the lunch took place 'on that first day of the war'; Beesly, *Room 40,* gives it as 'one day in the first half of August' (which of course includes a few days in the period before the outbreak of war as well as several more after the outbreak).

Strachan, *To Arms*, 381.

Ramsay, *'Blinker' Hall*, 29, citing 'Recollections' of Admiral of the Fleet, Sir Henry Oliver.

Ewing, *Man of Room 40*, 198.

Oldroyd, *Thinking About the Earth*, 230.

Ewing, *Man of Room 40*, 79-127.

Ewing, *Man of Room 40*, 144.

Ewing, *Man of Room 40,* 167-168.

HW3/3.

6   The spelling of surnames of Room 40 staff is inconsistent. I have stuck as closely as makes sense to spellings used in archive documents rather than those used by more recent authors.

7   Batey, *Dilly*, 33.

HW3/3; Hall papers; Denniston papers.

HW3/3; HW3/35.

Denniston papers.

ADM223/767. This file is an important source of information about MI5(b) between July 1914 and March 1915. It is a handwritten copy of various documents (including captured German military cipher instructions) and a log of important events. It appears to have reached the National Archives quite recently (but I have so far been unable to confirm the actual date it was opened to view) as it is not mentioned by ex-GCHQ historian Peter Freeman in his paper on the origins of MI1(b). Unlike the other recent releases on MI1(b) cited by Freeman and which are catalogued in the (HW) GCHQ series, this document is in the ADM (Admiralty) series of files. The National Archives catalogue has a misleading name: 'Room 40 OB Intelligence Division: Wireless Intercepts/Decrypts'. It is in fact about MI1(b) and it does not contain intercepts or decrypts.

WO32/10776, cited in Freeman, Origins, 208.

Freeman, Origins, 206-7. August 1914 to April 1915, under Director of Military Operations, as MO5(d); April 1915 to January 1916, under sub-directorate Directorate of Special Intelligence, as MO5; from January 1916, under Directorate of Military Intelligence, as MI5(b).

ADM223/767.

Freeman, Origins, 210.

Denniston papers.

HW3/6.

HW3/183.

ADM223/767.

Denniston papers.

Kahn, *Codebreakers*, 307.

Occleshaw, *Armour Against Fate*, 111.

Ferris, *British Army*, 5.

8   For the role of plain language intercepts by the Germans of Russian messages during the Battle of Tannenberg in August 1914, see Showalter, *Tannenberg*, 95, 99, 169, 229 and 328 ('the real importance of the often-sited radio intercepts [by the Germans of Russian army plain language transmissions] was as a security blanket, helping army and corps staff to execute decisions already made. For the Germans as much as for the Russians, attempts to change plans too often resulted in dangerous levels of confusion.')

ADM223/767.

HW7/3.

ADM223/767.

ADM223/767.

Taylor, *Storm and Conquest*, 284-291.

9   HW7/1.

10 HW7/1.

11 HW7/1.

12 The other two copies were numbers 145 and 974.

Churchill, *World Crisis*, 255-256.

13 HW7/1. In a draft chapter on codebreaking in a secret internal history of the naval war, written by Room 40 staff at the end of the war, this event is not described; however, there is a reference to the recovery of important documents with far-reaching consequences in Persia during the autumn of 1914. The author of that document wrote: 'the [VB code]book was actually taken from a consulate in Persia at an early period in the war'. However, this story does not seem to appear elsewhere, whereas the miraculous draft of the fishes does find its way in. It is worth pointing out that the SKM, HVB and VB were not the only codebooks in use by the German navy, military and government at the time. There were several diplomatic codes and ciphers as well as army and naval ones. Several such diplomatic codes and ciphers will figure later in our story. It is possible that the author of this post-war document has confused the acquisition of the VB with

some other codebook(s). Certainly some important secret documents including two diplomatic codebooks were captured in Persia in early 1915 (see Chapter 10), so possibly he has confused the two events. Or it may be that he has revealed the truth about how the VB was acquired.

[14] Hall papers.

[15] ADM137/4357.

Denniston papers.

[16] Clarke papers.

[17] Clarke papers.

Denniston papers.

Denniston papers.

ADM137/4065;ADM223/767.

ADM223/767.

Denniston papers.

Denniston papers.

Standage, *Victorian Internet*, 151.

The optical or semaphore telegraph, on the other hand, was invented for military purposes and, by and large, used for military/diplomatic/administrative applications in many European countries, and with only limited commercial uses in Britain and Sweden. A few codebooks had as many as 200,000 entries.

Kahn, *Codebreakers*, 844.

Kahn, *Codebreakers*, 850.

Fitzgerald, *Knox Brothers*, 82.

HW3/1.

ADM137/4156 *'Signalbuch der Kaiserlichen Marine'* 'Magdeburg Copy', '151'; ADM137/4331.

HW3/1; HW7/3; ADM137/4156; ADM137/4331.

HW3/1; HW7/3.

HW3/1; HW7/3.

HW3/1; HW7/3; ADM137/4329; ADM137/4388.

HW3/1; HW7/3; ADM137/4374; ADM137/4671.

[18] HW3/1; HW7/3.

[19] HW7/1.

HW137/4320.

HW137/4314.

[20] Examples of cipher intelligence gathered from intercepts: 15/5/1916, note by British intelligence from the Berlin/Madrid wireless link: 'The message begins with the Schieber set at 111, and in accordance with instructions for that case the 3rd digit is transposed on the last slider while the last digit is transposed on the middle slider. The message then switches on to the number what was communicated in April of last year which is 763, the process of schiebering the 3rd digit by means of the last 'slider and the 5th digit by means of middle slider continues' (ADM223/740); 24/6/1916 intercept, Madrid to Berlin: 'As much of the matter in telegrams 517 and 518, coded with the compromised cipher, has reference to the contents of secret telegrams – which can result in the compromising of the secret key also – I once more urgently request that such a procedure should be counter-ordered through the Cipher Office' (ADM223/738); 22/7/1916, intercept Madrid

to Berlin: 'As cipher correspondence with "Satzbuch" is at once recognised by the five-figure [code]groups, all of which begin with 9, I propose permanently to replace this initial figure 9 by figures 2 to 8 at discretion' (ADM223/738); 24/9/1916, intercept Madrid to Berlin, decipherment of a telegram was delayed because of a new cipher system. 10/10/16, intercept, Madrid to Berlin: 'Envelope marked 2225 is on the way to you, containing two separate shifts of page numbers 10 to 309 of cipher 2310. I suggest using the first shift for secret matter up to 1/1/1917 and that you should give me a recognition signal for this; and from 1 January the 2nd shift to come into force. In special circumstances the transposition in force up to the present could be used with this cipher. As there are two copies here of 2310, the old cipher could be simultaneously used for unimportant matter' (ADM223/739); 12/10/1916 intercept Madrid to Berlin: 'Please instruct the Cipher Bureau not to sent telegrams, contents of which are secret, with the most secret method and especially when the same [information] is also communicated by the News Service, as in the case of Berlin telegram 979 of 9/10/16' (ADM223/739); 19/10/1916 intercept Madrid to Berlin: Envelope 2225 received. 'The new cipher method will be indicated in respect of the 1st shift by the numbers 27082, for the 2nd shift by the numbers 21894; in the case of the use of the latest cipher procedure, the signal 400 will be used for both shifts' (ADM223/739).

The example and explanation is based on ADM223/767.

HW3/1; HW7/3.

Howard, *Franco-Prussian War*, 75; Wawro, *Franco-Prussian War*, 74–75; Tarrant, *Jutland*, 5.

Strachan, *To Arms*, 447–448.

Strachan, *First World War*, 375–376.

HW7/1.

Halpern, *Naval War*, 21; Strachan, *First World War*, 414.

Cited in Massie, *Castles of Steel*, 20.

HW7/1.

Strachan, *To Arms*, 406–407.

[21] Cecil Hampshire, *The Blockaders*, London 1980, 21–23.

Halpern, *Naval History*, 22.

HW7/1.

HW7/1.

[22] ADM137/4228.

Strachan, *To Arms*, 416.

Jolly, *Marconi*, 133.

Jolly, *Marconi*, 124.

Weightman, *Marconi's Magic Box*, 137.

Jolly, *Marconi*, 174–175.

Clapham, *Economic Development*, 308.

Headrick, *Invisible Weapon*, 120–124.

Gordon, *Rules of the Game*, 193–249.

ADM116/523; ADM116/567; ADM116/569; ADM116/570; ADM116/592; ADM116/595; ADM116/3403; Headrick, *Invisible Weapon*, 118.

Pocock, *British Radio Industry*, 170.

Hezlet, *Electron and Sea Power*, 38.

Bonatz, *Deutsche Marine-Funkaufklärung*, Darmstadt 1970.

ADM137/4065.

Denniston papers.

HW3/5.

HW3/5.

HW3/5.

HW3/5.

A. J. Alan, My Adventure at Chiselhurst, in Foss, *Best of A. J. Alan*, 105–117; this and other A. J. Alan stories can be seen at http://gutenberg.net.au/ebooks06/0609241h.html

HW3/35.

It is commonly suggested that Lambert, as a member of the staff of Room 40, was in some way involved in cryptography, but his contribution was to wireless interception procedures and techniques.

Denniston papers.

Denniston papers.

[23]   Baker, *Marconi*, 161–165.

[24]   ADM223/768.

[25]   HW3/3.

[26]   Baker, *Marconi*, 165.

[27]   HW7/1.

[28]   HW7/1.

Ewing, *Man of Room 40*, 160.

The original is in the Clarke papers at Churchill Archives, Cambridge; a copy is held in the National Archives in HW3/4.

Stafford, *Churchill*.

Beesly, *Room 40*, 18.

Denniston papers.

[29]   Denniston papers.

HW3/3. The background information I have used comes from a CV compiled by Montgomery himself at the end of the war. Beesly, *Room 40*, 125, says that Montgomery came to Room 40 from the Censorship; also that he was from Westminster Presbyterian College, Cambridge, not part of the University.

HW3/3.

HW3/3; Denniston papers.

HW3/3.

HW3/3.

HW3/3; Denniston papers.

Cited in Massie, *Castles of Steel*, 312.

Strachan, *To Arms*, 420–421.

ADM137/4065.

ADM137/4067.

Corbett, *Naval Operations*, vol 2, 28.

Cited in Massie, *Castles of Steel*, 353.

Gordon, *Rules of the Game*, 25.

Cited in Massie, *Castles of Steel*, 358.

ADM137/4067.

ADM137/4067.

ADM137/4067.

[30] Young, *With the Battle Cruisers*, 41–42, 54–55.

[31] HW7/1.

HW7/1.

ADM137/3958.

ADM137/3959.

ADM137/3958.

ADM137/3959.

[32] HW7/1.

[33] Pares, *Colonial Blockade*.

Chatterton, *Big Blockade*; Hampshire, *The Blockaders*.

Stevenson, *1914–1918*, 246.

ADM137/3958.

ADM137/3958.

ADM137/3959.

ADM137/3958.

ADM137/3958.

[34] Colin Simpson, *Lusitania*, London 1972.

[35] ADM223/740.

ADM137/3959.

ADM137/4066.

ADM137/3960.

HW7/1.

[36] HW7/1.

[37] Halpern, *Naval History*, 314.

[38] HW7/1.

[39] HW7/1.

[40] HW3/1; Clarke papers.

[41] HW3/1.

[42] Tucker, *The European Powers*, 390–393.

[43] Gordon, *Rules of the Game*, 397.

[44] Massie, *Castles of Steel*, 639.

[45] ADM223/737.

[46] ADM223/737.

[47] Massie, *Castles of Steel*, 659.

[48] Exchange Officer (Malcolm Hay), *Wounded and Taken Prisoner*, 69–70.

Harris, *Haig*, 91.

Pearton, *Knowledgeable State*, 155.

HW3/183.

HW3/183.

ADM223/767.

Ferris, *British Army*, 4.

HW3/183; Hinrichs, *Listening In*, viii.

N. Barr, Command in the Transition from Mobile to Static Warfare, in Sheffield and Todman,

Command and Control, 20–21.

[49] Peter Young, *Power of Speech*, 26.

HW3/183.

HW3/183.

[50] HW3/183.

[51] ADM223/767.

ADM223/767.

ADM223/767.

Freeman, Origins, 210.

[52] Hay, *Valiant for Truth*, 43.

[53] Hay, *Valiant for Truth*, 58.

[54] Hay, *Jesuits*, 124.

[55] Hay, *Jesuits*, 203–207.

[56] Hay, *Valiant for Truth*, 76–77.

[57] HW7/35.

[58] HW7/35.

[59] Freeman, MI1(b), cites examples of decodes seen by Lloyd George (when he first became Prime Minister in 1916), Maurice Hankey (cabinet secretary and a key policymaking figure) and the Foreign Office.

[60] Freeman, MI1(b), gives January 1916 as the first surviving US decode; this applies to the ADM files, but WO106/6072 contains decodes of several US messages about negotiations with Germany from May 1915 following the sinking of the liner *Sussex*.

[61] WO106/6072.

[62] Hay, *Valiant for Truth*, 59.

[63] Hay, *Valiant for Truth*, 77.

[64] HW7/35.

[65] HW3/185.

[66] HW3/186.

[67] HW3/1.

[68] Hall papers.

[69] Tilman Luedke, *Jihad Made in Germany*.

[70] Hopkirk, *Secret Service*, 105.

[71] Hall papers.

[72] Cited in Beesly, *Room 40*, 131.

[73] Cited in Beesly, *Room 40*, 132.

[74] HW3/1.

[75] Denniston papers.

[76] ADM223/773.

[77] Beesly, *Room 40*, 123.

[78] ADM223/768.

[79] ADM223/773.

[80] Cited in Beesly, *Room 40*, 134.

[81] Beesly, *Room 40*, 173.

[82] HW3/1; HW7/3.

[83] ADM223/773.

[84] ADM223/773.

[85] ADM137/4357.

[86] HW7/4.

[87] HW7/1 HW3/1; HW7/3; HW7/4.

[88] HW3/1; HW7/3.

[89] James, *Eyes of the Navy*, 132.

[90] Hall papers.

[91] Hall papers.

[92] Hall papers.

[93] ADM223/784.

[94] Hall papers.

[95] Freeman, MI1(b), 213.

[96] HW7/17

[97] HW7/1.

[98] Hall papers.

[99] HW3/177.

[100] Hall papers.

[101] HW3/184.

[102] HW3/184.

[103] HW3/184.

[104] HW3/184.

[105] HW3/186.

[106] William James, *The Eyes of the Navy*, xviii, xxiii-xxiv.

[107] HW3/8.

[108] Clarke Papers.

[109] Fitzgerald, *Knox Brothers*, 99.

[110] Fitzgerald, *Knox Brothers*, 127-128; 59.

[111] Batey, *Dilly*, 11-12.

[112] Fitzgerald, *Knox Brothers*, 99.

[113] Fitzgerald, *Knox Brothers*, 56.

[114] All quotes from Clarke in this section from HW3/3; copy in Clarke Papers.

[115] Denniston papers.

[116] Thompson, *White War*, 40-47.

[117] HW3/35.

[118] HW3/8.

[119] HW7/35.

[120] HW3/35; HW3/6.

[121] HW3/35; Clarke papers.

[122] HW3/35.

[123] HW3/183.

[124] HW3/183.

[125] This chapter has been drawn together using, in particular, ADM223/773 (history of Room 40 political branch; notable as the document which mentions codebreaking machinery), ADM137/4652 ('Solution of codes') and ADM137/4659 ('Solution of field codes, Enemy codes and their solution') and also, Friedman, *Solving German Code*, originally published in 1919. Some of these documents, including ADM137/4659 (cited as ADM137/4600),

have been published in Ferris, *British Army*.

[126] One important point is the frequency of words in the plain language and the implication of this for the ways in which codes would work in practice. In the German language the thirty most common 'wordforms'(*die, der, und, in, zu, den, das, nicht, von, sie, ist, des, sich, mit, dem, dass, er, es, ein, ich, auf, so, eine, auch, als, an, nach, wie, im, fur*)* account for 32 per cent of an average German language text (based on a count performed in 1911 of just under 11 million words of text from a variety of sources). The next 70 most common wordforms (including *man, aber, aus, durch ... ohne, eines, koennen, sei*) for 15 per cent and the next 207 words for another 7 per cent. Meaning: 30 most common: the (feminine), the (masculine), and, in, to, the/that, the (neuter), not, of, she/they/you, is, of the, self, with, to the, that, he, it, one, I, on, so, one, also, as, to, after, how, in the, for; next seventy most common: man, but, out/from, through ... without, one of, can/be able, are (in subjunctive form). So in all, these 207 wordforms account for just about 50 per cent of all words in a text. This average frequency applies to a wide range of text types. Koenig, *dtv-Atlas zur deutschen Sprache*, 114-115. The term 'wordform' is used rather than 'word' in the *dtv-Atlas* presumably as some of these basic words can combine with others to form new words, as adjectives, nouns, verbs, etc. The frequency statistics of German are thus skewed towards these common wordforms (mainly single syllable words) though they are still fairly similar to English where the fifteen most frequently occurring words account for 25 per cent of the text, the first 100 words for 60 per cent, the first 1,000 for 85 per cent and the first 4,000 for 97.5 per cent, Crystal, *Cambridge Encyclopedia of Language*,, 87.

[127] ADM137/4652.

[128] ADM137/4659.

[129] Cited in Ferris, *British Army*, 9-10.

[130] Ferris, *British Army*, 10.

[131] Cited in Ferris, *British Army*, 10-11.

[132] ADM137/4701.

[133] Ferris, *British Army*, 327.

[134] ADM137/4701.

[135] ADM137/4659.

[136] ADM137/4701.

[137] ADM137/4659.

[138] ADM137/4659.

[139] ADM137/4701.

[140] ADM137/4659.

[141] ADM137/4659.

[142] ADM137/4659.

[143] Ferris, *British Army*, 9.

[144] ADM137/4701.

[145] ADM137/4659.

[146] ADM223/773.

[147] HW7/4.

[148] Gannon, *Colossus*.

[149] ADM223/773.

[150] See Jon Agar, *The Government Machine,* for a discussion of the 'machine' as metaphor

for 'administration' and its reflection in the development of computerised administration.

[151] ADM223/738;ADM223/773.

[152] HW3/16.

[153] Ewing, *Ewing*, 269.

[154] Anne Somerset, *Elizabeth I*, London 1997, 541–542.

[155] Robert Hutchinson, *Elizabeth's Spy Master*, 99; John Hughes-Wilson, *Puppet Masters*, 69–90.

[156] James, *The Eyes of the Navy*; Ramsay: *'Blinker' Hall*; Beesly, *Room 40*.

[157] Hall papers.

[158] HW7/1; Beesly, *Room 40*, 187.

[9]   Tucker, *European Powers*, 171. Tucker claims that the extracts from the diary were circulated during Casement's trial, but this actually happened after trial and during the appeal process.

[159] James, *Eyes of the Navy*, 110–115.

[160] Raymond Carr, *Spain 1808–1975*.

[161] Salvado, *Spain*, ix.

[162] Salvado, *Spain 1914–1918*, 67.

[163] Salvado, *Spain 1914–1918*, 67.

[164] ADM223/736.

[165] ADM223/737.

[166] ADM223/737.

[167] ADM223/739.

[168] ADM223/737.

[169] ADM223/738.

[170] ADM223/738.

[171] ADM223/738.

[172] ADM223/739.

[173] ADM223/739.

[174] ADM223/737.

[175] ADM223/739.

[176] ADM223/739.

[177] ADM223/737.

[178] ADM223/739.

[179] ADM223/738.

[180] ADM223/736.

[181] ADM223/736.

[182] ADM223/739.

[183] ADM223/739.

[184] ADM223/736.

[185] ADM223/739.

[186] ADM223/739.

[187] ADM223/736.

[188] ADM223/736.

[189] ADM223/736.

[190] ADM223/737.

[191] ADM223/737.

[192] ADM223/740;ADM223/738;ADM223/739.

[193] ADM223/738.

[194] ADM223/740.

[195] ADM223/739.
HW7/1.

[196] Kennan, *Soviet-American Relations*, vol 1, 88.

[197] Brogan, *History of the United States*, 482.

[198] James, *Eyes of the Navy*, 124.

[199] Carr, *History of Germany*, 225–226.

[200] Cited in Freeman, The *Zimmermann Telegram* Revisited: A Reconciliation of the Primary Sources. *Cryptologia* 30, no. 2 (Apr. 2006): 98–150. p. 101.

[201] HW7/17.

[202] Kennan, *Soviet-American Relations*, vol 1, 28.

[203] HW7/17.

[204] HW7/34.

[205] HW7/17.

[206] HW7/19.

[207] Nickles, *Under the Wire*, 125–126.

[208] HW7/17.

[209] HW7/17.

[210] Tuchman, *Zimmermann Telegram*, 107.

[211] Tuchman, *Zimmermann Telegram*, 134.

[212] Joachim von zur Gathen, Zimmermann Telegram: The Original Draft, *Cryptologia*, 31, 2007, pp. 2–37.

[213] Thomas Boghardt, The Zimmermann Telegram: Diplomacy, Intelligence and the American Entry into World War I (*http://georgetown.edu/sfs/cges/working_papers.html*), 13.

[214] Gathen, Zimmermann Telegram, 18–19.

[215] Clarke papers.

[216] Freeman, Zimmermann Telegram, 115.

[217] Freeman, Zimmermann Telegram, 116–117.

[218] Gathen, Zimmermann Telegram, 24.

[219] CAB18/16.

[220] Headrick, *Invisible Weapon*.

[221] Freeman, Zimmermann Telegram, 119.

[222] HW3/35.

[223] Hall papers.

[224] HW3/35.

[225] HW3/187.

[226] Hall papers.

[227] Hall papers.

[228] HW3/177.

[229] Hall papers.

[230] Hall papers.

[231] Hall papers.

232 ADM223/738; sources differ on how many numbers made up a codeword in 7500; but this working document written at the end of the war puts 7500 in a category with six other 'four-figure [hatted] ciphers'; the five-figure codewords, as noted, use the additional figure for grammatical information.

233 HW3/177.

234 Freeman, Zimmermann Telegram, 26–27.

235 ADM223/773.

236 Freeman, Zimmermann Telegram, 122.

237 HW3/178.

238 ADM223/738; for more details on other diplomatic codes see ADM223/773.

239 HW3/35.

240 HW3/177.

241 HW3/182.

242 HW7/19.

243 HW7/19.

244 HW7/20; HW7/17; HW7/16.

245 Freeman, Zimmermann Telegram, 123.

246 HW7/8.

247 Freeman, Zimmermann Telegram, 125.

248 HW3/178.

249 HW3/178.

250 HW3/180.

251 Cited in Friedman and Mendelsohn, *Zimmermann Telegram*, 2.

252 HW3/180.

253 HW3/180.

254 HW3/180.

255 Hall papers.

256 HW7/8.

257 Beesly, *Room 40*, 234.

258 Hall papers.

259 HW3/181.

260 HW3/181.

261 HW7/20.

262 HW7/19; ADM223/742.

263 HW7/20.

264 HW7/20.

265 Holger Herwig, Total Rhetoric, Limited War: Germany's U-Boat Campaign 1917–1918, in Chickering and Foerster, *Great War, Total War,* 202–203.

266 Martin van Creveld, World War I and the Revolution in Logistics, in Chickering et al, *Great War, Total War,* 66–68.

267 Lieven, Russia, Europe and World War I, in Acton et al, *Russian Revolution*, 45.

268 Pearton, *Knowledgeable State*, 155.

269 Grigg, *War Leader*, 225.

270 Adams, *Arms and the Wizard.*

271 HW7/20.

272 Asprey, *German High Command*, 295–296.

273   Asprey, *German High Command,* 284-286.

274   Ferguson, *Pity of War,* 290.

275   Asprey, *German High Command,* 358.

276   ADM223/741.

277   HW7/21.

278   HW7/1.

279   Stevenson, *1914-1918,* 322.

280   The first 'hydrophone', manufactured by Standard Telephone & Cables Company was only ready for service in October 1917 (and was one of the first uses of electronic valve amplifiers). By the end of the war some 200 trawlers and destroyers were equipped with hydrophones, but though, in the words of a STC company historian, 'they made some kills [they] probably had a greater effect on the morale of enemy crews'. Young, *Power of Speech,* 27, 33, 61.

281   Stevenson, *1914-1918,* 321.

282   HW7/1.

283   HW7/24.

284   James, *Eyes of the Navy,* 172-173.

285   HW3/1.

286   James, *Eyes of the Navy,* 129.

287   Not all distant wireless signals were best intercepted closer to source. 'The great strides in wireless reception enabled the German communications in the Caucasus and South Russia to be intercepted with great accuracy in England itself, with greater accuracy and precision indeed than at Salonika or Egypt.' HW7/35.

288   HW3/8.

289   HW7/1.

290   ADM137/4699.

291   HW3/35.

292   HW7/35.

293   Ferris, *British Army,* 297.

294   Fromkin, *Peace to End All Peace, 276-281.*

295   HW7/1.

296   ADM223/782; HW7/32.

297   HW7/3.

298   HW7/3.

299   ADM223/782.

300   Stevenson, *1914-1918,* 339-340; Barr, *Setting the Desert on Fire,* 156, 176; Strachan, *First World War* (2006), 275-278.

301   Ferris, *British Army, 299, 341-342.*

302   HW7/32.

303   ADM137/4701.

304   HW7/1.

305   HW7/1.

306   John Ferris, 'Airbandit': C3I and Strategic Air Defence During the First Battle of Britain, in Dockrill and French, *Strategy and Intelligence,* 38.

307   HW3/88.

308   Ferris, Airbandit, 44-45.

309 Ferris, Airbandit, 45–46.
310 Ferris, Airbandit, 40:
311 Ferris, Airbandit, 44–49.
312 Figes, *People's Tragedy*, 537.
313 Wheeler-Bennett, *Brest-Litovsk*, 69.
314 Dowling, *Brusilov Offensive*.
315 Martin Kitchen, *German Offensives*, 256.
316 Asprey, *German High Command*, 398.
317 Asprey, *German High Command*, 403.
318 Kennan, *Soviet-American Relations*, vol 1, 401–402, 454–455.
319 Cited in Beesly, *Room 40*, 181–182.
320 William Carr, *History of Germany 1815–1985*, 225.
321 ADM223/789.
322 Jost Duelffer, Deutschland als Kaiserreich 1871-1918, in Martin Vogt, *Deutsche Geschichte*, 565.
323 Cited in Beesly, *Room 40*, 294–295.
324 ADM137/4164.
325 HW3/3.
326 HW7/1.
327 ADM223/773.
328 HW7/35.
329 HW3/1.
330 HW3/34.
331 Michael Smith, *The Spying Game*, 257.
332 HW3/1.
333 HW3/88.
334 HW3/34.
335 HW3/34.
336 HW3/34.
337 HW3/35.
338 HW3/34.
339 HW3/35.
340 It is possible that the situation could have been reversed if Hay had been appointed head of GC&CS's codebreaking unit and had retained the papers that formed his organisation's memory, also if Denniston had then burned Room 40 records in a fit of pique.
341 HW3/185.
342 HW3/88 contains a note from 1949 seeking memories and papers from people to help with a historical account of MI1(b): 'I have been chasing Pratt at intervals [about a rumoured history of MI1(b) written in 1925] and he now says his last hope is a man called Dixon (needless to say on leave) who was a clerk in MI1(b) for some time and may be able to recall the document.'
343 Clarke papers.
344 HW3/35.
345 HW3/35.

346   HW3/35.
347   Hay, *Valiant for Truth*, 183.
348   Gannon, *Colossus*, 75, citing Gordon Welchman.
349   Denniston papers.
350   Denniston papers.
351   Denniston papers.
352   HW3/13.
353   HW3/13.
354   Young, *With the Battle Cruisers*, 138-139.
355   Clarke papers.
356   White, *In Search of History*, 75; Yardley, *American Black Chamber*; Kahn, *Reader of Gentlemen's Mail*.
357   Kahn, *Reader of Gentlemen's Mail*, 98.
358   Yardley, *American Black Chamber*, 11.
359   HW3/13.
360   Yardley, *American Black Chamber*, 101, 217–219.
361   Kahn, *Reader of Gentlemen's Mail*, 138.
362   HW3/13.
363   The draft chapters of part of Hall's planned memoirs are held in the Hall papers at Churchill College Archives, Cambridge. They form the basis of accounts of Hall in: James, *Eyes of the Navy;* Beesly, *Room 40*; Ramsay, *'Blinker' Hall*. James wrote the first biography of Hall in 1955, using Hall's and Strauss's 1930s draft; when researching the book, he wrote to Denniston asking for information, explaining, 'I feel that a biography must not go at all deeply into technical matters. It was a most romantic business and I feel that much interest is attached to the development from small beginnings.' Denniston papers.
364   HW3/13.
365   HW3/13.

Bibliography

Archive references:
Clarke Papers, Churchill Archives Centre, Churchill College, Cambridge, UK.
Denniston Papers, Churchill Archives Centre, Churchill College, Cambridge, UK.
Hall Papers, Churchill Archives Centre, Churchill College, Cambridge, UK.

The National Archives,
   Kew, Richmond, Surrey, for file prefixes ADM, CAB, HW.

(*Details of works cited relate to the edition consulted*):

E. Acton et al (eds), *Critical Companion to the Russian Revolution*, London 1997.
R. J. Q. Adams, *Arms and the Wizard: Lloyd George and the Ministry of Munitions, 1915-1916*, London 1978.
Christopher Andrew, *Secret Service: The Making of the British Intelligence Community*, London 1985.
Robert B. Asprey, *The German High Command at War: Hindenburg and Ludendorff and the First World War*, Time Warner Books 1994.
W. J. Baker, *A History of the Marconi Company*, London 1970.
Arthur Banks, *A Military Atlas of the First World War*, London 2001.
James Barr, *Setting the Desert on Fire: T. E. Lawrence and Britain's Secret War in Arabia 1916-18*, London 2007.
Mavis Batey, *Dilly: The Man Who Broke Enigmas*, London 2009.
Patrick Beesly, *Room 40: British Naval Intelligence 1914-18*, London 1982.
Heinz Bonatz, *Die Deutsche Marine-Funkaufklärung 1914-1945*, Darmstadt 1970.
Hugh Brogan, *The Pelican History of the United States of America*, London 1986.
Judith M. Brown and W. M. Roger Louis, *Oxford History of the British Empire*, vol 4, *The Twentieth Century*, Oxford 1999.
Raymond Carr, *Spain 1808-1975*, Oxford 1982.
William Carr, *A History of Germany 1815-1985*, London 1987.

F. L. Carsten, *Revolution in Central Europe 1918-1919*, Aldershot 1988.

E. Keble Chatterton, *The Big Blockade*, London undated.

R. Chickering et al (eds), *Great War, Total War: Combat and Mobilization on the Western Front, 1914-1918*, Cambridge 2000.

Winston Churchill, *The World Crisis 1911-1918*, London 1943.

J. H. Clapham, *Economic Development of France and Germany, 1815-1914*, Cambridge 1936.

Grosvenor B. Clarkson, *Industrial America in the World War: Strategy Behind the Line*, Boston 1924.

Julian S. Corbett, *Naval Operations*, vol 2, *Official History of the Great War*, London 1921.

David Crystal, *The Cambridge Encyclopedia of Language*, Cambridge 1987.

John Dixon, *Clash of Empires: The South Wales Borderers at Tsingtao, 1914*, Wrexham 2008.

M. Dockrill and D. French (eds), *Strategy and Intelligence: British Policy During the First World War*, London 1996.

Timothy C. Dowling, *The Brusilov Offensive*, Bloomington 2008.

Christopher Duffy, *Through German Eyes: The British and the Somme 1916*, London 2007.

B. A. Ellerman and S. C. M. Paine, *Naval Blockades and Sea Power: Strategic and Counterstrategic 1914-1918*, Abingdon 2006.

A. W. Ewing, *The Man of Room 40: The Life of Sir Alfred Ewing*, London 1939.

Niall Ferguson, *The Pity of War*, London 1999.

John Ferris, *The British Army and Signals Intelligence During the First World War*, Stroud 1992.

Marc Ferro, *The Great War*, London 2002.

Orlando Figes, *A People's Tragedy: The Russian Revolution 1891-1924*, London 1996.

Penelope Fitzgerald, *The Knox Brothers*, Washington DC 2000.

Kenelm Foss (ed.), *The Best of A. J. Alan*, London 1954.

William F. Friedman, *Solving German Codes in World War I*, Laguna Hills, California 1977 (originally published in 1919).

William F. Friedman and Charles J. Mendelsohn, *The Zimmermann Telegram of January 16, 1917 and its Cryptographic Background*, Laguna Hills 1994.

David Fromkin, *A Peace to End All Peace: The Fall of the Ottoman Empire and the Creation of the Modern Middle East*, London 2000.

Paul Gannon, *Colossus: Bletchley Park's Greatest Secret*, London 2006.

Andrew Gordon, *Rules of the Game: Jutland and British Naval*

Command, London 2005.

J. Grainger (ed.), *The British Maritime Blockade of Germany in the Great War: The Northern Patrols 1914–1918*, Aldershot 2003.

Robert Grant, *U-Boat Intelligence 1914–1918*, London 1969.

John Grigg, *Lloyd George: From Peace to War 1912–1914*, London 1997.

John Grigg, *Lloyd George: War Leader 1916–1918*, London 2003.

Peter Gudgin, *Military Intelligence: A History*, Stroud 1999.

Paul G. Halpern, *A Naval History of World War I*, London 1994.

A. Cecil Hampshire, *The Blockaders*, London 1980.

Gerd Hardach, *The First World War 1914–1918*, vol 2 of *History of World Economy in the Twentieth Century*, London 1977.

J. P. Harris, *Douglas Haig and the First World War*, Cambridge 2008.

Peter Hart, *The Somme*, London 2006.

Alice Ivy Hay, *Valiant for Truth: Malcolm Hay of Seaton*, London 1971.

Malcom Hay (as 'Exchange Officer'), *Wounded and Taken Prisoner*, New York 1917.

Malcom Hay, *The Jesuits and the Popish Plot*, London 1934.

Daniel Headrick, *The Invisible Weapon: Telecommunications and International Politics 1851–1945*, Oxford 1991.

Arthur Hezlet, *The Electron and Sea Power*, London 1975.

Ernest H. Hinricks, *Listening In: Intercepting German Trench Communications in World War I*, Shippensburg 1996.

F. H. Hinsley and Alan Stripp (eds), *Codebreakers: The Inside Story of Bletchley Park*, Oxford 1993.

Peter Hopkirk, *On Secret Service East of Constantinople: The Plot to Bring Down the British Empire*, Oxford 2001.

Michael Howard, *The Franco–Prussian War*, London 1981.

John Hughes-Wilson, *The Puppet Masters: Spies, Traitors and the Real Forces Behind World Events*, London 2005.

Robert Hutchinson, *Elizabeth's Spy Master: Francis Walsingham and the Secret War that Saved England*, London 2006.

William James, *The Eyes of the Navy: A Biographical Sketch of Admiral Sir Reginald Hall*, London 1955.

W. P. Jolly, *Marconi*, London 1972.

David Kahn, *The Codebreakers: The Comprehensive History of Secret Communication from Ancient Times to the Internet*, 2nd edition, New York 1996.

David Kahn, *The Reader of Gentlemen's Mail: Herbert O. Yardley and the Birth of American Codebreaking*, London 2004.

John Keegan, *Intelligence in War: Knowledge of the Enemy from Napoleon to Al-Qaeda*, London 2003.

George F. Kennan, *Soviet-American Relations*, vol 1, *Russia Leaves the War*, Princeton 1956.

George F. Kennan, *Soviet-American Relations*, vol 2, *The Decision to Intervene*, Princeton 1958.

Paul Kennedy, *The Rise and Fall of British Naval Mastery*, London 2001.

Martin Kitchen, *The German Offensives of 1918*, London 2005. Werner Koenig, *dtv-Atlas zur Deutschen Sprache*, Munich 1978.

Andrew Lambert, *Admirals: The Naval Commanders Who Made Britain Great*, London 2008.

David Lloyd George, *War Memoirs*, vol 1, 2-volume 'new' edition 1938.

Tilman Lüdke, *Jihad Made in Germany: Ottoman and German Propaganda and Intelligence Operations in the First World War*, Münster 2005.

Giles MacDonogh, *The Last Kaiser: William the Impetuous*, London 2003.

Robert K. Massie, *Castles of Steel: Britain, Germany and the Winning of the Great War at Sea*, London 2005.

Gary Mead, *The Good Soldier: The Biography of Douglas Haig*, London 2007.

Richard Milton, *The Best of Enemies: Britain and Germany 100 Years of Truth and Lies*, Cambridge 2007.

Janet Morgan, *The Secrets of Rue St Roch: Hope and Heroism Behind Enemy Lines in the First World War*, London 2005.

David P. Nickles, *Under the Wire: How the Telegraph Changed Diplomacy*, London 2003.

Michael Occleshaw, *Armour Against Fate: British Military Intelligence in the First World War*, London 1989.

Avner Offer, *The First World War: An Agrarian Interpretation*, Oxford 1991.

David Oldroyd, *Thinking About the Earth: A History of Ideas in Geology*, Cambridge Ma 1996.

Edward Paice, *Tip and Run: The Untold Tragedy of the Great War in Africa*, London 2007.

Richard Pares, *Colonial Blockade and Neutral Rights 1739–1763*, Philadelphia 1975.

Maurice Pearton, *The Knowledgeable State: Diplomacy, War and Technology Since 1830*, London 1982.

Rowland Pocock, *The Early British Radio Industry*, Manchester 1988.

Andrew Porter, *The Oxford History of the British Empire*, vol 3, *The Nineteenth Century*, Oxford 1999.

Robin Prior and Trevor Wilson, *Command on the Western Front: The Military Career of Sir Henry Rawlinson*, Barnsley 2004.

David Ramsay, *'Blinker' Hall Spymaster: The Man Who Brought America into World War I*, Stroud 2008.

N.A. M. Rodger, *Command of the Ocean*, vol 2, *A Naval History of Britain 1649-1815*, London 2006.

Francisco J. Romero, *Spain 1914-1918: Between War and Revolution*, London 1999.

Matthew Seligmann, *Spies in Uniform. British Military and Naval Intelligence on the Eve of the First World War*, Oxford 2006.

Matthew Seligmann, *Naval Intelligence from Germany. The Reports of the British Naval Attachés in Berlin, 1906-1914*, Aldershot 2007.

Gary Sheffield and John Bourne (eds), *Douglas Haig: War Diaries and Letters 1914-18*, London 2006.

Gary Sheffield and Dan Todman (eds), *Command and Control on the Western Front: The British Army's Experience*, London 2007.

Denis Showalter, *Tannenberg: Clash of Empires, 1914*, Dulles Virginia 2004.

Michael Smith, *The Spying Game: The Secret History of British Espionage*, London 2003.

David Stafford, *Churchill and Secret Service*, Woodstock, New York 1998.

Tom Standage, *The Victorian Internet: The Remarkable Story of the Telegraph and the Nineteenth Century's Online Pioneers*, London 1999.

David Stevenson, *1914-1918: The History of the First World War*, London 2005.

Norman Stone, *World War One: A Short History*, London 2008.

Hew, *The First World War*, vol 1: *To Arms*, Oxford 2001.

Hew Strachan, *The First World War: A New Illustrated History*, London 2003.

V. E. Tarrant, *Jutland: The German Perspective*, London 1995.

Stephen Taylor, *Storm and Conquest: The Battle for the Indian Ocean, 1809*, London 2008.

Mark Thompson, *The White War: Life and Death on the Italian Front 1915-1918*, London 2008.

Tim Travers, *How the War Was Won: Command and Technology in the British Army on the Western Front, 1917-18*, London 1992.

Leon Trotsky, *How the Revolution Armed: The Military Writings and Speeches of Leon Trotsky*, vol 5, 1921-1925, London 1979.

Barbara Tuchman, *The Zimmermann Telegram*, London 2001.

Spencer C. Tucker, *The European Powers in the First World War: An Encyclopedia*, New York 1996.

Ferdinand Tuohy, *The Secret Corps: A Tale of "Intelligence" on all Fronts*,

London 1920.

Martin Vogt, *Deutsche Geschichte: Von dem Anfänen bis zur Widervereinigung*, Stuttgart 1991.

Stephen Wade, *Spies in the Empire: Victorian Military Intelligence*, London 2007.

Geoffrey Wawro, *The Franco-Prussian War: The German Conquest of France in 1870–1871*, London 2003.

Gavin Weightman, *Signor Marconi's Magic Box: How an Amateur Inventor Defied Scientists and Began the Radio Revolution*, London 2004.

Gordon Welchman, *The Hut Six Story: Breaking the Enigma Codes*, Shropshire 2000.

John W. Wheeler-Bennett, *Brest-Litovsk: The Forgotten Peace March 1918*, London 1938.

Theodore H. White: *In Search of History: A Personal Adventure*, New York 1978.

Dennis Winter, *Haig's Command: A Reassessment*, London 2001.

Herbert O. Yardley, *The American Black Chamber*, Annapolis 1931.

Keith Yates, *Graf Spee's Raiders: Challenge to the Royal Navy, 1914–1915*, London 1995.

Filson Young, *With the Battle Cruisers*, London 2002 (originally published 1921).

Peter Young, *Power of Speech: A History of Standard Telephone and Cables 1883–1981*, London 1983.

Index

ABC Code   18, 46
Abd El Malei   180
Adcock, Professor Frank   141
Admiralty resistance to convoys   222-223
Admiralty wireless stations
  Cape Town   26
  Chelmsford   27, 76
  Dover   13, 26
  Hunstanton   76-80
  Kingston, Ontario   26
  London   26
  Portpatrick   26
  South Lawn   35
  Stockton   27, 76
  Towyn   27
AFB Codebook (Allgemeines
  Funkspruchbuch)   66,
                                           132
Aitken, Lieutenant   248
Alan, A J - see Lambert, Leslie
Alfonso VIII, King of Spain   177, 179
Alice in ID25, see Birch, Frank
Allenby, General Edmund   230
Ampthill, Lord   23
Anderson, Brigadier General   31, 42,
                                113-114, 118, 124
Anderson, Miss   149, 248
Anstie, WH 'Bill'   30, 32, 42
Asquith, Herbert Henry   218
Aston, Sir George   253
Astor, J J   95

Babington Plot   172-173
Balfour, Arthur   108-109, 137, 189,
                          204, 206, 209, 252
Barclay, George   23
Barnes, Captain Ralph George   150
Bayley, Margaret   150
Beatty, Admiral David   91-93, 241, 252
  battle of Jutland   108-110
Beazly, Lieutenant J   149
Beesly, Patrick   7, 195
Bell, Edward   209

Benckendorff, Constantine, Count   39
Beresford, Charles Lord   29
Bernstorff, Count von   135-136, 191-194,
                              208, 213-214
Bethmann-Hollweg, Theobald von191, 195,
  219
Birch, Frank   47, 52, 56-57, 57-58, 85,
      126, 146, 147, 187, 221, 224, 246, 256
  Alice in ID25   85-86, 141-142, 144
Bletchley Park   7-9, 168
Bombe   168-169
Boulton, Harold E   149
Bright, Charles   44
British naval ships
  Garry   97
  Glasgow   12, 19-20
  Indefatigable   107
  Invincible   107
  Iron Duke   97
  Queen Mary   107
  Sirius   37
  Telconia   16
British interception, pre 1914   23
  Boer War   24, 31, 118
  China   24
  Persia   24
  Russia   23-24
  Turkey   24
British international telegraph cable network
  14, 23,
                                       198-199
British naval blockade of Germany   100-101
British submarine warfare   102
Brooke-Hunt, Captain   248
Browne, Lord Arthur   124
Bruges, German wireless station   71
Brusilov, General Aleksei Alekseevich   235
Bryans, C   31, 36
Bullough, Professor Edward   86, 149
Burnett, G Lieutenant   31

Campbell, R H L   126, 209
Carranza, President   187-188

Cape Town   13

Caroline Islands, German wireless station   15

Chamberlain, Joseph   86

Charles II, King of England   120

Charteris, John Brigadier General   26

Church, G R M Major   23, 31

Churchill, Winston 39, 42, 68, 83, 248, 249-250

   & Room 40's 'charter'   83-84

   exerts excessive control over Room 40 84, 90

   bombardment of Yarmouth   90

   Scarborough Raid   90-93

   battle of Dogger Bank   94-95

   involvment in sinking of Lusitania   103-104

Clarke, E Russell   76-81, 85

Clarke, William F   29, 32, 41, 47, 86, 106, 108, 142, 246, 248

   observations on colleagues   146-150

   post-war Admiralty censor   251-256

Cockerill, Colonel   127

codebreaking techniques   156-166

codebreaking machinery 132, 152, 168-171, 203-204

codes and codebooks   44-47, 156

   battlefield codes   114-115

   codes used in more applications   155-156

   two-part codes   167

Coleman, Edward   120-121

Colossus   8, 168-169

Coronel, naval battle   15, 19

Crocker, G C   31, 138

Curtis, naval instructor   30, 85

Curwen, Lieutenant Patrick J   246

Denniston, Alastair   29, 32, 41, 47, 95, 113, 129, 138, 142, 250, 255

   solves subtractor cipher   131

   becomes head of GC&CS   245-250

direction finding network/stations 13, 80-81, 104, 149, 224-228, 232-233

Dogger Bank, battle of   90-95, 252

Duala, German wireless station   16

Dubuisson, Major James   150

Duff, Admiral Alexander   222

Duke of York, see James II

Duse, Eleanora   149

Earnshaw-Smith   248

Eastern Telegraph Company, ETC   12-13, 26

Eckardt, German minister   214

Edmonds, C J   129

Eliabeth, Queen   172-174

Emergency War Code   26, 175

Enigma   168

Enver Pasha   117-118

Erzberger, Matthias   179

Ewing, Sir Alfred   21, 35-36, 39, 40, 41, 46, 83-84, 248, 250

   asked to set up codebreaking unit   27-28

   personality and background   28-29

   told to work with War Office unit   30-32

   withdraws staff from MI1(b)   41-43

   organises interception service   77-80

   begins to lag behind his staff   82-83

   fails to develop unit into intelligence centre 84

   looses influenece to Blinker Hall   126

   bad relations with Hall   130

   departs from Room 40   136-137

   Clarke on   148-149

   post-war views on machine age   171

   post-war leaks   252-255

Falkenhayn, Eric von   219, 230

Falkland Islands, naval battle   15, 19-20

Fanning Island, British cable station   14

Fashoda Incident, 1889   23

Faudel-Phillips, Benjamin   130-131, 149

Fetterlein, Ernst   239, 248

FFB Codebook (Flottenfunkspruchbuch) 66, 132-133

Fisher, Jack 'Jacky', Admiral 42, 83, 88, 90, 94, 252

Ford, Hugo R   248

Foy, Mr   254-255

Frnco-Prussian War   33-34

Franz Ferdinand, Archduke   10-13

Fraser, Professor John   124-125, 248

Freeborn, Frederick   249

Fremantle, Mr   147, 150

French, Colonel   124, 245

French, John Field Marshal   26

French navy   37, 67

French military codebreaking units   31-35

   first cipher broken on western front   34-35

Fryer, Lieutenant   248

Gage, Vera 146
Gaunt, Guy 209
GC&CS (Government Code & Cipher School) 244-250
GCHQ (Government Communications Headquarters) 8, 118, 135, 246
Geheimschreiber 168
Gerard, James W123, 135, 190-191, 197, 208
German air war on Britain 231-234
German ciphers 57-65
German communications links 14-17
via 'Swedish Roundabout' 134-135, 194
via US State department 135-136, 194
German diplomatic codebooks
13040 129, 135, 196, 200, 204-205
3512 131
5300 170
6400 169-170
7500 196, 203
89734 131
others (9972, 89934, 5950,) 153
German interception of British telephone traffic on Western Front 115-116
German merchant ships
Hobart 39
German naval codebooks - see AFB, FFB, HVB, Nordo, SKM, VB
German naval mutiny 1918 240-242
German naval ships
Albatros 98
Arcona 99
Braunschweig 98
Breslau 17, 19
Dresden 14, 20
Eber 13
Emden 19
Goeben 17, 19
Hohenzollern 13
Koenigsberg 12-14
Lutzow 110
Magdeburg 38-39, 89
Pommern 99
Roon 18
Rostock 110
Scharnhorst 13, 16

Strasburg 14, 97-105
German submarine warfare 182-184, 188-189, 208-209
reaction of neutrals to resumption of, 1917 216-217
resumption of, 1917 220-226
German submarines
U-12 98
U-18 97-98, 100
U-21 102
U-22 102
U-23 102
U-24 98, 101
U-27 102
U-28 101
U-29 102
U-30 101
U-32 101
U-35 U-35 195-196
U-109 132
Goeppert, Dr 214
Goodwin, Shirley Captain 31
Grand Vizier of the Ottoman Empire117-118
Greene, Sir Grhaam 136
Grey, Lord 10, 26
de Grey, Nigel 136, 142
Zimmermann Telegram 7, 195, 200-206
joins Room 40 86
joins diplomatic section 130-131
omits codebreaking machinery from accounts of career 171
sets up Mediterranean section 227-228
Gordon Highlanders 111

Haggard, G H M 150
Hale, William Baynard 210
Haig, Sir Douglas Field Marshal 26, 31
Hall, William Reginald 'Blinker' Captain (later Admiral) 32, 107, 123, 140, 141, 170, 225-226, 250
& capture of VB Codebook 40
suceeds Oliver as Director Naval Intelligence 84
& the Zimmermann telegram 7
involved in integrating Hope into Room 40 88
use of talkative agents to spread

disinformation
    95-96
restores relations with MI1(b)   137-139
guides Room 40's move towards diplomatic
interception   127
creates false story of capture of 13040
codebook
    128-129
identifies George Young   129-130
bad relations with Ewing   130

works on 13040 codebook   135
replaces Ewing   133, 136-137
compared with Walsingham   174
background and habits   174-177
creates misleading story of code broken for
Zimmermann telegram   195
Zimmermann Telegram   201-207
decides how to exploit Zimmermann
Telegram
    209-210
visits Mediterranean   227
response to Russian revolution   238-239
Hall leaves at end of war   245
later life   248, 254-255
autobiography censored   254-255
Hambro, Lady Ebba   150, 256
Hankey, Maurice   189, 223
Hanly, Captain E D   247
Hannam, Miss   149
Hardinge, Lord Charles   26, 126, 204, 209
Hardisty, Mr   248
Harvey, Joan   150
Hay, Captain Malcolm   122, 250
    early war service and wounding   111-112
    joins MI1(b)   118-119
    decodes Popish Plot letter   122
    takes charge of MI1(b)   123-124
    restores relations with Room 40   137-139
    rejected as head of GC&CS   245-246
    later life   246-247
Haylar, Miss   149, 248
Heinrich, Crown Prince   73-74
Henderson, Captain   33, 35
Henderson, Catherine   150
Henderson, General   26
Henderson, Professor   85
Herberthihe, German wireless station   16

Herschell, Lord   32, 85, 88, 179
Hindenburg, Paul von   219-220
Hipper, Rear Admiral Ritter von 90-93, 107-
    108
Hippisley, Baynton   77-81
Hochseeflotte (High Seas Fleet) 13, 68-72, 90-95
Hohler, Tom   204
Holtzendorff, Admiral Henning von   184
Hooper, Lieutenant John   153, 248
Hope, Lieutenant G L N   248
Hope, Captain Herbert   142
    joins Room 40   87
    initiated into the secret   87-88
    organises assessment of intelligence   88-89
    Clarke on   148
House, Colonel Edward   189-197
Hudson, Violet   150
Hunt, Captain   248
HVB Codebook
    (Handelsschiffsverkehrsbuch)   19,
    152, 232
    capture of   39-40
    structure of   52-54
    ciphers used with   58-60
    replaced 1916   66, 132-133
    used by Zepellin airships   52, 232

ID25 (Intelligence Division 25) - see Room
    40
Imperial German Navy, see Kaiserlichen
    Marine
Ingenohl, Admiral Friedrich von   90-93
Intelligence Section, GHQ, British
    Expeditionary Force   35, 42

Jackson, Admiral Henry   106-107
Jagow, Gottlieb von   135-136, 192
James II, King of England (Duke of York)
    120-121
James, Captain William 'Bubbles'   251
    biography of Hall   140
    takes over from Hope   142-143
    Clarke on   148
Jellicoe, Admiral John 68, 84, 90-93, 224, 251
    battle of Jutland   106-110
Jutland, battle of   104-110
Joffre, Joseph   33
Jopson, Mr   248

Kahn, David 47
Kaiser Wilhelm II - see Wilhelm II, Kaiser
Kaiserlichen Marine 67-68
Keigurn, R P 149
Kennan, George F 190
Keynes, John Maynard 143
King of Italy, see Victor Emmanuel
King of Spain, see Alfonso VIII
Kitchener, Lord 26, 42
Kleinkrieg ('Small War') 70, 98-100, 109
Knox, Dilwyn 'Dilly 131, 142, 248
  Zimmermann telegram 7-9, 200-202
  joins Room 40 86
  background and habits 143-146
Knox, Edmund 143
Knox, Ronald 143
Knox, Wilfred 143
Kruger, Paul President 24
Lambert, Leslie (aka A J Alan)78-79, 81, 248, 256
Lansing, Robert 193-194, 197, 209-210
Lawrence, Gerald 256
Lawrence, H W 'Harry' 86, 201
Lawrence, T E 231
Lenin, Vladimir Ilyich 235
Lloyd George, David 229, 248
  and start of war 10-12
  becomes prime minister 218-219
  overrules Admiralty on convoys 223
Ludendorff, Eric 219-220, 230, 235-237, 239
  Ludendorff Offensive' March 1918 235-237
Lunn, Miss 248
Lusitania 102-105
Lytton, Lord 23, 138, 148, 170

McCarry, Desmond 256
MacDonogh, Colonel 30, 113, 125
McGrath, Lieutenant 248
Marconi Company 21, 31
  & interception 27
  competiton with Germany 71-75
  direction finding equipment 80
Marconi, Guglielmo 71
  meets Kaiser in Rome 71
  technical & political conflict with Germany 71-75
  invention of wireless 75-76

  emphasis on receiver technology 75-76, 79
Marlowe, Lieutenant K 150
Marne, battle of and interception 33-34
Marreco, Miss 149
Marshall, C P O 77
Marwitz, George von der, General
Mary, Queen of Scots
Maude, General Frederick 230
Mason, A E W 201
Milne, General George Francis 26

MI1(b) 7-9, 22
setting up of 30-32
first interceptions and cipher breaking 32-35
relationship with BEF codebreaking unit113
relations with Room 40 41-42, 126, 133-134, 137-139
enters into diplomatic interception 117-118
interception of Turkish wireless traffic117-118, 128, 229-231
interception of US cable traffic 118
break US codebooks 122-123
widens diplomatic interception activities 124-126
breaks Greek codes 124-125
intercepts of neutrals' reaction to Zimmermann Telegram 216-217
exapnds overseas 228-231
Middle East operations 228-231
Versailles negotiations 242
statistics 242-243
post-war organisation 244-248
MI1(e) 125, 221-224
Molyneaux 256
Monkbretton, Lord 86, 147, 256
Montgomery, Rev. W H 86, 142, 248
  argues with Morrah over Home Rule 86
  joins diplomatic section 130-131
  range of codebreaking activities 151-153
  omits codebreaking machinery from CV
  Zimmermann Telegram 20, 203
Morrah, Herbert 85-86, 142, 147-148, 247
Morse code 48
Muley Hafid 180

Naval Intelligence Division 15
Falklands, planting false intelligence 19

setting up of 25
submarine tracking 104-105
Nauen, German wireless station 14, 17, 18, 71
Nauru, German wirless station 16
Nicholson, Arthur 26
Niedermayer, Dr. 129
Norddeich, German naval wireless station 14, 17,
66, 79, 91, 224
Nordo Codebook
Norman, Sir Henry 77
Norton R D 35, 85-86, 147, 256

Oliver, Henry, Captain (later Admiral) 21,
27-28, 29, 136
controls Room 40 after becoming chief of naval staff
83, 90-93
battle of Dogger Bank 94-95
battle of Jutland 104-110
Page, Walter Hines 189-190, 209, 218-219
Paget, Lady 95
Palmer, G S Captain 23
Parish, naval instructor 30, 32, 85
Pepys, Samuel 120
Pershing, General john 187
Persia 127-129
Phelippes, Thomas 172-173
Pletts, J St Vincent 31, 35, 122-123
Popish Plot 120-122

Quarry, A J Lieutenant 31
Le Quex, William 221
Quiggin 256

Rabaul, German wireless station 25
Raisuli 181
Ratibor, Graf (Count) 181-185
Rees, Lieutenant 248
Robertson, Miss 152, 169
Roddam, Olive 146
Romanones, Conde (Count) de 178-185
Room 40 7-9
legend of 21-23, 27
setting up of 27-36
capture of codebooks 37-43
first cipher breaking 40-41
relations with MI1(b) 41-42, 126,

133-134, 137-139
gets its name 43
receives its 'charter' 83-84
excessive control of output 84
Scarborough Raid 91-93
battle of Dogger Bank 94-95
submarine warfare intercepts 101, 102-104
battle of Jutland 104-110
enters into diplomatic interception 126-129
turns attention to German diplomatic traffic
126-127
capture of German diplomatic codebooks 128-129
setting up of diplomatic section 129-132
breaks replacements for SKM and HVB 132-133
intercepts reveal Germans breaking British naval
codes 133
discovery of German communications links 134-136
codebreaking machinery 167-170
intercepts German traffis with Spain 179-186
resumed submarine warfare, 1917 221-226
wider use of intellignece 225-226
ID25 226
expands overseas 226-228
Baltic section 141, 226-227
Mediterranean Section 227-228
German naval mutiny, March 1918 240-242
statistics 242-243
post-war organisation 244-248
Rotter, C J E, Paymaster RN 12, 27, 40-41,
85, 91, 167, 200
appointed to assess naval intelligence 87
Clarke on 148
Round, Captain H J 80-81, 226
Royal Australian Navy, capture of HVB
codebook 39
Royal Australian Navy, codebreaking unit 16, 19
Royal Navy 37, 67-72
promotion of wireless 75-76
Russian revolution 220, 234-235, 238
interception of communications during
Brest-Litovsk negotiations 238

Samoa, German wireless station   15
Sansom, Mr   248
Santoni, Alberto   22
Savory   256
Scarborough Raid   91-93
Scheer, Admiral Reinhard von   105-110, 240
Serecold, Claud   149, 201
Simla, British codebreaking unit based at 23-25
Sims, Admiral William S   223
SKM Codebook (Signalbuch der Kaiserlichen Marine)
Capture of codebook from Magdeburg 38-39
structure of   47-52
ciphers used with   62-66
codebook replaced May 1917   66, 132-133
SKM map grid information captured   89
Scarborough Raid   91
Slaby, Professor Adolf   74
Somers-Cocks, C   153
Somme, battle of   116
Spain, German diplomatic traffic to and from 127
Spee, Graf Maximilian von   14, 18-19, 71
Spurling, June   149-150, 248
Steel, H C   31
Strachey, Lytton   31
Strachey, Oliver   31, 122-123, 248
Strauss, Ralph   201, 204, 254-255
Stuart, Lieutenant RN   19-20

Tannenberg, battle of and interception 33, 219
Telefunken   15, 74
Thring, Paymaster E W   224
Tiarks, Commander F C   149
Tirpitz, Admiral Alfred von
delays introduction of wireless to German navy   75
Trafalgar, battle of   37
Travis, Edward   249
Trench warfare   113-117
Trotsky, Lev Davidovich 'Leon'   187, 234-5
Tryon, Admiral Sir George   75
Tsingtao, German naval base   14, 16, 18
Tuchman, Barbara   16, 195
Turner, J   248

Tyndale, H E C   31
Vaughan-Williams, Ralph   149
VB Codebook (Verkehrsbuch)
capture of   40
structure of   54-56
ciphers used with   60-62
partially replaced 1917   66
Scarborough Raid   91
use for diplomatic communications   129
Victor Emmanuel, King of Italy   73
Villa, Pancho   187-188
Walsingham, Francis   172-175
Wassmuss, Wilhelm   128-129
Watkin, Miss   149, 248
Welsford, R M   149
Western Front   112-13
military interception at start of the war 32-36
battlefield communications   114-117
wireless interception and decryption 113-114, 117
German interception of British telephone traffic   115-116
battle of Somme and communications 116-117
Ludendorff Offensive, March 1918 234-237
Western Offensive, August 1918   239-240
Wheatley, Frederick   19
Wilhelm II, Kaiser 13, 17, 18, 35, 67, 103, 110,
123, 178-179, 191-194, 219, 220-221, 236, 240
meets Marconi in Rome   73
promotes German wireless industry   73-74
Willoughby, Leonard   142, 144
Wilson, President Woodrow   219, 240
orders German communications link via State Dept.   135-136
diplomatic struggle with Germany 187-197
reacts to Zimmermann Telegram   209-211
Windhoek, German wireless station   16, 18
Wireless telegraphy   32-33, 73-76, 80-81

Yap
13, 15
Yardley, Herbert O   253-254

Young Filson   95-96, 253
Young, George   86, 129-132, 170
  Clarke on   148

Zalkind (Salkind)   238
Zeppelin airships 52, 100, 132, 156, 231-234
Zeppelin, Count   231
Zimmermann, Arthur   7, 127-128, 192-193
  Zimmermann drafts telegram   194-195
  decides which route to use   195-196
  decides which codebooks to use   195-197
  interview with US Ambassador   208
  sends second Mexico telegram   208-209
  acknowledges responsibility for 210-211
Zimmermann Telegram7, 128-129, 148, 152,
  251
  copied as passes through London 199-200
  De Grey & Knox start to decode   200-201
  US reaction to   210-211